How to Plan a Crusade

nonas nouembris capta est damieta siue defensi
one absq; tumultu 7 uiolenta depdatione. ut soli
filio dei uictoria ascribatur. Et cum caperetur ciui
tatis uiculis regis babilonis. u̅ fuit ausus more solito xpi
anos aggredi. s; confusus aufugiens ipsa castra combus
sit. Ego itaq; duas milicias xpi damietam ingressi. pla

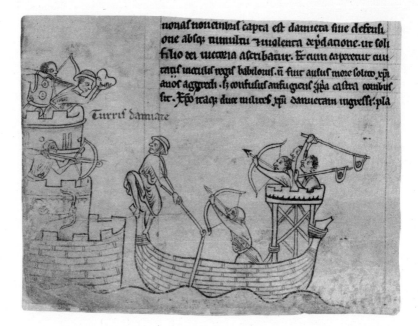

Turris damiate

Capta igitur damieta. missione castri thaphneos.
suut exploratores ad urbi uelle in festo sci cle
mentis in nauiculis p paruum flumen qued tap
uis appellatur. ut de castellulis 7 uillis uictuali
a quererent 7 situ locorum diligenti explorarent.
Cum aut appropinquassent ad castrum quoddam de

Ciuitas Damiete

CHRISTOPHER TYERMAN

How to Plan a Crusade

Reason and Religious War in the
High Middle Ages

ALLEN LANE
an imprint of
PENGUIN BOOKS

ALLEN LANE

UK | USA | Canada | Ireland | Australia
India | New Zealand | South Africa

Allen Lane is part of the Penguin Random House group of companies
whose addresses can be found at global.penguinrandomhouse.com.

Penguin
Random House
UK

First published 2015
001

Copyright © Christopher Tyerman, 2015

The moral right of the author has been asserted

Set in 10.5/14 pt Sabon LT Std
Typeset by Jouve (UK), Milton Keynes
Printed in Great Britain by Clays Ltd, St Ives plc

A CIP catalogue record for this book is available from the British Library

ISBN: 978-1-846-14477-6

MIX
Paper from
responsible sources
FSC
www.fsc.org   FSC® C018179

Penguin Random House is committed to a
sustainable future for our business, our readers
and our planet. This book is made from Forest
Stewardship Council® certified paper.

for Eleanor

Contents

CONTENTS

Preface

A dank, Oxford, early March evening in 1979; a tyro historian stumbling through a lecture in the Examination Schools; the sparse audience nodding; the speaker wondering why he had ever begun. The door bursts open. Enter medieval knights, mailed soldiers, minstrels, fallen nuns (in fishnets and habits split to the thighs), lepers (the effect achieved with the application of candle wax) and other exotica. They chant '*Deus lo volt!*', present the speaker with a splinter of wood (carried in a snuff box), beg him to lead them to Jerusalem, and then adjourn to the pub next door, quickly to be joined by lecturer and audience, united in relief at the destruction of his chain of thought. Later, splashed on the front page of the local newspaper, the reason for this trivial, youthful brouhaha was the lecture's title: 'How to plan a successful crusade'.

For the next three decades, similar provocation was avoided. Then, ambushed into presenting a paper to a seminar dedicated to planning in general, thoughts from times past revived. For the invitation that sparked the collection of ideas and material for this book, I have to acknowledge the ambushers, Mark Whittow and Nicholas Cole. Subsequent audiences in Oxford, Cambridge, Dublin, St Louis and New York have provided sympathetic sounding boards for my ideas. I must thank John Smedley for supplying the first opportunity to present my arguments for the payment of crusaders in print. For particular points, it is a pleasure as well as duty to record debts to Jessalynn Bird, Tim Guard and Kevin Lewis. More general obligations to other scholars working on related aspects of this book will be clear in the endnotes, but especial mention should be made of Martin Aurell, David Crouch, David d'Avray, Piers Mitchell, Alan Murray and John Pryor. Without the libraries and librarians in Oxford, there would be no book. Colleagues in my two colleges, Toby Barnard, Roy Foster, Ruth Harris, David Hopkin, Robin Lane Fox and David Parrott, have provided possibly unwitting support and inspiration. My agent, Jonathan Lloyd, has, as ever, proved an effective champion. My editor, Simon Winder, has kept me honest. He and his team at Allen Lane/Penguin have once again presented a model of sympathetic and efficient publishing. This book is dedicated to someone who currently understands more keenly than most the importance of adequate provisioning.

CJT
Oxford
11 November 2014

Chronology

*c.*400	Augustine of Hippo outlines a Christian theory of just war
638	Jerusalem is captured by the Arabs under Caliph Umar
800	Charlemagne the Frank is crowned Roman Emperor of the West
9th century	Holy wars proclaimed against Muslim invaders of Italy
11th century	Church approval for wars against Muslim rulers in the western Mediterranean
1053	Pope Leo IX offers remission of sins to his troops fighting the Normans of southern Italy
1050s–70s	Seljuk Turks invade the Near East
1061–91	Norman conquest of Muslim Sicily with papal support and spiritual privileges
1071	Seljuk Turks defeat Byzantines at Manzikert; they overrun Asia Minor and establish a capital at Nicaea
1074	Pope Gregory VII proposes a campaign from the west to help Byzantium against the Turks and to liberate the Holy Sepulchre
1095	Byzantine appeal to Pope Urban II for military aid against the Turks; Urban II's preaching tour of France (ends 1096); Council of Clermont proclaims Crusade

1096–99	First Crusade; Jerusalem captured (15 July 1099)
1101 onwards	Smaller crusades to the Holy Land
1104	Acre captured
1107–8	Crusade of the First Crusade hero Bohemund of Taranto against Byzantium
c.1113	Order of the Hospital of St John in Jerusalem recognized
1114 onwards	Crusades in Spain
1120	Order of the Temple founded in Jerusalem to protect pilgrims
1120s	Order of St John, the Hospitallers, beginning to become militarized
1123	First Lateran Council extends Jerusalem privileges to Spanish crusades and defines Church protection for crusaders
1144	Edessa captured by Zengi of Aleppo, leading to Eugenius III's bull *Quantum praedecessores* in 1145/6, which also outlines a range of crusader privileges
1145–9	Second Crusade of Louis VII of France and Conrad III of Germany; Dartmouth Commune and siege of Lisbon 1147
1149 onwards	Further crusades in Spain and, from the 1190s, the Baltic; small expeditions to the Holy Land
1163–9	The Franks of Jerusalem contest control of Egypt
1169	Saladin succeeds as ruler of Egypt
1174	Saladin begins to unify Syria with Egypt
1187	Battle of Hattin; Jerusalem falls to Saladin; Gregory VIII's bull *Audita Tremendi*
1188–92	Third Crusade of Frederick I Barbarossa of Germany, Philip II of France and Richard I of England; 1190 Philip II's treaty with Genoa; siege of Acre 1189–91; Richard I conquers Cyprus 1191

1190–91	Foundation of Teutonic Order
1193–1230	Crusades to Livonia in the Baltic
1195–6	Henry VI of Germany launches German crusade
1198	Pope Innocent III proclaims Fourth Crusade
1199	Church taxation instituted for the Crusade by Innocent III
1201–4	Fourth Crusade; Treaty of Venice 1201; fall and sack of Constantinople 1204
13th century	Crusades in the Baltic by Teutonic Knights (Prussia), Sword Brothers (Livonia); Danes (Prussia, Livonia, Estonia) and Swedes (Estonia and Finland)
13th century	Crusades against German peasants, Bosnians, etc.
1208–29	Albigensian Crusade
1212	Children's Crusade
1213	Innocent III proclaims Fifth Crusade in bull *Quia Maior*, which extends crusade privileges to those who contribute but do not go on crusade
1215	Fourth Lateran Council authorizes regular crusade taxation
1217–21	Fifth Crusade; siege of Damietta 1218–19
1228–9	Crusade of Frederick II of Germany
1231 onwards	Crusades against the Byzantines to defend western conquests in Greece
1234	Gregory IX's crusade bull *Rachel suum videns* consolidates vow redemption system
1239–68	Crusades against Hohenstaufen rulers of Germany and Sicily
1239–41	Crusades to the Holy Land of Theobald, count of Champagne and Richard, earl of Cornwall; Mongol attacks penetrate eastern Europe
1244	Jerusalem lost to Muslims; Louis IX of France takes the Cross

1245	First Council of Lyons held by Innocent IV grants crusade taxes
1248–54	First crusade of Louis IX of France; invasion of Egypt and defeat 1249–50
1251	First Shepherds' Crusade
1260	Mamluks repulse Mongols from Syria
1261	Greeks recover Constantinople
1267	Louis IX takes the Cross again
1270	Louis IX's second crusade to Tunis, where he dies
1271–2	Crusade to the Holy Land of Lord Edward, later Edward I of England
1274	Second Council of Lyons held by Gregory X; advice sought; crusade taxes agreed; collection regions fixed; crusade bull *Zelus fidei*
1291	Fall of Acre to al-Ashraf Khalil of Egypt and evacuation of mainland Outremer; failure of Pope Nicholas IV to launch crusade despite crusade taxes authorized; flood of crusade advice until mid-14th century
1330s	Aborted crusade of Philip VI of France

List of Illustrations

ILLUSTRATIONS IN THE TEXT

p. ii. Scenes from the siege of Damietta, 1219, including the floating siege-tower designed by the preacher and chronicler Oliver of Paderborn. (*CCC 16 fol. 55 verso (59 verso)*)

pp. 26–7. The defeat of the Christian army in Palestine by Khorezmians at Forbie following the loss of Jerusalem in 1244. (*CCC 16 fol. 170 verso*)

pp. 60–61. The defeat and captivity of French crusaders at Gaza, 1240. (*CCC 16 133 verso–134 recto (134 verso–135 verso)*)

pp. 124–5. Warriors practising and a preacher preaching illustrated in an early fourteenth-century treatise on how to recover the Holy Land. (*Tanner 190 fol. 189 recto*)

pp. 178–9. Knights attacking Muslim cavalry and a cargo ship. (*Tanner 190 fol. 17 verso-18 recto*)

pp. 228–9. Knights protected by Christ in an armed galley confronting Muslim forces. (*Tanner 190 fol. 22 recto*)

PLATE SECTION

1. An early fourteenth-century map of Jerusalem. (*Tanner 190 fol. 206 verso*)

2. The world as understood by crusader planners in the early fourteenth century. (*Tanner 190 fol. 203 verso-204 recto*)

3. A battle outside Damietta during the Fifth Crusade. (*CCC 16 fol. 54 (58 verso)*)

CCC = Matthew Paris, *Chronica majora*, Corpus Christi College, Cambridge MS 16 – old pagination listed first, followed by new pagination where appropriate

Tanner = Marino Sanudo Torsello, *Secreta Fidelium Crucis*, Bodleian Library, Oxford MS Tanner 190

Bayeux Tapestry reproductions from the Bridgeman Art Library

List of Maps

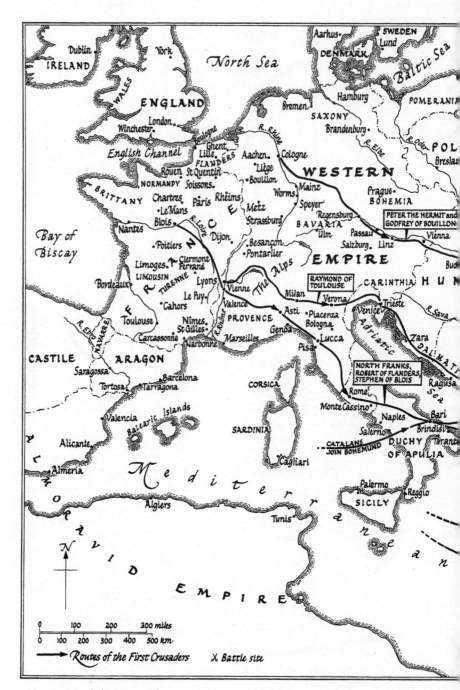

Dublin • York •
IRELAND
WALES
North Sea
Aarhus •
SWEDEN
Lund
DENMARK
Baltic Sea
ENGLAND
Hamburg
Bremen •
SAXONY
POMERANIA
London •
Winchester •
Brandenburg •
R. Rhine
R. Elbe
R. Oder
POL
English Channel
Boulogne
Ghent
Lille
FLANDERS
St Quentin
Rouen
NORMANDY
Soissons
BRITTANY
Chartres
Paris
Rhêims
Le Mans
Blois
R. Loire
Nantes
Poitiers
Dijon
Aachen
Cologne
Liège
Bouillon
WESTERN
Mainz
Worms
Metz
Strassburg
Speyer
Regensburg
BAVARIA
Ulm
Passau
Salzburg
Linz
Prague
BOHEMIA
PETER THE HERMIT and
GODFREY OF BOUILLON
Vienna
Breslau
Bud
Bay of
Biscay
FRANCE
Limoges
LIMOUSIN
TURENNE
Clermont
Ferrand
Lyons
Le Puy
Cahors
Vienne
Valence
Besançon
Pontarlier
The Alps
Milan
Verona
RAYMOND OF
TOULOUSE
CARINTHIA
HUN
EMPIRE
Bordeaux
Toulouse
Nîmes
St Gilles
Carcassonne
Narbonne
PROVENCE
Marseilles
R. Rhône
Asti
Genoa
Piacenza
Bologna
Lucca
Pisa
Venice
Trieste
Adriatic
R. Sava
Zara
DALMATI
CASTILE
ARAGON
Saragossa
Tortosa
Barcelona
Tarragona
R. Ebro
NAVARRE
CORSICA
NORTH FRANKS,
ROBERT OF FLANDERS,
STEPHEN OF BLOIS
Rome
Monte Cassino
Naples
Salerno
Bari
Brindisi
Tarant
DUCHY
OF APULIA
Ragusa
Sea
Valencia
Balearic Islands
SARDINIA
Cagliari
CATALANS
JOIN BOHEMUND
Alicante
Almeria
Algiers
Tunis
Mediterranean
Palermo
SICILY
Reggio
ALMORAVID EMPIRE

N

0   100   200   300 miles
0 100 200 300 400 500 km
→ Routes of the First Crusaders   ✗ Battle site

I. Europe and the Near East at the Time of the First Crusade and Preaching
Tour of Pope Urban II 1095–6

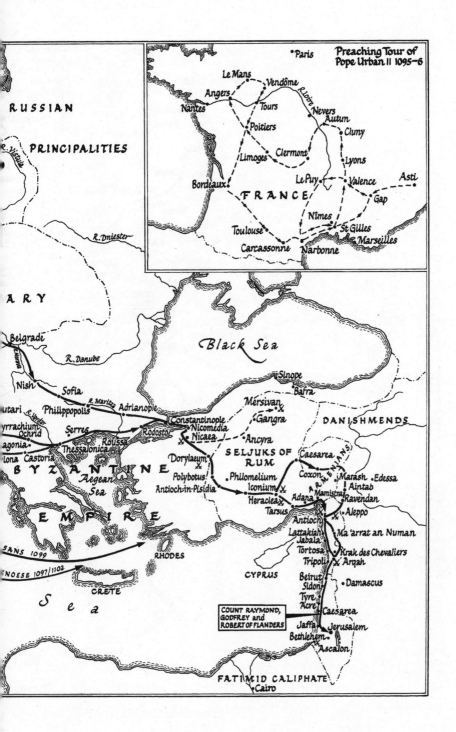

RUSSIAN

PRINCIPALITIES

R.Vistula

Preaching Tour of Pope Urban II 1095–6

Paris

Le Mans
Vendôme
Angers
Nantes
Tours
R.Loire
Nevers
Autun
Poitiers
Cluny
Limoges
Clermont
Lyons
Bordeaux
Le Puy
Valence
Asti
FRANCE
Gap
Nîmes
Toulouse
St Gilles
Marseilles
Carcassonne
Narbonne

R.Dniester

Black Sea

ARY

Belgrade
R.Danube
Sinope
Batra
Nish
Sofia
R.Maritza
Adrianople
Mersivan
Philippopolis
Gangra
DANISHMENDS
utari
R.Vardar
Constantinople
yrrhachium
Ochrid
Serres
Rodosto
Nicomedia
Ancyra
agonia
Roussa
Nicaea
SELJUKS OF
Caesarea
lona Castoria
Thessalonica
Dorylaeum
RUM
BYZANTINE
Polybotus
Philomelium
Coxon
Marash Edessa
Aegean
Iconium
Aintab
EMPIRE
Sea
Antioch-in-Pisidia
Heraclea
Adana
Mamistra
Ravendan
Tarsus
Antioch
Aleppo
SANS 1099
Lattakiah
Ma'arrat an Numan
Jabala
RHODES
Tortosa
Krak des Chevaliers
NOESE 1097/1102
Tripoli
Arqah
CYPRUS
Beirut
Damascus
CRETE
Sidon
Tyre
Sea
Acre
Caesarea
COUNT RAYMOND,
GODFREY and
ROBERT OF FLANDERS
Jaffa
Jerusalem
Bethlehem
Ascalon
FATIMID CALIPHATE
Cairo

2. Europe and the Near East at the Time of the Second Crusade and Bernard of Clairvaux's Preaching Tour 1146–7

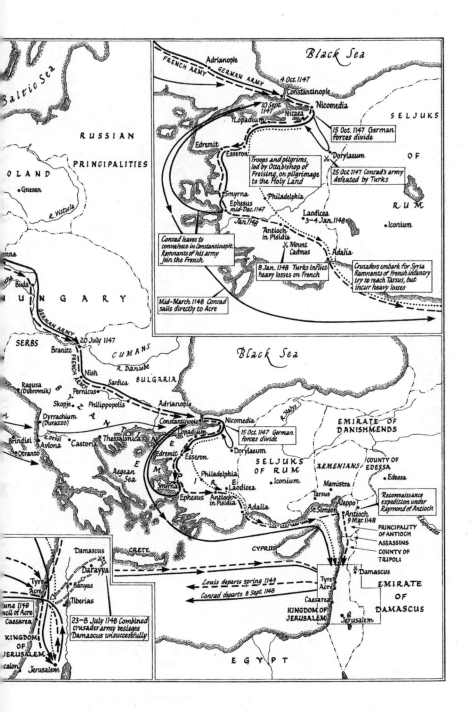

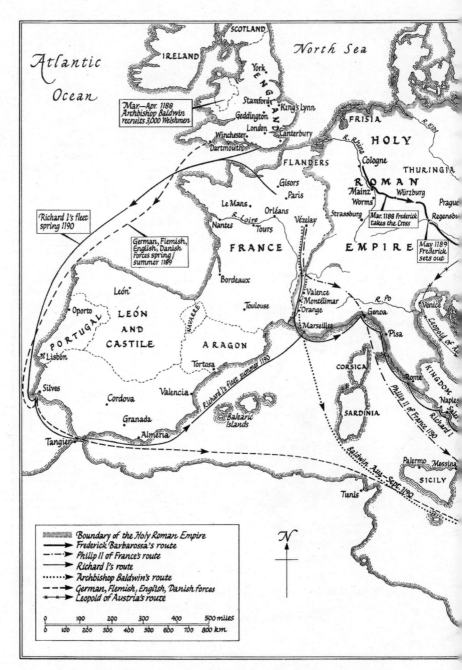

3. Europe and the Near East at the Time of the Third Crusade

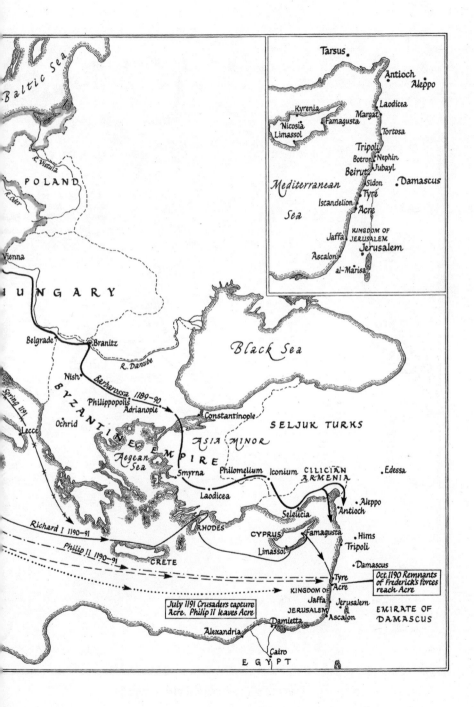

Tarsus
Antioch
Aleppo
Kyrenia
Laodicea
Margat
Famagusta
Nicosia
Tortosa
Limassol
Tripoli
Botron Nephin
Beirut Jubayl
Mediterranean
Sidon
Damascus
Sea
Tyre
Iscandelion
Acre
KINGDOM OF
Jaffa JERUSALEM
Ascalon Jerusalem
al-Marisa

Baltic Sea
R. Vistula
POLAND
R. Oder
Vienna
HUNGARY
Belgrade Branitz
Black Sea
R. Danube
Nish
Barbarossa 1189–90
Philippopolis
BYZANTINE EMPIRE
Adrianople
Constantinople
SELJUK TURKS
Ochrid
Spring 1191
Lecce
ASIA MINOR
Aegean
Sea
Smyrna
Philomelium
Iconium
CILICIAN
Edessa
ARMENIA
Laodicea
Aleppo
Seleucia
Antioch
Richard I 1190–91
RHODES
CYPRUS
Famagusta
Hims
Philip II 1190–91
Tripoli
Limassol
CRETE
Damascus
Tyre
Oct. 1190 Remnants
Acre of Frederick's forces
reach Acre
KINGDOM OF
Jaffa Jerusalem
EMIRATE OF
July 1191 Crusaders capture
JERUSALEM Ascalon DAMASCUS
Acre. Philip II leaves Acre
Damietta
Alexandria
Cairo
EGYPT

4. Europe and the Near East in the Thirteenth Century

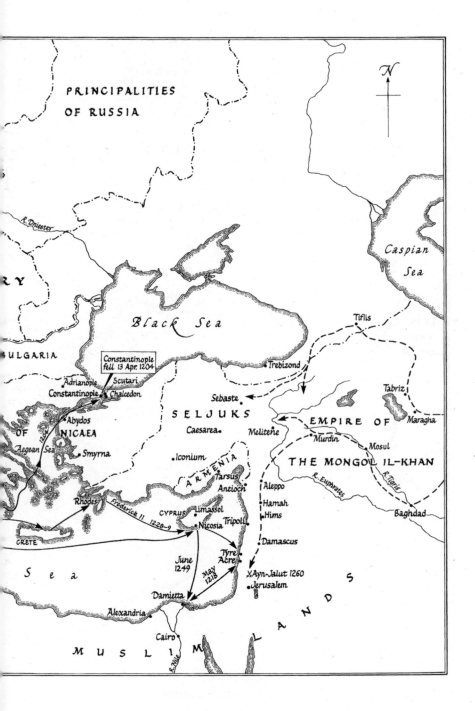

PRINCIPALITIES OF RUSSIA

R. Dniester

Caspian Sea

Black Sea

Tiflis

BULGARIA

Constantinople fell 13 Apr. 1204

Adrianople   Scutari
Constantinople   Chalcedon
                                  Sebaste
Abydos   Tabriz
OF   NICAEA   Maragha
Aegean Sea   Caesarea   Melitene   EMPIRE OF
           Smyrna
                                         Murdin   Mosul
                  Iconium
                           ARMENIA   THE MONGOL IL-KHAN
Rhodes   Frederick II Tarsus   R. Euphrates
             1228-9   Antioch   Aleppo
          CYPRUS Limassol   Hamah   Baghdad
CRETE   Nicosia Tripoli Hims
                                 Damascus
Sea   Tyre
              June   Acre
              1249   May   X Ayn-Jalut 1260
                     1218   Jerusalem
           Damietta
Alexandria   L
                                            A
      MUSLI M   N   D   S
   Cairo
          R. Nile

Introduction

This book is about how crusades were planned and organized, the application of reason to religious warfare. The culture of western Europe in the Middle Ages rested on the twin pillars of reason and religion. From the speculations of the learned and the politics of the ruling elites to the daily common puzzling at the point of existence or the problems of actually coping with the material world, faith informed behaviour and action while reason tried to explain why the supernatural made sense. Nothing illustrates this relationship more sharply than the history of the crusades.

This may at first glance seem eccentric. The crusades have frequently been portrayed as ultimate symbols of the power of credulity, witnessed by 'millions of men who followed the pillar of cloud and fire in the sure and certain hope of an eternal reward'.[1] They have encouraged a view of the Middle Ages as a period of naive energy and ignorance, 'a story touched by the pathos of an ignorant group of Latins who undertook a journey to recover the Holy Sepulchre'.[2] Most crusades to the prime objective, the Christian Holy Places of Palestine, failed, usually dismally. They have been portrayed as inept, failures of conception and implementation, hare-brained, feckless, extravagant mirages built on wishful thinking, not strategic reality, inspired by solipsistic cultural nostrums, not military or logistic common sense and cheered on by self-serving religious sophistry. Crusade armies may have comprised men accustomed to war but, the legend insists, they were led by commanders whose self-regarding vanity, meretricious ideology or greed were matched only by the absence of sound military intelligence or technological competence, the blind leading the deluded. What follows argues that in almost all respects this image is false. The intellectual as well as material effort involved in crusade organization contradicts such stereotypes. Viewed outside the frame of religious polemic or historical relativism, it becomes obvious that military expeditions as complex as the crusades were carefully, exhaustively and rationally planned.

Few periods of the past have suffered more from modern condescension than the rather patronizingly described Middle Ages, an imagined limbo of coarseness between the civilized worlds of classical antiquity and the Renaissance, a model carefully constructed by fifteenth-century humanists and lovingly polished ever since. These Middle Ages possessed value only as a mine from which nuggets of future modernity could be excavated by prospectors seeking thin veins of progress. Today, extremes of violence, bigotry, poverty, squalor or deprivation regularly attract the pejorative epithet of 'medieval', although the worst famines tend to delve deeper in the lexicon of bogus history to earn the title 'biblical'. Such labelling forgets that the most excruciating refinements in barbarism and inhumanity are historically recent. The period *c.* AD 500–1500 in Europe is dismissed, or occasionally praised, as an age of Faith, and thus, it is casually assumed, of ignorance. This misleads. Ignorance is no bar to reason, often the reverse. Modern society is not immune from the social force of religion. The assumption that faith or belief is antithetical to reason and vice versa is a canard given wings during the Enlightenment and the demolition of medieval (and, it might be remembered, classical) science. Yet no modern President of the United States would get elected if he publicly expressed the sort of rational religious scepticism shown by King Amalric of Jerusalem (r.1163–74), who was concerned at the absence of any external, non-scriptural evidence for resurrection.[3] Amalric's doubts hint at medieval faith as neither unthinkingly passive nor hostile to rational explanation. Equally, while his premises and world view may differ from those of later philosophers, Thomas Aquinas (d.1274) was, in his method, just as rational as, say, David Hume (d.1776), even, it has recently been argued, when dealing with the problem of miracles.[4] Nobody in the Middle Ages who thought about it imagined the world flat; intellectuals knew with near accuracy the circumference of the earth.[5] Literal interpretations of Scripture never held a monopoly. Logical and empirical reasoning were characteristic features of the world of the High Middle Ages, as they are of ours. Not, it should be insisted, in the same way or in identical forms (an anachronism that dogs so much historical fiction and drama) but nonetheless recognizable as rationality, a process of trying to discover objective truth.

The example of crusade planning provides compelling testimony. Many of the ingredients allegedly typical of later warfare can be found in crusade leadership, their preparations displaying rigour and conceptual focus to match their successors'. Causes for war were identified and elaborate propaganda employed to persuade public opinion. Diplomacy garnered allies and secured routes of march, supply dumps, markets and free passage. Campaign strategies were agreed at meetings of commanders briefed by intelligence sources, manuals of military and legal theory, and maps. Command structures were established, if often only painfully and uneasily. Recruitment was methodical. In conjunction with lordship, shared locality and peer-group pressure, it was based on pay and contracts. The devolved private armies of late medieval and early modern Europe were mirrored and anticipated by the fragmented paid companies of crusade lords. Before departure, money was raised by innovative schemes of taxation and borrowing. Funding wars on credit was hardly post-medieval. It has been noted that while 31 per cent of the costs of Queen Anne's War of the Spanish Succession (1702–13) were covered by loans, in the 1330s 90 per cent of Edward III's wars were.[6] From the start, crusade leaders frequently carried large debts both before and during campaigns. Pay scales and budgets were calculated. Transport, food supplies, logistics, materiel, even medical provision received careful and expert organization. Commercial fleets from the Baltic to the Mediterranean were mobilized or requisitioned. Internal markets within armies were created and regulated, if often ineffectually. Technology was employed, especially siege engines. On the Third Crusade, Richard I shipped with him to Palestine a pre-fabricated wooden castle and large throwing machines to be assembled on site.[7] The cosmic rhetoric of crusade promoters was matched by ambitious concepts of grand strategy that incorporated schemes for reordering the Near East, seeking alliances across Eurasia and dabbling with ideas for economic warfare. Not all of these techniques and methods were efficient or effective. Few produced the ultimate victories sought. But irrational they were not.

There are perhaps two main reasons why the orderliness of crusade planning has been generally downplayed. Both are rooted in the nature of the evidence: the didacticism of literary observers compounded by the absence of bureaucratic records. A secondary historiographical explanation rests with historians' understandable concentration on the drama of the campaigns rather than the prosaic methods that led to them. There have been some notable exceptions: among Anglophone scholars John France on the First Crusade; James Powell on the Fifth Crusade; William Jordan on Louis IX's crusade of 1248–50; Alan Murray on a succession of German expeditions; John Pryor on crusade logistics; and Piers Mitchell on medicine.[8] But even their interests have, sensibly enough, tended to be focused on the outcomes and consequences rather than the planning itself as a discrete activity. Others who have bothered to look closely at crusade preparations have been more concerned with what they reveal of participants' inspirations and motives. In this they have followed the literary sources, the bulk of surviving evidence for the earlier crusades.

Medieval writers, of chronicles, histories or academic commentaries, tended to present the enterprises in a religious or providential light, to concentrate on the 'why?' and the 'so what?' rather than explicitly on the 'how?' Only after the final defeat and evacuation of mainland Syria and Palestine in 1291 did it become widely fashionable to pay serious independent attention to logistics.[9] However, previous observers had not entirely ignored the mechanics of crusader warfare. Some clearly had a particular interest in such matters, such as Roger of Howden, an English royal official who went east with the Third Crusade.[10] Similarly, in contrast to most clerical accounts in Latin, those in the vernacular by laymen, such as Geoffrey of Villehardouin and Robert of Clari (for the Fourth Crusade) or John of Joinville (for Louis IX of France's attack on Egypt in 1248–50), included more information on planning and organization.[11] As knights and commanders, such things occupied them and probably interested them more than they did their clerical counterparts. Even so, logistical detail was included as part of the narrative rather than studied for any intrinsic interest of its own, or was presented as evidence of a leader's

4

especially admirable military acumen. Descriptions of crusades were dominated by models of bravery, chivalry and faith, with success and failure explained largely in moral terms, not the efficiency of planning or preparation. Similarly, preaching, recruitment and finance were assessed in terms of the probity of the propagandists, the devotion of the people and the honesty of the leaders rather than administrative acumen. Commentators tended to stick to a number of standard literary genres: the deeds of great men (*gesta*); the edifying collection of uplifting or admonitory lessons from the past (*historia*); linear narratives, often found in chronicles, that aped the historical patterns derived from the Bible; or chivalric adventure tales, epics and romances that revolved around abstract virtues – loyalty, bravery, generosity, etc. – of which crusaders' actions provided suitable exemplars. The lack of attention to the humdrum techniques of assembling effective military campaigns lent crusading a false air of spontaneity or improvisation, an impression encouraged by the second limitation of evidence.

The study of administration relies upon the creation and survival of archival records. These can reveal in intimate detail the planning process. So, for example, from a small dossier of documents preserved in the Archives Nationales in Paris it is possible to follow the development of a proposal to raise money for a putative crusade to the Holy Land in 1311. The plan was written by Guillaume de Nogaret, one of Philip IV of France's chief ministers and political fixers. One document in the dossier is covered in deletions, emendations and additions showing precisely how Nogaret's original ideas had been toned down, probably by a drafting committee, to fit more smoothly the immediate political and diplomatic context.[12] Without such material, understanding of Philip IV's regime's interest in crusading would be much more restricted. While, from around 1300, archives and libraries across Europe are littered with memoranda, tracts and treatises concerning the practical (and not so practical) means of organizing crusades, before then very little such material survives. Government records, with a few exceptions, are also notably exiguous. With rare interludes, such as Charlemagne's literate court around 800, until the twelfth century, and then unevenly, the restricted writing culture largely shielded processes of planning as lords and governments, although using writing to communicate, did not routinely keep written records once they became redundant. As a result, we can usually only assess results, not intentions.

Yet early medieval rulers at all levels, with their officials, agents and cronies, planned: for war; for governing; for exploiting material resources of land and commerce; for the administration of justice; for the control of subjects; or for the production of coinage. The physical results prove it. Great public works, such as Offa's Dyke or Charlemagne's incomplete Rhine–Danube canal, did not build themselves any more than churches, palaces, castles or city walls. The regular street plans of medieval London, Winchester or Oxford were not the product of some random building spree. Diplomats and merchants did not wander the landscape blithely hoping for coincidental encounters with politicians or trade. Noble households and armies were not assembled, maintained and fed by accident. The rotation of crops in village fields did not happen by chance. Law courts operated immemorially on precedent and convention before becoming confined by written record. So much is obvious. Narrative sources from all corners of Christendom frequently mention assemblies, conferences and council meetings, the occasions for planning, even if the detail of what was planned and how is largely omitted. Until the twelfth century, with the partial exception of England's royal administration, how civil or military projects were organized can only be reconstructed indirectly, from chronicles and histories, fiction, a few letters preserved for their style or significance of correspondent, visual art and archaeology. What documents do survive tend to be skewed towards matters affecting the Church and/or the transfer of property. None of these constitute very good sources for the mundane act of organizing men and resources. Yet the absence of written records of planning does not mean it did not occur. The great monuments of administrative endeavour, such as Domesday Book (1086), the English accounts, called the Pipe Rolls of the Exchequer (from the early twelfth century, surviving continuously from 1155) or the fiscal records (*computa*) of the counts of Catalonia (late twelfth century), did not emerge *ab nihilo*.[13] Although administrative historians sometimes find this difficult, the absence of written records or, importantly, written record-keeping does not necessarily imply a lack of previous efficiency, complexity or sophistication. Nor, conversely, does their appearance necessarily imply novelty or innovation in much except itself, i.e. record-keeping. The planning of the crusades bears this out, both before and after the deceptive watershed of written records.

Without government archives, there is a tendency to resort to 'they must have done x or y' arguments, reducing any assessment of the efficacy of planning to a deduction from the outcome. Thus William of Normandy's planning of the 1066 invasion of England has been held up as a model of efficient and effective preparation. It was; and would have been even if William not Harold had been killed at Hastings, and the Norman army had been driven back into the sea. Yet it is unlikely that historians – then or now – would have thought so if the Normans had not been victorious. Though Harold was defeated, his planning – although not necessarily its execution – may have been just as remarkable in its own way. We know of William's preparations not only from panegyric court historians and some fragmentary later documentary detail, but also from the visual evidence of the Bayeux Tapestry. In its detailed and careful depiction of the assembling of arms, armour, supplies, shipping and horses, as well as its scenes of conferences between commanders, the tapestry provides unequivocal testimony to the importance given at the time to the administrative effort behind the heroic campaign and to the centrality of the planning process from council chamber to the battlefield.[14] In essence, such pictures are not so very far from modern images of generals poring over maps, staff officers scrutinizing budgets and supply orders, or newsreels of factories manufacturing munitions or armies massing for war.

Writing in the early years of the fourteenth century, reflecting on the experience of two centuries of wars of the Cross, the Armenian prince, historian and ethnographer Hetoum (or Hayton) of Gorigos identified four prerequisites for a successful crusade to recover the Holy Land: an appropriate cause; sufficient resources; knowledge of the enemy's capacity; and suitable timing. These were the matters that 'reason requires anyone wishing to make war on his enemies to consider'.[15] The absence of medieval planning is a myth, a consequence of poor written evidence and a certain medieval cultural contempt for the bureaucrat and official. The lack of rationality in medieval warriors is another fiction. Both distortions envelop the crusade like heavy batter. Some responsibility rests with clerical commentators and clerics at the time, eager to portray commitment to the Cross as a Damascene conversion or epiphany. The prosaic reality of complex negotiation and laborious preparation usually made for poor didactic copy in medieval cloisters as in Hollywood studios. Across medieval Eurasia, war was woven into the fabric of society, a defining identity for the social and political elites. The crusades, although not simple, were simply wars. Those who launched and led them appreciated that their prospects depended, like most other wars, on at least seven associated but distinct considerations: establishing a convincing *casus belli*; publicity and propaganda; recruitment; finance; transport; a plan of campaign as far as could be predicted; and a wider geopolitical strategy. Each will be examined in turn. But first something must be said about the planners and warriors themselves and their culture of reason.

I

Images of Reason

Since the Reformation, critics and apologists alike have shared a fascination with the crusades' combined extremes of religiosity and violence. Whether judged noble or deluded, courageous or brutal, honest or hypocritical, faithful or naive, committed or corrupted, crusaders' religious mentalities have continued to excite interest.[1] Less attention has been paid to their intellectual hinterlands, mental capacities or education apart from military training. The modern image of a medieval knight too often resembles some cartoon cut-out of robust thuggery dressed up in gorgeous robes, shining (or bloodied) armour or extravagant gestures of martial or amorous gallantry, a wholly dated figure to be admired but only with a slight sneer of superiority. The crusader used to appear peculiarly alien because of his belief in salvation through fighting and in killing as God's work. Perforce, this incomprehension has recently begun to change. Crusading organization reveals a different aspect. Successful warfare requires experience, cool heads and the ability to reason, conceptually and empirically, as readily understood in the Middle Ages as it is today.[2]

AN INFRASTRUCTURE OF REASON

The exercise of reason requires an active mental organization, enquiry and deduction. Mere observation of phenomena or passive collection of information lack meaningful rationality unless ordered so that conclusions can be drawn. Otherwise, the information gathered constitutes mere random anecdotage. Reason seeks truth through enquiry. It is no coincidence that the two fashionable buzz words of twelfth-century scholarship, philosophy, law and even government were *inquisitio* (enquiry) and *veritas* (truth). It has been said that the social centrality of rational enquiry 'is a gift of the Later Middle Ages to the modern world ... the best kept secret of western civilisation'.[3] Reason can be applied to abstract thought and to empirical observation. Much modern rationality assumes its character as essentially intellectual, the gathering of evidence that aims to convince other rational people of a truth using a method that is transparent and available to all. In a society that understood the world to be God-created and divinely ordered, reason also possessed an ethical aspect – how best to live a decent life – alongside what Eugene Weber dubbed value rationality, or conviction, and formal, closed rational systems, such as law and the legal process.[4] Rationality is neither static nor immune to social influence. Alexander Murray famously ascribed the rise of reason in medieval culture to social aspiration and mobility allied to the commercialization of the economy and the consequent increasing role of mathematics.[5] Social and cultural context are central when assessing the exercise of reason in the Middle Ages. Reason may be absolute; its manifestations are contingent.

The opposite of reason is not ignorance, desire, appetite, emotion, experience or even denial but, as Edward Grant has suggested, revelation.[6] Much intellectual effort in the High Middle Ages was spent balancing these two forces. Acceptance of the existence of God the Creator did not exclude rational investigation of His world, i.e. nature, any more than the conviction that there is no God prevents examination of religion. However, belief in God inevitably involved confronting His interventions that appeared to override the natural order He had created, i.e. miracles. While these signs of God's immanence could be explained rationally, as Thomas Aquinas attempted, they were increasingly ascribed to a separate category of 'supernatural' events, a coinage of the thirteenth century in a backhanded compliment to the progress of the rational study of man and nature.[7] It is a common modern mistake to assume that because a premise is now regarded as false or unacceptable, any reasoning from that premise must itself be tainted as irrational. The integration of the scientific, political and ethical philosophy of the Greek philosopher Aristotle into Christian thought constituted the major academic project of the thirteenth century in western Europe. It formed the basis for the theology of Aquinas, the most influential thinker of the age. Aristotle's interpretation of the natural world may be untrue, but it is not irrational. Only if Aristotle had been acquainted with Copernican astronomy, Newtonian and Einsteinian physics, Darwinian biology and the rest and then had persisted with his theories would they have been unreasonable. Refusal to accept objective evidence is irrational; trying to make sense of what you think you observe or know is not. As already mentioned, ignorance, lack of information, is not per se irrational.

In fact a sense of inadequate understanding coupled with social ambition provided a spur in this period to intensified rational investigation in theology, philosophy and canon law. For example, the need to provide a rational proof of the existence of God, itself a commentary on actual or perceived medieval scepticism, was addressed by Anselm of Canterbury's ontological argument in his *Proslogion* (1077/8).[8] The formal technique of scholastic enquiry through the interrogation of authoritative texts to explore, explain and resolve contradictions and difficulties was pioneered by Peter Abelard, notably in his *Sic et Non* (i.e. 'Yes and No', *c.*1121) which included the classic formula for rational endeavour: 'by doubting we come to inquiry and by inquiry we perceive the truth'. The first question posed was 'Must human faith be completed by reason, or not?'[9] This interrogative technique formed the basis of the scholastic method that came to dominate academic enquiry at the growing number of universities that appeared in the twelfth and thirteenth centuries. University curricula rested on two modes of rational discussion, derived from classical education and together known as the Liberal Arts (*artes liberales*): literary, in the Trivium (grammar, rhetoric and logic); and mathematical, in the Quadrivium (arithmetic, geometry, music and astronomy, the last really meaning astrology). Men educated in these disciplines played central roles in crusading, as advisers, organizers and active participants.

Reliance on rational enquiry rather than deferential acceptance of revealed Truth was not just an attribute of schoolmen (and a few women). The use, benefits and imperatives of rational thought were apparent across society. The period of the crusades, from the late eleventh century onwards, coincided with a secular embrace of rational habits of thought and performance. At its most basic this amounted to little more than admiring thoughtfulness and circumspection, elevated into a virtue, prudence, *prudentia*.[10] This worldly wisdom could be attained by education, knowledge or experience, all useful whether in the merchant's counting house, the architect's or engineer's workshop or as judge or juryman in a court of law. Church courts sought witnesses, consulted documents and heard arguments before the judge reached a verdict. Increasingly, in England for example, traditional forms of trial in secular courts – by ordeal or combat – were, partly in imitation of Church courts, giving way to the hearing of evidence and the oaths of witnesses, with jurors attesting to facts. Even the most bone-headed lord was expected to dispense justice that, however loaded, could not necessarily afford to be wholly arbitrary. Equally, in running estates, ruling tenants and asserting rights, reason provided a handy tool, familiar to crusade leaders and their knightly followers.

Rational proof was not restricted to courts of law. Relics are often cited by critics as one of the more bizarre and benighted aspects of medieval religion, the devotion to slivers of wood, loose-chippings, soiled rags and body parts as conduits for divinity and contact with eternity. Some of these anxieties were shared by the medieval Church authorities themselves. The efficacy of relics and their surrounding belief systems crucially depended on authenticity. Christian doubt and the demand for proof have pedigrees as long as Christianity itself, witnessed by the story of Doubting Thomas. One of the most famous episodes of the First Crusade shows how controversial and disruptive authentication could become and how urgent the need to find objective resolution. The seemingly miraculous discovery of the supposed Holy Lance (the spearhead that was said to have pierced the side of Christ on the Cross) at Antioch in June 1098 was credited by some with inspiring the crusaders' crucial subsequent victory against the odds over the atabeg (or Turkic governor) of Mosul. Yet from the start sceptics questioned the relic's status and the validity of the visions allegedly visited on its finder, Peter Bartholomew. These uncertainties, fuelled by political rivalries in the crusader camp, threatened to break up the expedition. An attempt some months later to decide the issue by a judicial trial by fire of Bartholomew ended, as such ordeals often did, with conflicting opinions as to the outcome. The trial consisted of Bartholomew walking through a corridor of flaming timbers carrying the supposed relic.

His survival would prove the Lance was genuine. In the event, Bartholomew died after the ordeal. Yet his supporters insisted his injuries had not been caused by the fire but by his being mobbed afterwards. Years later, the bitterness created by the lack of an agreed verdict still flavoured chronicle accounts on both sides of the argument.[11]

Even though it failed, the attempt to resolve the Holy Lance controversy was conducted in a rational, judicial manner to address doubts as impartially as possible in order to arrive at a transparent, agreed, objective understanding of God's verdict. This mirrored the Church's general policy to winnow out the diabolic snares of bogus, bought or stolen relics. One of the most enthusiastic and academic chroniclers of the First Crusade, Guibert of Nogent (c.1060–c.1125), composed a bravura demolition of the claims of the church of St Médard, Soissons, to possess one of Christ's baby teeth. Relics were big business. By attracting paying pilgrims, an authenticated relic could make the fortunes of the church or monastery where it was exhibited. The problem became more acute after the capture of Constantinople by the Fourth Crusade in 1204, which released a glut of relics onto the market, including quantities of duplicates of some already venerated in the west.[12] This was not new. The 1098 Holy Lance of Antioch had competition from the Holy Lance on display at Constantinople that the crusaders themselves could have seen only a year before. The flood of Byzantine relics after 1204 sharply exacerbated the problem. Those receiving looted items had to reassure themselves they were genuine and not obtained for money. Rostang, a monk of the great Burgundian abbey of Cluny, carefully recorded the circumstances that led to the donation to the monastery of the head of St Clement in 1206.[13] To establish its credentials, Rostang received from the donor, a local lord, Dalmas of Sercy, a detailed oral narrative of how the head had been located and deftly stolen from under the noses of its Greek custodians. It makes for lively reading, but the point of the record was to prove the authenticity of the relic and the legitimacy of its new ownership. The problem of fakes was regarded as so severe and widespread that the Fourth Lateran General Council of the Church, held in Rome in 1215, promulgated a decree to control the relic industry. Newly venerated relics now required papal authentication. The aim was to prevent the faithful being deceived 'by lying stories or false documents, as has commonly happened in many places on account of the desire for profit', a desire from which the papal curia's licensing system was not immune.[14] It was just as well Rostang of Cluny had taken the trouble to write down the saga of St Clement's head. Both Rostang and the Lateran fathers knew the importance of written records.

The twelfth century's spread of recording documents profoundly affected the administration of justice and government, as written records gradually challenged memory as an accepted currency of recollection.[15] The new culture of record is most obviously manifest in official archives and new offices of administration, such as the audit office of the kings of England called the Exchequer (c.1106–10), named after the two-dimensional abacus used to calculate the amounts of revenue obligations and receipts. Exchequer accounts were kept on parchment rolls.[16] By the end of the century, judgments in lawsuits of the crown and diplomatic and other administrative documents were also beginning to be copied into central archives, and not just in England. What worked for kings was imitated by their wealthier subjects and society at large. By the early thirteenth century at the latest, crusade recruiting agents were writing down lists of those who had taken the Cross.[17] Commanders appeared to have kept written accounts of their followers' wages during the First Crusade a century earlier.[18] In law, commerce and government, at high or local levels, the standard of proof and record became more objective and, in that sense, more rational.

Like writing, medicine, architecture and engineering allied the intellectual and empirical aspects of reasoning. While the theories of the second-century AD Graeco-Roman physician and philosopher Galen and the four humours still dominated theoretical assumptions about how the body worked, and the role of the learned physician was recognized as superior to that of the artisan sawbones, surgeons and barbers, western medicine developed certain practical procedures that, while almost never curing maladies, alleviated symptoms. Hospitals or hospices proliferated in this period in which palliative care and the use of medicinal herbs combined in a regime of non-intervention, rest and good diet. Some experiences led to modest advances in treatment, notably in regard to battlefield injuries, not least during crusades. Beside the academic precepts of university medical schools, such as that at Salerno in Italy, and the shared wisdom of practitioners and

nurses, occasional bold, enquiring spirits conducted medical experiments. Basic surgical procedures were expected to succeed.[19] However
misguided or inadvertently homicidal, medieval doctors believed they
were following rational guides. As cure was not something within
their grasp anyway, the failure rate of their ministrations hardly
deterred their continuance. However, some conditions could be
approached in a more wholly intellectual rather than empirical manner. Discussing in the 1220s the suicide of an adolescent in Cologne,
the Cistercian monk Caesarius of Heisterbach drew a moral distinction
between depression ('sadness and desperation', *tristitia et desperatio*)
and madness 'in which there is no reason'. Victims of the former could
not expect divine forgiveness if they took their own lives, while the
insane, those 'out of their minds' (*mentis alienatio*), merited charity.
While Caesarius located the key difference in the presence or absence
of reason, the recognition of distinctive teenage depression indicates a
more general common sense, if harsh, observation of life.[20]

Architects, engineers, masons and carpenters did not rely on guesswork or avoid conceptual planning. The early twelfth-century treatise
De Diversis Artibus, while not devoid of eccentricities (such as advising tempering metal tools with the urine of small red-headed boys),
recognizes the need for the exertion of reason in describing techniques
of painting, metallurgy and glass making. Processes from bell founding to constructing an organ are pursued logically. Discussion of metal
work is prefaced by a description of how to build a workshop and
furnace.[21] The relevance of such metallurgical techniques to warfare is
obvious: armour, weapons, horseshoes and nails. The importance of
carpentry and the demand for skilled engineers to construct siege
machines is no less evident. The history of the crusades is peppered
with accounts of such engines and their builders. Some of the latter
were clearly professionals. At the siege of Nicaea in Asia Minor in
May and June 1097, a Lombard 'master and inventor of great siege
machines', to construct a protective shield, or 'cat', for the besiegers,
was paid 15 pounds of Chartres money (worth perhaps a quarter that
of pounds sterling, so a sum still equivalent of a very decent annual
income).[22] Some experts combined practical engineering skills with
elite education. In 1218, during the Fifth Crusade's siege of Damietta
in the Nile Delta, an amphibious siege tower, a sort of floating fortress,

was devised by Oliver of Paderborn, Paris-educated academic, propagandist, chronicler and later cardinal.[23] Whether the arithmetic and geometry of the Quadrivium assisted his engineering or it provided a private hobby is unknown. However, such skills were clearly not considered *déclassé*. Professional masons enjoyed relatively high social status. Architects attracted considerable reputations. The Frenchman William of Sens, a 'most cunning craftsman in wood and stone', won an international competition to become the designer of the remodelled Canterbury Cathedral in the 1170s.[24] An English master mason, Maurice, graduated from working on the keep at Newcastle in the 1170s to being the presiding engineer (*ingeniator*) at Dover Castle. There he was paid one shilling a day, suggesting an annual income that placed him almost in the knightly class. In addition, he received financial gifts from the king.[25] Such men and their professions also enjoyed a very particular gloss of reflected esteem. God the Creator appeared iconographically as the universe's architect, complete with a pair of compasses.[26] Jesus Christ had been a carpenter.

However, this was not a world of untrammelled freedom of thought. Rationality was accepted as useful but not elevated into a secular godhead. Limits appeared to where speculation and enquiry could go. Even though rational argument was employed by theologians, for example in staged theological debates between Jews and Christians,[27] the contest between reason and revelation claimed victims. Abelard was excommunicated for heresy.[28] In the later thirteenth century, the University of Paris spent much time and effort trying to define how far rational philosophy should impinge on theology, famously over the question of whether God could do anything that is naturally impossible. Against the official majority line, some Paris philosophers thought not.[29] Thought policing represented only one rather esoteric aspect of the mental framework that constrained reason. Another limit was exposed by divination and prediction. Rational enquiry was reckoned to be necessary to understand the natural world in order better to control it. If the world operated in an ordered, observable fashion, its future movements and events should, through the application of reason, be able to be predicted. Magic, alchemy and astrology were practised as rational enquiries into the operation of the natural world by some of the best brains of the period. Adelard of Bath (*c.*1080–after 1151) wrote or

16

supervised the production of works on Euclid, Boethius, natural science, the abacus, falconry and translations of Arabic texts on astronomy and astrology. He travelled extensively around the Mediterranean in search of texts. In the spirit of empiricism, he insisted on the primacy of reason rather than ancient authorities or the Bible to understand how things worked. Yet he also allegedly used to cast horoscopes, decked out in a special green cloak and ring.[30] For Adelard and his contemporaries, divination and reason were not opposites but aspects of the same intellectual endeavour of rational enquiry, as they were, much later, for Isaac Newton, another noted student of alchemy.

The failures of prediction if anything undermined confidence in the primacy of reason, ironically leaving revealed truth, scriptural exegesis, inherited nostrums, guesswork and prayer as alternatives to fall back on. In his treatise *De commendatione fidei* (mid/late 1170s) Baldwin of Forde launched a direct assault on the predictive use of reason, evidence, experiments and experience, for example in medicine or among sailors and farmers. Part of his attack was directed at the habit of 'prudent men of the world' making predictions about war and peace 'in accordance with what they remember having heard and seen', a medieval version of the adage that generals tend to fight the last war, not the one they are actually fighting. 'In all cases and others like them in which human skills play a part the judgement is uncertain . . . a doubtful outcome and a changeable result.' Baldwin's target was the reliance on 'human skills' (*humana ingenia*) and assumptions of cause and effect. 'The experiments of medics are false, evidence is ambiguous, the advice of men untrustworthy, and human providence uncertain.' In mid-career, Baldwin had joined the Cistercians, an Order congenitally suspicious of the rational debates of the schoolmen. He concluded his critique by asserting that the revelation of the Spirit of God and the holy prophets are 'above all human reason and above all natural things'.[31]

This did not make Baldwin an intellectual Luddite. His move to the Cistercians led to rapid promotion to abbot, bishop and finally to the see of Canterbury (1184–90), where he became locked in a vicious dispute with his own monks over the use of the diocesan income. He acted as a diplomat and arbiter in political disputes at the highest level. The waspish writer Gerald of Wales, who knew Baldwin well, rather uncharitably circulated the neat aphorism about him: 'most fervent monk, zealous abbot, lukewarm bishop, and careless archbishop'. His relegation of reason below revelation was entirely commonplace in the higher echelons of the educated clergy. Yet in practice he did not entirely dismiss the importance of experience. According to Gerald, who travelled with the archbishop, while touring Wales preaching the Cross and recruiting for the Third Crusade in April 1188, in a steep valley near Caernarvon, Baldwin insisted his party dismount and walk 'in intention at least rehearsing what we thought we would experience when we went on our pilgrimage to Jerusalem'.[32] Even for the slightly dour monk-archbishop, provided reason and empirical evidence did not come between man and God, they remained useful tools, not least in the transcendent cause of the recovery of the Holy Sepulchre.

THOUGHTFUL WARRIORS

The thinking knight was a recognized and respected type. Isidore of Seville, the great encyclopaedist of late classical learning in the medieval west, associated heroism with two qualities of rhetoric: *sapientia* and *fortitudo*, wisdom and strength or bravery, in military terms knowledge and skill. Later writers embroidered the duality: measured and rash; cautious and bold. In the *Song of Roland*, the seminal vernacular verse epic of the early twelfth century, these complementary attributes were embodied in the companions in arms Roland and Oliver: '*Roland est proz et Oliver est sage*', the one pure in defiance, headstrong but unassailably noble; the other pragmatic, less extravagantly heroic. One of the earliest chronicle accounts of the First Crusade, an anonymous work known as the *Gesta Francorum et aliorum Hierosolymitanum* ('Deeds of the Franks and other Jerusalemites', compiled by 1104), lists the qualities of Bohemund of Taranto, one of the book's heroes, as an outstanding general: wisdom (or perhaps experience/knowledge) and prudence, followed by power of personality and presence, strength, success, expertise in battle plans and skill at manoeuvring troops. Alongside conventional warlike epithets of courage, strength, bellicosity, etc., Bohemund is frequently characterized as wise (*sapiens*) and prudent (*prudens*) and twice as most experienced or skilled (*doctissimus*).[33] While bled of specific nuances, the choice of epithets was hardly meaningless, especially as the story of the crusade was littered with examples of the folly of human agency: the disasters that accompanied the first wave of crusaders in 1096 under Peter the Hermit; the near disastrous separation of the crusade contingents before the battle with the Turks at Dorylaeum in July 1097. In the very popular revised embellishment of the *Gesta Francorum* by Robert of Rheims (1106/7), the image of Bohemund as the thinking soldier is reinforced: circumspect, prudent and intelligent (literally 'capacious of mind'), astute, perceptive (literally 'seeing much'), very wise and eloquent.[34] Another editor of the *Gesta Francorum* (in *c*.1105), Baldric of Bourgueil, includes a scene in which Bohemund argues for the importance of prudence (*prudentia*) in dealings with the Greeks.[35] Technical expertise in the art of war, *ars bellica*, beyond simply the ability to split skulls, was presented as admirable.[36] Only the hero of these narratives – Bohemund – is so regularly afforded these qualities.

Literary type mimicked reality. One First Crusade commander, Baldwin of Boulogne, later King Baldwin I of Jerusalem (1100–1118), had been well educated in liberal studies (*liberalibus disciplinis*), although, as a younger son originally destined for the Church, he was an exception.[37] Just how exceptional, in an age of high mortality, is unknowable. More significant, perhaps, was the evident value placed on soldiers displaying careful thought, i.e. rationality, if not necessarily academic ability. A trawl through eleventh-century chronicles by P. van Luyn found that the epithet *prudens* only began to be applied to knights at all in the generation of the First Crusade, but then it became the single most frequent description. Thereafter the image of the thoughtful warrior became commonplace.[38] In a crusading context there was a special non-military reason for this. The clerical promoters of the crusade sought to present the enterprise as a means whereby the habitual violence of the increasingly assertive knightly class could be channelled towards a common good and personal salvation. For this conversion to possess any validity, in law or literature, it had to be a conscious transformation, a genuine, rational, considered choice. This emerges from numerous recorded deals by which monasteries provided departing crusaders with cash in return for property. The laymen are regularly described (by the monks, not the laymen themselves) as choosing the Jerusalem journey to expiate their sins and save their souls. The most famous literary expression of this model is Ralph of Caen's early twelfth-century account of the crusading deeds of Tancred of Lecce, Bohemund's nephew. On the one hand, Tancred is depicted as a homicidal thug. But he is also said to have possessed an *animus prudens*, a sensible soul or mind which allowed him to doubt his secular military vocation and accept the offer of redemption through commitment to the crusade.[39] Tancred was not alone. Thoughtful, contemplative warriors were not solely figments of propagandist imaginations. Henry II of England apparently hated the wars he was compelled to fight.[40] Over thirty years ago, Alexander Murray drew attention to the number of founders or other members of religious orders in the eleventh, twelfth and early thirteenth centuries whose conversion to the cloister involved, at some level, a conscious rejection of their own warrior culture, a list that includes the great Abbot Hugh of Cluny (1049–1109), Bernard of Clairvaux (d.1153) and Francis of Assisi (d.1226).[41] As with Tancred, the precise accuracy of these frankly hagiographic accounts is less relevant here than the fact that audiences were invited to recognize these heroic stereotypes as true to life.

We are not here talking about just anyone who could wield a sword, axe or spear. From the second half of the eleventh century, especially in the Francophone regions of western Europe, the term for a heavily armoured cavalryman, *miles*, or knight in English, gradually became associated with class not function. Nobles were increasingly defining themselves through their military identity, witnessed on their seals and monuments, in the development of heraldic badges that spoke of grand lineage as well as individual status, or in the growing enthusiasm for tournaments, a mixture of role-play, training and the assertion of social exclusivity. Nobles referred to themselves as knights (*miles*) in witnessing contracts and were ubiquitously described as such by chroniclers. The association of social power and knightly rank was evident from battlefield to law courts, where knights acted as judges and jurors; to administration, with knights serving as central or local agents of kings, princes and barons; and to the emergent literary genre of vernacular epic and romance. Although equipping and training a professional mounted warrior required wealth or patronage, the assertion of knightly prominence went beyond economic power. The function of fighting on horseback in full armour became the badge of a cultural as well as social elite, one characterized by habits of taste, expectation and behaviour. Broadly, while recognizing regional variations in the nature, degree and pace of change, by the end of the twelfth century these cultural attributes had coalesced into a delicate but clear code of conduct, chivalry. Entry and membership were defined by the ceremony of dubbing a knight, an act that set a clear separation between the knightly and others. In 1100 all nobles were knights, but not all knights, *milites*, were noble. By 1200 this had changed; all dubbed knights were by general acceptance noble and therefore socially, if not always economically, superior to other, excluded, freemen, even those who fought on horseback but lacked dubbed status.[42]

The image of the thoughtful knight was credible because of the education such nobles could receive. Anselm of Ribemont, a second rank commander on the First Crusade, sent letters home, no doubt dictated to a scribe, and was noted for his very great love of learning. Another knight on the First Crusade, Pons of Balazun, helped compile a chronicle of the expedition.[43] One of the knights who stormed Jerusalem on 15 July 1099, the Norman Ilger Bigod, had been a pupil at the abbey school of Bec under the great theologian Anselm, later archbishop of Canterbury. Ilger, who stayed in Syria as marshal of Bohemund's troops in Antioch, was later said to have corroborated the authenticity of Syrian relics by consulting written texts. Bohemund himself almost certainly spoke Greek to the extent he could pun in it. Gregory Bechada, a knightly follower of another First Crusade veteran, apparently knew Latin and spent a dozen years translating an account of the crusade into the southern French vernacular 'so that the populace might fully comprehend it'. Three generations later, Henry II of England was apparently conversant with many languages 'from the coast of France to the river Jordan'.[44] Linguistic skill was then far more an aristocratic accomplishment than now, partly the natural consequence of an internationally mobile nobility and clergy, lack of national frontiers and polyglot regions. The empire of Henry II stretched from the Cheviots and Dublin to the Pyrenees; that of his German contemporary Frederick Barbarossa from the Baltic to central Italy. Those born to rule were provided with the requisite education.

Noblewomen such as the mother and wife of Stephen of Blois, another First Crusade commander, were often well educated, acting as encouragers and disseminators of learning in their families and occasionally as rulers in proxy for male kindred or in their own right. With the culture of writing penetrating legal systems and administration, increasing numbers of laymen were required at the very least to become what has been described as 'pragmatic readers', i.e. possessing the ability to read and understand official documents in Latin. The government of Henry I and Henry II in twelfth-century England increasingly depended on laymen to act as royal justices and financial officials. All three heads of Henry II's administration, called justiciars, were laymen, two of them of knightly not baronial origin. Local royal agents, such as sheriffs in England or *baillis* in France, also had to be able to read to do their jobs, even as they asserted their social status through their warrior credentials. While in northern Europe levels of literacy grew as the culture of writing took firmer hold, formal lettered education was probably more common in southern France and Italy. It has been well observed that everyone's lives depended in some respect on reading and writing, even if by others; and everyone knew someone who could read.[45]

Higher up the social scale, great lords and kings could not function effectively if they lacked basic literacy. Some, like the Beaumont twins in England and Normandy, achieved more. Waleran of Meulan (1104–66) and his twin Robert of Leicester (1104–68) were famously well educated and academically precocious, even if their youthful performance in holding their own in disputation with cardinals in 1119 when they were young teenagers dazzled more brightly because of their status as the sons of Henry I's recently deceased leading minister and the indulged favourites of the king himself. Waleran read and researched Latin documents, possibly composed Latin verse and, with his brother, lived at the centre of an active literary and philosophical circle. He also defined himself as a military figure, was a pioneer of the use of heraldry and fought on the Second Crusade. Robert appears to have been of a more philosophical and legal bent, praised as a learned and meticulous administrator who ended his career as Henry II's justiciar, noted for his forensic skill.[46] While the Beaumont twins may have been exceptional both socially and academically, education in knights and commanders was not seen as incongruous. By the mid-twelfth century wealthy aristocratic laymen were reading, commissioning books and having them dedicated to them. The patronage of the noble knightly classes underpinned the explosion of vernacular poetry and prose. Some, like Geoffrey of Villehardouin, Marshal of Champagne, or the Picard knight Robert of Clari, composed vernacular chronicles of their own (in each case accounts of the Fourth Crusade, 1201–4, on which they both fought). Of course, beyond the basics of reading, further education was a matter of choice. Many members of the ruling classes, then as now, ignored things of the mind for less cerebral pastimes. While Dalmas of Sercy, the purloiner of St Clement's head, was described as very well educated (*valde literatus*), his companion on crusade was considered just a good chap (*virum fidelium et bonum socium*).[47] Walter Map, a gadfly observer of the court antics under Henry II, despaired of the general indifference and disdain towards learning displayed by the English aristocracy. Yet his alleged interlocutor was Ranulf Glanvill (d.1190). A layman of knightly origin who had fought for his king and was to die at the siege of Acre on the Third Crusade, Glanvill had acted as a sheriff, royal justice and, at the time of the conversation with Map, was the king's chief minister, a man of action and learning.[48]

'*Rex illiteratus, asinus coronatus*', 'an unlettered king is a crowned ass', was a popular saying in the twelfth century.[49] Rulers, certainly by the twelfth century, were expected to possess reading literacy, at least in their vernaculars. Presiding over written administration, capacity to engage with this form of business was essential. Solicitous parents hired smart tutors. Some kings, like two of the leaders of the Third Crusade, Frederick Barbarossa, king of Germany and Richard I of England, understood Latin.[50] Richard came from a remarkably academic family. His great-great-grandfather, Fulk IV le Réchin, or Fulk 'the Sour', count of Anjou (1067–1109), composed a chronicle of events of his own times.[51] His son, Count Fulk V (1109–29; king of Jerusalem 1131–43), although famously absent-minded, was praised for his patience and circumspection in military affairs.[52] He – or his wives – also seemed to believe in education for his sons: Geoffrey le Bel, count of Anjou (1129–51) and kings Baldwin III (1143–63) and Amalric of Jerusalem (1163–74). Geoffrey could read Latin, once during a frustrating siege consulting a copy of the late Roman manual on warfare by Vegetius. A contemporary eulogy noted his dedication to arms and to learning (*studiis liberalibus*), describing him as 'excellently educated' (*optime litteratus*).[53] He made sure his son, later Henry II of England (1154–89), followed suit with a first-class education from internationally renowned scholars.[54] Geoffrey's half-brothers, born after Fulk V relinquished Anjou in favour of becoming king-consort in Jerusalem, were cut from similar cloth. Baldwin III left a reputation as an intellectual, expert in the law, enjoying reading, listening to history and learned conversation. This praise may have owed something to convention, as his more lugubrious brother, Amalric, is described in almost identical terms. However, Amalric, as we have seen, was unafraid to question fundamental theological orthodoxy. He too believed in getting the best tutor for his son, the future Baldwin IV (1174–85), appointing William, later archbishop of Tyre. William, a Frank born in Jerusalem, had received a de luxe education in the schools of Paris and Bologna and later wrote a detailed history of the western settlements in Syria and Palestine, one of the most outstanding historical works of the Middle Ages.[55] If the court of Jerusalem nurtured intellectual monarchs, so too did those of their European relatives. Henry II, Geoffrey le Bel's son, spoke Latin and French, enjoyed reading and delighted in showing off his learning and quick wit. One witness described his court as 'school every day, constant conversation with the best scholars and discussion of intellectual problems'.[56] In turn, Henry ensured his sons were well schooled and literate, education that left its mark at least on some of them. Richard's intellectual skills ('Nestor's tongue and Ulysses' wisdom') were regarded by one eulogist as unusual in a knight, but were widely noted and admired, not least his enthusiastic interest in music.[57] John appears to have shared his Jerusalem relatives' interest in the law and legal procedures, while the illegitmate Geoffrey, a future archbishop of York, briefly acted as his father's chancellor, i.e. the head of his writing office.[58]

The extended Angevin dynasties in Europe and Palestine were not entirely atypical. Their standards both reflected noble practice and inspired imitation and were far from unusual among the great noble as well as royal families of the time. These families provided the commanders and planners of the crusades, men of experience and learning, with a culture of informed, circumspect militarism, well able to conceive and plan complex military operations. Relatively, many medieval commanders may have been better educated than some of their nineteenth- and even twentieth-century counterparts. They also had access to the advice of educated clerics, almost all of whom came from the same aristocratic, military social milieu. The papal legate on the First Crusade, Adhemar of Monteil, bishop of Le Puy (d.1098), had direct military experience before and during the campaign.[59] The attraction of the crusade for some of the most impressive intellects of the period tells its own story, from Bernard of Clairvaux through the brightest stars of the University of Paris and Innocent III to the great academic friars of the thirteenth century, including Albert the Great, crusade preacher and translator of Aristotle. Crusades were planned and accompanied by some of the sharpest minds available. While not ensuring success, their involvement secured a buffer against unreason.

When another lively intellectual, Gerald of Wales, sought to provide a (largely unoriginal) manual for princely behaviour, he insisted on *prudentia* as of the greatest practical use in war. In this he included skill at marshalling troops, the ability to anticipate enemy tactics, acquaintance with technical manuals (presumably with Vegetius in mind) and knowledge of past wars through the study of history. He went further by urging the practical importance of formal learning for successful generalship. Among all the victorious princes of world history the two that stood out, he claimed, were Alexander the Great and Julius Caesar, both men of outstanding academic erudition (*litterarum eruditione*). To drive the point home, he added the example of Charlemagne (768–814), the great, iconic early medieval conqueror of most of western Europe, and his tutor Alcuin. It may be less than surprising that an academic was advising the powerful to rely on academic learning for worldly success. Equally, Gerald's opinions, while those of a marginalized, embittered and failed church careerist, were derivative and largely conventional.[60] His alliance of reason and war was consonant with current intellectual opinion and with the social realities of the time, as were his examples with popular taste. To Gerald's contemporaries, as to those who first conceived of a war to conquer Jerusalem over a century earlier, Charlemagne was the prototype and ideal of the holy warrior, in legend the first to liberate the Holy Sepulchre from the infidels.[61]

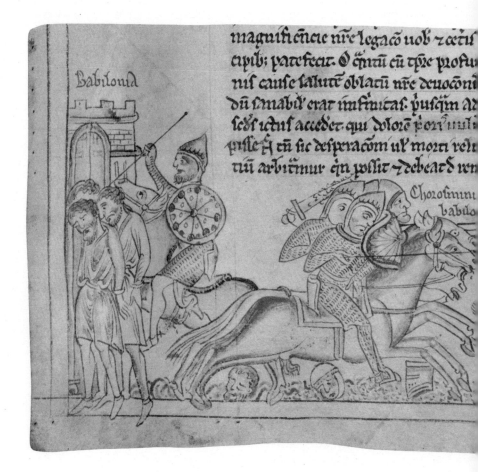

Babilonia

Chorofmini
babilo

magnifi cencie nře legacõ uob �ycētis
cipib; patefecit. O cēntū cū tpe profu-
nis cause salutē oblatū nře deuocõni
dū senabil' erat iusinitas. puſqñ ad
seõs ictus accedet. qui dolorē p en' uul-
piſſe Ħ cū ſic deſperacõm ul' morti reli-
tiū arbitrimur eū poſſit ꝫdebeat ð ren-

Justification

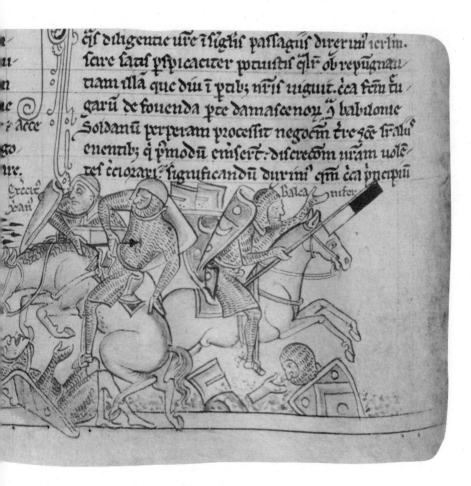

2

Establishing a Case for War

The idea of manufacturing arguments for war strikes a faintly sinister note, not confined to medieval history. Yet all wars require justification to secure the human and material means to fight them. Crusading was no different, except that, in promoting expeditions to the Holy Land, organizers needed to convince potential recruits that events 2,500 miles away were of immediate and urgent concern.

GOD WILLS IT

On 27 November 1095, at the end of an assembly primarily of clergy held at Clermont in the Auvergne in central France, Pope Urban II (1088–99) called for a new type of military campaign to relieve the Turkish threat to eastern Christendom and liberate – his word – Jerusalem from Muslim control. One of the most notorious and memorialized speeches in European history, Urban's sermon and attendant publicity provided the cutting edge to a carefully staged international campaign of propaganda and promotion.[1] Urban's project was radical, a special form of war, a *praelia sancta*, a holy war in answer to God's command in which those who fought with appropriate devotion were to receive spiritual reward. This appeared to contrast with the *legitime bella* or just wars previously sanctioned by the Church in its defence.[2] A critic of papal policy noted that Urban was attempting to convert secular warfare, the army of the world (*militia mundi*), into the army of God (*militia Dei*).[3] The temporal objectives of Urban's scheme were to help the Christians of the eastern Mediterranean in the empire of Constantinople, Byzantium; resist the invasions

29

of Asia Minor by the Seljuk Turks; and free Jerusalem from Muslim rule. Recruits would receive remission of all penance for confessed sins, a uniquely generous privilege. One witness at Clermont recorded that by the time Urban had finished speaking, elements in the congregation had begun to chant '*Deus lo volt*', 'God Wills It!'[4] This war was to be understood as God's special service, a holy act.

The call for war was unequivocal: 'we were stimulating the minds of knights to go on this expedition since they might be able to restrain the savagery of the Saracens by their arms and restore the Christians to their former freedom'.[5] However, the military appeal was wrapped in a specific image of penance and salvation, the Cross, and supported by a new ritual, the formal taking of the Cross in a liturgical ceremony that enhanced the distinctive nature of the enterprise and visibly signalled the creation of a novel religious community: 'soldiers of God' was now no longer a metaphor. The theological pedigree of the operation was unequalled – Christ Himself: 'Take up your Cross and follow me' (Matthew 16:24) appeared early as a slogan.[6] The Clermont remission of the penalties of sin addressed perceived and probably real anxieties among the arms-bearing ruling elite, whose culture of violence, on which their status depended, theoretically clashed with the tenets of their faith. Recruits were secured by swearing a specific oath to the enterprise, a legally binding vow which placed them under the jurisdiction and protection of the Church. The enemy were defined and demonized, but their victims were cast not only as distant easterners but as Christendom itself. In Urban's words, 'the knights who are making for Jerusalem' were going 'with the good intention of liberating *Christianitas*', which, conveniently, could mean either the Christian religion or the Christian community, Christendom. As a supreme act of Christian charity and confraternity, the political became the personal: 'they have risked their belongings and lives for the love of God and their neighbour', the twin, central tenets of Christ's teaching in the Gospels (Matthew 22:37–40). The political was also universal. Urban told counts in Catalonia, on a real frontier with Islam: 'It is no virtue to rescue Christians from the Saracens in one place, only to expose them to the tyranny and oppression of the Saracens in another.'[7] The temporal setting of the first and subsequent crusades was explicitly historical: the loss of swathes of Christendom to Islam since the seventh century and its recovery.

Placed at the centre of propaganda, the physical goal of Jerusalem straddled temporal and spiritual space: a goal of pilgrimage, the site of Christ's life, death and resurrection, its holy topography familiar to the faithful through Bible stories and the liturgy, simultaneously a military destination and a spiritual reward. The Holy Land existed as a virtual reality in the mentality of late eleventh-century western European Christians, a terrestrial relic, a metaphor for Heaven, a goal of life, the scene of the end of time and the Last Judgment as set out in the Book of Revelation. Simultaneously, Jerusalem provided a geographic destination for increasing numbers of western pilgrims, becoming, in the jaundiced lament of one observer, a fashion accessory for the vainglorious pious.[8] The parallel between holy war and pilgrimage, even if not explicit in Urban's own pronouncements, was drawn by many, helping render the novel and radical familiar and safe. Stories of the mistreatment of Jerusalem pilgrims circulated, depicting it as a scene of sacrilegious atrocities and desecration and providing impetus behind the recruiting campaign of Peter the Hermit, who toured central and eastern France in 1095 and led one of the first crusade contingents eastwards just a few weeks after the Clermont Council. The refined appeal of Pope Urban and the demotic outrage of Peter the Hermit together emphasized the direct command from God; the Cross; and Jerusalem, the Holy Sepulchre and their reduction to slavery. Congruency of message, coincidence of timing, Peter's ability to preach in areas ruled by anti-papalists and his later prominence on the campaign itself, suggest at the very least collusion between the two.[9]

The Jerusalem war was no sudden epiphany. It was carefully fitted into central polemical themes of the later eleventh-century papacy: 'liberation of the church' and 'imitation of Christ'. Urban possessed a keen awareness of the tides of Christian history and a special attraction to the relics of the Holy Land, the scene of the Early Church which the papacy sought to emulate and of the prophesied Last Days. Most elements in Urban's plan were already familiar. Spiritual merit in fighting infidels boasted a long tradition in western Europe and had been lent added recognition in the recent conquest of Muslim Sicily by the Normans (1061–91) and successful campaigns against the Moors of Iberia, notably the capture of Toledo by King Alfonso VI of Castile in 1085. Ideas of papal authority in mediating the will of God and authorizing legitimate warfare had gained currency over the previous couple of generations with popes asserting their political and juridical prominence within Christendom. William of Normandy had thought it prudent to acquire papal blessing for his invasion of England in 1066, as had his compatriots in their conquests in southern Italy and Sicily from the 1050s. The promotion of warfare as salutary penance, rather than as a sin requiring expiatory penance, emerged as one of the radical ideas of the papacy of Gregory VII (1073–85) in the long conflict with the German emperor Henry IV (1056–1106) over Church government, known as the Investiture contest.[10] Rumours of the irruption of the nomadic Turks into the settled communities of the Muslim Near East and Christian Byzantine Empire had circulated for more than a generation, fanned by pilgrims' tales of harassment and repeated requests for assistance from the Byzantine emperor, the latest one being received by Pope Urban at Piacenza in March 1095. Twenty years earlier, Gregory VII had floated a scheme to send military aid to Byzantium and to press on to the Holy Sepulchre in Jerusalem that appeared very similar to the plan announced by Urban at Clermont. Gregory's scheme failed through inadequate diplomacy, insufficient political support, lack of slogans and obscure incentives: there were no specific spiritual privileges, just a generalized promise of 'eternal reward'; no vows creating a protected status and sense of special community; no distinctive ritual such as taking the Cross; and no international populist campaign of propaganda. Gregory's emphasis on martyrdom spoke more of his own robust temperament and contrasted with Urban's positive image of bearing the Cross to follow Christ, a clear message with strong and familiar liturgical resonance.[11] Given Urban's close association with Gregory, it is tempting to regard the care and precision vested in constructing a new case for an eastern war as owing something at least to lessons learnt from the failure of 1074.

Nonetheless, Urban II's correspondence shows that he wished to project his scheme as distinctive, a 'new path to salvation' as one close observer put it.[12] The pope's surviving correspondence, although meagre, reveals clarity of intent and purpose, unencumbered by too much detail: crisis; atrocities; obligation; plan; reward. Details, such as the proposed muster on 15 August 1096 under the papal legate Bishop Adhemar of Le Puy, risked being altered or being ignored.[13] No mention was made of an appeal from the Byzantine emperor Alexius I, even though it provided Urban with a suitable crisis to ignite the expedition and show him performing the universal role he claimed was his, thus stealing a march on Henry IV and his client the anti-pope Clement III (1080–1100). Even though Alexius may have spiced his request with reference to the plight of Jerusalem, Urban suppressed the Greek's role to such an extent that news of the Piacenza request has survived in only one contemporary monastic chronicle, from Constance in southern Germany.[14] Urban's letters talk of beleaguered eastern brethren, but not the Byzantine initiative, if such it was, in sharp contrast to Gregory's appeals of 1074. Urban sought to elevate his message above diplomacy or territorial politics. He succeeded. The response was huge. Perhaps as many as 100,000 people were moved to answer the pope's call over the eighteen months following the Clermont Council, a large proportion of whom set out eastwards. In this process, the delicate construction of the case for the Jerusalem war was crucial. Even sources that omitted or diminished the pope's role, including 'eyewitness' chronicles and Latin and vernacular poems, reflect the essentials of Urban's manifesto.[15] In its muscular leanness, the call to Jerusalem in 1095–6 came to provide a model for an extraordinarily resilient habit of violence and religious expression that over the subsequent half-millennium left few corners of Europe or the Mediterranean unscathed.

URBAN'S LEGACY

Crusading offered an unusual model of conflict. If the desire was simply to fight Muslims, Spain was a far closer frontier, but it scarcely took precedence over Jerusalem even when crusading rituals and privileges were extended to Iberia from the early twelfth century. Middle Eastern Islamic rulers between the eleventh and fourteenth centuries posed little direct threat to western Europe. It took a very sophisticated – or sophistical – grasp of what might be termed theopolitics to find a danger to western European safety, prosperity, security or way of life in the Turkish occupation of Palestine, Syria or even Asia Minor in the late eleventh century; in the unification of Syria and Egypt in the twelfth; or in regime changes in the Near East in the thirteenth. Ironically, the two really genuine threats, the non-Islamic Mongols in the thirteenth century and – at least to the eastern and southern fringes of western Europe – the Ottomans from the fourteenth, attracted only feeble or local crusading responses. Nonetheless, the justifications for wars of the Cross resonated throughout medieval Europe, combining two of the most familiar features of secular life: military action and religious gesture. As examples of confected causes for war, those for crusading rank among the most egregious in Eurasian history, considerable monuments to their planners' intellectual, political and promotional ingenuity.

Just as some later historians sought reasons for the crusades in mass hysteria, millenarian enthusiasm or supposed credulous superstition, contemporary commentators, ignoring the practicalities of marketing a cause, were rather taken by the image of a mysterious, divinely inspired 'great stirring' (*motio valida*).[16] Rumour inevitably played its part, as with other instances of popular enthusiasms, medieval or modern, such as the 'terror' of 1064 that inspired mass pilgrimages towards Jerusalem or the revivalist 'Great Alleluia' in Lombardy in 1233 down to *la grande peur* in France in the summer of 1789.[17] On numerous occasions, news of crusades fought, failed or planned incited popular action outside official or elite authority or control: the Children's Crusade of 1212 from France and western Germany at a time of anxiety at repeated Holy Land failures and the supposed threat of heresy in southern France; the Shepherds' Crusade of 1251 in reaction to Louis IX of France's defeat in Egypt; or the similar risings in 1309, in response to the Hospitaller Crusade that conquered Rhodes, and in 1320 in answer to published French schemes for a new Holy Land expedition.[18] However, these communal excitements demonstrated precise causes with clear links to actual crusade plans or campaigns. Even at some remove, they shared the essentials of official propaganda: combating the enemies of Christ; wearing the Cross; and the liberation of Jerusalem. Similarly, if awkwardly for medieval and modern apologists alike, the link between papal crusade rhetoric and populist attacks on the Jews in the Rhineland in 1096 or again in 1147 was direct.[19] All crusades, popular and elite, showed planning and as Hetoum of Gorigos identified, a 'just and reasonable cause'.[20]

In theory, recruitment rested on individual enthusiasm as, legally, taking the Cross was voluntary. Although in practice conditioned by employment, dependency and access to resources, this recruiting culture of ostensible volunteerism imposed on organizers the need to present an agenda of threat, menace and peril. This revolved around the concept of a particular imagined community, Christendom, in which a perceived threat to one part – Byzantium, Jerusalem, the Holy Land, Spain, the lands around the Baltic or the faithful of Languedoc – could be construed as an affront and danger to the whole.[21] Temporal space could be ignored or, with the Holy Land, subsumed in the rhetoric of religious nostalgia for the familiar places of the Bible. The dominant image was Christian victimhood, from Christ on the Cross to His faithful surrounded by enemies 'visible and invisible', as a charter of one departing crusade put it, echoed in one of the various liturgical rites for taking the Cross.[22] As victims of infidels or their own sins, loyal followers of Christ ought to seek redress or reform, even vengeance, through wars couched in terms of repentance and a restoration or assertion of God's order, whether in the Mediterranean, Iberia, the Baltic or within Christendom itself. This Christian obligation imposed sacrifice, effort, fear, suffering, danger and death. However, the reward was great: God's favour, spiritual cleansing, even Paradise itself.

LAW

Within this almost metaphysical understanding of the significance of crusading, planners consistently referred to a corpus of related incentives and justifications. The central idea transcended the limits of just war: good intent; legal cause – defence, or restoration of rights – legitimate authority; proportionate violence. By contrast, holy war represented a spiritually meritorious, transcendent act of devotion and obedience to divine command, a religious duty, not (as with just war) a legal category mitigating an essential sinful activity. Instead of fighting requiring subsequent penance, this violence was itself a penitential act.[23] Holy war scarcely fitted the legal standardization being developed in the twelfth century. It allowed Bernard of Clairvaux to stretch a basic canon law injunction against forcible baptism when he urged people to take the Cross to wipe out or convert pagan Slavs in the Baltic.[24] The great collection of canon law, Gratian's *Decretum* (first drafted in *c.*1139), while having much to say about religious just war, perhaps pointedly avoided wars of the Cross.[25] However, with the arrival of a new breed of Church lawyers, not least on the throne of St Peter, such as Alexander III (1159–81) and Innocent III (1198–1216), crusade justification evolved from its original radical simplicity. Crusading war as legally just as well as holy gained currency among an increasingly university-educated intellectual elite. Proponents included the Jerusalemite chronicler William of Tyre (c.1130–86), educated at Gratian's own university of Bologna, the influential canonist Huguccio of Pisa (d.1210) as well as Innocent III, whose great crusading bull *Quia Maior* (1213) took pains to explain that most of the Near East, including Palestine, had once been Christian until conquered by the 'treachery' of Muhammed. Jesus' purchase of the Holy Land with His blood is coupled with an analogy of a king deprived of his kingdom.[26] Just war interpretations attracted observers some distance from elevated academic circles. In the remote north-east Baltic, Henry of Livonia (c.1188–c.1260) fashioned his creation myth for the Latin Christian conquest of Livonia around not just spurious claims to the region as the heritage of the Virgin Mary, but by careful depiction of the pagan and Russian Orthodox indigenous peoples as *perfidi*, contumacious apostates who thus forfeited their rights to ownership or security.[27]

By the mid-thirteenth century, crusades were decked in the juridical robes of just war and, by 1300, the imperatives of natural law and the laws of nations.[28] New crusading fronts, especially those not involving infidels, demanded slightly different formulae than the Jerusalem wars, with a greater emphasis on just rather than holy war, evident in the language used to promote the crusade against heretics in Languedoc from 1209 to 1229. Here the euphemistic slogan 'the business of faith and peace' was employed instead of the 'business of God' phrase associated with the Holy Land, implying a clearly canonical legal restoration of Christian order.[29] Justifications for wars against infidels developed in similar legalistic fashion. Innocent IV (1243–54), another lawyer pope, placed crusading in the context of inter-faith relations and natural law, to which infidels, like Christians, should adhere. Muslims had rights but not if they contravened natural law, such as condoning sexual perversion, idol-worship, the rejection of Christian missionaries or the persecution of Christians. Idolatrous pagans, therefore, were outside the pale of natural law and thus fair game for conquerors. Furthermore, popes, by virtue of their office, possessed the authority actively to secure the spiritual health of all people. Crusading was legitimate in so far as it conformed to the tenets of just war, being fought defensively to assert or protect rights under natural law and to punish infidels who broke it. The Holy Land did not legally belong to Muslims as it had been bought for Christians not by conquest, as had Muslim dominion, but by Christ's blood and peaceful, voluntary conversion. Furthermore, as it had once been ruled by the Roman Empire and Constantine had, according to the eighth-century forged document known as the *Donation of Constantine*, handed temporal power to the pope, Palestine lay within the patrimony of the pope as both the Vicar of Christ and heir of Constantine. In case the *Donation*'s status was questioned, as some contemporaries did over two centuries before it was finally exposed as a forgery in the fifteenth century, Innocent argued that the current western emperor, Frederick II, was also the legitimate king of Jerusalem and so deserved support in rescuing the Holy Land.[30] Such attention to natural rights presaged later systems of international law developed from the sixteenth century onwards.

Other contemporaries such as the canonist Hostiensis (Henry of Seg-usio, *c*.1200–1271), a pupil of Innocent IV's before he became pope, adopted a more straightforward approach. Although forced conversion remained forbidden, after the Incarnation infidels had no rights to lordship. Yet even this assumed the possibility that non-Christians could possess, or could have possessed, rights, a position taken by the greatest theologian of the age, Thomas Aquinas (1225–74). Like others, Aquinas regarded the Holy Land as an exception, but even so the removal of Muslim rule over Jerusalem was cast as a matter of law as well as religion, the one supporting the other.[31] This assumption of natural law and the rights of non-Christians, even if severely circumscribed, although not contradicting the tradition of Urban II, reflected a changing intellectual climate. Academic subtlety may have lacked popular appeal, but organizers took account of it. Ideology moved on no less than politics.

REVENGE

One juridical category present from the start was vengeance: revenge for the conquest of Christian lands and the sufferings of eastern Christians; for the insult to Christ; and for the deaths and defeats of crusaders.

In theory, vengeance operated within a moral framework of retribution for injury which could lead to the related but distinct legal act of punishment. Throughout the Middle Ages, revenge provided a mechanism of social control in resolving disputes, restoring equilibrium and achieving redress, from blood feuds to judicial combat, of which war could be an enlarged version. The language of vengeance used by crusade promoters and commentators tapped into a common understanding of moral and social obligation to enforce right: duty and justice. Although absent from Urban II's surviving correspondence and many of the frontline narratives of the First Crusade, the idea of couching this holy war as revenge for past and present wrongs proved irresistible to Latin chroniclers and composers of vernacular verse narratives and songs alike. Vengeance conveniently possessed scriptural and religious as well as secular and legal pedigrees, as familiar in monasteries as in law courts or feasting halls. It appealed emotionally to the desire for retribution, and intellectually to the instinct for the restoration of rights. Vengeance embraced general outrage at the ills suffered by Christians, Christ and the Cross – injuries to God, as even the anti-papalist chronicler Sigebert of Gembloux described it within a decade and a half of the First Crusade.[32] Or it focused on specifics: the conquest of Christian lands, the occupation of Jerusalem, the loss of a Christian stronghold or the death of a fellow crusader. An insult to Christ invited parallels with the obligation to fight for one's secular lord, a comparison milked by Innocent III. Vengeance allowed for the ready use of atrocity stories to fuel recruitment, a tactic ascribed to Peter the Hermit. In harnessing vengeance, crusade enthusiasts were recruiting a ubiquitous mentality.[33]

Vengeance as a technique to justify crusade war and engage recruits grew from 1100 onwards. It provided the mainspring for the ideology expressed in the great vernacular epic La Chanson d'Antioche (collated c.1180), as well as for prominent themes in vernacular crusade poems from the Second Crusade to the elite verse of the crusader Count Theobald IV of Champagne (1201–53) in the mid-thirteenth century. Revenge hardened the excuses for the conquest of Livonia in the chronicle of Henry of Livonia and formed the keystone in propaganda for the Third Crusade. Bernard of Clairvaux mined the language of biblical revenge in his letters advocating support for crusades to the Holy Land and the Baltic in 1147, quoting Psalm 149:6–7: 'Let the high praises of God be in their mouth, and a two-edged sword in their hand; / To execute vengeance upon the heathen and punishments upon the people.'[34] Gratian of Bologna's acceptance of vengeance as a legitimate response to injuries to Church and faith, including by unbelievers, possessed clear implication for crusade apologists, including the former Bologna alumnus William of Tyre in his *Historia* of twelfth-century Outremer, as the lands 'over the seas' in the Levant, settled by western Europeans, were known.

However, until Innocent III, who displayed consistent enthusiasm for revenge as a recruiting motif, official papal pronouncements avoided it, preferring the language of defence, liberation, Christian charity and love towards fellow believers. This discrepancy between papal rhetoric and popular attitudes may deceive. Although neither papal bull that launched the Second and Third Crusades (*Quantum praedecessores*, 1145–6 and *Audita Tremendi*, 1187) explicitly called for revenge, they operated within propaganda campaigns that did.[35] The bulls presented the evidence of the atrocities others urged should be avenged. It is hard to imagine Eugenius III (1145–53) distancing himself from the revenge rhetoric of his mentor Bernard of Clairvaux. While Gregory VIII's *Audita Tremendi* emphasized penance, the loss of the Holy Land and the charitable duty to love and aid fellow Christians, his legate promoting the crusade in Germany, Henry of Albano (c.1136–89), in a letter to the faithful in Germany and in one of his associated propagandist tracts, asserted the need to avenge the insult to the Cross. The message got through to the crusader who announced his intention to go on crusade 'to avenge the outrage to the Almighty'.[36] To the legally minded Innocent III, the canon law pedigree of revenge, stretching back past Gratian to earlier interpreters of Augustine of Hippo's just war theories, such as Anselm of Lucca (in his *Collectio canonum*, c.1083), would not have made this appear inappropriate in the slightest. As the historian, canonist, liturgist and crusader Sicard of Cremona (1155–1215) commented, one category of just war was indeed vengeance. Bernard of Clairvaux – no lawyer – went further. When praising the new military Order of the Templars in the 1130s, he argued that Christ gloried in the death of infidels, quoting Psalm 58:10–11: 'The righteous shall rejoice when he seeth the vengeance: he shall wash his feet in the blood of the wicked. So that a man shall say, "Verily there is a reward for the righteous: verily he is a God that judgeth in the earth." [37]

CHIVALRY

This fusion of vendetta and holy war, the profane and sacred, was typical of crusading and central to its promotion. Crusades were designed to exploit the culture, skill and resources of warriors by focusing on their possible anxieties at the contradictions between their lives and the precepts of the Scriptures, 'the Gospels or the world?' as one early twelfth-century writer put it, fears fuelled by clerical advisers eager for penitential profit. [38] As an explicitly military endeavour, crusading was inescapably couched in terms of valour and martial reputation. By sanctifying martial prowess, crusading helped cast arms-bearing as a profession blessed by religion, an *ordo pugnatorum*, defined as complementary to the clerical order by a pro-papal publicist, Bonizo of Sutri, in the late eleventh century. Such men fought 'for their salvation and the common good' against enemies of the Church and defended the helpless, widows, orphans and poor. [39] The sanctification of arms was picked up enthusiastically in accounts of the First Crusade. In his biography of the First Crusade commander Tancred of Lecce, Ralph of Caen summed up the effect of Urban II's new deal. Tancred's violent, predatory military life no longer contradicted God's commands, now 'his experience in arms recalled him to Christ' (*experientia vero armorum ad Christi obsequium revocata*). [40] Vernacular versions of the story of the First Crusade are drenched in the language and culture of martial heroics and honour. Christian knighthood was not invented by the First Crusade. It enjoyed a long history, back to Charlemagne or even Constantine the Great. Byzantine emperors had evolved a doctrine of holy war in the seventh century. Popes had blessed campaigns against Muslims in the ninth century, and more recently in wars in Italy in the 1040s, Sicily, England and possibly Spain in the 1060s. Gregory VII had tried, not very successfully, to recruit a *militia Sancti Petri* during his struggle against the German emperor. However, the First Crusade and its successors, in song, prose, sermon and verse, as well as in action, provided a new yardstick, a focus of exemplary models, a pool of admirable stories to illustrate what was punningly described as the *militia Christi*, a righteous, if equally bloody alternative to secular *malitia*, the evil of secular war.[41]

Crusading became a feature of the increasingly exclusive knightly habits and institutions known as chivalry, an aristocratic code of conduct and mentality that by 1200 provided the badge of identity for the ruling caste of western Europe. Crusading in the east became part of a knightly career, attracting such figures as the future Conrad III of Germany or Fulk V of Anjou in the 1120s, or Count Thierry of Flanders (in 1139, 1147, 1157 and 1164) and his son Philip (in 1177 and 1190). Famously, around 1143, the English baron Brian FitzCount, mired in the moral ambiguities of bloody civil war between Matilda and King Stephen, cited the *boni milites* of the First Crusade as paragons of honour and virtue. Eugenius III, in his bull launching the Second Crusade, emphasized the achievements of the warriors of 1096 and their successors in conquering and defending the Holy Land.[42] Bernard of Clairvaux picked up the theme in a recruiting letter, exhorting 'mighty men of valour', 'mighty soldiers', 'men of war' to 'a cause for which you can fight without danger to your souls; a cause in which to conquer is glorious and for which to die is gain' (a familiar play on Paul's Epistle to the Philippians 1:21, 'For to me to live is Christ, and to die is gain').[43]

Some tension between clerical rhetoric and chivalric practice remained. Tournaments were repeatedly banned by Church councils as harmful to the 'business of the Cross'.[44] However, increasingly, and according to some sources, from the very start, crusading came to be regarded not as an alternative to secular knighthood but as a supreme chivalric act. Robert of Rheims, a participant at the Council of Clermont, may have echoed elements of the preaching campaign of 1095–6 when he had Urban II praise the martial reputation of the Franks and their ancestors: 'most strong soldiers and the offspring of unvanquished parents'.[45] If vernacular and Latin verses composed in the generation immediately after the First Crusade are indicative, the message that the Jerusalem campaign represented the height of martial glory had been very effectively disseminated and enthusiastically received. The Occitan *Canso d'Antiocha*, possibly compiled by a Limousin knight, dwells on the details of fighting in a manner reminiscent of the *chansons des gestes*. First Crusade leaders such as Bohemund and Robert of Normandy were praised for military prowess as much as for piety. Albert of Aachen's portrait of Godfrey of Bouillon's deeds of arms provides a classic depiction of a *Christi athlete*, champion of Christ. According to the English chronicler William of Malmesbury, writing *c.*1125, Robert of Normandy's deeds of arms led to his being offered the crown of Jerusalem itself. Geoffrey Gaimar's vernacular French verse chronicle, written in Lincolnshire *c.*1136–7, unambiguously described Robert's crusading deeds as illustrative of his '*mainte bele chevalerie*' (much good chivalry). Not the least attraction of war was the opportunity to enhance one's reputation.[46]

This could be played out in competition with ancestral martial glory, as Eugenius III had recognized. At the crusaders' siege of Lisbon in 1147, en route to the Holy Land, the East Anglian lord, Hervey of Glanvill, reportedly tried to persuade his fellow Anglo-Norman crusaders to act together, by appealing to 'the virtues of our ancestors', the Normans' 'glorious deeds' and the 'military spirit' (*militia*): 'we ought to strive to increase the honour and glory of our race'.[47] Forty years later, in an account of Danish recruitment for the Third Crusade, the nobleman Esbern was described as exhorting his audience to action by reference to the great if violent deeds of their pagan Viking ancestors, sustained not by religion but by the desire for fame, 'worthy of perpetual glory'.[48]

Secular imagery became commonplace. A song composed at the time of the Second Crusade described it as a tournament between Heaven and Hell. During the Fourth Crusade (1199–1204), one of the commanders, Count Hugh of St Pol, wrote to Duke Henry of Brabant from Constantinople in the summer of 1203:

> You should also know that we have accepted a tournament against the sultan of Babylon in front of Alexandria. If, therefore, anyone wishes to serve God ... and wishes to bear the distinguished and shining title of 'knight', let him take up the Cross and follow the Lord, and let him come to the Lord's tournament, to which he is invited by the Lord himself.[49]

A verse chronicle of the Third Crusade, possibly composed within a decade of the events by a layman known as Ambroise, portrays it as a series of chivalric adventures, with Richard I as hero. Here and else-where, Richard and other leaders are favourably compared with iconic heroes of chivalric epics including Roland and Oliver. The com-pilation known as the *Itinerarium Ricardi Regis*, constructed from a selection of immediate sources and eyewitness recollections a gener-ation after the Third Crusade, and probably intended as a spur to encourage recruits for the Fifth Crusade (1217–21), provided a hand-book of chivalry.[50] Other thirteenth-century texts, especially (but not exclusively) those in the vernacular by laymen such as Geoffrey of Villehardouin and Robert of Clari on the Fourth Crusade or John of Joinville on the crusades of Louis IX of France, followed suit.[51]

A poem by Conon of Béthune, a crusader on both the Third and Fourth Crusades, *Ahi! Amours, con dure departie* ('Oh, Love! How hard will be the parting') captures the spirit of chivalric crusading. Pack-aging the official message in the more accessible medium of vernacular song, probably as part of the propaganda effort in 1188–9, Conon imagined the crusade entirely within the conventions of chivalry:

> Let great and small alike know
> that it is the place [i.e. the Holy Land] where one wins paradise and
>   honour,
> merit, reputation and the love of one's beloved
> that one must do deeds of chivalry
> . . .
> He who returns will be fortunate:
> honour will be his companion all his days.

Yet Conon's lover, separated from his lady, does not ignore the basic religious imperative and incentives: 'No man must fail his Creator.' Duty, revenge, the promise of salvation, the redemption of the Cross: all are woven into what appears superficially a traditional love song. The Holy Land is 'that place where God will cleanse my heart'. Conon touched on another prominent secular feature of the crusade message:

> If we now leave our deadly enemies there
> we shall suffer the disgrace for the rest of our lives.
> Let the man who would not live a shameful life here
> go and die for God, happy and joyful

. . .

. . . those who are healthy, young and wealthy
cannot remain here without being shamed.[52]

The lure of reputation and the infamy of dereliction of duty suffused
both clerical and secular propaganda. Papal bulls repeatedly cited the
fame of biblical or historical military exemplars as goads to action.
The status of effective crusade leaders – the heroes of 1099, Richard I
or Louis IX – supplied their own incentive. The disgrace of backsliders, such as Stephen of Blois and others who abandoned the siege
of Antioch in 1098, was equally plain. The vehemence of Villehardouin's
castigation of those who failed to join or stay with the main crusade
force that diverted to Constantinople in 1202–4 rested on his conception of the Fourth Crusade as a fulfilment of a series of oaths: taking
the Cross; the treaties with the Venetians and then with the Byzantine
pretender. Honour and good repute acted as central moral yardsticks.
An observer of the massive recruitment drive for the Third Crusade
noted that those regarded as potentially reluctant to join up were sent
wool and distaffs as signs of craven effeminacy, a medieval version of
the white feathers of 1914.[53] In the thirteenth century, the armchair
crusader and the *descroisié*, the man who redeemed his vow for cash
with no wish to leave home and comfort for the risky passage east,
became familiar literary – and actual – archetypes. The French poet
Ruteboeuf's *descroisié* in the 1260s argued that God could be found
in France as well as in Outremer.[54] However, as Philip V of France
warned a cousin in 1319, failure to turn crusade promises into action
would provoke '*la honte du monde*', the world's shame.[55]

While Joinville's portrait of Louis IX, the overtly chivalrous and
essentially saintly crusader, depicted the supreme refinement of the
union of secular and spiritual, stories of knightly valour were not
the exclusive preserve of the laity, or even of chroniclers. They feature
prominently in thirteenth-century crusade sermons, particularly as
exempla, morally uplifting anecdotes to illustrate the preacher's arguments. In an early thirteenth-century English crusade-preaching manual,
such anecdotes, in the vernacular for direct impact, dealt with deeds
of arms against the odds, brave knights courting death and salvation for God's sake, including stories of well-known crusade heroes

such as James of Avesnes, a much-fêted crusade commander killed at Arsuf in 1191.[56] The elevation of crusading as a chivalric enterprise, the pinnacle of knightly ambition, deliberately followed the grain of aristocratic culture and social mores, part of a more general Church policy to evangelize the laity, raise their religious awareness and control their observance. The simultaneous militarization of the faith and apotheosis of knighthood was succinctly captured by the veteran French crusade preacher, papal legate, crusader and cardinal, Odo of Châteauroux (c.1190–1273). In one of his collected sermons *De Inventione Crucis*, 'On the Discovery of the Cross', on a text from the Second Book of Maccabees 15:16 ('Take this holy sword, a gift from God, with which you will strike down your adversaries'), Odo explained God's approval of war in his service, in this instance against the Mongols who were threatening eastern and central Europe. He argued that the holy sword – i.e. God's war – was not just sanctified by the Cross but '*Crux enim gladius est*'; the Cross is the sword.[57]

MATERIAL REWARD

The crusade decree at Clermont explicitly excluded from the promised spiritual reward those who undertook the Jerusalem war hoping for 'honour or money' ('*pro honoris vel pecunie*'), the Latin *honor* here probably meaning lands or titles rather than reputation or glory. In his subsequent letters Urban II confirmed this, talking of the reward in terms of religious obligation and penance. However, the Clermont decree was concerned with crusaders' motives, not their actions on crusade or the consequences of them. Thus rewards need not solely be spiritual. The compiler (or compilers) of the *Gesta Francorum* recorded an early crusader battle cry: 'Stand fast all together, trusting in Christ and the victory of the Holy Cross. Today, please God, you will all gain great riches (*omnes divites*).' The ambiguity of *divites* was apt. Soldiers of Christ could expect rewards temporal as well as divine, and those promoting the crusade acknowledged the fact.[58]

Some close to the papal court, including participants at the Council of Clermont, recorded Urban offering specifically material incentives. Fulcher of Chartres, a northern French priest who went on crusade, had met Pope Urban in 1096 and apparently enjoyed access to papal documents. He suggested that Urban implied, if only metaphorically, landed prosperity for those who answered God's call as well as eternal reward. Two witnesses to Urban's sermon were more explicit. According to Baldric of Bourgueil, Christian knights were promised their 'enemies' possessions' (*facultates*), i.e. a normal incentive of war. This formula is reflected in the *Canso d'Antioca*, parts of which may date to within twenty years of the crusade, where material profit and wealth are considered just reward for victory according to 'due process of law'. Robert of Rheims, whose chronicle of the First Crusade was the most popular version in the twelfth century, had Urban appeal to Frankish knights' self-respect and desire to gain reputation and imitate the glories of their ancestors, promising them the Holy Land 'flowing with milk and honey' (Exodus 3:8) to conquer and colonize (*'vobis subjicite'*).[59] The attraction of new lands was couched in economic terms. Western Europe was overcrowded, and unable to support its agricultural workers. Competition for scarce resources lay behind violent internecine feuding. Thus the crusade would resolve material, social and economic as well as religious, spiritual and political problems. After a succession of poor harvests this was a compelling analysis. However, all these accounts were compiled after the establishment of Latin rule in Syria and Palestine. Whether or not Urban himself presented his expedition in such terms, others clearly did, as many who started the journey east appeared to be emigrants, taking with them their families and portable possessions. A German abbot, Ekkehard of Aura, also noted that dire economic circumstances had encouraged many recruits, in some cases stirred up by local, self-appointed preachers independent of the official recruiting campaign.[60]

Material incentives varied across the theatres of operations. Wars in the Baltic to which crusade institutions were attached represented unequivocal and unashamed land grabs veneered with religious overlay. Support for crusade ventures in the eastern Mediterranean from the maritime cities of Italy, Pisa, Genoa and Venice was encouraged by prospects of commercial privileges in the conquered ports of the Levant, such as Acre (the Pisans and Genoese in 1104) or Tyre (the Venetians in 1124). Venetian enthusiasm for the Fourth Crusade was sparked by the prospect of helping the crusaders invade Egypt and breaking into the fabulously lucrative trade network centred on Alexandria. The Albigensian Crusades after 1209 developed into an exercise in regime change and the seizure of southern French lordships by northerners (and ultimately by the French crown). In none of these cases was territorial acquisitiveness the sole or, for many, presiding incentive. However, the crusade mentality never excluded profit. The conventions of official crusade rhetoric insisted on the transcendent not the temporal. Recruiters were not so squeamish. Gunther of Pairis happily quotes Abbot Martin of Pairis's crusade address at Basel in 1201 setting out a temporal case for taking the Cross:

> the land to which you are headed is by far richer and more fertile than this land, and it is easily possible that ... many in your ranks will acquire a greater prosperity even in material goods there than they will have remembered enjoying back here. Now, brothers, look at how great a guarantee comes with this pilgrimage. Here, in the matter of the kingdom of heaven, there is an unconditional pledge [i.e. the plenary indulgence]; in the matter of temporal prosperity, a better than average hope.[61]

Material incentives were further provided by crusaders' temporal privileges. At or shortly after the Council of Clermont, the pope placed each crusader and his (almost invariably his, although there appears to have been no barrier to, or absence of, women taking the Cross from the start) family and property under the protection of the Church, an extremely prudent move given the risks inherent in leaving home for a such a lengthy, unspecified period.[62] Until the completion of his vow, the crusader enjoyed a quasi-clerical relationship with the rest of society. This attracted a series of immunities and other privileges, legal and, enticingly, financial. By the 1140s, a comprehensive system had emerged, increasingly understood and recognized by both ecclesiastical and lay authorities. Eugenius III listed the most prominent privileges in 1145–6: Church protection for the crusader's property, wife and children; immunity from civil law suits against a crusader's property for the term of his crusade or until the crusader's death; exemption from payment of interest on all previous loans; and freedom to raise money for the crusade by pledging property as collateral.[63] These core privileges were repeated for subsequent Holy Land expeditions.

The consequences of these temporal privileges indicated their significance. The legal immunities and the provisions regarding usury and borrowing clashed with secular law and customs, provoking a series of negotiations between local and regional lay and ecclesiastical authorities to agree limits. Critics argued – and law courts wondered – that immunity from civil law suits constituted a criminals' charter, with defendants taking the Cross to avoid facing trial. So, various local restrictions were set on the nature of the litigation and the duration of the immunity from appearance to answer charges. Provision regarding crusaders' debts were similarly curtailed, not least because the initial exemption from usury inevitably undermined a crusader's creditworthiness and seriously challenged the validity of contracts, a point recognized in the Fourth Lateran Council's crusade decree *Ad Liberandam* in 1215.[64] It may be no coincidence that the council was attended by representatives of local clergy and lay rulers who actually had to cope with these problems. In 1188, the kings of England and France had had to clarify the implied papal grant of crusaders' immunity from taxation. The precise details and scope of the crusade privileges continued to be modified over time and in different places.[65] However, their general purpose was clear and deliberate, 'providing peace of mind' (*vestrorum quieti*), in Eugenius III's words, or, as Innocent III had it, a 'special right' (*speciali prerogativa*).[66]

SPIRITUAL REWARD

The central distinguishing privileges were spiritual: the remission of the penalties of confessed sin in this world and the next.[67] Away from the legal and theological niceties of what precisely was being remitted – the temporal penance or the guilt of the sin itself – the nature of the offer was clear in promotion and reception. Salvation for those who died in the service of the Cross and, for all survivors who fulfilled their vows, satisfaction and remission of all confessed sins: as Bernard of Clairvaux wrote in 1146, 'a bargain: the cost is small, the reward is great'. The privilege was symbolized by the Cross, crusaders, in the words of Fulcher of Chartres, 'signing themselves with the image so that they might attain its reality (*rem speciei*)'. The Cross was variously promoted as a victorious ensign, a 'heavenly sign', a 'sign of

salvation'.[68] While lacking the technical trappings of the fully elabor-
ated penitential system of the later medieval church, the reward
offered was clear enough to participants. One of them, Geoffrey of
Villehardouin (*c.*1160–*c.*1212), a veteran of the Third and Fourth
Crusades, attributed the popularity of the Fourth Crusade to the offer
to crusaders of being 'quit of all confessed sins they had committed . . .
because the pardon was so great (*si granz*)'. Although still canonically
equivocal, Innocent III's formula, followed by his successors, provided for a complete pardon (*'plenam suorum peccaminum veniam
indulgemus'*) of confessed sins.[69] To people taught that they were all
sinners, the attraction of avoiding excruciating punishment post mor-
tem cannot be exaggerated.

Yet further inducements may have been introduced. Villehardouin
claimed the indulgence on offer on the Fourth Crusade was for anyone who served in the crusader army for a year. The papal bull of
1198 made no such offer, the nearest to it being the grant of the plenary indulgence to those who sent and paid for proxies provided these
served for at least two years. The length of qualifying service became
a matter of local interpretation and academic debate. In English and
French law courts, varying terms were accepted for crusaders' immunity from appearance to answer lawsuits: three years; five years; seven
years; or indefinite. During the Fifth Crusade, crusaders adopted a
very flexible approach to what constituted fulfilment of their vow,
as had Philip II of France and others during the Third Crusade. No
longer did all crusaders feel the need to see the campaign through to
its end; nor, increasingly, were they expected to. To match local conditions and, so one observer had it, lukewarm recruits, on the campaigns
against heretics and others in Languedoc, the qualifying term was
only forty days, on the model of secular military obligation.[70] In the
Baltic, one season of campaigning appears to have sufficed.

This flexibility or relaxation of the crusaders' physical obligation was
matched by variations of the scope of the spiritual privileges. From
the Third Crusade, and clearly established by Innocent III, indulgences
were extended to those who assisted the crusade in ways other than
personal service, by providing proxies, money or materiel. From 1213,
crusaders could redeem their vows for material contributions, usually
cash. Extending access to the uniquely generous crusade indulgence

suited the thirteenth-century Church's attempts to evangelize the laity. Now the old, the sick, the infirm, the young and women could be enrolled in the project via the spiritual benefits without having to join up. By the end of the thirteenth century, indulgences were sold outright, without the need to take the Cross. Fractions of the crusade indulgence had begun to be pedalled much earlier: in 1188 to those who paid the crusade tax (the Saladin Tithe) and, from 1213, even to those who attended crusade sermons. Fifty years later, the propagandists/preachers themselves were rewarded with the full indulgence. By then, not only did crusaders' wives and children enjoy the indulgence, but on occasion so did loved ones (*caros suos*, according to one crusade preacher in the 1240s) and even dead relatives.

Taking the Cross was good for you – and for those dear to you. An additional raft of formal and informal spiritual benefits increased the attraction: exemption from the penalties of excommunication and interdict; the power to appoint personal confessors who could then absolve crusaders from an eclectic range of penances and crimes. More inventively, some ascribed to taking the Cross – by combating the Devil – power to heal deformities and cure illness.[71] While no entirely coherent legal theory of crusading emerged in the High Middle Ages, the burgeoning apparatus of justifications and privileges constituted an easily recognized pragmatic ideology, part military, part religious, part social, a normative cultural activity. Planners had to marry ideological vision with administrative necessity. Even where crusade institutions covered palpably and predominantly material and avaricious intentions, as in the Baltic, the language and conceptualization of holy war reflected more than immediate cynical exploitation. Albert of Buxhövden, the aggressive and acquisitive bishop of Livonia (1199–1229), intended to establish an ecclesiastical empire by force if necessary. He may also have believed that he was performing God's will.[72] Only anachronistic sensibilities find this contradictory. Elastic application of crusade language and institutions depended on general contemporary acceptance of an elaborate, inclusive Christian code of thought and moral behaviour that characterized the European High Middle Ages, in theory addressing all aspects of life, sex, marriage and death; economic, personal and political relationships; and attitudes to God, spiritual vocation, learning and the natural world. Crusading emphasized God's immanence and His scrutiny of believers' individual and collective conduct, a relationship sealed by the offer of spiritual reward for faithful service, rational responses to the implications of belief in what was assumed to be a divinely ordered world.

POLITICS

While spiritual and temporal incentives underpinned every crusade war appeal, manifest crises provided the immediate excuse: the threat to Byzantium in 1095; the loss of Edessa in 1144; the defeat of Hattin in 1187; the final fall of Jerusalem in 1244; the loss of Antioch in 1268; the final evacuation of Acre in 1291; the capture of a stronghold; the end of a truce. News of each disaster was usually spiced with stories of atrocities and desecration of relics and portrayed as a danger to all Christianity. The problem lay in how to make remote or complex political crises appear sufficiently catastrophic and threatening. For all its religious freight, the crusade, like any other war, required a plausible temporal cause. Without a convincing narrative of imminent or actual disaster, even the defence of the Holy Land could fail to elicit support. Between 1149 and 1187, despite repeated requests from Jerusalem for aid and vocal papal backing, no substantial expedition went to help the beleaguered Latin states in Syria and Palestine.[73] Concrete events rather than general conditions of weakness were needed, however trivial in themselves. In 1198 Innocent III used the conclusion of the German crusade (1195–8) and the renewed threat of Muslim attack as an excuse to launch the Fourth Crusade. In 1213, he cited the construction of an Ayyubid fort on Mount Tabor near Acre as the reason to launch the Fifth Crusade.[74] The importance and sensitivity of identifying a suitably popular war objective was evident in the nervous concealment of Egypt rather than the Holy Land as their target by the leaders of the Fourth Crusade.[75] Public opinion had not yet been softened up to accept this new-fangled strategy as it was to be in subsequent decades.

Recruitment for the Third Crusade showed the power of clear strategic justifications. In July 1187, the Christian army of Jerusalem had been annihilated at Hattin in Galilee by the army of Saladin, sultan of Egypt and ruler of Damascus. Most of the Christian Holy Land soon fell, the Holy City itself capitulating in October. Writing before news of the fall of Jerusalem had reached the west, Pope Gregory VIII's bull *Audita Tremendi* described Saladin's victory in lurid detail: the loss of the relic of the True Cross habitually carried by the Christian Jerusalemite armies as a totem of God's favour; the slaughter of bishops; the capture of King Guy of Jerusalem; the executions of Templars and Hospitallers after the battle; the dire consequences for the rest of the Holy Land. The pope noted the indifference to the plight of the Holy Land since the Second Crusade. Now he insisted that the disaster in Palestine was not just a crisis in a far-away country but an immediate responsibility for all believers.[76] While coming to the relief of fellow Christians in Outremer was presented as a gesture of spiritual renewal, subsequent propaganda stressed more tangible Muslim atrocities, notably the killing of Reynald of Châtillon allegedly by Saladin himself.[77] Reynald, in life pugnacious rather than conspicuously pious, was transformed in death into an improbable unofficial martyr. Saladin, although later glamorized in the west, was demonized in papal bulls, sermons and propaganda tracts. Some preachers allegedly even employed large painted canvas cartoons of Saladin's horse fouling the Holy Sepulchre to whip up feeling.[78] Such was Saladin's identification as the bogeyman of the war, the Napoleon or Hitler of the day, that the tax levied in parts of western Europe to subsidize the crusade was known even at the time as the Saladin Tithe.

Tens of thousands joined the Third Crusade, perhaps more than any previous eastern expedition. However, such successful branding became harder to replicate as the crusade and the defence or recovery of the Holy Land became the permanent 'business of the Cross'.[79] A hint of wishful thinking may have informed Innocent III's use in 1213 of apocalyptic prophecy to foretell the fall of Islam: the time of 'the beast', i.e. Islam, according to the Book of Revelation, is 666 years 'of which nearly 600 have passed'.[80] Yet biblical prophecy, regarded as wholly rational by even the best educated, remained central to crusade polemic. During the Fifth Crusade in Egypt (1217–21), the morale of the army was buoyed by a series of optimistic prophecies signalling the overthrow of Islam enthusiastically promoted by the crusade leadership, including intellectuals such as James of Vitry, academic, preacher, bishop of Acre and future cardinal.[81] Elsewhere, the prominent if maverick mystic theologian Joachim of Fiore briefly interpreted the crusade in millenarian terms.[82] Inevitably the divine mathematics of chronological prophecies shifted with passing years. Into the early fourteenth century, the prophecy of Daniel 12:12 became popular: 'Blessed is he that waiteth, and cometh to the thousand three hundred and five and thirty days.' After 1335 its popularity faded. Prophecy played well with potential recruits and suited the increasingly wide, global, almost cosmic strain in crusade rhetoric. 'Now is the accepted time' (2 Corinthians 6:2) was a familiar cry. Yet, as with all crusade polemic, prophecy staled with repetition and failure.

The extension of crusade institutions to other theatres of religious or ecclesiastical conflict further complicated the substance and effect of war propaganda. In 1213, Innocent III cancelled the spiritual privileges for the crusades in Spain against the Almohads and in Languedoc to concentrate on his new Holy Land enterprise, only to be thwarted in the latter by local politics and the determination of the pope's erstwhile champion, Simon of Montfort (d. 1218), to carve out a dynastic principality for himself in southern France.[83] Gregory IX (1227–41) authorized crusades against German and Frisian peasants, Bosnians, Russians, Mongols, Livonians and Frederick II of Germany, as well as to defend the Holy Land and the Latin empire of Constantinople established after the Fourth Crusade.[84] In the late 1230s some French counts refused to swop Jerusalem vows for Greece and a group of English crusaders apparently swore oaths confirming their Holy Land destination 'lest their honest vow be hindered by the objections of the Roman Church and diverted to shedding Christian blood in Greece or Italy'.[85] In 1229, Frederick II had negotiated the return of Jerusalem to Christian rule as an open city. When the city was again lost in 1244, a new crusade was announced in traditional terms. However, a few days after calling for a new Jerusalem crusade, Pope Innocent IV (1243–54) summoned a general council of the Church to Lyons to discuss, in addition, expeditions to Greece, to resist the Mongols and to combat Frederick II.[86] Pope Alexander IV (1254–61)'s attempts to divert Holy Land crusade taxes towards an anti-Hohenstaufen campaign in 1255 led by Henry III of England (1216–72) provoked vocal protests.[87] Too much politics, perhaps. In the event, the recruitment of the subsequent eastern Mediterranean crusade of 1248–50 largely rested with the king of France, Louis IX (1226–70).

Louis himself had taken the Cross, in the gilded memory of his associates, not because of the loss of Jerusalem or papal injunction, but in thanks for a seemingly miraculous recovery from near-fatal illness.[88]

Crusade planning exposed the reactive nature of the medieval papacy. Increasingly, the application of crusade privileges derived from local requests as much as papal initiatives or urgent international crises: crusades on demand. It was on the instigation of regional princes and clerics that popes attached crusading privileges to attempts to suppress troublesome social elements in the Netherlands (the Drenther 1228–32), the Lower Weser region of north-east Germany (the Stedinger 1232–4) and Bosnia (from 1241).[89] The cases for war here came from those already eager to fight, the reverse of the traditional model. Papal rhetoric merely provided the necessary authorization for recruitment through preaching and the incentives of crusade privileges and taxes – as was even more apparent when the local power seeking the authority of the crusade was, self-referentially, the pope himself, in the series of Italian wars conducted against a succession of political opponents in the peninsula from the 1230s to the early fifteenth century.[90]

Lending secular and ecclesiastical politics spiritual dimensions required delicate manipulation. Crusading in Spain followed the often vertiginous contours of regional politics, even to the extent that wars of the Cross were promulgated against Christian kings. In 1197 Pope Celestine III issued Holy Land indulgences for those who fought Alfonso IX of León who, seeking aid in his wars against his Christian neighbours, had allied himself with the Almohads of Morocco. Popes repeatedly lamented the damaging Christian internecine feuding while entrenching the crusade against the Moors. These complexities were well embodied by Alfonso IX himself who died in 1230, by then a fêted crusader.[91] In another political contradiction, Peter II of Aragon, a hero of the great crusading victory over the Almohads at Las Navas de Tolosa in 1212, was killed at the battle of Muret in 1213 fighting the anti-Cathar crusading champion in Languedoc, Simon of Montfort, for control over the county of Toulouse. Whatever else it was, the so-called *Reconquista* was far from one long sequence of Christian wars against the infidel inspired by faith alone.

In the Baltic, commercially ambitious Lübeck merchants, empire-building German clerics and territorially expansionist Danish kings drove the early thirteenth-century conquest of Livonia (now Latvia and Estonia).[92] Livonia was rebranded as the land of God's Mother, its inhabitants either backsliding pagans who rejected conversion or aggressive 'schismatics' (i.e. Russian Orthodox Christians). Wars of colonial invasion were portrayed as necessary defence against wilfully evil enemies of God and His people and were projected as holy, a task rendered easier once the initial German colony had been established. This exercise was wholly self-conscious, led by Cistercian missionaries and the militant bishops of Riga, lauded by clerical hagiographers and chronicled by a German cleric, Henry of Livonia. Henry distorted papal policy to make it seem more consistently committed to the Livonian crusade than in fact it was. His account of Innocent III's enthusiasm for a crusade to protect the land of the Virgin Mary at the Fourth Lateran Council, for instance, is contradicted by the pope's own corres- pondence, in which he carefully distinguished the needs of the Christian bridgehead in Livonia from his great Jerusalem enterprise.[93]

The Livonian concealment of territorial conquest behind defensive crusading was paralleled later in the thirteenth century by the violent German colonization of Prussia. In effect a brutal and lengthy land seizure by competing German and Polish rulers, the conquest of Prussia was designated a legitimate religious exercise. As in Livonia, secular imperialism literally under a religious banner (the Cross and the Virgin Mary) became institutionalized. In Livonia, initially this had centred on the Sword Brothers, founded by the bishop of Riga around 1202. In Prussia, which attracted papal crusading bulls from 1217, the conquest was increasingly vested in the Teutonic Knights, originally a hospitaller religious order founded by German contingents in the Holy Land during the Third Crusade. Militarized by the early thirteenth century, a series of papal bulls from 1226 onwards gave the Order autonomous lordship in Prussia, in 1245 being granted the power to call for crusades without requiring specific papal permission. From 1237, the Teutonic Knights assumed the military and political role of the Sword Brothers in Livonia following the latter's near-annihilation by the pagan Lithuanians. Thereafter, the Teutonic Knights consolidated linked 'order states' in an arc stretching from Pomerania in the west to Estonia in the north-east. Crusading's ideological fusion of the temporal and spiritual reached a material consummation in members of a professed religious order operating as temporal rulers. The Virgin Mary, patroness of Livonia and the Teutonic Order, was re-imagined as a war goddess and the Teutonic Knights portrayed as the heirs of the Apostles. Such transformations were inherent in the crusading enterprise of holy politics. Not everybody was convinced. In the 1260s and 1270s the Oxford don Roger Bacon suggested that crusading and the aggressive colonial policies of the Teutonic Knights were counterproductive, making less likely the conversion of pagans, while Humbert of Romans, a former master general of the preaching order of the Dominicans and a powerful apologist for wars against Muslims, argued that the threat posed by Baltic pagans to Christendom was, in any case, exaggerated.[94]

Universal acceptance of official crusade justifications could not be assumed, especially where they were directed at fellow Christians. Legal legitimacy of papal authorization, Cross-taking, spiritual and temporal privileges associated with the Jerusalem war, etc., were not enough.[95] Ingenuity was required to thread domestic political crises into a satisfactory narrative of threat and subversion that required the purgative force of crusading to restore divine order. Crusades directed against Frederick II of Hohenstaufen and his sons between 1239 and 1268, partly in Germany but mainly and decisively in Italy, resulted in the wholesale transfer of power in southern Italy and Sicily to papal allies. Unlike the general Holy Land appeals, preaching and recruitment for the anti-Hohenstaufen crusades tended to be directed more narrowly, at audiences and rulers liable to share papal concerns. The rhetoric mimicked that for the Holy Land. Gregory IX branded Frederick II's threat to Rome as a danger to the Christian name; Innocent IV accused Frederick of 'whipping with the hammer of tribulations not only the church but the whole Christian people'.[96] Innocent's lurid thesaurus of invective was honed to combine his opponent's earthly destruction with eternal damnation. Frederick II was a 'wicked man', an 'enemy of the church', its 'persecutor', 'treacherous and impious', an 'enemy of God and contemptuous of the Catholic faith'. For his stubborn disobedience and hostility towards the Roman Church, Frederick was branded a heretic, a 'disturber of the public peace', compared with the worst biblical and classical oppressors and villains, Pharaoh, Herod and Nero, and labelled a 'limb of the devil, minister of Satan and calamitous harbinger of the Anti-Christ'. Typical of overheated medieval polemic, the flight from the mundane to the apocalyptic was rapid and immediate. Innocent, a distinguished canon lawyer, was adept at eliding arguments of natural law and just war (disobedience, breach of faith and contract, disturber of the public peace, etc.) with the crowd-pleasing language of God's unanswerable purpose and the fate of the World.[97] Urban IV (1261–4) followed suit. Launching a new anti-Hohenstaufen crusade, he rehearsed the familiar accusations of persecution of the Church and pope, accusing Frederick's son, Man-fred of Sicily (ruled 1254–66), of promoting Islam and Muslim rites (a feature of anti-Hohenstaufen propaganda), referring to Frederick II's employment of Muslim troops settled at Lucera in Apulia.[98] Whether many believed that the Hohenstaufen were closet Muslims or Islamic fellow-travellers is hard to know. Pockets of scepticism and dissent were evident from Italy to Germany to England.[99] If the shifting diplo-matic and military alliances in Italy and Germany are a guide, supporters of the anti-Hohenstaufen crusades, while happy to enjoy the crusade privileges on offer, tended to be driven by political advan-tage rather than unalloyed religious fervour. Changing sides was common. When the kings of England and France successively embraced the papal cause in the 1250s and 1260s, their objectives appear less than transcendent, the crusade operating as a shield for less elevated political calculation.

THE FAILURE OF JUSTIFICATION

Not all crusade appeals worked. Failures emphasized the importance of getting the message and its presentation right. One common myth of the Middle Ages assumes that popular audiences, chiefly the rural peasantry, lived in a perpetual state of murky ignorance of the con-cerns of high politics. The crusades give the lie to this. They induced widespread enthusiasm, informed popular political action and inspired social dissent. No crusade initiative was guaranteed support. Responses confirmed that contemporaries were not particularly unthinking, defer-ential or credulous. Timing, context and presentation were essential.

Both the Second Crusade (1145–9) and Fourth Crusade (1198–1204) got off to limp starts before generating any marked enthusiasm, the key resting in adequately prepared political co-ordination. Crusade failures often cast deep shadows, as with the dismal outcome of the Second Crusade. Until the catastrophic defeat at Hattin and the loss of Jerusalem, repeated crusade appeals fell on near-deaf ears and the rhetoric of crusade was in danger of contradicting itself as the theoretical assumptions of divine providence obscured political reality. While the Holy City remained in Christian hands, as God apparently willed, what need was there for any further outpouring of men and treasure? The defeats of 1147–8 in Asia Minor and Syria signalled His disapproval not of the purpose but of the execution and executors. Only the unimagined loss of Jerusalem in 1187 changed the dynamics of the crusade appeal. Ironically, the failure of the Third Crusade to recapture Jerusalem, and the increasing emphasis after Gregory VIII's *Audita Tremendi* on crusading as a personal as well as a communal responsibility, sustained the popularity of the eastern Mediterranean holy wars in the first half of the thirteenth century, despite repeated failure. However, the abject disaster of Louis IX's first crusade in Egypt (1249–50), a highly professional, well-funded and widely supported expedition led by a man of conspicuous piety, honesty and bravery, dampened enthusiasm for subsequent large-scale enterprises including Louis's own second crusade of 1270. The initial inability to galvanize sections of the French nobility between 1267 and 1270 signalled inadequate immediate preparation of propaganda as well as doubts as to the crusade's feasibility. The unrelenting message was of the Holy Land in danger, a fact now inescapable from well-publicized reports of the rapid erosion of Latin power in Palestine and Syria from 1260, including the loss of Antioch in 1268. But this was no longer enough to disguise the practical difficulties of recruitment, finance and strategy, considerations that similarly helped determine the collective inaction of western Europe in the face of the loss of the remaining Frankish bases on the Syrian and Palestinian mainland after 1274. Not even the fall of Acre and the final evacuation of 1291 overcame political constraints at home. No rhetoric, no amount of earnest devotion and no brilliance of expert advice could provide the necessary political and financial circumstances for a new crusade. Contemporaries knew this and agonized over it, notably at a general council of the western Church at Lyons in 1274.[100] Even for those willing to heed the call, the exercise had become increasingly negotiable, its political and administrative context less tractable.

At least from the failed Second Crusade onwards, sceptics had voiced suspicion that justifications for war covered political self-interest and masked the corruption of those involved. Such doubts were reinforced where crusading became politicized within western Europe. Incomprehension or rejection of crusade justification, familiar among Muslim or Jewish victims, was paralleled by Languedoc poets lamenting the rape of their culture or by partisans of the Hohenstaufen. At its most extreme, resistance to particular crusading initiatives resulted in armed opposition, even, for example in Germany in 1240 and in England in 1263–5, stimulating what could be called anti-crusades, with crusade opponents adopting the Cross against crusaders.[101] At the other end of the emotional and political spectrum, hostility to holy war manifested itself in a condemnation of violence altogether. Francis of Assisi's conversion to pacific mendicancy came after his withdrawal from a crusade in Italy. Some intellectuals, such as the Dominican William of Tripoli (in Syria, *fl.*1270s), came to argue that the war in the Holy Land, by alienating Muslims, had even hindered the desired goal of the collapse of Islam and the restoration of Christian rule over the Holy Places.[102] Alongside the failures of some appeals and recurrent periods of indifference, such rejectionist attitudes, while never dominant and often very local or partisan, constituted a backhanded compliment to those who laboured to provide convincing cases for crusade war. Ideas and arguments mattered, whether accepted or challenged. Creating a successful, popular crusade justification was not necessarily all smoke and mirrors, relying on hucksters' conjuring tricks to seduce or fool a biddable, deferential public. Support for crusading depended on the rational as well as emotional case advanced for it.

·7 recrēn̄ŏ·ßi h̄ dīferīmen ab ū̄ō fūpfir p̄ōnātū̄. Jṅ
miliēie fue ī ēra fēa. ne fōrtuiī̄ cafib̄ ŕ
ad rep̄mēēd̄ īp̄ē̄ īmīnīcō̄ p̄ūēīaliū̄·ŕ
Frānci per fugā̄ elap̄ fi· 7 biy fā̄luatī ᵹ̄ miliēes

Propaganda

3
Publicity

Crusade promotion employed a full range of senses, involving speaking, listening, seeing, singing, reading, performing and touching. The written word was integral. There were official instructions, news-sheets, letters, pamphlets, polemics, hagiographies, treatises, handbooks, chronicles, poems and songs. There were also the records of administration: enrolled lists of recruits; accounts; schedules of pay; contracts; and wills. Oratory and literature were complemented by painting, sculpture, drama, ritual and liturgy. While taste does not seem to have featured, the crosses handed out were touched by giver and receiver, both probably shrouded in clouds of incense. Propaganda knew few boundaries: formal sermons and private chat; newsletters; travelling circuses; hymns; love songs; eloquence; bullying; the bush telegraph of commerce and international religious corporations; local gossips; magnificent public ceremonies; parish harvest festivals; royal courts; great cathedrals; counting houses; marketplaces. Persuasion involved high art and low humour; stained glass and tattoos; orators and mountebanks; saints and stand-ups; intense emotion and cheap bribery; following Christ and follow my leader.

Publicity was not random. The First Crusade set the pattern and exposed the difficulties. Urban II arranged a coherent campaign to promote the call to arms, co-ordinate propaganda and manage the politics and diplomacy of leadership. Yet he failed to control recruitment or conduct. Although his fourteen-month tour of France and wider correspondence suggest he hoped for a substantial response, the eventual size, diversity and nature of recruitment dwarfed expectations, challenging central planning. This administrative gulf remained for most subsequent international crusades. Local circumstances determined responses in each region. Nonetheless, the ambition to present a defined prospectus for war met with considerable and consistent success in what constituted the first practical attempt to implement policy on an international scale in western Europe since the heyday of the Carolingian empire three centuries earlier.[1]

ASSEMBLIES

Combining promotion, consultation and consent, from the start assemblies provided the most convenient focus for organization, such as the substantial Church councils of Piacenza and Clermont, to which secular lords were invited (although few went), to more overtly secular conferences, such as that held in Paris in February 1096 by Philip I of France.[2] Shadowed by smaller regional gatherings, they constituted normal medieval methods of conducting public business. In the absence of rapid communications and subordinate local bureaucracies, compliance with any general political initiative – most obviously decisions to go to war – relied on the authority that only came from direct contact with those most concerned. Although later dressed up in the vestments of Roman Law tags (such as '*Quod omnes tangit ab omnibus approbetur*', 'What touches all should be approved by all'), the requirement on rulers to obtain the counsel, consent and assistance of their chief associates was embedded in long custom and practice across Latin Christendom.[3] Crusading theoretically transcended customary obligations of lordship and service, so seeking the widest approval and co-operation assumed even greater importance.

Assemblies publicized the cause in ceremonial display and rhetorical exhortation while acting as a stage for diplomacy, political negotiation and fiscal bargaining. Before the Second Crusade, assemblies in 1146 at Vézelay at Easter and Speyer at Christmas provided a platform for Bernard of Clairvaux's preaching, Cross-taking by the French and German nobilities and opportunities for both Louis VII of France and Conrad III of Germany to assert political leadership. The same combination of preaching and politics informed the so-called Court of Christ held at Mainz under the auspices of Frederick I Barbarossa in March 1188 at the start of the Third Crusade. The conference held at Gisors in the Vexin between Normandy and the Île-de-France in January 1188 finessed the reconciliation of the kings of France and England and the count of Flanders under the auspices of taking the Cross. Henry II of England used a council at Geddington in Northamptonshire a few weeks later to announce preaching and details of the Saladin Tithe, an income tax on non-*crucesignati* to pay for the expedition. In a distinct reminder of the 1090s' pattern, the lack of royal involvement in the Fourth Crusade (only King Imre of Hungary apparently pledged to go in 1200, although never did) was reflected in the succession of regional gatherings, at tournaments or religious festivals, that saw Cross-taking, as at Ecry-sur-Aisne on Advent Sunday 1199 or Bruges on Ash Wednesday 1200, or that forged alliances and planned action, as at Soissons and Compiègne in the summer of 1201. The preaching role of the Cistercians made their General Chapter meetings in 1198 and 1201 natural foci of support for the crusade; on both occasions, in the presence of leading lay crusaders, the charismatic preacher Fulk of Neuilly played a central role.[4]

While the Fourth Lateran Council of 1215 authorized a tax to be levied on Church property and a council held in Paris in March 1215 by Philip II modified crusaders' legal immunities, with preaching increasingly devolved on to local panels (and, from the 1230s, the friars), the need for grand deliberative assemblies became less urgent. Nonetheless, they persisted as rituals of commitment and common endeavour. The tradition of 1215 was maintained in Church councils of Lyons in 1245 and 1274 and Vienne in 1311–12 providing the framework for propaganda and finance. Lay attendance at these councils could be patchy; only one king, James I of Aragon, attended Lyons in 1274, although ambassadors from other monarchs were there. Cross-taking by great men still provided a ceremonial context for preaching, just as conferences to discuss taxation kept the crusade issues in the public eye. However, the Westminster parliament of 1270, which granted a lay tax for the crusade of the future Edward I, while representing a significant confirmation of the role of the knights in matters of general taxation, appears a long way from the Council of Clermont.[5] Stylish and stylized crusade jamborees punctuated the later Middle Ages: the French Cross-taking festivals of Philip IV (1313) or Philip VI (1333); the papal crusade summit meetings of the 1360s; the

Feast and Vow of the Pheasant at Lille and the conference at Frankfurt in 1454 in response to the fall of Constantinople the year before; or Pius II's conference at Mantua in 1459. These were replicated locally across Latin Christendom, although more as familiar ceremonies of communal identity than as serious precursors to military action.[6]

Although the famous mid-thirteenth-century crusade preacher Humbert of Romans expressed purist suspicion of declaiming in 'public places and crossroads where men carry on business', practice determined otherwise. The friars instructed to preach the Cross in the diocese of York in 1291 were sensibly directed to visit places with crowds.[7] Whether watching Bernard of Clairvaux in the shadow of the great church at Vézelay or listening to a Franciscan friar proclaiming the Cross in the parish church at Pocklington in the East Riding of Yorkshire almost a century and a half later, such gatherings continued to be crusading's public platform.

LEGATES AND PREACHERS

To impose order on the planning process, Urban II and his successors used surrogates – messengers, diplomats and preachers. Urban despatched legates to north Italy, Normandy and England as locals could not always be relied on. During a second wave of recruitment in 1099–1100 Archbishop Anselm of Bovisio in Milan found local clerical leaders reluctant to preach the Cross themselves.[8] Some legates and preachers were expected to accompany those they recruited, as did Peter the Hermit in 1096 and archbishops Hugh of Die and Anselm himself in 1101. The model campaign legate was Adhemar, bishop of Le Puy. He had been one of the first French clerics to be consulted by Urban in the summer of 1095, was first to take the Cross at Clermont, and was formally designated by the pope as his representative for the projected campaign. Adhemar was attached to the army of the count of Toulouse.[9] Clerics in other contingents appear to have received some sort of papal licence or approval.[10] Such delegation provided the only possible means of even notional control.

This could prove elusive. Bernard of Clairvaux did not accompany the Second Crusade, and took it upon himself to appoint others to preach in distant regions such as Brittany, Bohemia and Austria. By contrast, Cardinal Bishop Theodwin of Santa Rufina, a papal insider who had been closely involved in pre-crusade diplomacy, was appointed legate to the German army. Yet he and the legate assigned to the French army, the retiring, donnish Cardinal Guido of San Grisogono, cut somewhat dim figures on the crusade itself, in contrast to the squabbling French bishops Arnulf of Lisieux and the acerbic Godfrey of Langres, who both claimed some sort of legatine authority, according to one gossipy commentator, as an excuse to line their own pockets by fleecing the sick and dying by selling absolutions. Godfrey insisted on his Cistercian credentials and the delegated authority of St Bernard. The different chains of authority and the passive role observers ascribed to Pope Eugenius III suggest an element of improvisation and a fragile chain of command.[11] Notoriously, when Radulph, yet another Cistercian, attracted vigorous crowds and golden opinions with his anti-Jewish demagoguery in the Rhineland in 1146, he was disciplined but only for being unlicensed.[12]

Difficulties of control increased as new fronts for wars of the Cross opened and crusade preaching became endemic. Unlicensed charlatans exploited the new market in preaching. With the proliferation of wars of the Cross, preaching campaigns overlapped in time and place, muddying the separate appeals and attracting profiteering sharks selling crusade vow redemptions, instigated during the Fifth Crusade from 1213.[13] These problems arose from a system of increasing regulation developed from the time of the Third Crusade. Alongside the papal legates such as Cardinal Henry of Albano, who died before the expedition embarked, or Joscius, archbishop of Tyre, who had brought the bad news from Palestine, local bishops were recruited to preach the Cross on a regional basis, such as Bishop Henry of Strasburg in Germany or Archbishop Baldwin of Canterbury in England and Wales, prefiguring the elaborate preaching networks of the thirteenth century. However, despite the unquestioned success of propaganda in 1187–90, the scale of the operation and response outstripped the meagre administrative resources of the papacy and regional dioceses. Before the arrival of any official legate or preacher, Count Richard of Poitou, the future Richard I of England, took the Cross in November 1187. Judging by his father's fury, this had not been officially co-ordinated.[14] Archbishop Baldwin found his preaching in Wales pre-empted by local initiatives. Surviving rites for taking the Cross show marked regional variations indicating the prevalence and force of local response rather than central direction, such diversity being common in the medieval western Church.[15]

Launching the Fourth Crusade in 1198, Innocent III addressed some of the difficulties. In addition to two chief legates, he authorized local archbishops and bishops to organize preaching in their regions, even identifying individuals to help them, such as, in the diocese of York, Roger Vacarius, the veteran academic who had introduced Roman Law into the English higher academic curriculum. In each province preachers were to recruit the aid of a Templar and a Hospitaller, living symbols of the Holy Land conflict and, more helpfully, members of international organizations with access to revenues and credit. Innocent recruited the celebrity preacher Fulk of Neuilly, whose explicit terms of his appointment avoided the uncertainties surrounding Bernard of Clairvaux's powers fifty years earlier.[16] Once again co-ordination proved elusive. When Abbot Martin of Pairis preached at Basel early in 1201 he was duplicating the work a year earlier of the local bishop, and his sermon, as recorded, ignored Innocent's 1198 crusade bull beyond the central offer of eternal salvation.[17] Further problems included allegations of embezzlement levelled against Fulk of Neuilly, exposing a tension between preachers' rejection of materialism and their de facto role as alms-collectors. The charges may have been genuine. Either way, Fulk's example was soon used to emphasize the need for preachers to live blameless lives.[18] The crusade's puritan dimension, the conversion of the faithful to a more holy life, could obscure the extraction of military and material support. The Cistercian Abbot Eustace of St Germer de Fly in Picardy, recruited by Fulk of Neuilly to preach in England, was chiefly remembered there for his promotion of the need to observe the Sabbath and hostility to commercial malpractice, not his crusade sermons.[19] Contradictions between words and deeds haunted Innocent III's instructions to preachers in 1213.[20] The theme was echoed in later preaching manuals. 'Nor should the preacher's own life be out of harmony with his words' insisted the Dominican crusade preacher Humbert of Romans (c.1200–1277). Earlier (c.1221–2), Thomas of Chobham (c.1160–1233/6) condemned financial hypocrisy of the sort insinuated against Fulk of Neuilly. He warned against sermons that solicited donations without explicit spiritual purpose and the consequent 'suspicion of greed' (*suspicio avarite*).[21] Legates as well as messages could become confused. Cardinal Peter Capuano provided the classic example. In 1202, he appeasingly acquiesced in the crusaders' attack on the Christian Dalmatian city of Zara, in the face of papal prohibition. He then contrived to be absent in the Holy Land during the crucial months surrounding the actual capture of Zara and the diversion to Constantinople in 1203–4. A year later, on his own initiative, he absolved the crusaders in Greece of their remaining vows to proceed to Jerusalem, effectively cancelling the crusade. Innocent was incandescent but impotent.[22]

By the time a new campaign was proclaimed in 1213, Innocent III had become a veteran of promoting crusades. Papal-sponsored wars against political enemies in Italy and Sicily (in 1199), the Almohads in Spain (1212) and heretics in Languedoc (from 1209) honed both rhetoric and organization. The consequences of undisciplined crusade propaganda were evident in the Children's Crusade of 1212, a response to the wide publicity given to the general perception of Christendom in danger (from Moors and heretics), to Christian failure in the east, and to the need for social humility and moral reform.[23] For Innocent's new eastern crusade, the mechanisms employed for the Third and Fourth Crusades were expanded and systematized. Legates on the old model were appointed, as in France, or local archbishops or bishops were relied upon, as in Hungary, Denmark and Sweden. The pope himself took responsibility for Italy. Elsewhere, teams of regional clergy, not necessarily bishops, were appointed, empowered to recruit between four and six additional preachers. To avoid scandal, preachers were selected for their supposed honesty, integrity and faith. They were to refuse all gifts, live simply and accept only modest hospitality. All donations were to be directed to a religious house or church. Preaching was to adhere to the 1213 crusading bull *Quia Maior*. Questions arising from papal instructions or the offered privileges were to be referred directly to the pope.[24]

Innocent recruited some of the leading intellectuals and publicists of the day. Many, like the pope himself, were alumni of the University of Paris, the leading centre for the study of pastoral theology and of the application of Christian ethics to practical, temporal experience. The influence of Paris-trained experts on thirteenth-century preaching is hard to exaggerate. Some of those available to Innocent, like the Englishman Robert Curzon, the Frenchman James of Vitry or the German Oliver of Paderborn, were teachers and writers who went on to become cardinals. The Italian Cardinal Ugolino, Innocent's nephew, who preached and raised funds across northern Italy, became Pope Gregory IX (1227–41).[25] The presence of these highly educated intellectuals on preaching teams and papal legations pointed to a close association between crusading and prevailing academic developments in western Europe. The so-called Scholastic method of enquiry that had been articulated during the twelfth century, particularly in the cathedral schools and universities of France and Italy, sought to impose a structured approach to understanding God and His creation. Enquiry led to truth through the study and reconciliation of contrasting ideas, explanations and authorities in theology, law and philosophy: reason applied to revelation. The incorporation of Aristotelian philosophy and natural science into the western curriculum from the later twelfth century opened new, wide horizons, not least in logic and natural science. This expansion of the tools of rational enquiry affected crusading and its presentation, at least by and to social and intellectual elites. Crusading's combination of moral theology, pastoral evangelism, Christian action and providential eschatology rendered it an awkward legal category. The new intellectual fashion, represented by the preachers of the Fifth Crusade, sought to corral the concept of crusade away from free-ranging divinely inspired holy violence into a reasoned structure of legal sanction and natural law. Surviving thirteenth-century crusade sermons were rooted in measured, rational processes of argument.[26]

However, the ordered thought of academic orators did not always match messy reality. Preaching talent was neither limitless nor evenly spread. Constant referral to the pope for clarification of details imposed unsustainable pressure on the papal curia's bureaucratic resources, let alone the pope's stamina. The 1213 bulls had confirmed easier access to the fullest indulgence; instituted a panoply of special liturgical ceremonies; and introduced the element of redemption of vows for money and material assistance. Each generated lengthy correspondence.

Letters to the curia by Gervase, abbot of Prémontré in 1216–17 alone showed how almost every aspect of the crusade – privileges, timing, money – incited argument, conflicting advice (including, unhelpfully, from Paris dons) and muddle. Local agents were frequently inadequate: 'In other provinces I know few men whom I dare to recommend for carrying out this business.' This problem did not go away. Experienced thirteenth-century operators repeatedly complained of low standards of preaching and preachers' conduct.[27] The diocesan structure failed to cope. Abbot Gervase was reduced to pleading for new instructions and fresh teams of papal agents to be despatched. From such entrenched confusion it is remarkable that crusaders embarked at all.

Crusade promoters assumed a variety of roles in addition to publicists, recruiting officers and fundraisers. During the Fifth Crusade they acted as arbiters in local disputes, the crusade providing a neutral context for resolving conflicts. Robert Curzon and his successor, Archbishop Simon of Tyre, did this in France, as did Cardinal Ugolino in north Italy, James of Vitry in Genoa and Oliver of Paderborn, then *scholasticus* of Cologne, in western Germany. This arbitration assisted recruitment. The legates who claimed to have recruited 30,000 *crucesignati* in Marseilles in 1223–4 had gone there to negotiate an end to the city's excommunication over long-running disputes between the citizens and the local clergy and bishop.[28] Such flexibility helped ensure that no decade and almost no region of western Europe failed to see some sort of crusade promotion in the thirteenth century. Preachers received pay and some had their own seals for preaching business.[29] As crusading and its promotion developed into a familiar social institution, so it soon became associated with the new active force in thirteenth-century religion, the friars.

The two mendicant orders of St Francis and St Dominic were founded in the early years of the thirteenth century in the shadow of crusading.[30] Francis of Assisi briefly joined the Fifth Crusade in Egypt in 1219 and was reported as having tried to convert the Sultan al-Kamil. Dominic Guzman had been a member of the papal legation preaching against heretics in Languedoc before and during the Albigensian Crusade. Committed to following the *via apostolica* in poverty and evangelizing, the friars channelled precisely the spiritual energy crusade planners sought to tap. Dominic's order was known as the Order of Preachers. The centralized hierarchical structures of the orders and their direct allegiance to the pope fitted neatly with the administrative needs of crusade promotion. Committed to engaging with the secular world, friars became familiar presences in the streets of towns, rural highways and, increasingly, in the courts of the great as confessors and in the lecture halls of the universities as scholars. Since the Second Crusade, the monks of the Cistercian Order had taken the lead, individually and collectively, in providing an international network for crusade propaganda from southern France to the eastern Baltic. Now, the friars offered greater focus and flexibility as, unlike monks, evangelizing the laity was their *raison d'être*.

The election of Innocent III's nephew, veteran crusade recruiter and established patron of the new mendicant orders, Cardinal Ugolino, as Pope Gregory IX in 1227 established the friars as major figures in crusading.[31] Starting with Frederick II of Germany's long-delayed crusade in the mid-1220s, Dominicans, and later Franciscans, were employed to preach the Cross for campaigns across the arc of crusading: Spain (1228–9); the Baltic (from 1230); the Holy Land (from 1234); the Balkans and Greece (from 1234 and 1237); and against others designated enemies of the Church (e.g. the Stedinger peasants near Bremen in 1232–3 and the Hohenstaufen from the 1240s). Apart from the usual perils of preaching, such as audience indifference, scepticism or occasional hostility, the task could be dangerous. According to an admittedly hostile and distant witness, Matthew Paris of St Albans, two Franciscans were hanged by Frederick II in 1243 for fostering opposition to him.[32] Paris said they were acting on the orders of superiors. The centralized command and provincial structures of both orders recommended them to organizers impatient with often recalcitrant diocesan clergy. Friars acted as specially commissioned individuals or in local teams. The extent of their annexation of crusade promotion may be gauged by the vitriol heaped on them personally and collectively by a writer such as Matthew Paris, who at some stages in his career regarded them as agents of an alien, grasping and exploitative power – i.e. the papacy – acting to the corporate disadvantage of the faithful in general and of his own Benedictine Order and monastery in particular. Many crusade legates were still drawn from traditional ecclesiastical backgrounds of monastery, university or court, such as Odo of Châteauroux, legate for Louis IX's first crusade to the eastern Mediterranean (1248–54). However, direction of preaching passed from the Paris-trained secular clerics and future cardinals such as James of Vitry (1160/70–1240) or Oliver of Paderborn (c.1170–1227) or regional religious entrepreneurs such as Bishop Albert Buxhöven of Riga (c.1165–1229) to equally erudite and academically polished friars such as the Dominicans Humbert of Romans or the theologian and translator of Aristotle, Albert the Great (c.1206–80).

Such luminaries provided the vanguard of a preaching army, suitably equipped, and available more or less on demand. In 1252 Henry III of England asked the leaders of the mendicant orders in England to send to him in London a sufficient number of friars 'who have knowledge of preaching the cross'.[33] The friars were now the recognized experts. Humbert of Romans composed a special manual on how to preach the Cross. A generation later, in 1291, Archbishop Romanus of York wrote to all the Dominican priors and Franciscan wardens in his archdiocese requesting they send a certain number of friars to thirty-five named places to preach the Cross on the same day as the archbishop himself intended to deliver a crusade sermon in York Minster, 14 September, Exaltation of the Holy Cross Day, a festival especially suited to crusade appeals. By then it was assumed that general public sermonizing was a job for the friars. However, their near-monopoly did not necessarily produce higher standards of delivery or behaviour. Experts still railed against incompetence, and the image of the ascetic mendicant inspiring by example was rather compromised by the prosperous, well-fed reality. The provisions accounts of the troupe of forty-five preachers in northern France in 1265 reveal a rich, elite diet for men who, besides their gourmet meals, were simultaneously enjoying the temporal reward of pay and the spiritual benefit of the crusade indulgence. Nice work if you could get it.[34]

The use of the friars consolidated the clergy's closed-shop control over crusade – as over other – preaching. In the early years, laymen occasionally presented the case. Famously Bohemond of Antioch, dominant figure of the First Crusade, conducted a celebrity lecture tour of France in 1106 to publicize his new crusading venture east.

His address at Chartres was vividly recalled. In 1128, Hugh of Payens, founder of the Templars in Jerusalem a decade earlier but not an ordained priest, presented his own publicity for a new crusade tied to advertising his new order. At the Danish king's Christmas court at Odense in 1187, on receipt of Gregory VIII's crusade bull, it was left to the nobleman Esbern, brother of the archbishop of Lund, to rouse the assembly to remember the heroism of their Viking ancestors and commit to this new great adventure for God.[35] By the early thirteenth century, however, such blurring of functions had become increasingly difficult. Preaching manuals were insistent that preaching could only be conducted by men in holy orders, certainly not by laymen or women. Humbert of Romans argued that preachers required knowledge of scripture, theology, history, hagiography and geography, attainments he reserved to those with formal higher education: male clerics.[36]

Women played active roles in religious and financial activities associated with crusade preparations and crusading in general: supporting (or, according to a favoured trope of misogynist preachers, hindering) their male partners and kindred; keeping crusaders' families and lands intact; cherishing the memory of dynastic crusade involvement; taking the Cross; redeeming vows but also joining and even fighting on crusade. In stereotype and reality, women featured as grieving wives or lamenting widows; devout pilgrim *crucesignatae*; heroic camp followers; distracting sexual partners; and field camp prostitutes. The story of Adela of Blois bullying her husband Stephen into redeeming his desertion of the First Crusade by returning east was well known.[37] Crusade preaching manuals specifically challenged love of family, with its obvious association with women, as an impediment to service of the Cross. Innocent III envisaged women as paymasters and even as leaders of troops on crusade. However, with the exception of the famous, well-connected mystic Abbess Hildegard of Bingen (1098–1179), consulted by the count of Flanders over his proposed crusade of 1176, it is difficult to find much evidence of women being shown as taking prominent parts in crusade planning, even though such politically active figures as Eleanor of Aquitaine in 1189–90 hardly left everything to the men.[38] However, public preaching, as opposed to private persuasion, women did not do. They were absent from the crusade hustings, except as decorative or symbolic *crucesignata* (viz.

74

Eleanor of Aquitaine's presence on the platform at Vézelay in 1146, reassuring her Aquitainian vassals as much as supporting her husband Louis VII of France). There was more to this than habitual cultural misogyny. Laymen were similarly reduced to attend crusade sermons as clients, witnesses and guarantors, not as orators. Even the passionately committed, such as Louis IX of France, demonstrated their devotion in public but only as largely mute performers in choreographed clerical rituals.

WRITING

The laity was more actively engaged in using the written word. Writing was central to crusading from its inception as a medium of instruction, information, propaganda and memorialization. In the generation before the First Crusade, letters, pamphlets and tracts had provided key polemical weapons in the contest for control over the Church between popes and the German emperor. Now lost networks of written communication underpinned the extensive diplomatic exchanges and the summoning of the papal councils of Piacenza and Clermont in 1095. Although no official version of Pope Urban's speech has survived, and the Clermont crusade decree boasts a very tenuous manuscript tradition, the other conciliar decrees were circulated in writing. Some of the previous 'reports' (*relatione*) of Muslim outrages Urban II referred to when writing to his supporters in Flanders in December 1095 had taken the form of letters, some to lay rulers.[39] Among the earliest surviving groups of non-royal lay correspondence are the two surviving letters from the crusade leader Count Stephen of Blois to his wife Adela and those of another crusader, the Picard knight Anslem of Ribemont.[40] Such people inhabited a literate culture.

At least one First Crusade general kept an account book or roll of his expenses to which he referred when arguing his case for a greater share of the spoils.[41] It is improbable he was alone. Military commanders were likely to have been very conversant with the existence of written lists of followers, their obligations and their pay; written summonses date from at least Carolingian times at the turn of the eighth and ninth centuries. Detailed written recording in the

Anglo-Norman realm, home to numerous crusaders led by Duke Robert of Normandy, survive from precisely the period of the First Crusade. These range from a list of ships and soldiers provided to William of Normandy by his nobles for his attack on England in 1066, probably compiled c.1067–72 in the Norman abbey of Fécamp, to official government records such as Domesday Book or the Pipe Rolls of the Exchequer.[42] The ubiquity of administrative writing at any propertied noble's court partly explains the large-scale secular employment of clerics, not least on crusade. In the background of any aristocratic or military enterprise clerics compiled accounts and per-haps correspondence, tasks not necessarily demanding very high levels of literary skill.

As well as for record, information or instruction, writing was employed creatively. Urban II used letters to explain the nature, pur-pose and rewards of his new enterprise; to project a very precise image, to shape ideas and direct opinion. Recipients would be expected to further disseminate the contents in more copies, through oral pres-entation and, where necessary, translation, thus reaching audiences beyond the formally literate in Latin. Letters could act as propaganda in their own right. Peter the Hermit was said to have brandished one from the patriarch of Jerusalem describing Muslim atrocities in the Holy Places and calling for western aid. Peter's letters, fictive in fact or fictional in the telling, fitted a pattern. Letters from crusaders were preserved and in at least one case, those of Anselm of Ribemont to Archbishop Manasses of Rheims, were circulated to encourage fur-ther recruitment for the crusade of 1100–1101 with their testimony of divine approval and Christian heroism. Manasses also cited letters from Pope Paschal II (1099–1118), Godfrey of Bouillon and the new Latin patriarch of Jerusalem to encourage new recruits and old back-sliders to join up.[43] Such techniques became standard.

If letters could supply basic texts for crusade evangelism, the role of a distinctive form of writing associated with the crusade is more uncertain. The First Crusade generated a uniquely extensive body of Latin and vernacular narrative accounts, prose histories, travelogues, war stories, *gesta* (literally 'deeds'), verse epics, hymns and songs. Through such books, songs and hymns, so one northern French monk insisted in the 1130s, the story of the Jerusalem campaign was so well known that further detailed repetition was unnecessary.[44] From an early stage, the First Crusaders realized the need to control the image of what they were doing. In addition to letters home, the earliest 'official' version of what had happened was composed under the auspices of the remaining leadership in September 1099, two months after the capture of the Holy City. This briefly related events from the siege of Nicaea in the spring of 1097 to the victory over the Egyptian relief army at Ascalon in August 1099. The message was repetitively clear: God's hand in victory, without which there could be none; His displeasure at sin; the vindication of God's retribution and the remission of sins. The crusade is carefully depicted as confirming the most central tenets of Christian polemic and belief; positive, tangible proof of God's direct immanence, from overcoming numerical odds to booty gained; even the camels, sheep and cows supported God's army; even the elements. The letter was probably employed to encourage subsequent recruits to help the fragile and vulnerable Latin conquests.[45]

Less obvious was the use of the equally artfully crafted longer narrative accounts that soon appeared from the pens or dictation of veterans and observers. Arguments that one of the earliest of the immediate accounts, the so-called *Gesta Francorum*, in some version dating from perhaps as early as 1099/1100, had been actively used to promote Bohemund of Antioch's projected crusade of 1106, may not convince, but it clearly helped burnish his later reputation.[46] As Bohemund himself demonstrated in his publicity tour of 1104–6, immediate public impact was best achieved theatrically, through speeches, sermons and ceremonies. Unlike letters, long texts such as the *Gesta*, even if subdivided, were unwieldy for direct publicity purposes. Their function was more to memorialize past heroics and to mould and move future opinion. The manuscript transmission, both of the earliest by self-styled veterans and of the more upmarket, re-fashioned versions that quickly followed, indicates their audience was far from demotic. Networks of transmission were courtly and monastic, initially Benedictine and later Cistercian, an order especially linked with promoting holy war at least from the 1120s onwards.[47] These texts helped establish an elite vision of crusading to which laymen and clerics alike could and did refer. A knight from Vélay in the Auvergne, a veteran of the First Crusade, presented Louis VII of France, probably in 1137, with a de luxe illustrated copy of three Holy Land chronicles, including two by fellow witnesses to the Jerusalem journey, Fulcher of Chartres and Raymond of Aguilers. His intent was clear:

> the countless eminent deeds and saying of our ancestors need to be committed with a worthy pen to an honourable memory . . . in this way you might look in this book with the eye of reason (*rationis oculis*) as if in a mirror at the images of your ancestors and you might follow their footsteps on the path of virtue.[48]

The written message of these texts – stressing Jerusalem and knightly piety – combined with visual and oral memorializing to create the cultural context within which subsequent crusade decisions were reached. In Louis's case he took the Cross eight years later and, arguably, tried to conform to these ambient stereotypes. His chaplain, the monk Odo of Deuil, who wrote a detailed account of the first stage of the Second Crusade, certainly prepared for his task by reading narratives of 1095–9, taking one of them with him on the expedition.[49]

This targeted use of crusade chronicles as mines of information, sources for exhortation and models for emulation lent the practice of crusading a veneer of intellectual and ideological unity, precisely what organizers sought to achieve. Eugenius III couched his appeal for the Second Crusade in the context of the glorious memory of the First. The abbot of Schäftlarn in Bavaria presented Frederick Barbarossa with a very grand copy of Robert of Rheims's account of the First Crusade, possibly in the context of the 'court of Christ' in March 1188 at which Frederick took the Cross for the Third Crusade. Robert of Rheims's book was by far the most copied account of the First Crusade in the twelfth century and production of many of the surviving manuscripts appear to cluster around the recruiting and preaching campaigns of 1145–7 and 1188–90.[50] Crusade sermons were saturated with references to crusade history. The influence of these first written chronicles on the crusade mentality of the time was evanescent, but on subsequent accounts of later expeditions it was profound. Thus James of Vitry, an eyewitness, described the misery in the crusade camp at Damietta in Egypt during the Fifth Crusade (1217–21) in the words of the twelfth-century writer William of Tyre's account of the deprivations suffered on the First Crusade. William had borrowed his material from Albert of Aachen's chronicle complied in the early twelfth century from the memories of veterans.[51] The self-referential nature of the crusade enterprise was inescapable. This was as true for the increasing bulk of vernacular epics, poems and songs which coalesced into written versions in the twelfth and thirteenth centuries as with the impressive corpus of Latin chronicles. Thirteenth-century crusade preachers were advised to play on the memory of heroic ancestors and to use stories from historical texts to enthuse their audiences.[52] As well as being lived experiences, the crusades were defined through literature, some motifs of which were popularized through preaching and the emergence of a specific crusade liturgy. Whatever else, crusade literature provided a resource of ideology and moral example, a bank of selective, tendentious memories that framed responses of successive generations by providing a rationale for action: the deeds of ancestors; the favour of God.

The more immediate use of writing remained administrative. Papal bulls provided consistent direction. Eugenius III's *Quantum praedecessores* initiating the Second Crusade required two editions, the first having flopped. It served as a model for Eugenius's successors Alexander III (in 1165, 1169 and 1181) and Lucius III (in 1184/5). The convenience of a pre-existing written template for the temporal and spiritual crusade privileges was confirmed in the following century when the crusade decree of the Fourth Lateran Council of 1215 (no. 71 *Ad Liberandam*) was copied by the councils of Lyons in 1245 and 1274. These bulls were intended to supply the core message. In 1181, Alexander III ordered the clergy, whom he hoped would promote the crusade, to publicize his letters. In 1213, Innocent III insisted that the details of his bull *Quia Maior* be transmitted 'carefully and effectively'.[53] In the thirteenth century, if not earlier, the texts were translated into local vernaculars. Chroniclers recognized the importance of papal letters by incorporating copies sent to their regions; before 1198 these are often the only versions that survive. Authorization of legates and preachers, as well as attempts to answer queries and control the course of preaching, relied on the exchange of letters. Legates in the field fired off written enquiries on matters from transferring vows to one theatre of conflict from another, dispensing with the need for wives' permission for a crusader to take the Cross and the precise circumstances for Cross redemption to the size of a preacher's entourage (Bishop Conrad of Regensberg requesting a larger one). The abbot of Rommersdorf in Austria collected *Quia Maior* and other relevant papal letters in a dossier for future reference and preachers were enjoined to record their activities and recruits.[54] By the mid-thirteenth century, and probably earlier, friars preaching the Cross in France and Germany were issued with portfolios of relevant papal bulls – in one surviving case with a German translation.[55]

Although administrative correspondence was almost exclusively conducted in Latin this did not necessarily exclude the laity. Knights and clerics shared a social milieu, which for some included education; witness Richard I's correction of Archbishop Hubert Walter's Latin.[56] As already seen, lesser nobles and aristocrats could also be well educated.[57] Knightly virtue embraced the liberal arts, and learning was not a dirty word but a social adornment.[58] Various types of literate skill can be identified among crusaders: the mercurial Waleran of Meulan, a crusader in 1147, the precocious philosophy student, who composed letters in Latin and may even have dabbled in Latin verse, or Ranulf Glanvill, from East Anglian lesser nobility, who ran the Latin-based English royal bureaucracy, presided over the compilation of a Latin law book and oversaw the successful academic (if not political) training of the future King John.[59] As already seen, other lettered knights composed vernacular verses or prose histories, suggesting a partial education in Latin at least, and a definite facility in literary technique, men such as Gregory Bechada, Geoffrey of Ville-hardouin, Robert of Clari and John of Joinville.[60] In the thirteenth century, functional literacy – the ability to read at the very least – would have been expected and hardly worthy of mention, although still the concept and presence of the *miles literatus* could arouse clerical resentment, as a moral example of superficially antithetical talents. A third group were those whose own education may have been very limited but who acted as interested patrons, such as, according to William of Tyre, Raymond of Poitiers, Prince of Antioch (1136–49).[61]

Written correspondence facilitated preparations for the Second Crusade, following precedents displayed in papal bulls for campaigns against Muslims in Spain and the Balearics in the 1110s and 1120s. In 1146–7, Bernard of Clairvaux orchestrated his preaching tours and those of his surrogates through letters, for example to England, Franconia and Bavaria. Accompanying such letters were copies of the papal bull. Bernard's delegate Abbot Adam of Ebrach read both the bull and Bernard's letter before preaching and giving the Cross at an assembly at Regensburg in February 1147. Bernard assumed that some at least of his lay recipients required help with translation or comprehension.[62] During the Third Crusade the papal call to arms was circulated from the Atlantic to the Baltic, providing the blueprint for preaching. Letters and short narratives of events in the east were circulated, some, if not all of those claiming to be from eyewitnesses, rewritten or freshly composed to suit the official lines of propaganda. Their consistency of content and language in copies across Europe suggests careful construction, probably in the circles around the papal curia and the crusade legates.[63] From the same or similar groups of publicists came recruiting tracts in deliberately contrasting registers, aimed at those promoting recruitment, some by seasoned controversialists. Peter of Blois, scholar, poet, writer, legal adviser, seasoned polemicist and administrator whose public experience stretched from Sicily to England, was at the papal court when news of the disaster at Hattin had arrived. He composed three pamphlets in 1188–9 using different approaches – hagiography on Christian martyrdom, reasoned debate and passionate invective – to urge concerted and immediate retaliation against Saladin and challenging backsliders and the fainthearted. Peter was not just an armchair pundit. He accompanied his employer, Archbishop Baldwin of Canterbury, to the desperate siege of Acre in 1190.[64]

Like its predecessors, the Third Crusade inspired literary narratives that were used to inspire subsequent expeditions. Some commemorative accounts were planned even before the crusade embarked. Archbishop Baldwin optimistically commissioned prose and verse accounts from writers in his entourage (who never wrote them).[65] As well as Latin descriptions, one lengthy history was composed in the 1190s in French verse by one veteran, Ambroise. Stories of the heroism of figures such as James of Avesnes, killed at Arsuf in 1191, entered the stock of standard moral tales prescribed for use by crusade preachers. Literary underpinning of crusade efforts began to assume an air of solid familiarity. The Fourth and Fifth Crusades, as well as those directed against heretics in Languedoc, attracted their crop of histories in Latin and the vernacular. None were neutral or disinterested. Geoffrey of Villehardouin's vernacular account of the diversion to Constantinople by the Fourth Crusade presented a highly tendentious lionizing of great deeds of arms. Writers on the Albigensian Crusades wrote as partisan exponents for or against the contentious events being described. Oliver of Paderborn's history of the Fifth Crusade, based on his letters as a preacher and subsequent leader of crusaders from Cologne, sought to explain the providence of God in the context of later repeated calls of the Cross.[66]

Written news also played a dynamic role in publicity. Oliver of Paderborn, one of the team of preachers in the diocese of Cologne, circulated to fellow preachers and others, including the legate to France, Robert Curzon, and the count of Namur, descriptions of visions and miracles that had accompanied crusade sermons, including his own, in Frisia in 1214. This form of 'live' news informing fellow publicists and their audiences of miraculous events occurring during a current preaching campaign added immediacy to preachers' ammunition. These circulated stories informed subsequent chronicles, in the Rhineland and beyond, including as far afield as St Albans in England. Oliver himself included an edited version of the miracles in his history of the Fifth Crusade, a compilation of his newsletters from before and during the expedition. As recruiter, publicist and crusader, Oliver demonstrated the interdependency of written and oral language and, in the instance of the Frisian celestial signs, visual aids as well. Oliver's preaching supplied the raw material for a raft of uplifting, quasi-miraculous stories that were soon preserved in writing, for example at the Rhineland Cistercian monastery of Heisterbach where the abbot and monks were closely involved in Oliver's preaching campaign.[67] Memory was not left to oral recitation but deliberately given almost instantaneous literary permanence.

Gathering men and money further consolidated the importance of writing. A detailed register of *crucesignati* and payments survives from Cardinal Ugolino's activities in northern Italy, as do some papal accounts regarding the 1215 clerical tax.[68] However, keeping records of muster and accounts was no novelty. Nor was the habit restricted to the papal bureaucracy. Bohemund's accounts, his *compotus* of expenses during the First Crusade indicates as much.[69] Any fundraising by putative crusade commanders of whatever status probably entailed some form of accounting: the crusade tax in England in 1096 or those levied on their lands by Louis VII in 1146 or Frederick Barbarossa in 1188. Henry II established a separate accounting office at Salisbury for the Saladin Tithe in England in 1188. The precocious archival tradition in England reveals careful accounting of men, payments, supplies, requisitioned ships and other accoutrements of crusading for Richard I's grand expedition in 1190.[70] However, half a century earlier, the confraternity established by the crusader fleet at Dartmouth in 1147 with oversight of monetary distribution, discipline and legal judgments probably possessed the means to verify past decisions and record new ones, if only to prevent or mitigate disagreements within a fractious polyglot force.[71]

Chroniclers were fond of listing crusaders. Their information came from somewhere, not necessarily by word of mouth. The most obvious need for written records was to inform commanders and the community at home. Lords mustering troops, churchmen trying to enforce oaths, courts eager to prosecute felonies or adjudicate civil disputes, or creditors seeking debtors: all needed to know. As the records of secular courts in England and France in the thirteenth century reveal, the implications of a crusader's vow extended to the furthest reaches of social activity. While it might be presumed that military officials such as constables would have found lists of those under their command useful, tangible examples are hard to discern from the earlier expeditions.[72] Governments, such as those of England and Sicily, were compiling lists of obligations by the mid-twelfth century, largely for fiscal reasons. The technology was available; scribes were at hand and the cultural acceptance of written records gaining prominence. Numbers in medieval chronicles are notoriously inventive. However, when Gerald of Wales estimated that 'roughly' 3,000 Welshmen had taken the Cross during Archbishop Baldwin's preaching tour in Lent 1188, this was a far from ridiculous figure and may have been based on written records. In the late 1190s or early 1200s, Archbishop Hubert Walter of Canterbury compiled lists of *crucesignati* in Cornwall and Lincolnshire, hangovers from the Third Crusade who had failed to fulfil their vows. These may have been new, but equally he may have simply checked them against existing records. The records of the English Exchequer for 1190, 1191 and 1192 list fifty-nine knights exempt, as crusaders, from a tax levied to fight the Welsh. The same accounts for 1207 and 1208 appear to list eighty crusaders (*cruisiati*) from Yorkshire being fined for reasons that are not at all clear. Their names, however, are.[73] The St Albans historian Roger of Wendover described how a crusade preacher in 1227, Master Hubert, kept a roll of the names of those he had signed with the Cross, improbably estimated by Wendover at 40,000. Given the size of the educated teams of preachers sent out during and after the Fifth Crusade, such a practice was probably standard. Oliver of Paderborn, in his circular recounting the celestial visions that accompanied his preaching in Frisia in 1214, estimated not only overall numbers but attempted to identify different categories – knights, sergeants and squires. While he gave different figures in the various versions of this letter, the scale – a few thousand – was not incredible. He assumed that counting crusaders was part of his brief. A well-informed contemporary close to the Fifth Crusade recruiting operation in his area noted that 'up to eighty' took the Cross as a result of a preaching coup by a priest from Mainz, a wholly realistic number.[74]

Other lists would have concerned pay or other rewards, fundamental recruiting techniques from the First Crusade onwards. Yet written archival evidence for them only surfaces during the Third Crusade.[75] The unusual terms for crusaders signing up for the Albigensian Crusade – forty days – operating as they did outside customary lordship obligations, would have been suitable for written confirmation; still more so those who decided to extend their service. In seeking a metaphor for the way taking the Cross guaranteed a crusader's enjoyment of the heavenly inheritance of Christ, an early thirteenth-century preaching manual likened it to a written charter ('*quasi per cartam*'), while one version of the Cross-taking rite used the technical term for a certain type of written contract 'by cyrograph' (*de cyrographo*).[76] While contracts for crusade service probably existed as far back as the eleventh century, the earliest surviving draft of a written contract for service between one crusader and another dates from 1239–40, with further examples emerging from the archives of the French and English royal administrations in the late 1240s and early 1250s.[77] Centralized command structures, whether papal or royal, as in the 1190s or 1240s, may have been more likely to keep detailed written records as crusading constituted merely an extension of their normal governmental and bureaucratic practices. Yet it would be misleading to assume that earlier or humbler networks of crusade planning relied any less on writing because they did not consistently collect or retain copies that were then preserved by their heirs and successors. The importance of writing at a local level is witnessed in the records of monasteries preserving the fundraising expedients of wealthy crusaders, or in the regional variants for the rite of taking the Cross in diocesan registers. The bureaucratic culture of institutions inclined to systematic long-term record retention more than private individuals or families. However, crusade organizers had employed writing in almost every aspect of their activities long before the prominence of the culture of archives.

The legend that Peter the Hermit began the crusade tradition with a letter from the patriarch of Jerusalem is not inappropriate. Newsletters, genuine or doctored, continued to provide information and incitement to action. The friars' centralized hierarchy, international contacts and chapter assemblies supplied fresh channels of written communication. The seals carried by crusade preachers in the mid-thirteenth century must have been used to authenticate documents, not just for securing bags of donations or redemption money.[78] Increasingly, self-consciously bureaucratic secular and ecclesiastical regimes extended their refined archival procedures to the mechanics of crusading. Writing, from the very beginning an active element in long-distance and large-scale mobilization of public opinion, diplomacy, military planning, finance and recruitment, continued to occupy a central place in crusade preparations. The weapons of persuasion – *excitatoria*, letters, tracts, pamphlets, model sermons, chronicles, hymns and poems – complemented the tools of business – charters of land deals, lists of crusaders, contracts of service, diplomatic correspondence and financial accounts. However, writing played only one part. The local worthy's property deal with neighbouring monks may have been recorded in writing but was likely to have been contracted in a public ceremonial exchange of objects – a dagger, a clod of earth – symbolizing the transfer of rights. Diocesan officials may have transcribed the neighbourhood liturgy for taking the Cross, but the act of becoming a *crucesignatus* or *crucesignata* involved a liturgical rite acted out in front of a congregation. Mobilizing support for a crusade depended on writing and systems of delegated authority, but also on performance.

4

Persuasion

Medieval images of crusade preachers reflected contrasting traditions of Christian evangelism: hierophant and demagogue; teacher
and pastor; didacticism and charisma; St Paul and John the Baptist;
Urban II and Peter the Hermit; Bernard of Clairvaux and Brother
Radulph. By the early thirteenth century, stories of Fulk of Neuilly,
the Paris-trained populist, or academics and intellectuals such as Gerald of Wales, James of Vitry or Oliver of Paderborn, allied the two
strands in vignettes of direct engagement, with the anxieties of individuals set alongside statements of theological stringency. Gerald of
Wales described confronting the doubts, obstacles and dilemmas of
individual prospective crusaders, the Cross a panacea for private difficulty not just public crisis. During his preaching in Frisia in 1214,
Oliver of Paderborn dealt with personal and domestic problems: the
skinflint usurer who paid under the odds for his vow redemption; the
life-threatening pregnancy of a crusader's wife; the bullied servant
who sought the protection of the devil; the impact on local recruitment of the murder of a Frisian lord.[1] Preachers voiced crusaders'
concerns to Innocent III and Honorius III over details of the crusade
vow, important for those considering such potentially serious personal or material investments. Attention to the effects of crusading on
the lives of ordinary believers suited the didactic and pastoral evangelism devised by the same academic clerical elite who led the crusade
publicity campaigns, as theories and conventions were crafted to
advise practitioners and combat public indifference or hostility.

THEORY

Boosted by a growing supply of ecclesiastical careerists eager to prove their pastoral as well as intellectual credentials, from the Third Crusade the preaching industry burgeoned. Theoretical analysis and prescriptive manuals flowed, composed mainly by coteries of Paris-educated scholar priests whose common touch was often more conceptual than actual. Self-congratulation was endemic, a literary trope if not a personality flaw. Just as Oliver of Paderborn boasted of his effectiveness in Frisia, so James of Vitry congratulated himself on charming the matrons of Genoa. In 1224, the provost of Arles circulated a newsletter lauding his recent triumph in Marseilles. He had been told he would be lucky to get one recruit, but his team had netted, he claimed, hundreds each day and more than 30,000 in five weeks. By their own account, their preaching inspired celestial visions and miracles of healing. Impediments raised by partners of crusaders (of both sexes) were overcome. Local women were convulsed by trances during which they saw 'many secret things of the cross'.[2] Ecstatic women apart, these were familiar trappings of crusade evangelism. This hubris was presented as the work of God, success attributed to His immanence.

Reality could be very different. Accounts of preaching are speckled with instances of disruptive behaviour, such as the English mason, a veteran of the Holy Land, who heckled in an attempt to dissuade fellow listeners from taking the Cross.[3] Some crusades aroused opposition as being illegitimate or excuses to leach money from the faithful. Preachers might be incompetent or have off days, as Gerald of Wales rather gleefully noted of Archbishop Baldwin of Canterbury in 1188.[4] The pitfalls for unskilled, poorly prepared or ill-equipped orators were familiar. Audience boredom and inattention vied with outright hostility. One Cistercian abbot, after managing to put his own monks and lay brothers to sleep, only woke them up by a gratuitous reference to King Arthur. An English crusade preaching manual of c.1216 explained how exciting anecdotes, *exempla*, were necessary to grab attention and avoid tedium.[5] Care was taken to ensure the intellectual consistency and oratorical effectiveness of both message and medium.

Difficulties were addressed in a wave of theoretical preaching literature from the late twelfth century onwards, supported by sermon
collections from stars of the genre, including crusade preachers such
as James of Vitry, Odo of Châteauroux, papal legate for Louis IX's
1248 crusade, or the Dominicans, Stephen of Bourbon, an expert in
anti-heretic oratory, and Humbert of Romans.[6]

Theoretical prescription was detailed and formulaic. Sermons followed set patterns: an introductory explanation or text, or *exordium*;
the purpose of the sermon or *narratio*; the arguments and counter-
arguments or *divisio*; then the proofs and refutations, *confirmatio*
and *confutatio*; and ending with the conclusion or epilogue. The
model could be adapted to suit different audiences: princes and
nobles; soldiers; lawyers; freemen; serfs (no point for crusade preachers as *crucesignati* technically had to be free); women (with distinctions
drawn for widows and the unmarried); clerics; academics; towns-
people; young; old; rich; poor. Sermons should be clear and tightly
structured. Preachers should avoid patronizing their audiences, speaking over their heads, baffling them with verbiage, using rhetorical
tricks, lying or employing irrelevant sophistry. Narratives and *exempla* should not be prolix but, as one manual put it, 'brief, lucid and
plausible', advice, to judge from surviving examples, regularly ignored.
Words and gestures should match meaning; describing disasters, the
voice should tremble in simulated fear. Preachers needed good dic-
tion, strong voices, verbal fluency, a capacious memory and competent
Latin. Exaggerated expressions and gestures were discouraged; they
made preachers look like fools, jesters or actors.[7] Here, too, the ideal
seems to have been honoured in the breach.

In sermon compendia, those on the crusade were not grouped separ-
ately but collected with those on penance. The language of redemption
through the Cross and penitential imitation of Christ crucified transferred easily from crusading to other genres of sermons *de cruce*.
Baldwin of Forde, before preaching the crusade in 1188, had composed a sermon 'de Sancta Cruce' in which he described the Cross
spiritually as a 'military banner, trophy of victory and sign of triumph', in context metaphorical but of obvious ambiguity. A century
and an half later, in 1333, Archbishop Pierre Roger of Rouen, the
future Pope Clement VI, in a crusade address delivered in front of

Pope John XXII, recycled verbatim one of his penitential sermons *de cruce* for his peroration.[8] The distinctive radicalism of crusade ideology, lauded as an ultimate expression of the secular Christian life, was polemically subsumed in normal pastoral theology. Humbert of Romans, in his general sermon treatise, compared preachers to 'soldiers of Christ', 'a courageous militia' like the Maccabees (a familiar parallel with crusaders), for 'to preach is to fight, for [preachers] make war on the errors against faith and morals'.[9]

However, crusade preaching was distinctive. Humbert composed separate advice for it, *De praedicatione s. Crucis contra Saracenos*, in around 1265. As his own surviving crusade sermons display, Humbert was concerned to provide flexible themes adaptable for different audiences and situations rather than a fixed model, although he possibly appended a version of Urban II's Clermont speech to show how it should best be done.[10] The tract is a practical reference book not an archetype. Whether it reached a wide audience is less certain, given a modest manuscript tradition, although, as a former head of the Dominican Order, Humbert enjoyed the widest of contacts. *De praedicatione s. Crucis* tackled preaching mechanics: when certain specified hymns should be sung; at which point the congregation should be asked to take the Cross; where the Cross should be worn (the right shoulder) and why. Obstacles to taking the Cross are combated: sin; fear or apprehension at the likely hardships and dangers; love of home and family; peer-group hostility, indifference or derision; material incapacity; or doubt. Some of the refutations were laced with homely images. Those who wished to stay at home for love of domesticity are likened to chickens that never leave their hutches, Flemish cows who stayed tethered to houses, or freshwater fish fleeing the salt water of the sea. The advice ends with remarks on the necessary religious acts and spiritual state required to fight Muslims. The key elements are clear: Christian obligation to avenge injuries to God, his Holy Land and fellow Christians in the east; the crusade as the supreme pilgrimage, good employment for Christian knights and the faithful as a whole; the Cross, both a protection and a pledge of grace. The offer of salvation and indulgences was fundamental, captured in the summons to receive the Cross: 'Come; who desires the blessing of

God? Who loves the company of angels? Who yearns for the crown incorruptible? To all who approach, those who come to take the Cross will obtain all these things.'[11]

Preachers needed to be good salesmen with the necessary oratorical skills. To encourage their audiences, they must take the Cross themselves and explain the details and effects of the indulgences and privileges on offer. Their priestly authority to grant absolution provided a necessary prerequisite for administering the Cross. Humbert made ambitious academic demands on preachers. In addition to relevant Bible passages, they should command a grasp of regional geography and world maps (*mappae mundi*, then in vogue, like the one preserved at Hereford Cathedral). Along with texts such as the *Chanson d'Antioche* and William of Tyre, preachers ought to be conversant with the life of Muhammed and the history of Islam, including the Koran. This may have become standard. Oliver of Paderborn, who preached the Fifth Crusade in western Germany, professed knowledge of the Koran's teaching on Christ and the Virgin Mary. Humbert's useful texts showed off his academic credentials: they included Eusebius; Cassiodorus; Augustine; Gregory of Tours; Gregory the Great; Bede; Pseudo-Turpin on Charlemagne as a proto-crusader; and a selection of hagiography.[12] For all its pragmatic tone, Humbert's treatise, like the sermon collections, was severely academic, more rarefied than demotic.

Yet a sermon treatise from half a century earlier suggests that the demand for these sophisticated skills was neither unusual nor unique. The *Brevis ordinacio de predicatione s. crucis in Angliae*, probably dating from 1213 to 1216, may be associated with the team of preachers appointed by Innocent III to preach the Fifth Crusade in England. King John took the Cross at Easter 1215 mainly as a political ploy to cement a papal alliance and wrong-foot his opponents, given the war with France in 1214. But subsequent war with France, rebellion, civil war and the French invasion of 1215–17 made effective preaching for the Holy Land crusade unlikely until hostilities ceased, although some royalists appear to have adopted the language and perhaps the formal status of crusaders against the rebels.[13] The *Brevis ordinacio* may have been simply a scholarly exercise. However, it does indicate how it was thought a popular message should be conveyed. Theological niceties were dressed in crowd-pleasing imagery to confront listeners' anxieties, chiefly about sin and death. Examples and analogies stressed that, for those bearing the Cross of redemption, death led to life, a fate not to be feared but embraced. The benefits of the crusade indulgence combated the snares of sin for the penitent and contrite, the lynchpin of crusading's economy of redemption. Striking by its absence was any suggestion that spiritual virtue might reap material gain.

Exposition and communication were bound together. A lengthy discussion of the eucharist and the Real Presence recognized that crusade preaching habitually occurred in the context of the celebration of the Mass, with its appropriate emphasis on Christ crucified, sacrifice, redemption, confession and absolution. The crucifix linked esoteric analogies with a common religious tool. In another home-spun image, taking the Cross was said to confirm the crusaders' reward of heaven 'as if by a charter'. A final section, 'On the call of men to the Cross', provided a model sermon on the redemptive power of the Cross: service to God in heart and deed; and salvation and eternal life through a martyr's death in battle. Acceptance of eternal life through a crusader's death is illustrated in two *exempla*, one involving Godfrey of Bouillon and his brother from the First Crusade, another about the French hero James of Avesnes from the Third. The section is punctuated by oratorical refrains inviting the adoption of the Cross, each beginning 'Therefore, rise up' (*Surge ergo*), based on Matthew 16:24: 'Therefore arise, take up my cross'. The treatise concludes with six further death and glory *exempla*, with the same refrains. The anecdotes combined Latin with vernacular punch lines, reflecting live practice and a knightly audience. One, about a crusader urging his horse 'Morelle' into battle and thence to Paradise, was also used by James of Vitry. Each describes apparently historical crusading martyrs eagerly embracing a heroic death confident in the reward of everlasting life. One produced a dreadful Anglo-French pun. Hugh of Beauchamp charges the Saracens crying 'Although my name is Beau Champ, never was I in a good field (*bello campo* i.e. *beau champ*) until today.'[14] The groans are almost audible.

TIMING

The liturgical year provided crusade publicity with a calendar of appropriate seasons and feast days to focus on repentance, penance and redemption through Christ and the Cross. The penitential seasons of Advent, leading to Christmas, and Lent, leading to Easter, suited Christ-centred calls to penance, despite inclement weather for travel, let alone outdoor oratory. Urban II preached during Advent, Christmas, Lent and Easter in 1095–6. The Second Crusade was first publicly preached at Christmas 1145. *Quantum praedecessores* was re-issued and Bernard of Clairvaux began his preaching in Lent 1146, culminating in the great Cross-giving festival at Vézelay on Easter Day. Conrad III of Germany took the Cross from Bernard the following Christmas. In 1188, key moments in preaching the Third Crusade coincided with Epiphany and, in Wales and western Germany, Lent. Frederick Barbarossa took the Cross at his 'Court of Christ' at Mainz on *Laetare Jerusalem* – Rejoice Jerusalem – Sunday (the fourth in Lent), the same day that Philip II of France held an assembly in Paris to discuss the crusade. During the Fourth Crusade, the counts of Champagne and Blois received the Cross on Advent Sunday, 28 November 1199, while the count of Flanders followed suit on Ash Wednesday, 23 February 1200. Innocent III issued the bulls *Quia Maior* during Eastertide 1213, and *Ad Liberandam* in Advent 1215, the year King John of England took the Cross on Ash Wednesday and Frederick II of Germany at Easter. Examples proliferate. The provost of Arles's five-week preaching mission to Marseilles in 1223–4 coincided with Advent and Christmas. Henry III of England took the Cross on *Laetare Jerusalem* Sunday in 1250.[15] In 1267, Louis IX of France took the Cross on a date with dual resonance, 25 March, mid-Lent and the Feast of the Annunciation to the Virgin Mary, increasingly the presiding mistress of the crusading spirit.

Rolling preaching campaigns of the sort organized from the Fifth Crusade onwards were less bound to seasonal timetables. However, individual festivals remained important, producing crowds off work, gathered to worship, trade or have fun. Urban II's visits to

Limoges, Poitiers and the Loire valley in the winter of 1095–6 coincided with the feast days of local saints or re-dedications of churches to them. In 1214, Oliver of Paderborn exploited the crowds gathered at Dokkum in the diocese of Utrecht for the Feast Day (5 June) of St Boniface, a local martyr. In early September that year, Oliver's colleague John of Xanten gate-crashed a harvest festival in the valley of the Meuse.[16] He did not wait for the crusaders' special festival, 14 September, Holy Cross Day, the feast of the Exaltation of the Cross. In 1198 and 1201 the traditional Holy Cross Day meetings of the General Chapter of the Cistercians at Cîteaux became focal occasions in the preliminaries of the Fourth Crusade. At the other end of the social scale, the preaching initiative across in Yorkshire in 1291 was orchestrated for 14 September. Philip IV of France, not one to miss a propagandist trick, ordered the arrest of the Templars on the same day in 1307. Continued enthusiasm for the crusade in Tournai into the fourteenth century may be connected with its annual festival of the Holy Cross that culminated on 14 September.[17]

Festivals supplied occasional opportunities. The Mass provided a regular and familiar ceremonial setting, specified in some surviving rites for taking the Cross. Its imagery and language evoked the main themes of the crusade: the presence of Christ; His sacrifice; the Cross; confession; absolution; the promise of redemption; and the crucifix, employed by crusade preachers rhetorically and as a prop. The Mass and crusade propaganda acted in dialogue. Bernard of Clairvaux, whose Easter Day sermon at Vézelay in 1146 followed the Easter High Mass, wrote with clear Eucharistic overtones of Palestine being made holy by Christ's blood where 'the flowers of His resurrection first blossomed'. At Clermont, Urban II's sermon may have been accompanied by his audience reciting the general confession from the Mass. Thereafter, the Mass regularly provided the preamble and the setting for calls to take the Cross. The great sermon and Cross-giving ceremony at Regensburg in February 1147 was prefaced by a High Mass, 'as was customary' noted one *crucesignatus*. Preachers often acted as celebrant, as at Regensburg. In Flanders and Wales during Lent 1188, crusade sermons were preached after Mass. At Bedum in Frisia in 1214, Oliver of Paderborn's sermon formed part of a celebration of 'a high mass of the Holy Cross' decorated by an alleged apparition of the crucifix in the sky, although the member of the congregation apparently most convinced was an eleven-year-old girl.[18]

Whatever the occasion, advance warning was essential. Congregations needed to know what to expect; local clergy to incorporate the sermon into their liturgical programmes; preachers to set up their props and apparatus and perhaps rehearse; potential crusaders to settle their determination and overcome any domestic opposition; crowds to plan their day out. Spontaneity was unhelpful and impractical. For long tours, preachers needed to organize itineraries, hospitality and venues. Time was required to gather large assemblies or conferences. Odo of Deuil tells how, after the damp squib of Louis VII's declaration of his crusading intentions at Christmas 1145, 'another time was appointed, Eastertide at Vézelay, where all were to assemble on the Sunday before Palm Sunday [i.e. Passion Sunday], and where those who should be divinely inspired were to take up the glorious cross on Easter Sunday'. To add effect, the king obtained a cross from the pope beforehand. Divine inspiration required some assistance.[19] Similarly, the impeccably well-connected but religiously austere Bishop Otto of Freising attributed the success of the Regensburg ceremony at which he took the Cross in 1147 not to rhetoric but to preparation:

> For there was no need of persuasive words of human wisdom or the ingratiating use of artful circumlocution, in accordance with the precepts of rhetoricians, since all who were present had been aroused by previous report and hurried forward of their own accord to receive the cross.[20]

Literary insistence on spontaneity concealed reality. According to one of his monks, Abbot Martin of Pairis's sermon in Basel in 1201 came as no surprise. Those gathered in Basel cathedral,

> stimulated by current rumours ... had heard for quite a while how other regions round about were being summoned to this army of Christ at well-attended sermons ... Consequently, large numbers of the people of this area, prepared in their hearts to enlist in Christ's camp, were hungrily anticipating an exhortation of this sort.[21]

Martin's sermon adorned a well-understood ritual in which the congregation affirmed decisions already reached elsewhere. Such ceremonies were rarely innovative, and were often conscious re-enactments. The model of Urban II was still referenced two centuries later. Gerald of Wales in 1188 deliberately re-created a famous scene from Bernard of Clairvaux's preaching tour in 1146–7. Oliver of Paderborn's celestial visions of 1214 were widely imitated. As preachers were ritualistically playing Christ in calling on his followers to take up crosses, argument could be less important than form and setting.[22]

PLACE

Preachers were advised to operate in towns, large villages and any-where with an audience, however modest.[23] As crusade preachers had to sign up as many volunteers as quickly as possible, maximum popu-lar exposure and geographical coverage were of the essence, hence the restlessness of preaching tours, such as in Wales in 1188 or Frisia in 1214, and their attention to centres of population, nobles' courts, festivals, churches and cult sites. The main locations were towns. Ecclesiastical centres, the towns ('*civitates*' his successor Paschal II observed) of western France, played host to Urban II in 1095–6. Peter the Hermit was said to have preached in cities and small towns ('*urbs et municipia*').[24] The Rhineland cities of Cologne, Mainz, Worms, Speyer and Strasburg repeatedly featured in promotional campaigns. In England, London provided a focus for publicity and recruitment in a long tradition from the Second Crusade onwards. Cardinal Ugolino's 1221 mission in north Italy revolved around cities: Lucca, Pisa, Padua, Pistoia, Genoa, Bologna and Venice. Florence, like Cologne, Genoa and London, embraced a long crusading inheritance. Lübeck and Bremen were the centres for proselytizing and recruit-ment for the Livonian crusades after 1200. Major assemblies occurred in towns and cities: Clermont (in 1095), Vézelay (1146), Speyer (1146), Frankfurt (1147), Regensburg (1147), Paris (1096 and 1188) and Mainz (1188). Some of the most vivid accounts of preaching in the early thirteenth century concerned cities: James of Vitry in Genoa in 1216 or the provost of Arles in Marseilles in 1223–4. Oliver of Paderborn and John of Xanten criss-crossed from small town to small town in the archdiocese of Cologne in 1214. Archbishop Baldwin's troupe did the same in Wales in 1188. The famous Dominican translator of Aristotle, Albert the Great, in Germany in 1263–4 as 'predictor et promotor crucis', stuck to major urban centres, using the network of religious houses in them as his bases: Augsburg, Donauworth, Würzburg, Frankfurt-am-Main, Cologne, Strasburg, Speyer, Regensburg, Mainz.[25]

Secular sites were employed for crusade ceremonies, including castles, as at Usk in Wales in March 1188, tournament fields, as at Ecry in November 1199, and market places, as at La Vieille-Tour in Rouen in 1268, despite worries at such proximity to commerce.[26] Gisors, where the kings of France and England took the Cross in January 1188, was the traditional site for summits between French monarchs and the dukes of Normandy. However, just as the diocesan structure supplied preaching circuits, so churches, cathedrals and occasionally monasteries (Marmoutier in 1096, St Denis in 1146, Clerkenwell in 1185, Cîteaux in 1198 and 1201, etc.) provided the grid for their itineraries.[27] Churches provided natural meeting places and the largest public buildings. Their staff could prepare the venue, publicize the event and supply hospitality and local information. Preaching followed the growth of towns and cathedral and church building and the establishment of a secure parochial system. In churches, relics in altars or separate shrines created a suitably encompassing religious atmosphere. This could be especially exploited during the translation of relics or church re-dedication, from (for example) St Martial at Limoges in December 1095, St Hilary at Poitiers and St Nicholas at Angers in January 1096 to Mary Magdalen at Rouen in March 1268.[28]

One cliché of crusading was the open air sermon. Urban II seems to have enjoyed this, perhaps to emphasize Christ-like evangelism. A sense of preacher machismo pervades some accounts. One witness remembered that Urban had to preach in the open air at Clermont because 'no building was large enough to contain all those present'. Odo of Deuil repeats this trope in his account of Bernard of Clairvaux's speech at Vézelay: 'since there was no place within the town which could accommodate such a large crowd, a wooden platform was erected outside in a field, so that the abbot could speak from an elevation to the people standing round about'.[29] Acoustically and logistically, as thirteenth-century manuals noted, preaching inside a church was preferable. However, many churches would simply have been too small to house a congregation drawn from beyond the immediate vicinity. Even substantial civic churches could be inadequate. Equally, not all preaching operations possessed the manpower to cover individual parish churches in the way the Yorkshire friars did in 1291, so they organized large gatherings in convenient centres.[30] In Wales in 1188, most of the sermons were delivered outside.

Other factors influenced decisions where to hold crusade ceremonies. The special religious processions instituted after 1212–13 in aid of Spain and the Holy Land were sometimes conducted in the open. In England in the spring of 1295, Holy Land processions were to be held outside if the weather were fine; inside if wet.[31] Tournaments, as at Ecry in 1199, presented publicized rendezvous for ready-made audiences of fighting men. A field of chivalry offered a highly pointed ceremonial setting for transmuting sinful secular violence into redemptive holy warfare. The contrast between the *malitia* and *militia*, especially as tournaments were banned by the Church between 1130 and 1316, could hardly have been missed. The ambivalence of the crusade's clerical promoters towards knightly culture, embracing it ostensibly to reform or redirect it, was nowhere more manifest. In summer months, open-air picnics provided acceptable ways to listen to the word of the Cross. Oliver of Paderborn paints a relaxed picture of his audience gathered in a meadow outside Bedum in 1214, a family outing with three generations sitting together with their neighbours. At Dokkum that June the open air may have been for preference. Oliver's claims of celestial visions cannot have diminished the crowds' enjoyment. His colleague John of Xanten was less fortunate: on one occasion his words were carried away on the wind (conveniently blamed on diabolical intervention). One enterprising Franciscan incorporated a flagpole in his preaching platform so listeners could see where the wind was coming from and position themselves. Audibility exercised preaching experts. Many listeners, perhaps most, would miss exactly what was said, another incentive for theatrical business and props. Oliver of Paderborn admitted that only about a hundred people saw the crosses in the sky at Bedum, presumably those close enough to hear the speaker suggest the clouds' meaning.[32]

AUDIENCE

Promotional success depended on getting audiences. Itinerant preachers, often covering large swathes of territory very rapidly, staying in each place for very short times, often inside a day, had to rely on locals rustling up an audience. James of Vitry recounted a story of Fulk of Neuilly arriving at a French town to preach only to find there was nobody about. So he started to shout: 'Help! Help! Robbers! Robbers!' That brought people running, asking where the criminals were. Fulk neatly explained that demonic thieves had come to the town to steal their souls and proceeded to preach as planned, now to a substantial audience.[33] No audience; no crusade. From the Fifth Crusade onwards, nervousness over attendance may have lain behind the offer of indulgences for those who simply turned up to listen. On one level, this recognized the spiritual nature of the process, in line with redemption of vows and partial indulgences for other assistance. By the mid-thirteenth century preachers and even collectors of crusade taxes were allowed to enjoy remission of sins. Yet, at the same time, there were worries of sermon fatigue as crusade preaching became almost normative, its conduct by friars more institutional, its causes ever more varied, and its object increasingly financial – concerns openly voiced in the 1270s by the Franciscan Gilbert of Tournai. The tariff for audiences grew from between 10 and 20 days' remission of the penalties of confessed sin under Honorius III (1216–27) to between 100 and 450 days under Gregory X (1271–6).[34]

Whether or not this inflation reflected a growing indifference or hostility to non-Holy Land crusades, which some contemporaries identified, or was simply incorporating all aspects of the crusade industry into a comprehensive penitential system, the incentive of spiritual rewards for attending sermons underlined their ritualistic aspect. This generous scattering of indulgences still attracted customers. One (admittedly hostile) observer noted how friars preaching the Cross in England in 1249 announced that those who came to hear them would receive an indulgence of 'many days'. This drew a crowd across age, gender, wealth and social status. The Cross was given indiscriminately to invalids, the sick and the old who next day redeemed their vows with cash.[35] The chronicler may have been scandalized, but the beneficiaries gained free indulgences along with those they bought; a decent bargain. In any case, not all who heard sermons intended to take the Cross or did so, preachers aiming beyond potential *crucesignati* to their relatives. As with other such commitments – marriage for example – crusading required public approval by those most affected. Only sections of any congregation actually took the Cross, even with cash redemptions increasing the proportion of temporary, non-combatant *crucesignati*. The rest participated by their witness and acquiescence or, especially if they lived on Church lands, by paying taxes. All needed reassurance of the merits of the enterprise.

Propaganda was crafted to suit different audiences. The bellicose imagery of Urban II and Bernard of Clairvaux set the pattern for the *ordo pugnatorum*: princes, lords, knights and lesser fighting men. Bernard, when mentioning merchants, presented the crusade offer of salvation in terms of a commercial bargain. Bishop Albert of Riga appealed to the commercial groups (*negotiores*) in western Baltic and northern German towns.[36] In other cities, crusading appealed across social and economic strata, to those with property, however modest, or enjoying wages. Paupers did not queue up to take the Cross, even if some who did subsequently fell on hard times before they fulfilled their vows.[37] The alliance between crusading, the apostolic poverty movement and anti-materialist campaigners so apparent in the generations around 1200 was less socially radical than it may seem. The *Brevis ordinacio* likened the rich to fish wallowing in mud who, stung by the preacher's words, fled God's net, i.e. the Cross. Pursuing the aquatic metaphor, large fish got caught in the devil's nets while small fish – the poor – swam through to the Cross and to God.[38] If taken literally, the idea that the wealthy were estranged from crusading was absurd, self-defeating and untrue. Such anti-materialist rhetoric caused difficulties. The crusaders' exemption from usury and immediate repayment of debts, current at least since the 1140s, awkwardly undermined their creditworthiness just at the moment they were most in need of loans. However, attacks on the wealthy were not quite what they seemed. In a crusade sermon designed for use on Holy Cross Day – 14 September – composed around the time of the Third Crusade, Alan of Lille made it clear that Christ's favour was bestowed on the humble not the indigent by quoting Matthew 5:3 (rather than Luke 6:20) 'blessed are the poor

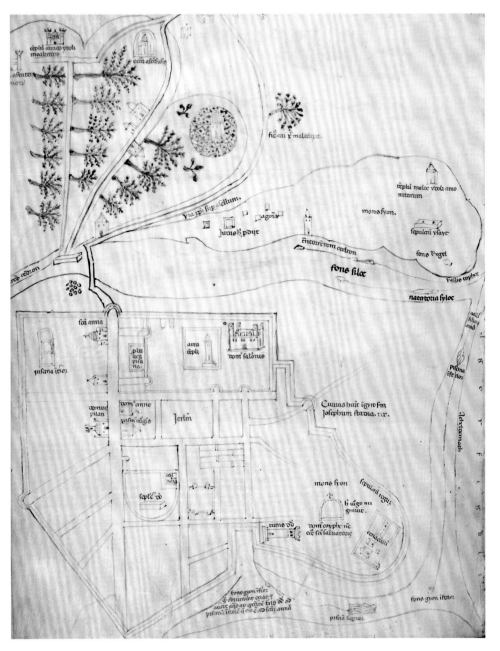

1. Idealized geography: an early fourteenth-century map of Jerusalem.

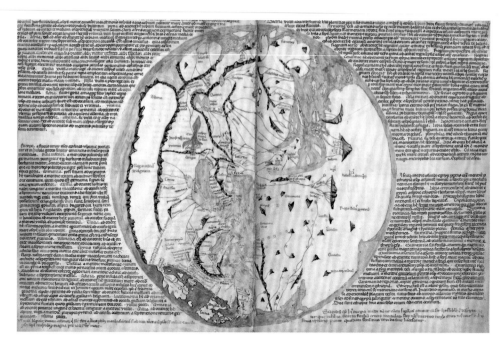

2. The world as understood by crusader planners in the early fourteenth century.

3. Crusade and chivalry: a battle outside Damietta during the Fifth Crusade.

4. Louis IX of France taking the Cross on his sick-bed, 1244.

5. Planning crusades: the First Council of Lyons, 1245.

6. Preachers of the crusade: a thirteenth-century image of a Franciscan friar.

7. Louis IX of France displaying relics linked to the Holy Land: the True Cross and the Crown of Thorns.

de cōsilio ducis Burgundie. Comitis Walti de Brene
a agrī hospital'. z cecoẓ nobiliū. maioẓ scilicz par
tis excerci' paci z treuge cōsensū subscepte. Que li
cet i pīmo aduentu nīo difficil' fieri apparebat:
cōmendabil' est cū z are see subsidio fructuosa. Am
pauperibz z pegnantibz leta est z secura. medioebz

¶Ereunt franci a sarracenorum liberati.

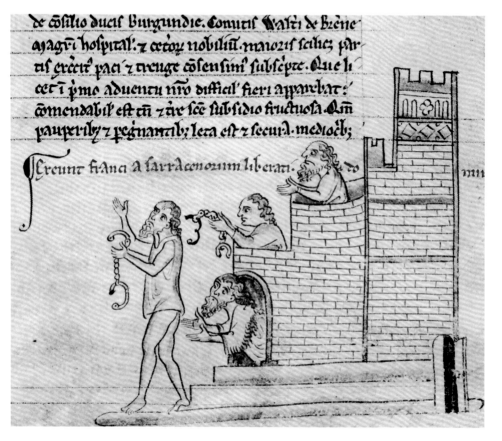

12. Crusade diplomacy: the release of French prisoners from Egypt, 1241.

13. Communications: late eleventh-century messengers.

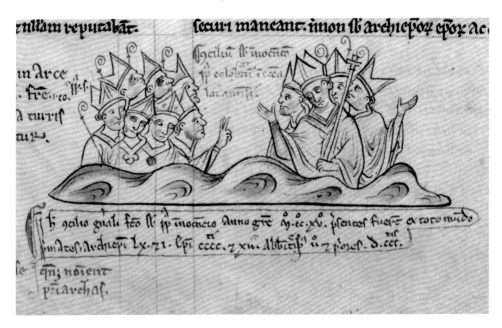

14. Planning crusades: the Fourth Lateran Council, 1215.

in spirit' (*beati pauperes spiritu*).[39] Carnality not coffers was the target. Preaching poverty to the destitute was not good policy.

The wealthy and propertied provided the core audience for crusade promoters. A Genoese crusader noted the attraction of the First Crusade for the 'better sort'. Over a century later, James of Vitry consorted with Genoese high society.[40] Around nobles, lords and prelates were their households, clients and servants. Listeners and future crusaders came from a full array of occupations in what was an increasingly specialized economy: bakers, blacksmiths, bowmen, butchers, carpenters, carters, chaplains, chefs, cobblers, ditchers, dyers, fishmongers, knights, masons, merchants, notaries, physicians, potters, sergeants, skinners, squires, tailors, usurers. Sensitivity was shown to regional interests. Local crusade heroes appeared in *exempla* and, in one, the Flemish custom of pole-vaulting over canals became a metaphor for the crusader in death vaulting over purgatory 'as if in one leap they pass into heaven'.[41]

Women attended sermons – three generations of one family at Bedum in 1214. Although often cast as impediments to male partners taking the Cross, many became *crucesignatae*. Some chroniclers, as if to highlight the gender divide, portrayed women as urging their men to go on crusade while they kept the home fires burning.[42] Holding sermons on feast days made whole family outings easier and more likely. The co-opting of the Virgin Mary as a patron of holy war may also have encouraged the support of women, although it is likely that the gender-blind offer of vow redemptions and indulgences proved more tangibly persuasive. Most crusade preachers probably shared the often virulent institutional misogyny of the academic classes of the time, so their references to women tended to be negative, as in the story of the mother who accidentally smothered her baby in punishment for trying to stop her husband taking the Cross. Even the more cheerful account of how agreeing to allow her husband to go on crusade saved a mother in labour assumed initial wifely opposition. In the imagined world of crusade propaganda, obstructive women invited life-threatening illness or terrible misfortune on themselves. Such anecdotes were clearly pitted against the experience of the real risk to hearth, health and happiness presented by the absence of a husband, and one reason no doubt some wives attended sermons was to keep an eye on feckless spouses. Faced with such difficulties, Innocent

III effectively re-wrote canon law to allow male crusaders to depart without their wives' consent, thereby unilaterally denying them their conjugal rights. Nonetheless, both James of Vitry at Genoa and the provost of Arles and his team at Marseilles used women to further the cause, acknowledging their closet influence. As further incentive, during the first half of the thirteenth century it became established that a crusader's wife and children shared in his plenary indulgence.[43]

The physical conditions and attention span of the listeners aroused concern. Unless sprawled across summer meadows, most audiences, like that at Basel in 1201, stood, as they did during church services and as crowds at mass rallies have always done. Preachers had to take account of this. Humbert of Romans warned that any audience could include people who did not want to be there, left early, could not stay still, wandered about disturbing others, were not listening but were doing something else, or were simply bored. In advising how best to capture listeners' interest, he admitted that not every cleric was up to it, from the ignorant to the over-educated.[44] Congregations could be noisy, whistling, interrupting, applauding, talking, or just dozing. From Urban II's whipping up cries of '*Deus lo volt!*' at Clermont, vocal reactions were integral to many sermons. This could get out of hand. Heckling was inevitable, sometimes derailing dialectic sophistication, as the smart canon lawyer Hostiensis encountered to his cost when preaching a crusade against the Hohenstaufen in Germany in 1251. Crowds could get out of control. Gerald of Wales recorded a posse of over-excited Welshmen chasing Archbishop Baldwin after his sermon at Hay-on-Wye demanding to receive the Cross.[45] Overall numbers drummed up by a preaching tour might have been in the thousands, especially if local lords led their followers into the commitment. However, individual congregations might produce only a few dozen or scores. Even the self-satisfied preachers in Marseilles in the winter of 1223–4 only claimed one or two hundred a day, even though apparently hardly a household failed to produce a *crucesignatus*. This might imply preachers had gone round door to door, as James of Vitry did in Acre in 1217. Personal canvassing appears in accounts of preaching elsewhere. Although private proselytizing was associated with heretics, supplementing the chance dynamics of mass meetings with private conversations was approved and made sense.[46]

At large set-piece orations, despite the vocal projection of trained preachers, probably only those at the front heard properly. Details would have been passed to those further away. To achieve any wider coverage, speeches' content was signalled in advance or circulated subsequently, orally or by newsletter, a common-enough technique for public meetings until the twentieth century. Although written versions of actual live crusade sermons, known as *reportationes*, were compiled from notes taken at the time, it is unclear if any were deployed for immediate promotional purposes or just reserved as academic models for future use.[47] However, precise meaning may have been less important than stage management. Prudent preachers left little to chance or oratory. Apart from setting an example by taking the Cross themselves, some ensured a pre-selected member or members of the congregation would come up first to take the Cross; as one such plant put it, 'to give strong encouragement to the others and an added incentive to what they had just been told'.[48] Preachers travelled with entourages, and local clergy were on hand, so finding stooges would not have presented a problem. Claques could be organized; at Clermont one such reportedly began the chanting of '*Deus lo volt!*' Community singing could be arranged to heighten the revivalist atmosphere and add peer pressure on the reluctant. Crowds were additionally encouraged to heap insults on the standoffish, a nasty exercise in deliberately contrived mob tyranny.[49]

Such devices could misfire. Demotic crusade evangelism courted social unrest with its manifesto of violence and equality. If all *crucesignati* were equally liberated from sin through personal contrition and fighting for the Cross, officially, there could be no social hierarchy in salvation. Encouraging emotions of fear, guilt, violence and revenge, undifferentiated calls to attack the 'enemies of Christ' provoked massacres of Jews in Germany in 1096 and 1146 and in England in 1190. Provocation for the so-called Children's Crusade in 1212 in northern France and western Germany came from devotional crusade processions and overlapping preaching campaigns stressing the threats to Christendom in Spain, Languedoc and the Holy Land.[50] Faced by preachers celebrating the divine mission of the faithful poor to succeed where the military elites had failed, audiences were propelled into collective action challenging traditional social discipline. In part, Innocent III's careful regimentation of preparations for the Fifth Crusade from

1213 sought to counter such unlicensed enthusiasm. However, his offer of indulgences for cash redemptions of vows and other donations still excluded many from crusade action, contradicting the rhetoric of inclusive salvation. Popular demonstrations from excluded crusade enthusiasts, in northern France in 1251 and 1320 or among the urban poor on the streets of London in 1309, showed that audiences could not always be taken for granted.[51] One hostile but baffled observer of the First Crusade publicity campaign noted how excitement over the Jerusalem project spread out of control, by word of mouth, one person to another.[52] In this detonation of rumour, crusade ceremonies provided the ignition; they could not necessarily confine the combustion.

LANGUAGE

Promotional events offered ritualized engagement, not invitations to public debate; direct but formal communication. While most sermons survive in Latin, they were not necessarily delivered in Latin. A famous story about Bernard of Clairvaux's preaching the Second Crusade in Germany described how he was understood by people who did not know the language he was preaching in. This suitably miraculous memory was recycled by Gerald of Wales when recalling how he wowed an audience at Haverfordwest in 1188 despite speaking only in Latin and French, languages unknown to his Anglo-Welsh listeners. Gerald noted that Bernard had been speaking French (*lingua Gallica*) to his German audience, not Latin. Bernard's own secretary's recollection of the same event did not explicitly deny this; and he may have been taking notes. Whichever language Bernard spoke, the need for intelligibility dictated the presence of interpreters, even though their efforts reportedly fell completely flat. The story was designed – and repeated – to highlight the superiority of divinely inspired spiritual response over literal understanding. It also exposed a genuine problem.[53]

In polyglot landscapes regional languages and dialects overlapped and co-existed with elite vernaculars – such as Anglo-Norman French in England – and Latin, the language of learning, the liturgy and the Bible, the language of God. If, as claimed, preachers spoke with the voice of God (*vox Dei*), it had to be in Latin. Clerical audiences could be expected – sometimes wrongly – to understand Latin. However, given the Latinate culture of courtly life, aristocratic education, financial accounting, contracts and administration, many lay people may also have been able to follow a basic Latin speech, especially one that relied on a few key words – *Deus, Christus, crux, redemptio, salvatio, Terra Sancta, milites Christi, diabolus, infideles, ultio, devotio, contritio, remissio, peccatum, peregrinus, accipio, sequor, paradisus* – and employed simple repeated tropes, as in the *Brevis ordinacio*'s '*Surge ergo*'. As Humbert of Romans commented, 'a good preacher . . . will see to it that he does not say many things, and will say them in few words'.[54] Meaning was enhanced with ritual, props, vocal emphasis and gestures. Crusade preaching and Cross-taking shared a lexicon and choreography with the familiar Latin liturgy. In Romance-speaking areas Latin may not have seemed alien or far removed from vernacular speech, for example in Italy where the Frenchman James of Vitry scored a success in 1216. Latin provided an international language, a lingua franca suitable for international publicity and polyglot groups, such as armies. When the Portuguese Bishop Peter Pitões addressed cosmopolitan crusader forces at Oporto in 1147, he used Latin so that interpreters for each individual regional contingent could understand what he was saying. At Llandaff in south Wales on 15 March 1188, Archbishop Baldwin of Canterbury and his team were confronted by a segregated audience: on one side the English; the Welsh on the other.[55] Using Latin and leaving the rest to interpreters probably seemed the best thing to do.

Nonetheless, to ensure God's faithful understood His word, preachers employed the vernacular or a mixture of languages. The vernacular made addresses by the laymen Bohemund of Antioch in Chartres Cathedral in 1106 or Esbern at the Danish court at Christmas 1188 especially powerful.[56] Innocent III preached in Italian as well as Latin, on one, non-crusading, occasion forced into extempore translation from a Latin text when his memory failed him.[57] In medieval Europe the well educated were all at least bilingual in Latin and their own vernacular. Many were polyglot. Abbot Samson of Bury St Edmunds in Suffolk, Paris-trained but not the most overtly scholarly of monks, reportedly preached in Latin, French and his native Norfolk English dialect.[58] Increasingly in the twelfth century the vernaculars themselves were becoming respectable literary languages in verse and prose epic, romance, history and chronicles. By 1200 a bishop of Paris had produced a sizeable compendium of French vernacular sermons. Three generations later, Humbert of Romans insisted that an effective preacher needed 'to express himself well in the vulgar tongue'.[59] While sermons directed at fellow clergy were likely to have been in Latin, crusade preaching was aimed primarily at the laity whose Latinity could not be assumed. This attention to preaching in the vernacular reveals itself in macaronic (i.e. mixed Latin and vernacular) texts, such as the *Brevis ordinacio* with its French punch lines to Latin *exempla*. Papal bulls were translated for preachers' use. Preaching circuits traced linguistic rather than political boundaries: northern or southern French; High or Low German. French-speaking areas of the western empire might be lumped together with dioceses in the kingdom of France; preachers in Germany might be assigned German-speaking parts of Flanders but not French ones. In 1214 Oliver of Paderborn concentrated on Low German-speaking areas of the vast archdiocese of Cologne, while Albert the Great in 1263–4 spent his time in High German-speaking regions. Speaking the local language, they would have expected to use it.[60] The use of local diocesan clergy and mendicants confirmed a prudent linguistic sensitivity.

Nonetheless, interpreters were ubiquitous. Gerald of Wales, who preached in Latin and French, noted Archbishop Baldwin's need for interpreters, not necessarily because he used Latin but because, like Gerald, he did not speak in Welsh. Help came from the local clergy led by the archdeacon of Bangor. The divide between different vernaculars was possibly more of a problem than that with Latin. In Germany, Bernard of Clairvaux could only preach in French, not in German, so he required interpreters, an exact parallel to Archbishop Baldwin in 1188. After preaching in French-speaking Flanders, Cardinal Henry of Albano faced identical difficulties on his arrival in Germany in 1188, one contemporary commenting that, being French, Henry knew no German but managed well enough through interpreters.[61] Forging an emotional link with a crowd of strangers was easier if you could speak their language. Foreign grandees operated at a disadvantage. When preaching the Cross at Lincoln in 1267, Cardinal Ottobuono Fieschi (the future Pope Adrian V, July to August 1276, one of the few popes never to have been ordained a priest) needed two friars and the cathedral's dean to get his message across. Inability to engage in vernacular banter or argument with his German audience may have contributed to the Italian Hostiensis's problems in Germany in 1251. As the account of the bishop of Oporto's address in 1147 makes clear, some crowds expected their sermons to be in their own language.[62] Crusade organizers obliged.

PROPS, PERFORMANCE AND DRAMA

Crusading became materially embedded in the cultural landscape. Certain saints' shrines or relics possessed crusade associations (such as that of the Crown of Thorns in Louis IX's Sainte Chapelle in Paris). So too did tombs of former crusaders or churches constructed in imitation of the Holy Sepulchre or the al-Aqsa mosque (e.g. the late twelfth-century Temple Church in London). Sites recalled crusade connotations (such as Vézelay, site of Bernard of Clairvaux's iconic sermon in 1146 and the joint departure point for the crusades of Richard I and Philip II in 1190). Memories were decorated and preserved in sculpture (e.g. the well-known portrayal of a crusader and his wife at Beval in Lorraine), stained glass (famously the First Crusade cycle in the mid-twelfth-century glass at St Denis near Paris), murals (e.g. the famous Templar series at Cressac-sur-Charente or scenes of the Passion in the chapel of the Holy Sepulchre in Winchester Cathedral, c.1227, or the scenes of the Third Crusade on the walls of the palaces of Henry III of England) and other church and domestic decoration (e.g. the mosaic commemorating the taking of Constantinople by the Fourth Crusade in 1204 in Ravenna or Henry III of England's floor tiles depicting Richard I and Saladin). Crusading was paraded in regular special liturgies and processions instituted by Innocent III; in the chests placed in parish churches for crusade donations; and through prayers and masses for the dead that included the liberation of Jerusalem, regular demands for money, and offers of indulgences. Such presence in the normal social lives of western Europeans provided an increasingly rich private backcloth for public attempts to rouse enthusiasm.[63]

To secure such active support called for the populism of the circus not the dialectic of the study. Words were complemented by visual and theatrical display. Performance was essential. The rites for taking the Cross, in all their local and regional variety, were intrinsically theatrical: declamatory dramas.[64] Unlike the ceremonies of dubbing knights, where the clergy blessed the symbols of knighthood that were then bestowed on initiates by laymen, in granting the Cross the role of the priest was central throughout, from the Mass, to the sermon, to the blessing and actual giving out of the crosses. Tricks were legion. Sermons were carefully staged. Platforms served as more than just pulpits. At Vézelay at Easter 1146 one collapsed under the weight of the grandees on display to support Bernard of Clairvaux. Preachers used pulpits as stages. They employed an array of facial expressions, hand and body gestures and vocal modulations to suit the words, as if taking different parts in a dramatic monologue or play. Experts' pleas for discretion and moderation suggest more than a few performances went over the top. John of Xanten preached with his eyes shut as if in a divine trance.[65] The act could begin with elaborate prayers and holy water being scattered liberally as a prelude to the main show. Histrionics came with props. The most common were crosses or crucifixes, held up to emphasize key points in the argument. In Wales in 1188, a cross was passed to each speaker in turn, almost like a microphone. One late fourteenth-century showman, Bishop Henry Despenser of Norwich, apparently heaved a large life-sized replica cross onto his shoulders, which he later erected on the chancel steps to encourage his congregation. Some claimed their cross contained a relic of the True Cross. Urban II carried samples with him in 1095–6. During the siege of Lisbon a preacher claimed to be brandishing 'a sacred piece of the wood of the Lord'.[66]

Such claims could backfire. A possibly apocryphal story circulating in English monastic circles told of a French abbot, during the preaching of the First Crusade, who was struck down with cancer for trying to pass off a cross he had made himself as a gift from God, the dangers of forgery presumably being the point of this story. Whether many preachers went as far as another French abbot, who gave himself a nasty life-long wound by branding or cutting a cross on his forehead at the time of the First Crusade, is unknown. Tattoos of the Cross seemed to have been popular among early crusaders, acts of devotion or, alternatively, literal-mindedness sniffed at by the *bien pensant.*[67] The customary visual aids were, of course, the prefabricated crosses that were handed out. Stories of preachers, such as Bernard at Vézelay, running out of these – they were usually made of cloth, sometimes silk, occasionally metal – reveal preparation. When things went wrong, the desired group hysteria could boil over into riot, as at Rouen in 1096.[68]

One means of crowd control was to direct audience participation. Repeated refrains (e.g. '*Surge ergo*' in the *Brevis ordinacio*) invited joining in. Building to repeated verbal climaxes was a standard rhetorical ploy to excite an audience, employed successfully, so he claimed, by Gerald of Wales in 1188. The manuscript of Humbert of Romans's *De predicatione s. Crucis* indicates where in a sermon certain appropriate hymns should be sung. Community singing or chanting were – and are – familiar ways to galvanize and unite a crowd. Archbishop Anselm of Milan got his audiences in 1101 to 'sing the song of *Ultreia Ultreia* (Onward! Onward!)'.[69] Songs, hymns and verses, sacred and profane, punctuated crusade propagandizing from the Council of Clermont's *Deus lo volt!* to the masses for Jerusalem sung by chantry priests in the fifteenth century to the verses of poets and troubadours. Their core messages displayed marked homogeneity: obligation, reward through suffering, the generosity of God, the true worth of spiritual gain against material pleasure. Consistent repetition of these tropes indicate that audiences attended sermons less to be persuaded than to be entertained and given the chance to sign up for the benefits. Novelty could play badly.[70]

Visual aids added further spice. Two distant Muslim writers, disdainful of iconodule infidels, claimed propagandists for the Third Crusade used pictures to alarm audiences. The chief judge of Saladin's army, Baha al-Din Ibn Shaddad, in a laudatory biography of his master, recorded that preachers in the west displayed a large image (presumably on wood or canvas) of a Muslim cavalryman trampling the Holy Sepulchre, which his horse was fouling. A contemporary Syrian historian, Ibn al-Athir, described how crusade promoters hawked around a placard of Christ being beaten up by Muhammed: 'They put blood on the portrait of the Messiah and said to the people: "This is the Messiah with Muhammed, the prophet of the Muslims, beating him. He has wounded and slain him."'[71] Despite their source, neither story is inherently unlikely. Sermons were delivered in churches covered in frescoes and sculptures showing relevant scenes from the Bible or more directly pertinent crusade stories in stone, glass or paint. Audiences were attuned to reading such visual narratives.

Elements of drama added to the impression of popular entertainment. According to Ibn al-Athir the placard of Christ and Muhammed was accompanied by clerics, nobles and knights from Outremer dressed in mourning black. What better advocates than penitent sufferers of the disasters that needed avenging? Although letters from Outremer veterans were circulated, public guest appearances by them, with one exception, have largely escaped record. Archbishop Joscius of Tyre brought the bad news of the Hattin disaster to Italy and then preached in France. His witness lent authority to his appeals to the kings of France and England and the count of Flanders at Gisors in January 1188. He also could speak northern French. Joscius cannot have come alone. He did not sail the black-sailed ship he travelled in from Tyre to Sicily by himself and he would have been supported by an entourage. Joscius's mission may in fact have provided the inspiration for Ibn al-Athir's story, although he put Patriarch Heraclius at its head instead, an understandable error.[72] The use of veterans and victims was not exclusive to 1188. In 1106 Bohemund, whose own reputation guaranteed a sympathetic audience, trailed in tow his pet claimant to the Byzantine throne.

The drama of preaching expanded into actual theatre. In 1207, Innocent III seemed to acknowledge the legitimacy of devotional plays, provided clerical actors did not overdo the theatricality. This recognized the parallel development of Easter, Christmas and other theatrical presentations designed to flesh out and explain biblical stories and Christian teaching. In many of these, the cross would literally have taken centre stage.[73] One of the more eccentric devotional dramas was performed one winter, probably that of 1205/6, at Riga, newly built command centre of the missionary crusade to Livonia. Appropriately, this *ludus magnus* portrayed biblical warriors smiting infidel foes. Interpreters were on hand to explain the moral of the show to the apparently disconcerted and probably bemused audience of recently (and forcibly) converted ex-pagans.[74] Given their intrinsic showiness and devotional context, staged crusade presentations could slide easily into overt theatricality. Taking the Cross was itself a dramatic performance. The reported scenes of religious fervour at Speyer at Christmas 1146 when, with carefully prepared ceremony, Bernard of Clairvaux gave the Cross to Conrad III of Germany are unmistakably theatrical. Bernard presided over the Mass and then preached the Cross, adopting the role of God: 'O man, what is there that I should have done for you and did not?' Conrad assumed the part of the penitent convert, replying 'I am ready to serve' before taking the Cross and a military banner that was lying on the altar: ritual as drama.[75]

Few sermons, prayer meetings, processions or other crusade ceremonies competed in dramatic impact with that in Venice in 1258 recorded by the Franciscan writer Salimbene de Adam. In order to inflame his audience to take the Cross to fight the Hohenstaufen-supporting ruler of Treviso, Alberigo of Romano, Cardinal Ottaviano degli Ubaldini, the papal legate, produced thirty noblewomen Alberigo had allegedly sadistically abused. They had been stripped naked in public and forced to watch their husbands, sons, brothers and fathers being hanged. Apparently Cardinal Ottaviano milked their plight for all it was worth: 'in order to anger the people more against Alberigo ... the cardinal ... had the women come forth in the same shameful and nude condition that the wicked Alberigo had reduced them to'. This macabre display worked. The crowd was roused into a suitable frenzy of outraged self-righteous fury, complete with chants of 'So be it! So be it!', before taking the Cross en masse. Salimbene attributed the success of this operation to the cardinal's skill, revulsion at Alberigo's atrocities, the plenary indulgence and 'because [the people] saw the shameful dishonour that those ladies suffered'. Despite his reputation as a tough partisan in the messy papal/Hohenstaufen conflicts in Italy, it may be doubted whether the cardinal actually paraded a troupe of naked well-born ladies in front of the Venetian populace. He may have used actors. Or Salimbene, who enjoyed gossip, exaggeration and a good story, may be an untrustworthy witness. Nonetheless, this improbable alliance of sado-erotic drama with liturgical ceremony only stands at one extreme of a system of persuasion by performance that characterized all crusade appeals.[76]

If profane theatricals provided one means to grab attention, divine intervention remained even more sensational. Stories of miracles were a normal accompaniment to preaching tours, even clustering around the less than charismatic Archbishop Baldwin of Canterbury. They emphasized the redemptive and curative power of the Cross and the role of preachers as mediators of God's grace. Miracle propaganda aimed to convince its audience of the temporal as well as spiritual efficacy of the enterprise. Miracles of healing and pain relief addressed matters of immediate, universal and daily concern. Crusade miracles were no exception, healing the blind, lame, deaf, dumb and deranged. Bernard of Clairvaux was reported to have performed well over four hundred cures of the sick and, in one case, the dead. Rumours of thaumaturgy worked as illustrations of God's immanence and were highly popular. Miracles were consumer-led; clients sought out the miracle worker. After his tour of Germany, Bernard of Clairvaux had to turn away crowds who sought his healing.[77] In the drama of giving and receiving the Cross, the miraculous confirmed the preacher's Christ-like role.

More evanescent, celestial visions, conjured up on cue, visible to all, not just the halt and the sick, provided some of the most enduring copy for crusade commentators. Matthew Paris placed Oliver of Paderborn's apparitions in his list of most memorable events between 1200 and 1250. Paris also noted how the story had been carefully circulated in official letters read out publicly.[78] Imaginative interpretations of meteorological activity had provided a usefully apocalyptic dimension to the preaching of the First Crusade. Heavenly signs appeared to order. A 1096 charter of the Poitevin abbey of St Maixent was dated 'when Pope Urban was at Saintes [13 April] and the sign of the cross appeared in the sky'.[79] Not all were persuaded. The suspicion lingered that believing was seeing, not vice versa. Guibert of Nogent, a fierce critic of phoney relics and what he called 'vulgar fables', noted with contempt the wishful thinking of a crowd he was in at Beauvais who imagined the clouds overhead formed a cross; he only saw what looked a bit like a stork or a crane. Guibert was also deeply sceptical about claims of miraculous signs of the Cross appearing on crusaders' bodies; he attributed them to self-mutilation or tattoos.[80] Yet crosses – in the sky, on bodies, on stage, in the pulpit – became adhesive companions to the publicity of words. At about the same time as crosses were appearing over Frisia in 1214, the Cistercian abbot of Bonneval conjured one up to coincide with his call to take the Cross against the Albigensian heretics. According to the abbot, who helpfully spread the story, the cross usefully pointed towards Toulouse, the alleged centre of heresy.[81]

The abbot's care in passing on the story was significant. By themselves, visions served as transitory *coups de théâtre*. To be effective propaganda, they required publicity. Chroniclers, like the one who recorded the abbot of Bonneval's account, necessarily exerted a narrow and delayed influence. The letters circulated by Oliver of Paderborn wielded a greater immediate impact. A stack of references to his visions appeared in near-contemporary chronicles across northern Europe. Visions became a staple. Occasionally, drama outstripped theology, as with the heavenly dragons over Cologne that accompanied preaching a crusade to resist the Mongols in 1241. Some accounts reached *exempla* collections, such as that of a vision of the Virgin and Christ-child accompanying cross-taking included in Stephen of Bourbon's (d.1261) preaching manual.[82] The laity became complicit, accustomed to expect such miraculous signs and accordingly seeing them apparently without prompting. Roger of Wendover, a monk of St Albans, recorded how the preaching campaign during the summer of 1227 was accompanied across southern England by numerous visions of Christ crucified. A fishmonger and his son saw one in the sky on their way to market near Uxbridge in north-west Middlesex, later regaling their customers with the story. Not all believed them until further apparitions overcame the doubters. Wendover summed up the point of these stories: 'in these [visions] the Crucified One himself deigned to open the heavens and to show the incredulous his wonderful glory with immense splendour'.[83] For the clerical elites involved in crusade preparations, that was precisely the effect they strove for.

TWO PREACHERS AT WORK

Although crusade propaganda campaigns were fully systematized only after 1200, a taste of the complex methods of inducement can be sampled through the activities of two very different agents of the

Third Crusade, Henry of Marcy, cardinal bishop of Albano, and Gerald of Barry, usually known as Gerald of Wales.

Henry of Albano 1188–9

Cardinal Bishop Henry of Albano was an energetic, doctrinally muscular prelate and former abbot of the Cistercian monastery of Clairvaux whose career had been marked by militant activism in promoting orthodoxy. Between 1178 and 1181, he had led preaching and armed repression against supposed heretics in southern France. His reward was to be made a cardinal in 1179. Henry represented a new sort of career cleric. Not content with the abbacy of one of the most famous religious houses in Europe, Henry attached himself to the international authority of the papacy, giving him the freedom to act as a roving agent of Church discipline and reform. His effectiveness was recognized in a later, possibly spurious story that on the death of Pope Urban III in October 1187 Henry had been offered the papal throne. In the event, the new pope, Gregory VIII, appointed him papal legate to France and Germany to preach the Cross and exercise authority over the whole process of diplomacy, propaganda and recruitment. Between November 1187 and March 1188, Henry travelled from Ferrara in north-east Italy to eastern France and western Germany. At some point he met Frederick Barbarossa of Germany and with him summoned the 'court of Jesus Christ' at Mainz on 27 March 1188. Henry may have shared in negotiations between the German emperor and the French king in December 1187 and either he or another legate assisted at a recruitment rally at Strasburg the same month. Henry meanwhile travelled in a great arc through Hainault to Mons, Nivelles, Louvain and Liège before reaching the Rhineland in time for the assembly at Mainz. There the German emperor took the Cross with large sections of the German nobility. Cardinal Henry continued his evangelizing efforts until his death at Arras in January 1189.[84]

During this period, Henry's role was as much administrative as propagandist. His activities engaged a variety of media: performance, spectacle, spoken word, written text, possibly visual display. There were ceremonies, at Strasburg and Mainz, and sermons, as in Hainault. Papal letters, primarily Gregory VIII's bull *Audita Tremendi*, provided the central theme on which preachers could extemporise. The verbal images of desecration of the Holy Places may have inspired or copied posters of atrocities. While private diplomacy, such as the deliberations with Frederick I, was crucial to the adherence of rulers and their followers, publicity reached beyond personal engagement through correspondence, newsletters and pamphlets. The dissemination of *Audita Tremendi* and other related bulls, such as that sent to the Danes, *Quum divina patientia*, can be traced through the copies in contemporary chronicles, particularly those associated with royal courts. For all its importance, *Audita Tremendi* survives only in two English and one German chronicle, emphasizing papal dependence on local acceptance.[85] The bull's puritanically penitential moral and sumptuary injunctions only received currency through publication by Henry of Albano in Germany and Henry II in England. Propaganda spread effectively along the interlaced networks of the lay and ecclesiastical elites, central crusade messages being carried in diverse strata of exhortatory literature, including vernacular verses by a French civil servant, Berthier of Orleans, or the noble Picard *literatus* Conon of Béthune, with his call to arms masquerading as love poetry.[86]

In this operation, Henry performed a variety of roles. He preached, although not at the grand state occasions at Strasburg and Mainz, deferring to locals such as the bishops of Strasburg and Würzburg. During Lent in Hainault, Limbourg and at Liège, Henry encountered mixed success. Although the sermons do not survive, during these months he wrote letters and a substantial exhortatory tract, which may indicate something of what he said. The letter summoning the Mainz assembly, probably written before Christmas 1187, owed a general debt to *Audita Tremendi* of late October and early November, which Henry may have helped compose: loss of the Holy Land and the Cross; desecration of Holy Places; the sins of Christians redeemed by Christ's offer of repentance through avenging the insult to God. The Mainz summons struck a more personal note by incorporating the language used by Henry's Cistercian predecessor, Bernard of Clairvaux, promoter not only of the Second Crusade but also the Order of the Templars. Henry addressed the Germans as 'knights of Christ' adopting, like the Templars, the 'breastplate of faith and the helmet of salvation'. He borrowed Bernard's famous punning contrast between bad and good knighthood, *malitia* and *militia*, proclaiming the Cross as the 'banner of Christian knighthood'. Such inter-textual wordplay may have escaped the letter's recipients, but it shows the care taken in constructing a message specifically designed to attract fighting men.[87]

A more extended advocacy was contained in Henry's lengthy meditation on the spiritual journey to the City of God, i.e. Heaven, *De peregrinante civitate Dei*, addressed to the Cistercian monks at Clairvaux and probably completed in the second half of 1188. In Tract 13, 'A Lament on Jerusalem captured by the infidel', Henry turned from the spiritual to the political.[88] The Cistercians, in Bernardine tradition, remained closely associated with crusading, providing international support as well as recruiting agents. Cistercian liturgy included regular prayers for *crucesignati*. Archbishop Baldwin of Canterbury, who led the Church's crusade effort in England and Wales, was another former Cistercian abbot and used at least two Cistercian abbots to assist him. In France, the Cistercians' role was recognized in their exemption from the Saladin Tithe.[89] Henry's intended audience was therefore likely to be wider than just his confrères.

The *De peregrinante* picked up a theme in his letter to the Germans, one only briefly mentioned in *Audita Tremendi*, the loss and desecration at Hattin of the True Cross. This was one of the many splinters or fragments believed to be from the wood of the cross of the Crucifixion that the Franks of Jerusalem carried with them into battle as a talisman of God's favour and protection. Throughout the 1188–90 recruitment drive, the symbol of the Cross dominated, the term *crucesignatus* to describe a crusader now becoming standard. In his tract, Henry echoed the Mainz summons, describing the Cross as 'the medicine for sins, the care of the wounded, the restorer of health', and, more grandly, the 'ark of the vassal of God, the ark of the New Testament'. Henry's stock phrases were copied, at times verbatim, by other crusade publicists, such as Peter of Blois, then Latin secretary and legal adviser to Archbishop Baldwin. Peter had travelled with the papal court in the autumn of 1187; the language he uses in his own pamphlets lamenting the disaster of Hattin, the loss of the Holy Land and the sluggishness of the Christian response, closely echo Henry's.[90] Such similarities were hardly random. The propaganda tone was set by a small circle; both Henry and Baldwin were ex-Cistercian abbots; Baldwin employed Peter of Blois; Peter could well have encountered Henry at the papal curia; both Baldwin and Peter had been pupils at Bologna under Uberto Crivelli who, as Pope Urban III, had received the news of Hattin. In the following months, Henry, Baldwin and Peter all spent considerable time with the secular rulers of Germany and the Angevin empire respectively. Personal contact was supplemented by the written word, especially letters that framed crisis and response. The propaganda campaign was thus orchestrated by a close circle of clerical writers, academics, administrators and diplomats. At its inception, the crusade appeared as much a contrived intellectual concept as a populist call to arms. The trick was to translate the one into the other. Judged by the massive numbers who signed up, it worked.

Weaving the metaphorical with the political, the *De peregrinante* demonstrated a range of publicity techniques. Muslim desecration of the Holy Places (and in particular the True Cross) appeared as a sort of second crucifixion, the Cross 'captured, mocked, dishonoured with the filth of all its enemies'.[91] Baha al-Din Ibn Shaddad's and Ibn al-Athir's posters come to mind. The latter's description of a placard showing Christ being beaten up by Muhammed mirrors a passage in Henry's tract in which Muhammed glorifies Christ's ignominy at the loss of the Cross, a triumph over Christ himself. Desecration, defilement and insult supplied emotional bite to crusade propaganda, ultimate atrocities demanding redress. Christ had willed this to test His faithful. Moral reform was essential; so too military action. To drive the point home, Henry drew a comparison with soldiers fighting for their temporal lords: in the Heavenly Lord's war, the reward is immortality, a familiar crusading trope. The choice lay between the followers of God and a demonized Saladin, an instrument of the devil, a combat of right versus wrong. Using the history of the True Cross from its discovery by St Helena in the fourth century, Henry cited successive heroes who had confronted the infidel: Heraclius, restorer of the Cross to Jerusalem in 630 after its capture by the Persians; Charlemagne; the First Crusade. Academic flashiness then gave way to immediate politics in a final diatribe against delay and backsliders, of whom there were many. In constructing a coherent programme of propaganda and persuasion offering possibilities for oral, written or pictorial presentation, Henry's language could appeal to separate audiences on different levels. Complex theological issues were arrestingly summarized – and, in phrases such as '*Christi martyres*', glossed over. Many of the polemical motifs foreshadowed the more extensive preaching of the following century. Anxiety at the progress of preparations pointed to perennial obstacles to translating preaching into crusaders. Henry himself had encountered recidivist local banditry among those he had signed with the Cross in Limbourg in early 1188.[92] Before his death in January 1189, he would have witnessed much more.

Gerald of Wales 1188

Henry's experiences exposed an asymmetry between intellectual endeavour and the untidiness of practical organization, a contrast that similarly haunted the preaching of Baldwin of Canterbury in Wales. One dimension of this was speed of response. However, medieval communications were not necessarily as sclerotic as post-industrial observers sometimes imagine. News of the defeat at Hattin (4 July 1187) reached Sicily perhaps in September and the papal court at Ferrara by mid-October. Immediately letters were sent out warning of the catastrophe. Despite the difficulties of an itinerant court and the sudden death of Urban III, his successor Gregory VIII's papal bull was drafted and despatched in late October and early November. Individuals, such as Richard of Poitou, the future Richard I, were taking the Cross north of the Alps as early as November, while the pope's representatives, armed with *Audita Tremendi*, fanned out across Europe. They reached the German court at Strasburg in December, Denmark by Christmas and Gisors on the borders of Normandy and the Île de France on 21 January 1188. Although the Danish court was apparently stunned by the news, elsewhere it had been anticipated. Before Christmas, Henry II of England had tried to commandeer the profits of the Becket pilgrim trade at Canterbury for the crusade and Henry of Albano had conducted preliminary talks with Frederick Barbarossa.[93] The German nobility had been signed up by the end of March, less than six months after the Cross had begun to be preached. Official preaching began in England at Geddington in Northamptonshire on 11 February 1188. By 4 March, Archbishop Baldwin had left

Hereford on the road into Wales. At the same time diocesan bishops were at work. By the time the archbishop reached the northern Welsh marches in mid-April, the local bishop, Reiner of St Asaph's, had already scooped the pool of recruits.[94]

Almost everywhere Baldwin went he encountered audiences waiting and primed. Details of his itinerary evidently circulated in advance. At the start, he was met by the prince of south Wales, Rhys ap Gruffydd, who later chaperoned the archbishop for some of his journey. At Cardigan Rhys was waiting for the archbishop to arrive. At one time or another, Baldwin encountered all the major princes of the region, bar one, who was excommunicated. These prior arrangements were necessary to secure audiences and recruits, but not sufficient. Without the involvement of lords, crusade vows were easily, probably necessarily, left unfulfilled by their dependants, as happened when Rhys abandoned his commitment (which had not in the event extended to actually taking the Cross himself). Without a lord's approval, the Cross might not be adopted in the first place. Rhys's son-in-law asked his permission before taking the Cross at Radnor.[95] No leadership; no crusade. Only two minor princes actually took the Cross. Eagerness to greet the archbishop probably owed as much to the need to keep Henry II sweet as to a desire to avenge the insult to Christ.

The significance of securing noble support was reflected in the strenuous efforts made to obtain it. One lord took the Cross one evening after private persuasion by the archbishop.[96] For the social elite, adopting the Cross was not solely a matter of conviction or piety. The bishop of Bangor was publicly bullied into becoming a *crucesignatus*, compliance implying he acknowledged the authority of Canterbury over the Welsh church and Henry II over the Welsh princes.[97] Baldwin's masses in every Welsh cathedral united the political and the pious. The secular agenda of Baldwin's tour compares with that of the king of France's attempt to tax his kingdom for the crusade, or Frederick Barbarossa's use of the court of Jesus Christ to consolidate imperial power within Germany. Baldwin's contact with local nobility and clergy conformed to experiences elsewhere. Only local leaders could provide the necessary audiences in an overwhelmingly rural setting with only small towns and villages. Not all Baldwin's large set-piece gatherings occurred in cathedrals, some of the largest being held at Radnor, Cardigan and Haverfordwest (Rhys being in attendance on two of these occasions). Taking the Cross required the approval, not always forthcoming, of close family, kindred and lords, all of whom Baldwin encountered. Crosses were given out in a variety of settings and circumstances: during or after public High Mass; as a result of apparently impromptu petitioning; at an improvised service on an Anglesey beach; after individual discussions following sermons; or even at nocturnal conversations in the archbishop's lodgings. A decision often represented a conclusion as much as a beginning – for the crowds at the big preaching performances as for those convinced in private discussion – each one involving careful calculation and preparation. However, this was not how it was presented.

Baldwin's Welsh trip yields such detail about the mechanics of crusade publicity because of the presence of the archdeacon of St David's, Gerald of Barry, or Gerald of Wales. A fluent, vivid, engaged if by no means entirely reliable narrator or witness, Gerald wrote a detailed account of Baldwin's Welsh tour, the *Itinerarium Cambriae* (*Journey Through Wales*, first redaction c.1191) and referred to the trip in other works. Prone to prejudice and self-aggrandizement, Gerald possessed an alert eye, sharp pen and an analytical mind. From the outset, deliberation and planning emerge clearly. In recalling that he had been the first to take the Cross from the archbishop at Radnor after the initial sermon of the tour, he explained the circumstances:

> I threw myself at the holy man's feet and devoutly took the sign of the cross. It was the urgent admonition given some time before by the king [Henry II] which inspired me to give this example to the others, and the persuasion and oft-repeated promises of the archbishop and Chief Justiciar [Ranulf Glanvill, who was present at the Radnor sermon], who never tired of repeating the king's words. I acted of my own free will, after anxiously talking the matter over time and time again, in view of the insult and injury being done at this moment to the Cross of Christ. In doing so I gave strong encouragement to the others and an added incentive to what they had just been told.[98]

Successful ritual depends on efficient choreography. By showing the native audience (Baldwin's sermon had been translated into Welsh) what to do, Gerald was providing important non-verbal guidance in demonstrating how to receive the Cross. However, Gerald was more than a necessary extra in not-so-amateur theatricals. He had been ordered to take the Cross by his masters because of his political status. A well-connected Anglo-Welshman, Gerald's relatives were spread among the powerbrokers of Church and state in south Wales and Ireland. Rhys ap Gruffydd was his first cousin once removed. Gerald's example was thus political as much as it was pious. Neither Gerald nor Rhys actually went on crusade. Yet Gerald's retrospective insistence that he was moved to avenge the insult to the Cross of Christ, even if literary embellishment, linked his account of Cross-taking in rural Wales with Henry of Albano's elevated rhetoric to the monks of Clairvaux in southern Champagne.

Gerald's commentary exposes many of the techniques that sustained crusade preaching across generations. Aristocratic and ecclesiastical affinities provided congregations and settings. Baldwin summoned an audience to Haverfordwest 'as being in the centre of the province', accessible.[99] Context was carefully contrived. Preaching and Cross-giving usually followed the Mass. The two religious acts shared being essentially spectator performances, communion rarely being taken by laymen at the time, participation in both being largely passive and occasionally vocal. The miracle of the real presence of Christ appropriately framed the call to defend His name and Cross. The memory was reinforced by stories of miracles associated with Baldwin's preaching recorded by Gerald only three or four years later. An array of preaching devices, props and techniques were described. Preachers brandished a cross to illustrate the twin themes of revenge and repentance. Style mattered. Gerald – at his most vain – later noted how he succeeded in lighting up a curmudgeonly audience at Haverfordwest where the archbishop had signally failed. Speaking first in Latin, then French, he divided his address into three parts, probably following the pattern of the papal bull: the *casus belli*; the obligation; the remedy. Each was rounded off with a rousing, possibly repetitive refrain, perhaps in the manner of the later English *Brevis ordinacio*. Apparently, at the end of each section, Gerald was interrupted and forced to pause as the crowds pressed forward to take the Cross. Gerald's artful performance conformed to standard rhetorical models.[100] There was nothing random about any part of it.

Positive responses could not be taken for granted. Gerald's account is peppered with stories of preaching failure and audience reluctance. Although resistance to the crusade message, often misogynistically attributed to the malign influence of women, was, in Gerald's triumphalist account, repeatedly overcome by eloquence or quasi-miraculous conversion, even the best-planned campaign met opposition or indifference. Baldwin and his team's reliance on local interpreters led by Archdeacon Alexander of Bangor posed performance difficulties. Near-simultaneous translation interrupted the flow of the ritual, especially if speeches in Latin or French required more than one translation to cater for segregated English- and Welsh-speaking audiences, as at Llandaff. In his aping the famous story of Bernard of Clairvaux, Gerald cast doubt on the efficacy of translation altogether.[101] In a replay at St David's, Gerald recalled, the translated Welsh version of his sermon actually repelled those who had just been moved to take the Cross by his own incomprehensible address.[102] To provide a respectable theoretical gloss, Gerald emphasized the transcendent rather than rational nature of the conversion to the Cross, the internal working of the Holy Spirit, as he called it, which operated beyond words. By contrast, at exactly the same time, the perhaps more practical Henry of Albano, a native Frenchman, was content to use German speakers in Germany, preaching himself only in largely French-speaking areas.

Despite the insistent literary and propagandist pretence of spontaneity, Gerald's experience matched Henry of Albano's in revealing how the crusade preaching carefully and deliberately harnessed the senses. The spoken words were heard, seen, written about, and even physically commemorated, as in the chapel erected on the site of Baldwin's sermon at Cardigan.[103] Cardinal Henry and Archdeacon Gerald carried papal letters that informed the sermons they staged and created visual and aural impressions both immediate and lasting. Descriptions were soon disseminated: Henry's treatise to the monks of Clairvaux; Gerald's compendious account of the Welsh tour. Each element connected and enhanced the others. Letters, pamphlets, written versions of sermons and descriptions of preaching were integral to the process of crusade evangelism. For future edification, Archbishop Baldwin planned to commission a prose history of the anti-Saladin crusade from Gerald himself, while a verse edition would be produced by the archbishop's nephew, Joseph. Across Europe, others were preparing to do precisely the same.[104] Yet, despite all the effort, many, possibly most, who signed up in Wales failed, like Gerald himself, to fulfil their vows. A different set of tactics and techniques was required to translate promises into action.

Recruitment

5

Recruiting and Reward

Successful recruiting for a crusade relied on organization, not emotion. Planning to undertake a crusade to the east with Louis IX of France in the late 1240s, Count Raymond VII of Toulouse prepared a file containing written copies of the contracts agreed with the knights and sergeants who were to accompany him, although in the event illness and death prevented the count from setting out.[1] Contractual recruiting methods, commonplace in crusading in the 1240s, were traditional features of wars of the Cross. A hundred and fifty years earlier, in the autumn of 1098, the count's great-great-grandfather, Raymond IV, was contesting Bohemund of Taranto's right to rule the newly conquered Syrian city of Antioch. During heated exchanges, Bohemund, to support his claim, produced his contract of agreement with the other leaders and his accounts of expenses (*compotus*).[2] Such documents most likely contained lists of payments for equipment and provisions; wages for troops or other servants and followers; and details of loans or subsidies paid or owing. Medieval armies, like their successors, were recruited through a combination of enthusiasm, loyalty, ambition, coercion and cash. Those for the crusades were no different. In his great crusading bull *Quia Maior* of 1213, Pope Innocent III identified three categories to which he offered the full crusader's remission of sins: those who paid for themselves; those who paid for others; and those who were paid to go.[3] Closely following the contours of the affluent society of noble, knightly and urban elites, recruitment relied on planning, not spontaneity. Whatever the emotional or ideological response to preaching and propaganda, the translation from crusade vow to battlefield required the mediation of customary secular military organization. In late eleventh-century western Europe and beyond, this revolved around obligation and reward.

Until the emergence of modern war states from the later seventeenth century, armies in western Europe rode an often ungainly pantomime horse of public command and private enterprise. Even where an over-all commander might provide payment, recruiting and leadership devolved onto patronal and regional groups. Service tended to be conditional and contractual for those with social or professional clout, compulsory for their paid or impressed followers. While in theory voluntary and almost uniquely international, in practice crusading relied on interlaced networks of lordship, kinship, locality, community, subservience, employment, opportunity, profit and pay. Recruitment and finance were, almost literally, two sides of the same coin. While taking the Cross may have been a private decision, its implementation could not be. Beyond the necessary consent of priest, lord, employer or family, to be a *crucesignatus*, leader or led, meant submission to a structure of necessity: access to funds and material support. None would have reached destinations without money, the people who possessed it and those with the social clout to raise it. Loyalty, community, kinship, peer pressure, acquisitiveness, reputation, hope for temporal or eternal benefit, expiation of sin, honouring family tradition, escaping domestic difficulties, debts or litigation, compulsion by force, a sense of shared purpose: any or all may have underscored decisions to enlist.[4]

The image of recruitment drawn by crusade promoters emphasized, with perhaps suspicious uniformity, crusaders' freedom of choice and purity of intent. Critics similarly tended to concentrate on motives not logistics. Intent lay at the centre of the legal justification for the privileges offered to *crucesignati* and the whole concept of penitential warfare. Yet realities of recruitment challenged the autonomy of commitment, pious or otherwise. Most crusaders were constrained by service and obedience to social superiors or driven by loyalty, necessity or self-advancement. For crusaders obliged to follow their lords or compelled to serve for pay, freedom of choice was notional. Secular incentives and pressures remained persuasive. Religious intensity may have been significant as a motive, but in practice incidental for career knights, paid sergeants, footsloggers, the footloose *iuvenes* who crowd chronicle accounts, household officials or servants and artisans employed by the great. Occasionally, the image slipped. Troops from Nevers were alleged to have been forced to go on crusade in 1101, and over a century later a Norman knight, Baldwin de Montibus, admitted having been forced (*compulsus*) to serve for pay against the Albigensians in 1226.[5] For the regiments of those in service requiring pay or those hired as stipendiaries, the crusader's spiritual and temporal privileges acted as added bonuses to subsistence and wages, but of themselves were hardly sufficient. This is not to deny the role of religious faith, without which the whole edifice of crusading would not have survived or been constructed in the first place, but rather to demythologize its role in the practical process of recruitment. Conviction may thrive in both the abstract and in action but does not exist in a vacuum. If crusades were exercises in mass private enterprise, the entrepreneurs of the operation set terms that often left their dependants with little power to abstain, only paymasters enjoying genuinely independent choice.

Motives and money were inescapable partners, tied together by rewards, pay and rations, the commerce of arms. Writing from Constantinople in the summer of 1203, Count Hugh of St Pol made this clear. He described how, a few months earlier, the leadership of the Fourth Crusade, although in a tiny minority, had overcome the resistance of the bulk of the crusade army against diverting the expedition to the Byzantine Empire. The majority had wanted to proceed immediately and directly to the Holy Land. However, Count Hugh recorded, he and his fellow commanders 'clearly demonstrated to the entire army that the journey to Jerusalem was fruitless and injurious for everyone insofar as they were destitute and low on provisions and no-one among them could retain the services of knights and pay the men-at-arms'.[6] The mass of articulate crusaders may have desired Jerusalem but they all needed pay to get there, knights and sergeants as well as infantry. No pay; no crusade.

THE CONTEXT OF WAR

The appearance of international crusading depended on more than the coincidence of aristocratic existential guilt, the culture of warfare, ecclesiastical radicalism, or the geopolitical upheavals around the

Mediterranean. In response to the developing agrarian and commercial economy of western Europe, changing social and financial organization of war created methods of military recruitment, retention and action capable of sustaining such extensive campaigns. Particularly in Italy, northern Iberia, France, Flanders, western Germany and southern Britain – the heartlands of crusade recruitment – the culture of warfare increasingly relied on well-funded, trained mounted knights; structures of local power reliant on aggressive and acquisitive military lordship; expansive, mobile noble ambition that encouraged a fluid market in military personnel; the ready availability of moveable profits and assets convertible, if required, into bullion or cash; access to credit; and familiarity with techniques of accounting and contracts to secure service and loyalty beyond customary associations of household or tenure. It was precisely to these knights that Urban II deliberately addressed his Jerusalem appeal.[7] Gathering large, cosmopolitan armies of the sort assembled from the 1090s onwards relied on these expanding opportunities to convert agricultural and trading wealth into armies, in the words of a contemporary biography of a hero of the First Crusade, '*de argento milites creare*' (to create soldiers from silver).[8]

Medieval armies were assembled through a variety of incentives: loyalty; kinship; friendship; obedience; coercion; negotiation; or obligation. Military service was performed by tenants, servants, household employees or campaign retainers. These would be paid, as were those without formal obligation, the stipendiaries that comprised increasing proportions of western armies from the eleventh century: cavalry, infantry and archers, both bowmen and crossbowmen. All but the smallest companies were coalitions of otherwise often discrete groups of followers of lords and paymasters. The collective leaderships of many crusades have often attracted modern criticism. In fact they mirrored normal medieval command structures. The fiscal limitations of even the most monetized or surplus-led agrarian economy precluded the existence of standing armies: financially and logistically they could not be sustained except for small regiments based on noble households. Larger forces required the mobilization of dependants and their respective retinues and clients. Medieval political societies could not be run on centralized autocratic lines, nor could their armies. Even when, from the thirteenth century, regional or national governments could deploy more financial resources and institute some degree of central control over funding and recruitment, operational leadership remained in the hands of often powerful and independent-minded commanders, as witnessed, for example, during the Hundred Years War, the sixteenth-century Wars of Religion, or the seventeenth-century Thirty Years War or English Civil War. In the Middle Ages, no general could ignore the opinions or interests of his captains. Nor was collective leadership necessarily detrimental to military effectiveness. The most disparate and contested crusade command structure – that of the First Crusade – proved resilient and successful. Conversely, the most unified command, that of Louis IX in 1249–50, was one of the most calamitous, corroded by personality clashes and scarred by divisions over tactics and strategy.

Military expeditions depended on pay. The period from the second half of the tenth century was distinguished by an increased use of money, in coin not just bullion. More silver was mined, particularly (but not exclusively) in Germany, and circulated around western Europe, mainly through trade. The increased use of coinage was evident in western Germany, Frisia, southern France, northern Spain, Italy and parts of northern France, as well as in England and, after 1066, the cross-Channel Anglo-Norman realms. Regional mints were established, some controlled by regional powers, such as kings in England, some by local rulers, as in France. Even when the supply of coin appeared to diminish towards the end of the eleventh century, the developed culture of money persisted in normal commercial and social transactions, such as paying rent. Coinage affected almost all sections of society, through mints, markets, money-changers, the need to sell surplus produce to generate cash payments for rent, and, notably in England, taxation. In this monetary system, which included bullion, a multiplicity of different mints, money-changers and currencies of account became familiar. The basic monetary divisions and proportions of pounds, shillings and pence, although established as early as the eighth century, now became entrenched in the financial system, in varying regional values operating in parallel with units of weight, such as marks, or silver content, such as sterling.[9]

As the actual physical coins were silver pennies of varying purity of precious metal, calculations of wealth and value required often sophisticated mathematical computation. One crusader's report noted seven different currencies circulating in the Provençal camp in early 1099 from Poitiers, Chartres, Le Mans and Lucca as well as three southern French mints. This did not take account of the indigenous currencies or those of other contingents. Godfrey of Bouillon may have travelled with specially minted coins from Lower Lorraine.[10] Coin finds along the route of the Second Crusade in central Europe reveal a similar pattern of different coinages – pennies from Normandy, Champagne, the Rhineland, southern Germany and Austria. Such diversity was hardly eccentric and is shared by surviving eleventh-century Scandinavian coin hoards. One method of avoiding contested exchange rates was to use an internationally recognized currency of value such as sterling, as leaders of the Fourth Crusade did in Venice in October 1201.[11] Domestically, faced with such increased complexity, keeping records of tax, rents, income, expenses and revenues and other financial transactions became more common. Rendering account became more technical, not just for the growing ports and commercial centres of the Mediterranean, Flanders and the Rhineland, where financial business was far from being confined to growing Jewish communities. As payments in money, including cash, became more common, so too did the instruments used to authorize or confirm them, increasingly taking the form of written accounts and contracts. The requirement for basic numeracy increased and with it varying degrees of functional literacy across all those who handled or relied on money: landlords, estate managers, household officials, merchants, traders, shopkeepers, artisans, employees, taxpayers – and soldiers.

Discussion of paid troops in the Middle Ages has tended to be vitiated by describing them as mercenaries, a term loaded with pejorative overtones of fickleness and brutality. As such it is a confusing misnomer. Medieval writers usually referred neutrally to stipendiary troops – *stipendiarii* – rather than mercenaries – *mercennarii*. Clause 51 of Magna Carta banned foreign *stipendiarios* from England not because they were paid but because they were aliens. Horror stories attached to mercenaries focused on their violent and licentious behaviour rather than their paid status.[12] Criticisms of the mercenaries that terrorized England during the civil wars of the reign of King Stephen

(1135–54), or those professional bands or *routiers* that ravaged southern France in the later twelfth century, or the notorious Free Companies of the fourteenth, were political and moral. Mercenary companies were taken as symptoms of a collapse of an idealized and largely fictional social order, a crisis in lordship, discipline and hierarchy. Hostility was fuelled by snobbery and social anxiety rather than distaste of rampant materialism on which, in practice, all lords and their armies relied. Critics of crusade finance targeted peculation, abuse or hypocrisy, not pay. Despite the aspersions cast on untrustworthy 'hirelings' in the parable of the Good Shepherd (John 10:12–13), pay was not of itself regarded as amoral. John the Baptist urged baptized soldiers to 'be content with your wages' (Luke 3:14). As it developed by 1200, the code of chivalry emphasized conduct not its means of support. Many knights at one time or another in their careers served in military households, armies or princely retinues for money. Paid status in no way diminished knights' honour or that of their paymasters. The well-known experiences of William Marshal during the 1170s and 1180s in the commercial tournament team of Henry II's eldest son, Henry the Young King, stand witness to this.[13] Profit sustained lords' authority and their networks of dependants. By 1100, if not before, money was as much a feature of lordship as the holding of land. Paid service enhanced rather than challenged the moral dimension of the relationship between lord and retainer. In his influential 1150s political treatise, *Policraticus*, John of Salisbury (d.1180), the bibulous, gossipy English networking intellectual, friend of popes, saints and prelates and shrewd observer of the secular scene, regarded payment of knights as necessary to secure their loyalty and a privilege of their order.[14] According to a well-informed contemporary observer, the Norman commander Odo Borleng stiffened the resolve of the royal garrison of Bernay in the face of a rebel army in 1124 by arguing that 'if we lack the courage to resist, how shall we ever dare to face the king again? We shall rightly forfeit our wages (*stipendia*) and honour and shall never again deserve to eat the king's bread.'[15] Loyalty, subsistence, honour and pay provided mutually supportive privileges of service and lordship.

Payment covered a wide social spectrum, from hired peasant with a strong arm to royal princes. Until the later twelfth century, perhaps, the term *miles* still could indicate military function and status not social class. Flanders provides two contrasting examples of hired knights. The *milites* who assassinated Count Charles the Good of Flanders (1119–27) in Bruges in 1127 were offered four marks each for their pains. They came from relatively modest but not servile backgrounds, drawn from the household (*familia*) of one of the chief conspirators, bound by wages and hand-picked for their ferocity (*animosiores et audaces*), a feature many crusaders evidently shared. One of those crusaders, Charles's uncle, Count Robert II of Flanders (1093–1111), potentially one of the wealthiest lords in north-west Europe, was himself hired by successive kings of England to provide troops in 1093 and 1101.[16] Elsewhere, in 1085, to repel a threatened Danish invasion, William the Conqueror collected an army of paid knights, archers and infantry that included another future crusade commander, Count Hugh of Vermandois, brother of King Philip I of France.[17] In Germany, such 'service for gain' became a literary trope in twelfth- and thirteenth-century vernacular literature where even a king's son 'offered his service for pay, as a knight very often does'.[18] This was not just artistic licence. Bishop Benzo of Alba, in about 1089, advised Emperor Henry IV of Germany (1056–1106) of the need to ensure he had the funds to pay his troops, important advice given Henry's dependence on stipendiary forces in his Italian wars of the 1080s, campaigns that involved another crusade leader, Godfrey of Bouillon.[19] All medieval military commanders included some, often many, paid troops beyond their own, also paid, military households. While holding land could impose military obligations on tenants variously satisfied in person, by proxy or through cash redemption, the idea that anyone relied on raising an army solely from geographically widely scattered tenants or sub-tenants with their own domestic ties and varying degrees of fitness, military training or skill is both inherently unlikely and contradicted by evidence. A host based simply on land tenure did not exist.

Within military households of the great, membership of a *familia* could be rewarded with equipment, housing, board (such as free meals, bread, wine and candles) and spending money, in contemporary German chivalric poetry '*lîp und gût*', board and pay.[20] Beyond the household or *mesnie* of permanent or semi-permanent retinues of paid warriors, other knights, some with tenurial obligations, others with wider, looser affinities of kindred or locality, some freelance, were recruited into larger companies for particular campaigns. These knights could expect pay beyond basic rations, including items such as cloaks. The pay and status of followers exhibited the moral dimension of a lord's *magnanimitas*, his largesse: the richer the followers, the grander their lord. The socially more elevated knights would have their own retainers, supported out of the pay they themselves received, pay acting as a powerful cohesive force in these often disparately assembled armies. Alongside knights came mounted sergeants, either directly associated with knights to form cohesive fighting units or as more general regiments of supporting cavalry. When shipping his household to the Holy Land in 1190, Philip II of France assumed a ratio of two sergeants to every knight, while in his scheme to pay recruits for his planned crusade in 1195, Henry VI of Germany assumed a ratio of 1:1, calculating pay and provisions accordingly.[21] Beyond the knights and mounted sergeants, money would provide specialist troops such as archers and crossbowmen, as well as infantry and the necessary support artisans: engineers, carpenters, cooks, laundresses, etc.

A medieval army of any size resembled a moving village or town, with its clergy, hierarchy, justice, markets, sex trade, etc. The inherent flexibility of such a system, both in manpower and specialisms, matched the shifting requirements of any warlord and proved especially well adapted to lengthy campaigns such as crusades where allegiances shifted as commanders died, departed or went bankrupt. The primary unit of social organization was the shared mess, based on the extended households of paymasters. The range of some lords' *familia* could be extensive. Landgrave Louis of Thuringia's entourage, assembled for an aborted crusade in 1227, included four counts, eighteen named and numerous other unnamed knights, chaplains, clerks and various unfree knights characteristic of German aristocratic society, known as *ministeriales* and including four household officials, the butler, marshal, seneschal and chamberlain.[22] Not only would all these expect to receive payment of some sort, in cash or kind, Louis himself probably hoped to receive financial support from the putative commander of the crusade, Frederick II, who had promised 100,000 gold ounces for the expedition and in the event paid for at least 1,000 knights. Frederick's father, Henry VI, had offered 60,000 gold ounces for 1,500 knights and 1,500 sergeants for his crusade in 1195. Five years earlier, Frederick's grandfather, Frederick I, had placed a monetary budget of a minimum of 3 marks per head on departing crusaders.[23]

Crusading conformed to patterns of secular warfare. Evidence for the ubiquity of payment for military service from the late eleventh and early twelfth centuries is clear. Paid troops, including knights, are familiar from warfare in Languedoc; in Germany and Italy during the so-called Investiture Dispute between the German kings and allies of the papacy from the 1070s; and in southern Italy during the eleventh-century conquests by the Normans, where they were described by an early twelfth-century commentator as 'stipendiaries against the pagans'.[24] In the Anglo-Norman realms it was later alleged that William the Conqueror's need for knights' 'wages and rewards' (*stipendia vel donativa*) (note the distinction) and Henry I's need for coined money (*numerate pecunia*) to suppress rebellions led to a change in the way income from royal lands was received, from food renders to coin. English taxes for war had been paid in coin since the 990s. William of Poitiers, a former knight turned chaplain and biographer of William the Conqueror, noted the vast sums the duke paid his troops in 1066.[25] Money and other payment suffused the whole network of legal dependency. Eleventh-century evidence from Normandy and the Beauvaisis in northern France to the abbey of Fulda in Hesse in Germany shows lords paying for, or otherwise subsidizing, the service owed to them. From this it appears that tenants were expected to provide their own horses and arms while the lord supported them during the period of their service. Outside any stipulated term of service, such as the widespread forty days limit of obligation, the lord would be expected to pay.[26]

English evidence confirms this. From the returns of Henry II's grand enquiry of 1166 into the amount of knight-service owed by those holding land from him, the so-called *Cartae Baronum*, it is clear that the service of knights to their lords, and ultimately to the king, was redeemable for cash, at 20 shillings per unit of knight-service, known as a knight's fee. If these knights served the king, they expected to provide their own horses and arms from the revenues of the lands they held, but beyond that they were paid. If a tenant was obliged to retain in his own household the notional quota of knights owed his lord or the king, they too were likely to be paid as well as provisioned: '*victum cotidie . . . atque stipendia*', 'daily subsistence and pay', i.e. more than just rations. Knights receiving wages for prescribed service also appeared in the returns to Henry II's Inquest of Sheriffs in 1170.[27] A century earlier, before the Norman Conquest, the same formula of 'subsistence and pay' (*victum vel stipendia*) applied to a thegn's sixty-day obligation in the *fyrd* and was priced at 20 shillings.[28] It was said of William II of England that he was so spendthrift that he allowed his knights to fix their own rates of pay. Abbot Suger of St Denis famously described him as a 'wonderful merchant and paymaster of knights'.[29] By contrast, Suger commented that his hero, the future Louis VI of France, could only afford a much smaller retinue. Almost half a century later, Suger was himself praised for providing the knights of the royal household with their accustomed wages, robes and gifts during Louis VII's absence on the Second Crusade.[30]

While legal contracts emphasized the tenurial, landed ties of loyalty and obligation, in reality armies were raised and lordship expressed through the payment of troops, those obliged to serve as well as those hired specially. The armies of this period, including crusade armies, were confederations. Greater lords recruited lesser lords who recruited knights, some of whom were of sufficient status and wealth to have their own banners and retinues of lesser knights. Attached to each company were sergeants and squires, less armoured than knights but mounted, as well as perhaps specialist infantry, such as archers or pikemen, in addition to the less differentiated footsoldiers. Beyond them were the necessary supporters, artisans and servants. All were held together by the chains of command. Pay supported rather than undermined or contradicted this lordship, securing not challenging loyalty, a tangible demonstration of the moral bond of mutual aid and faith between lord and man as much as (in many cases more than) an anonymous financial transaction. This was the world of the crusades. The combination of social rather than legal ties of lordship and reliance on money and pay to secure followers made possible recruitment for crusading's non-obligatory war service. The techniques of finance, accounting and the administration of paid armies that developed during the eleventh century provided the means to gather and maintain such large forces over long periods under different lords, vital to crusading as an effective military enterprise.

THE CONTEXT OF REWARD

To admit the incentive of material gain is not to set God against Mammon. Piety is not an exclusive state of mind or action. Religious enthusiasm could be, can be, expressed through concrete acts of public or political action and personal, private temporal ambition. As one of the founders of modern crusade scholarship, the great German historian Carl Erdmann, remarked in 1935, 'the crusading idea did not eliminate natural human self-interest' (*den natürlichen menschlichen Eigennutz*).[31] The sacred and the profane complement each other, a matter not of 'either/or' but of 'and/and'. This was understood by crusade promoters and planners who consistently employed allusive language of spiritual and material reward. The vocabulary of holy war reflected social, economic and financial reality. Service to God was, certainly from the Third Crusade onwards, regularly compared and contrasted with service to secular lords. Preachers employed metaphors of charters and chirographs (a particular form of written deed drawn up in duplicate or triplicate familiar especially in contracts of service).[32] Proselytizing the Second Crusade, Bernard of Clairvaux used the language of financial bargaining to appeal to merchants: 'the cost is small; the reward is great'. In his sermon to *crucesignati* at Basle in 1201, Abbot Martin of Pairis offered his audience 'certain pay' and 'great and eternal pay'.[33] The development of crusaders' temporal privileges in the twelfth century addressed explicitly material interests. As we have seen, *crucesignati*, their families and possessions received ecclesiastical protection and were allowed to postpone litigation in courts, avoid repayment of debts, acquire interest-free loans, enjoy certain tax exemptions, and freely sell or mortgage property. The attraction of crusading as a legal and financial benefit was neatly summed up by a Somerset *crucesignatus* in 1220, who argued in court that 'the crusade (*crussignatio*) ought to improve my condition not damage it'.[34]

Concrete, temporal reward served as an inducement from the beginning. Its nature can be separated into two distinct categories: subsistence and profit. Both appeared among the incentives and expectations of crusaders and the requirements of campaigning. No large-scale, long-distance campaign drawn out over an extended period could survive without the repeated augmentation of new sources of funds. Such re-endowments were integral to the whole process, including planning. Hence, the search for money and wealth was not a desideratum of campaigning, more a *sine qua non*. Generally, the material necessities of war were well recognized. Urban II and his successors specifically aimed their appeal for active crusade service at lords and the arms-bearing classes: 'stimulating the minds of knights', as Urban put it, or the 'more powerful and the nobles', in the words of Eugenius III. Preachers, when aiming at military recruits rather than financial contributions, pitched their rhetoric directly and flatteringly at 'renowned knights' (*milites egregii*).[35] The 1095 Clermont crusade decree implicitly recognized the lure of material ambition, insisting that the remission of penance would only be gained by those who embarked 'for devotion alone, not for the acquisition of honour or money' (*pro sola devotione, non pro honoris vel pecunie*), honour, as we have seen, in this case being ambiguous, possibly implying, in the common usage of the time, possessions – fiefs, lands, status or office – rather than an honourable reputation.[36] Gregory VIII in 1187 was more precise: 'do not go there for wealth or worldly glory' (*ad lucrum vel ad gloriam temporalem*).[37]

The key was right intent and purity of motive, the necessary legalistic trappings of penance and just war. However, by recognizing less elevated soldierly aspirations, the popes acknowledged a central conundrum of the crusade project. While almost all literary, promotional and contractual sources take pains to emphasize spontaneity, free will and religious enthusiasm, recruitment and service were determined by secular responses and material means. Guibert of Nogent, among others, characterized the tension between ideal and practice as a new form of war that promised salvation through conformity with, rather than rejection of, the habits of the *milites*, as with Tancred of Lecce, for whom the First Crusade resolved the dilemma between following the Gospels or the military life in a 'two-fold opportunity': 'his experience in arms recalled him to the service of Christ'.[38] Thus, given devout intent and consequent heavenly favour, all aspects of warfare – recruitment, funding, fighting, slaughter, booty and conquest – were legitimized, sanctified even. In their letter celebrating the triumphant campaign of 1097–9, the commanders of the First Crusade explicitly associated God's help not just in military victory but in the attendant killing of enemies and capture of possessions, booty and lands.[39] This became a key point of the crusade message: habitual military behaviour transfigured by serving divine command, in Bernard of Clairvaux's infamous pun, no longer a secular curse, *malitia*, but a *militia Dei*, a knighthood of God.[40]

It is unknowable what sort of additional material incentives, if any, Urban II proffered to attract recruits in 1095–6. However, within a decade or so the prospect of material gain in return for service in a divine cause was well established, a reflection of what actually happened. A model of opportunity was created. As the Benedictine commentator Baldric of Bourgueil imagined Urban II putting it, he used the images of payment and reward both as metaphor and material incentive: 'God distributes his penny at the first and eleventh hour'; 'the goods of your enemies will be yours, because you will plunder their treasures and either return home victorious or gain an eternal prize purpled in your own blood': salvation, wealth, fame; a potent cocktail.[41] Expected or desired rewards could include anything from basic wages for service, to material loot, to gilded reputations, to offices or possessions gained in conquered territory. Relics were a popular commodity, most blatantly witnessed by the frenzied mass larceny at Constantinople in 1204 but also found in the stream of items liberated from the Holy Land from the 1090s onwards. Many came in sumptuously adorned reliquaries. While not obviously commercial, such sacred booty provided significant tangible benefits, memorials to the returning crusader's great deeds and valuable counters in the market of social advancement. Donors of impressive relics attracted considerable communal kudos. Some crusaders were at least reputed to have returned more conventionally wealthy. A few appear in the sources rather like English nabobs of the eighteenth century, bearing back silks, gold, gems, precious rings, arms, military fittings and other exotic oriental riches. Some, like Gouffier of Lastours, who according to later legend also brought back a lion from the First Crusade, enhanced their status by showing off their Jerusalem booty, in his case displaying cloth hangings in a tower at Pompadour in the Limousin. Egyptian Fatimid embroideries of linen, silk and cloth of gold acquired or looted during the First Crusade found their way to the abbey of Cadouin in Perigord and Apt cathedral in Provence. In the 1180s, William Marshal (1147–1219), later regent of England, brought back from Palestine a silk cloth which he destined for his shroud. Others may have converted such treasures and booty into cash or property.[42]

Relics apart, tangible profits left little surviving trace. However, regardless of the actual amount of wealth acquired, the crusade offered potential material profit in terms of social prestige. From 1099 it became more or less *de rigueur* for powerful lords to acquire crusading credentials. It has been argued that this lay behind the otherwise eccentric decision of Philip I of France in 1106 to allow his daughter to marry Bohemund of Antioch, a previously disinherited upstart son of a self-made parvenu transformed into a European Christian hero by his deeds on the First Crusade.[43] The story of the First Crusade and the pious commitment and bravery of its veterans were indelibly inscribed onto western European culture in prose, verse, song, hymns, liturgy, local legends, family history, relics, sculpture, stained glass and wall-painting. No mere indulgence of memory, crusade credentials could translate into material benefit. It was alleged that after his defeat and capture by his usually remorseless brother Henry I of England in 1106, Robert of Normandy was spared worse punishment than imprisonment because of his status as a Jerusalemite.[44] Great lords regularly sought tours of service in the Holy Land: five out of six counts of Flanders went east between 1095 and 1205, one, Thierry (1128–68), four times. Similar association can be traced across the nobilities of France and Germany, family traditions and habits not confined to the grandest. Domestic reputation could be matched by colonial opportunism. The example of the Lusignans from Poitou showed what could be achieved. Two younger sons of Count Hugh VIII, a lord of modest regional prominence, became kings of Jerusalem: Guy (1186–92) and Aimery (1197–1205). Aimery's descendants reigned as kings of Jerusalem in the thirteenth century and ruled as kings of

Cyprus from 1205 to 1473. The crusade commitment of other minor French comital families, such as the extended Montlhéry kindred from the Île de France in the early twelfth century or the Briennes from Champagne over the following century and a half, displayed comparable trajectories of individual promotion and dynastic advance.[45]

In high politics, every king of France between 1137 and 1364, of England between 1154 and 1327, and of Germany between 1137 and 1250 (when there followed an interregnum), took the Cross. The political dividends of command of a crusade were obvious and telling. For Louis VII of France the crusade of 1146–8 provided a unique opportunity to act as a king, to preside over assemblies of lords from across his disunited kingdom and to lead a truly national force beyond the frontiers of his kingdom, the first event of the sort since the ninth century. His chaplain noticed that in eastern France, where his predecessors had rarely ventured, as head of the crusade Louis was received as overlord. Similarly, Conrad III of Germany, another monarch challenged by internal dissent, was able to use the cloak of the crusade to impose an agreed general peace in his kingdom and even to outface powerful opponents.[46] The prestige of Louis IX of France, both in his lifetime and as a royalist icon after his death, hardly needs emphasis. Such political dividends, while not automatic or universal, nonetheless remained a feature of political calculation well into the fourteenth century, even after realistic opportunities for active mass crusading expeditions had lapsed. Those who reneged on crusade commitments, such as Henry II of England, could expect hostile reviews. King Edward III (1327–77), the first English monarch not to take the Cross since King Stephen (1135–54), remained nervous of the omission.[47] Even at the other end of the political scale, to be a Jerusalemite operated as a useful, uncontested badge of honour and status at the level of local courts, where the legal privileges and immunities of absent or returning *crucesignati* were habitually recognized.[48]

Crusaders could expect rewards across a range of informal as well as formal patronage during and after any campaign. In 1177, William of Mandeville, earl of Essex, offered a potential recruit for his crusade, the prior of Walden, 'a place at his table every day'.[49] A central dynamic of aristocratic society in this period lay in the creation of loosely constructed affinities whereby lords attracted followers bound not just by tenurial, dynastic or regional bonds but with temporary or permanent contracts of association. Crusade recruitment provided fertile opportunities to form such affinities. The evidence from the First Crusade alone is littered with references to such agreements or contracts, *conventiones*, sometimes described as monetary arrangements, *conventiones solidorum*. These *conventiones* proved fundamental in securing the cohesion of crusading enterprises. As lords died or ran out of money, their followers of necessity sought new patrons and paymasters, just as other lords eagerly sought to capitalize on this fluid market in potential clients to enhance their own standing. Great lords such as Raymond of Toulouse or Godfrey of Bouillon extended their influence within the crusade armies in this fashion. Lesser figures could advance up the social hierarchy by doing the same. A Limousin lord in the Provençal army, Raymond Pilet, briefly asserted independent command at Antioch towards the end of 1098 when he retained (*retinuit*) many knights and infantry for a raid towards Aleppo. The severe losses suffered by this force reduced Raymond to his former subordinate status, however.[50] More striking were the gains made by Tancred of Lecce, the young well-connected Italo-Norman lord of modest means, who successfully established a significant position for himself during the campaign through accepting money from other leaders and then, with these funds, booty and loans from fellow crusaders, offering lucrative employment to knights outside his immediate household. As a result, the size of Tancred's military retinue varied from between forty and one hundred knights, the core of an influential regiment. On the way he was able to recruit figures from well beyond his southern Italian social milieu, including knights from the Chartrain and Normandy. As Tancred benefited, so did those he recruited. The mutual reciprocity of gain was well caught by Tancred's contemporary eulogist Ralph of Caen, who has Tancred declare:

> My soldiers are my treasure. It causes me no concern that they are provided for when I am in need, so long as I command men for whom provision is made. They load their pouches with silver; I load them with cares, arms, sweat, tremors, hail and rain.[51]

This model of affinity-building and hiring of recruits formed a staple of crusading warfare, offering any recruit the prospect of a good chance of profitable, if strenuous employment. Examples feature prominently in the accounts of the Second Crusade, where both the king of Portugal and Conrad III of Germany took into their paid service knights beyond their own military establishments.[52] The Third Crusade similarly saw kings hiring additional troops, at which Richard I was especially adept.[53] Subsequent crusade leaders, such as Henry VI of Germany in 1195 or Louis IX in 1248–9, were open in their offers of pay and good conditions of service. In the latter case, recruits may have been attracted both by the prospects of making a profit from the enterprise and, if that proved impossible, of petitioning the king to be bailed out. In the event, between 1249 and 1251 Louis stood surety for at least ten followers to the amount of 25,000 *livres tournois*.[54]

These associations of reward could extend beyond the battlefields and campaigns of the Cross. On the First Crusade, the Norman Ilger Bigod, who presumably embarked with his duke, Robert of Normandy, at some point transferred his allegiance to the southern Italian Norman lords, acting with Tancred of Lecce at the assault of Jerusalem in 1099 and subsequently finding high office under Bohemund at Antioch as his 'magistrate of knights'.[55] In the intricate weave of incentives that formed part of this gift culture, the rewards of service could be material even for longstanding dependants. In 1100, the Tuscan Raimondo of Montemurlo was granted a new fief by his lord, Count Guy V of Pistoia, for his service (*pro servitio tuo*) on the Jerusalem journey. Less concrete, but no less attractive, could be the fresh contacts and patronage channels opened by shared experience on campaign.[56] Hubert Walter's promotion to the archbishopric of Canterbury in 1193 may have owed much to Richard I witnessing his efficient administration of English troops at the siege of Acre. The Champagne lord John of Joinville, in addition to being rescued by Louis IX from financial embarrassment over his inability to pay his own military retinue in Cyprus in 1249, owed his subsequent close access to Louis and the royal court to their shared service and friendship developed on crusade and in the east in 1248–54.

From his own testimony, Joinville's experience neatly encompassed the gift and reward culture without which the crusade would have remained stillborn. Although acquainted with Louis IX before the crusade, Joinville's later intimacy with King Louis and political preferment could not have been anticipated. Prior to the crusade Joinville had refused royal patronage. However, the reality of crusade finance soon caught up with him. On arrival in Cyprus, Joinville found himself running out of money. He had contracted to pay for a retinue of nine knights and two knights-banneret, these last having the right to display their own banners, presumably in turn retaining their own *équipe* or band of followers. He had paid for the ship that transported his retinue. This left him, he revealed, with only 240 *livres tournois*, not enough to keep paying his knights some of whom consequently threatened to abandon him. At this moment King Louis intervened and retained (*'et me retint'*) Joinville in his service for 800 *l.t.* which, he admitted, left him with more money than he actually needed.[57] The knights were paid; Joinville scooped a profit and royal patronage; and King Louis gained a valuable new servant from outside his customary sphere of influence. This does not mean that people took the Cross simply as a career move, or in search of pay or employment. Joining a crusade carried serious physical and material risk to crusaders and to their families: death, debt, disparagement. However, as a contributory influence on recruitment, the prospect of advancement was inescapable.

The most obvious opportunity for reward lay in booty and conquest. This was admitted by the earliest commentators on the First Crusade and ran as a consistent theme of crusading thereafter. All early medieval military operations offered profit as a consequence of success. Robert of Clari's anxiety and anger at the unequal distribution of the spoils of Constantinople in 1204 probably spoke for most crusaders. Division of spoils was not simply a welcome bonus but, for extended campaigns, a necessary process of re-endowment without which the whole enterprise could falter and fail. The imperative of material as well as spiritual, God-granted riches, *divites*, determined the course of action.[58] The need to renew sources of income led the First Crusade to accept massive subsidies from the Greek emperor in 1097 and to exploit the lavish booty following the victories at Dorylaeum (1097), Antioch (1098) and Ascalon (1099), as well as extracting protection money from local rulers, such as the emir of Tripoli (1099). One leader, Stephen of Blois, admitted in a letter home to his wife that, as a result of Greek largesse, he was wealthier in 1097 than he had been when he left northern France the year before.[59] The army's anger at the lack of looting at Nicaea in 1097 and at the unequal division of the spoils at Ma'arrat in northern Syria in the winter of 1098/9 reflected not just thwarted greed but legitimate anxiety over future resources. Patterns were repeated. Conrad III received vital subventions from Emperor Manuel I at Constantinople in 1148, allowing him to refit an army in Palestine that spring. Frederick Barbarossa secured his army's prospects by occupying the rich Byzantine province of Thrace in the winter of 1189/90 and by his victory over the Turks at Iconium the following spring. Richard I forced King Tancred of Sicily to part with the huge sum of 40,000 ounces of gold in 1191 and seized further treasure following his conquest of Cyprus later that year. The diversion of the main crusade army and fleet to Constantinople in 1203 was driven by the prospect of Byzantine wealth to support the Jerusalem war, acceptance of the plan being driven, according to one supporter, 'partly by prayers and partly by price' (*tum precibus tum precio*).[60] In such circumstances, profit was neither distraction nor distortion; it was essential.

For some, the prize went beyond campaign profits. In the Baltic holy wars, permanent lucrative gains were achieved by the Lübeck merchants and ecclesiastical imperialists who underwrote the conquest of Livonia, and by the Teutonic Knights who took up rule there and conquered Prussia. Control of the trade in furs, timber, amber and slaves acted as a clear economic incentive, even if the regular temporary recruits of western European nobles answered to more overtly chivalric and pious appeals.[61] Commercial gain and temporal rule were hardly regarded as inimical to the extension of Christendom and Catholic orthodoxy there or in Iberia or Greece. The crusade against heretics in Languedoc (1209–29), largely supported by short-stay and paid soldiery, attracted an element of freebooters. It also offered the chance to carve out a semi-independent principality to its first commander, Simon of Montfort, himself a member of a family whose members seized opportunities for profit and social advancement from the British Isles to Syria. In the 1220s, this so-called Albigensian Crusade was subsumed into the regional expansionism of the French kings.[62] Even if not realized, the Levant crusade presented similar prospects for conquest and economic gain, features not lost on planners. The image of the fabulous riches of the east played into this. On his tour of the west in 1106, Bohemund cut an extravagant dash, even though he had apparently bled Antioch dry to achieve this. His crusade against Byzantium in 1107 was overtly one of conquest, and the image of Greek wealth remained a constant draw for crusading armies and organizers for another century.[63] One element that undermined the diplomatic efforts of Patriarch Heraclius of Jerusalem to elicit western aid for the beleaguered kingdom of Jerusalem in 1184–5 was his entourage's gaudy public display of gold, silver and perfumes.[64]

The lure of eastern treasures attracted the maritime cities of Italy and southern France. In particular, Pisa, Genoa and Venice invested men, money and ships in crusading in the eastern Mediterranean, both on their own commercial behalf and as carriers of crusaders and pilgrims, activities intended to produce material returns as well as spiritual benefits. Contracts with crusaders show the high levels of investment involved, from the Genoese deal with Philip II of France in 1190 (5,950 marks plus wine for an army of just under 2,000), to the famous treaty of Venice with the leadership of the Fourth Crusade (a massive 85,000 marks for a supposed, unrealistic force of 33,500), to the extensive series of contracts agreed with Marseilles, Genoa, Aigues Mortes and other ports by Louis IX, whose naval expenses between 1248 and 1254 probably far exceeded 100,000 *livres tournois*.[65] The risks, as the Fourth Crusade vividly demonstrated, came from defaulting clients not honouring their contracts. Lasting trade advantages accrued from helping to capture trading ports in the Levant, in the form of commercial privileges and control of whole sections of the captured ports, such as the Genoese in Acre after 1104 or the Venetians in Tyre after 1124. While far from immune to religious incentives, trading cities unashamedly celebrated material profits, such as the share of the booty ('gold, silver and gems') brought back to Genoa from the battle of Ascalon (in August 1099) by the Embriaco brothers.[66] The mixed incentives of wealth and salvation were prominent in accounts of the Venetian crusade of 1122–5 in the Adriatic, Aegean and Levant, part terrorist raid, part crusading armada, part relic hunt. An apparent eyewitness saw the Genoese fleet, returning from the capture of Caesarea and Arsuf in 1101, proclaim 'the triumphant victory which had come their way with God's help' and show off 'the great wealth and treasures which they had seized there'.[67] Such bonanzas were not confined to Italians. The return of crusaders to Cologne in 1189 laden with booty taken from Iberian Muslims was noted by locals with approval.[68] To these direct profits could be added the potentially huge proceeds from the support industries of ship building, ship chandlers and the employment of sea captains and crews. For these commercial centres, crusading offered not competitive but simultaneous spiritual attraction, costly investment and abundant business opportunity.

Calculations of material return and how to deal with conquests and other profits were not confined to Mediterranean or Baltic merchant elites. At Vézelay in July 1190, Richard I of England and Philip II of France entered a sworn agreement to share any conquests made on their forthcoming crusade. Similar agreements to share the spoils of war were reached between the leaders of the Fourth Crusade and the Venetian Republic. These deals recognized that material acquisition was integral to the project. During the First Crusade, the western leaders swore oaths to the Byzantine emperor regarding lands they expected to conquer. Commanders such as Raymond of Toulouse or Bohemund strenuously manoeuvred to acquire estates and principalities, ambitions which had probably formed part of their motivation from the beginning. Minor or landless nobles, such as Tancred of Lecce or Baldwin of Boulogne, unashamedly sought their fortunes. Issues of paid service and the share of booty formed part of the preparatory communal arrangements of the North Sea crusade fleet in 1147.[69] Subsequently during the Second Crusade, the pursuit of private gain drove events at Lisbon and, apparently, later, at the siege of Damascus. At least one version of what happened there ascribed the failure of the campaign to competition for control of the city between local Jerusalemites and the count of Flanders. He was said by the same hostile account to have lobbied hard for the city to be given to him despite his rich possessions in the west.[70]

Even if a libel, the story recognized a material dimension to crusade warfare hardly concealed in the widely circulated descriptions of such expeditions, still less in the associated adventure stories popular in vernacular verse. The conquest and retention of the Holy Land,

'Christ's heritage', was the intrinsic point of the Jerusalem crusade, a temporal ambition for a transcendent reward – and, inevitably, vice versa. At the start of the Fourth Crusade, Innocent III worried lest there be insufficient land and population in the Holy Land to support crusading artisan and agricultural settlers. By the late thirteenth century, the secular means to achieve and secure territorial conquest and occupation dominated much of the lively contemporary strategic debate. At least one possibly well-informed observer was reported as claiming that in 1248 Louis IX had transported a mass of farm equipment with him to Egypt, and was distressed that he lacked the manpower to effect a full secure colonization.[71] Beneath the shadow of serious spirituality, crusades were presented and directed for what they were: wars of conquest.

6

Who Went On Crusade?

A veteran of the First Crusade described the Christian host assembled at the siege of Nicaea early in 1097: warriors with coats of mail and helmets – the knights; those 'accustomed to war', but lacking full metal armour – the mounted sergeants and infantry; and those not bearing arms – clergy, women and children. A century and a quarter later, a description of the different tariffs allotted from the booty of the capture of the Egyptian port of Damietta during the Fifth Crusade identified four similar categories: knights; priests and turcopoles (i.e. local recruits); *clientes*, meaning either dependants or non-knightly men-at-arms/sergeants or both; and, finally, wives and children. The official arrangements for the Saladin Tithe of 1188 in England and France assumed the bulk of *crucesignati* would be well-to-do knights and clerics.[1] From Urban II onwards, planners wished to recruit effective military forces. In theory, all *crucesignati* required permission to take the Cross from parish priests or licensed preachers-cum-recruiting officers.[2] Although, as recognized by the Saladin Tithe ordinances, this stipulation could be ignored, in practice crusading was neither an expression of mass hysteria nor a movement of communal spontaneity but an essentially elite activity, sustained by recruitment from wider social groups. In contrast to chroniclers' vapid generalizations and moralizing wishful thinking, while a 1215 French inquiry into the operation of crusader privileges noted urban, rural and merchant *crucesignati*, the core of recruits remained the *bellatores*, the arms-bearers.[3] Even in the thirteenth century, when the system of purchasing vow redemptions copied secular reality by focusing on raising money for troops rather than troops directly, and despite crusade rhetoric saturated with fashionable themes of poverty and humility, campaigns were dominated by the propertied, and those they supported.

LORDS AND LORDSHIP

Extensive evidence of named *crucesignati* in chronicles and in the archives of Church, state, law and lordship abundantly confirms this. The names of well over five hundred individuals have been identified as crusaders on the First Crusade alone.[4] Recruiting agents recorded the names of *crucesignati* on parchment rolls at least from the 1220s. Accurate-seeming figures for those taking the Cross suggest that preachers in the diocese of Cologne in 1214 and in Wales in 1188 did the same. In 1221, the future Pope Gregory IX recorded the names of those northern Italian crusade captains in receipt of Church taxes. By 1200, the archbishop of Canterbury and the king of England had access to the names of *crucesignati* in their jurisdictions.[5] Chroniclers, historians and poets delighted in sonorous lists of holy warriors. Literary, administrative, financial and legal records are obvious skewed towards those with something to sell, mortgage, protect, donate or abandon: those with social standing. The scale of wealth could be modest. Some charters describe transactions involving no more than a few acres, *sous* or shillings, yet distinguish those involved from the penumbra of unnamed dependants, troops, servants and hangers-on.[6]

Crusading's constituency revolved around lords and knights, their households, relatives, friends and retainers, armies bound unevenly together by loyalty, employment, kinship, geography and sworn association confirmed or supplemented by pay. The additional expense of war distinguished crusaders from pilgrims, as did the distinct rituals of enlistment. Preachers' discourses on poverty and their *exempla* anecdotes were designed for propertied, martial audiences. The preponderance of military units based on aristocratic households is overwhelming and unsurprising, from Godfrey of Bouillon's or Bohemund's *familiares* in 1096, to the extensive noble and royal military *équipes* of the Third Crusade, to the retained households of Louis IX and the magnates who followed him in 1248 and 1270. The English Pipe Rolls for 1190–92 grouped crusaders according to region and lordship.[7] Crusaders sought lords as much as lords imposed lordship. A southern Italian noticed at the time how, once Bohemund had taken the Cross in 1096, young warriors flocked to his service. Three-quarters of a century later, the Jerusalemite historian William of Tyre analysed the process:

> For whenever it was rumoured that a prince had taken the vow to make the pilgrimage, the people (*populi*) flocked thither in throngs and begged permission to join his company (*comitatui*). They invoked his name as their lord for the entire journey and promised obedience and loyalty.[8]

A great lord invited service. At the siege of Acre in 1191, it was alleged, seeing the way the political wind was blowing, the Pisans volunteered to perform homage to the newly arrived Richard I, presumably antici-pating a reciprocal act of generosity from their new master.[9]

Patterns of lordship recruitment ran in concentric circles. The widest were displayed at the grand set ceremonial adoptions of the Cross. The great aristocratic assemblies that punctuated the start of inter-national expeditions established or confirmed in a very public manner bonds of mutual complicity. Potential recruits frequently waited to see how the leaders in their communities would jump before commit-ting themselves. At Strasburg in 1188 a stuttering start to Cross-taking was transformed once the magnates signed up.[10] As a recruiting event, the Clermont Council in 1095 was hardly even a modest success in this respect, its international reach being largely ecclesiastical, not, as hoped, secular. By contrast, the assemblies at Vézelay and Speyer in 1146 brought together large sections of the higher nobility of France and Germany, identified command structures and imposed political reconciliation. In January 1188, taking the Cross at Gisors both sealed the necessary peace between the kings of England and France and the count of Flanders and set in train official efforts to raise money and men. Frederick Barbarossa's Court of Christ, three months later, pre-sented the crusade as part of an assertion of royal and imperial power in Germany, a precedent imitated by Frederick's son and grandson in 1195, 1215 and 1220.[11] The higher calling of the Cross, while impos-ing obligations that could prove awkward if ignored, provided useful contexts for resolving rivalries and disputes without either party losing face. The sequence of Cross-takings in 1199–1200 at Ecry and Bruges joined former rebels against the French king with faithful royalists. The regional Cross ceremonies of the Fifth Crusade and the so-called Princes' Crusades of 1239–41, as well as those associated with Louis IX's crusades in 1246–8 and 1267–70, shared these characteristics of conflict resolution.[12]

Cross-taking expressed communal identity as well as personal commitment. Recruiters' descriptions of the preaching campaigns in Wales in 1188, in the diocese of Cologne in 1214–17 and in Marseilles in 1224 registered how existing social group dynamics – lordship, kinship, location or community – swayed responses.[13] Urban recruitment could consolidate corporate solidarity which then continued on campaign: the Venetians in 1101, 1122 or 1202; the Genoese in 1097; Pisans during the Third Crusade; Cologne in 1147, 1189 and 1217; Bremen in 1189; Florence in 1188; Londoners in 1147, 1189 and 1190; Lübeck in the Baltic. Civic identities feature prominently in an account of the Second Crusade: Bristol, Hastings, Southampton, Cologne, Rouen and Boulogne, and young men 'from the region of Ipswich'.[14] Most of these contingents were led by local aristocrats or civic grandees, as the Genoese veteran Caffaro put it, 'the better sort' (*meliores*) in cities and towns. His account of the 1097 Genoese expedition of twelve galleys prepared, equipped and supplied with 'fighting men of the best quality' by the leading citizens who had taken the Cross could be replicated across Europe.[15] The shipload of at least eighty Londoners that embarked on crusade in 1190 was led by two members of the urban elite, Geoffrey the Goldsmith and William FitzOsbert, nicknamed Longbeard. (The latter was a literate, educated and propertied citizen, later infamous as a leader of popular civic agitation.) The Londoners further emphasized their autonomy on crusade by adopting Thomas Becket as their patronal saint and founding a hospital dedicated to him at Acre.[16]

Chroniclers delighted in catalogues and necrologies of crusaders. Three lists of the living illustrate the dominance of social elites: a German and an English one from the Third Crusade and a French one from the Fourth. Each derived from participants or sources very close to them. The *Historia de Expeditione Friderici* (*History of the Campaign of Frederick*) was, like most contemporary accounts of twelfth-century crusades, a composite text. The basis for the first part may have been written by the end of 1189. It includes a long list of the German crusaders assembled at Pressburg on the Danube, modern Bratislava, on the frontiers of Hungary in late May 1189. Arranged in rough hierarchical order, it included, beside the Emperor Frederick and his son Duke Frederick of Swabia, a dozen prelates, three margraves, twenty-seven counts, twenty-five other non-comital nobles, plus an unspecified number of unnamed dependent *ministeriales* and distinguished knights ('*electorum militum*'). The list recognized the nature of recruitment, grouping names in regions – Swabia, Bavaria, Franconia, Saxony, Carinthia, Alsace – and noting where nobles travelled with close relatives, brothers, sons and uncles.[17] Similar catalogues from the Third Crusade confirm the pattern. A later English compilation, the *Itinerarium Peregrinorum et Gesta Regis Ricardi* (*The Journey of the Pilgrims and the Deeds of King Richard*), based on sources close to the action, recorded the names of nobles, mainly from Angevin lands in France, who arrived at the siege of Acre after Richard I in 1191. A prominent feature of this list were kinship groups: the brothers Corneby; knights with the name Torolens or Tozelis; the knights of the des Preaux family (in fact three brothers); the de la Mares; the Stutevilles ('*Stutevillenses*').[18]

When a veteran of the Fourth Crusade, the Picard knight Robert of Clari, came to record his war memories, he prefaced them with an extended register of the *haus homes*, the 'high men', those of sufficient standing and wealth who 'carried banners' (*portient baniere*), i.e. those who led their own armed companies, the key component of any crusade or other medieval army. Like the German Third Crusade list, this was arranged hierarchically, beginning with the counts of Champagne, Flanders, Blois, St Pol and Montfort, the bishops and abbots. Next the barons were paraded by region: Picardy and Flanders; Burgundy; Champagne; the Île de France; the Beauvaisis; the Chartrain. Again, accompanying brothers and sons figure. Naming these grandees provided a suitably resonant noble setting for subsequent events, lists of great knights being commonplace in chivalric literature to which Robert's chronicle bore some resemblance. Robert singled out those who performed deeds of conspicuous bravery on campaign, distinguishing between the 'rich' and those he called 'poor'.

These 'poor' crusaders were in fact chiefly knights of some local prominence in Robert's home provinces of Picardy, Artois and Flanders, definitely members of the aristocracy, socially below the nobles but with close links to local barons and the count of Flanders. The poverty of such men was distinctly relative.[19]

All three lists described the leadership and patronage of rich lords. Beyond them were, in Robert of Clari's phrase, the *'boine gent a cheval et a pié'*, 'good men on horse and foot'.[20] These were no paupers. In other contexts *'boni homines'* suggested property; here Robert at least implies military skill. Elsewhere he explained that in 1202, to make up the shortfall in the agreed payment to honour the transport treaty with the Venetians, each crusader was expected to contribute according to rank: a knight 4 marks (1 mark being equal to two-thirds of a pound); a mounted sergeant 2 marks; the rest 1.[21] These structures were evident from the First Crusade to the written agreements for retaining and allegiance in the 1240s and beyond: great magnates surrounded by lesser lords and prosperous knights linked by kinship, affinity, service or contract, or a mixture of each.[22] Surrounding them were troops who served out of loyalty or obligation, who were supported by their own funds or by subsistence and pay from others, or a combination of both. The whole was woven together by contractual agreements or prior arrangements of association, service and clientage.

Some English evidence shows how this operated. On the Third Crusade Richard I retained great lords such as Duke Leopold of Austria and Count Henry of Champagne, the king's nephew. He did not incorporate their troops into his household, any more than Louis IX did when he paid for his great magnates and their followers fifty years later. Yet the lesser knights Richard contracted with at Acre were directly attached to his command as stipendiaries to join his existing army of paid troops, to fight under his banner.[23] In 1239–40, King Richard's nephew, Richard, earl of Cornwall (1209–72), embarked on his crusade with his brother-in-law Simon of Montfort (son of the leading commander of the Albigensian Crusade) and William Longspee and at least eighteen 'bannerets', knights who commanded separate retinues under their own banners. All of these who embarked with Richard, Simon and William were described by one close observer, who knew Earl Richard, as members of his household, 'de familia comitis Ricardi'.[24] These included John of Neville, chief forester of England, and Philip Basset. These two seemed to have reached a separate bilateral agreement under which Philip agreed to accompany John at his own expense to the Holy Land with two knights. Once there, he and his knights would serve John as members of his familia.[25] Similar networks of interlaced contracts secured the participation of the future Edward I of England and his contingent in Louis IX's crusade in 1270. Edward received what was couched in terms of a loan of 70,000 lt from Louis, promising in return to serve him on crusade, an agreement which some saw as tantamount to Edward joining the French king's household as one of his barons. Edward, in his turn, recruited by contract 225 paid knights.[26] The Basset–Neville deal of 1240 survives as the first written crusading contract, if only in draft. Yet Louis IX's crusade of the late 1240s was raised through a similar chain of contracts, from those with great lords such as his brother Alphonse, count of Poitiers, to the Joinville deal already discussed. While as late as 1270 not all such agreement were written down, that did not impede the tight construction of crusade bands.[27]

Leaders paying for their own household troops, hiring others and subsidizing their transport presented a long history. The language of retaining appears in accounts of all Holy Land crusades from the 1090s onwards. Such bonds worked horizontally as well as vertically. On the First Crusade, Bohemund took kinsmen of equal status into his familia, while Count Raymond of Toulouse offered cash to recruit fellow commanders. On the Third Crusade, Richard I, Philip II and Frederick Barbarossa all lavished subsidies on crusading magnates, in essence little different from the contracts of the 1240s or 1270. The huge crusade treasure amassed by Count Theobald of Champagne in 1201–2 may have been intended for a similar purpose.[28] Transport costs were traditionally concerns of commanders. Bohemund paid for his followers to cross the Adriatic. Louis VII apparently toyed with using a Sicilian fleet. Richard I hired a fleet of upwards of 100 ships for his crusade in 1190. Count Baldwin IX of Flanders invested in a Flemish crusade fleet in 1202 that shipped many of his best troops. In 1228–9, Frederick II paid for the sea transport east not just of his own military entourage but of all his followers.[29]

Within the confines of lordship, contractual dependence provided merely one element in reciprocal relationships characterized by sentiment as well as gain. Recruiting undifferentiated regiments of stipendiaries or hiring fleets was a largely anonymous process. By contrast, dealing with household troops, close clients and *familia* could involve personal responsibility, affection even. Lords travelled with administrative and domestic staff, military retinues, social dependants and friends. Medieval lordship and government retained a peripatetic quality well suited to enterprises such as crusading. It was natural for Richard I to take with him his seneschal, his chamberlain, the clerk of the chamber and his vice-chancellor, Roger Malceal, who drowned in a storm off Cyprus in April 1191 still wearing the royal seal around his neck. (An irony, as Roger had sealed a royal charter concerning the king's right of wreck only six months before.)[30] Military households on campaign could be large, such as Landgrave Louis of Thuringia's in 1227: four counts; eighteen named knights; numerous *ministeriales*, including his butler, marshal, seneschal and chamberlain, as well as priests, chaplains and other knights. A hundred and thirty years earlier, Godfrey of Bouillon had similarly been accompanied by his butler, seneschal, chamberlain, clerical staff and an extended clientage of lords and knights and a group of client monks.[31] However, a *familia* could possess intimacy.

The retinue of Leopold V of Austra in 1190, besides the count of Moerl and a freeman called Dietmar, contained eight of his *ministeriales*, some if not all old family retainers.[32] When Count Guy V of Forez's drew up his will as he lay dying near Brindisi on his return from the Holy Land in 1241, the witnesses from his close entourage included his chaplain, a friar, his clerk, a knight, his chamberlain and his master of sergeants; among the legatees were two squires and a physician, presumably also from the count's retinue.[33] In newly conquered Damietta in December 1219, the concerns of a dying Bolognese crusader, Barzella Merxadrus, centred on the immediate security, comfort and material needs of his nearest companions, followers and, in particular, his wife Guiletta, not least her right to stay in the tent they shared.[34] The will drawn up at Acre in October 1267 by the Englishman Hugh of Neville is equally eloquent of the care shown towards followers, including paying for their passage across the Mediterranean. Among the beneficiaries were three knights, friends or otherwise attached to Hugh's retinue, two of whom acted as executors; two more executors, his page, Jakke the Palmer, and Walter his chaplain; Colin his clerk; his cook, Lucel; his groom Thomas; and two marshals, John and Master Reimund. Among the goods bequeathed by Hugh were horses, armour, a sword, jewelled buckles, a goblet, a gold ring and large quantities of cash, in a variety of currencies – sterling silver, marks and gold bezants (Byzantine coins) – a commentary on the complex bimetallism that faced westerners in the Levant and the expense of running even a modest company. Hugh was expecting further money to come from England, as well as 500 marks promised from Church crusade funds. When, nearly twenty years earlier, William Longspee embarked from England on his fatal crusade with his saddlebags stuffed with money, he was merely being prudent.[35]

NON-NOBLES

Hugh of Neville's will maps the social contours of recruitment. Despite chroniclers' trumpeting of mass enthusiasm, precise evidence is underwhelming for active independent crusaders from the poorest, most oppressed sections of the community beyond household servants and military retinues that included archers and infantry as well as knights and sergeants. This exclusiveness was recognized after 1200 by the introduction of vow redemptions and partial indulgences for small donations from those of modest means. Independent *crucesignati* who did come from lower down the social scale from the arms-bearing elites, the *burgenses* and *rustici* mentioned in the ordinance for the Saladin Tithe in 1188, held one thing in common with their social superiors: negotiable property.[36] Surviving fiscal and archival evidence, which almost invariably concerns the propertied, may not distort reality. Legally, a crusader had to be free. If, like the Nottinghamshire peasant Hugh Travers, he were a serf, taking the Cross implied manumission (confirmed in this case).[37] If self-funded, a crusader required resources. English court records from the early thirteenth century are peppered with references to *crucesignati* who were poor. Too poor to embark, they nonetheless employed the shield of crusade privilege to resist lawsuits. A list from around 1200 of Lincolnshire *crucesignati* who had failed to fulfil their vows identified in 20 out of 29 cases poverty as the main cause of non-compliance, some described as very poor or beggars. Even so, one *crucesignatus* claimed he had been robbed of goods in Lombardy. Another, who insisted he had fulfilled his vow, was listed as a *pauperissimus*, a consequence perhaps of his five children.[38] The social and economic identities of audiences and *crucesignati* revealed in accounts of preaching and in sermons indicated means. The temporal crusade privileges assumed the same: the ability to sell or mortgage property; immunity from interest on loans and repayment of debts; delay in answering civil charges.

The social profile of the response to crusading from wide swathes of free society reflected the upward mobility of non-noble land-holders, merchants and artisans as much as that of arms-bearers. In 1200, Innocent III distinguished between the feeble and poor ('*debiles et inopes*') who should not be forced to embark, and others who had taken the Cross: nobles, magnates, warriors ('*bellatores*'), and artisans and farmers ('*artifices et agricolae*').[39] Crusader privileges allowed tenants as well as landowners to raise money freely by sale or mortgage.[40] Deals could be piecemeal, raising as little as a few shillings, or, as with a *villicus* or steward from the Loire valley around 1170, involve a whole patrimony, in this case worth 300 *sous*.[41] Beyond farmers and landed *rentiers* of one sort or another, artisans feature prominently. Many of them could expect to work on campaign. Lists of crusaders in English Exchequer records for 1207 and 1208 identify a dyer, a bowman and a butcher alongside merchants, provosts, squires, sergeants and chaplains. A *c.*1200 list of Cornish *crucesignati* noted a blacksmith, a miller, a cobbler and a tailor, while a contemporary Lincolnshire list adds a skinner, a potter, a butcher, another blacksmith, a vintner, a ditcher and a baker. In the 1220s, the master carpenter of Chichester Cathedral sought permission to go on crusade.[42] According to Robert of Clari, the crusaders' camp outside Constantinople in 1203 was defended by horse-boys and cooks, equipped with quilts, saddlecloths, copper pots, maces and pestles. Butchers in the crusader camp raised the alarm when the count of Poitiers was surrounded by Turks at the battle of Mansourah in 1250.[43] Laundresses – old women ostensibly beyond sexual allure – doubled as de-lousers on the Third Crusade.[44] Alongside the usual household officials such as butlers, seneschals, stewards, marshals, constables, chamberlains, notaries and physicians, the Fifth Crusade was joined by judges, academics (*magistri*) – a telling indication of the rise of universities over the previous century – a carter, a barber, a tanner, a cook, a schoolmaster (*grammaticus*) from York-shire, a Gloucestershire franklin (or freeholder) and a German master chef (*magister coquinae*). From other sources appear fishmongers, physicians, surgeons, masons, fowlers, doghandlers and engineers.[45]

Besides service in the entourages of the well-to-do, artisans had access to cash as wage earners. Many proved professionally useful in crusader armies, and some were unashamedly entrepreneurial. At the siege of Nicaea in 1097, the Lombard engineer who volunteered his services did so on condition he was paid and all expenses be provided from the crusade's general funds. He received the substantial sum of 15 *livres* of Chartres money, which helped pay his team of workmen (*opifices*).[46] The crusade veteran and chronicler Raymond of Aguiliers noted, with a whiff of asperity, that while most of those who helped build the siege engines at the siege of Jerusalem in June and July 1099 did so freely ('*spontanei*'), the professional artisans, the '*artifices*', were paid, some from public collections, others by the count of Tou-louse.[47] Businessmen might hope to secure a good living on crusade. One witness accused merchants ('*li marcheant*') at the siege of Acre in the winter of 1190/91 of deliberately hoarding grain to drive prices up. To underline his moral point, he recounted a story of a Pisan profiteer whose plan to keep hold of his grain store until he could exact max-imum profit came unstuck when it was completely destroyed by fire, ruining him.[48] Less pejoratively, merchants and money-changers pro-vided commercial and financial services in the markets that fed the armies.

Towns remained the centres for recruits as for preaching. By no means confined to maritime trading cities, recruiting was directed along inland networks of politics and trade to urban centres that acted as magnets for surrounding regions. In 1247, crusaders from Châteaudun in northern France between Chartres and Orleans sig-nalled their corporate identity by forming a confraternity, *confratria*, to organize funding and to attract non-crusaders' donations.[49] In twelfth- and thirteenth-century Oxford, a well-connected inland market town hosting religious houses, a royal palace and a nascent university, townsmen traded houses, meadows and rents for funds to pay for their journeys east.[50] One of the more misleading assumptions about the crusades is that its idealism was less attractive to those engaged in urban or commercial activities except in so far as those ideals promised new markets or the chance for material profit. In fact, incentives of faith and reward gained similar if not greater traction in town as in country.

Two other groups of recruits fit later stereotypes more easily: youths and clergy. In chronicles, *iuvenes* described literally young men or, more obliquely, as-yet-un-dubbed or not-yet-landed knights. As with armies everywhere, young men were enticed by prospects of fighting and adventure in the service of an exciting and noble cause. Albert of Aachen blamed military failings of Peter the Hermit's expedition in 1096 on the intemperate indiscipline of crowds of excitable *iuvenes*. Seven *iuvenes* from the Ipswich area were singled out for their conspicuous bravery at the siege of Lisbon. In 1190, young crusaders apparently played a leading role in the attacks on Jews in England.[51] Propertied crusaders frequently travelled with their sons and younger brothers. Young *crucesignati* could persuade their non-crusading parents to provide funds for their adventure, like Robert of Marsh in 1201 or John Pacche of Oxford in 1247–8. Others were probably less independent than commentators portrayed them. The habitual structure of noble and knightly households included aristocratic youths as squires or pages, a form of in-service knighthood training, men such as Hugh of Neville's page (*vallet*) at Acre, Jakke the Palmer. Under his master's will, he received a horse and full knightly armoured apparel appropriate for a '*gentil home*'.[52]

Predictably, clergy comprised another major component of any crusade. During recruitment, they assisted in preaching, crusade liturgies, processions and Cross-giving. As parish priests they granted recruits permission to go on crusade. On campaign, like their lay colleagues, they fell into three general categories: those serving in the households of the wealthy as chaplains and clerks; those of independent means associated in various ways with lords, other clerics or local crusading companies; and grand prelates whose households were, at least in the early years of crusading, indistinguishable from those of secular lords. The clergy from England on the Third Crusade who actually reached Palestine included an archbishop, a bishop and an abbot, archdeacons, cathedral canons, chaplains, parsons, clerks and the vicar of Dartford.[53] Although Urban II had disapproved of the involvement of cloistered monks, that did not prevent their participation. Former monks who had been elevated to bishoprics, and thus freed from the cloister, provided much of the ecclesiastical leadership of the Second and Third Crusades as well as the Albigensian crusade of 1209. Archbishop Baldwin of Canterbury, who helped lead the English advance guard to Syria in 1190, had been a Cistercian abbot.[54] For secular clergy crusading became acceptable and common. Many behaved like other aspiring crusaders. To make crusading easier for them, from around 1200 beneficed clergy were permitted to raise money on their income to pay for other crusaders or to subsidize their own journeys. They were also allowed to enjoy the income from their benefices during their absence and, after 1215, to use proceeds from the general revenues of their churches generated by the new system of ecclesiastical crusade taxes.[55]

Clergy on crusade served the spiritual needs of individuals, households and the armies at large through regular rounds of quasi-monastic devotions: prayers; private confessions; public processions; penances; liturgies. They exhorted and encouraged. Crusade campaigns were punctuated by public rituals of re-dedication or supplication, often crucial in maintaining morale during moments of crisis. Prayers and sacraments before battle at least addressed the most immediate anxiety of the soldiery, sudden death. The physical presence of a significant number of priests overtly demonstrated the holy nature of the endeavour. Clergy did not form an undifferentiated mass. Even at humbler levels, varying contemporary designations indicated a variety of functions. In one mid-thirteenth-century list of crusaders, three adjacent clergymen are identified as 'priest', 'chaplain' and 'clerk'.[56] They did much more than pray and reassure. The ubiquity of lesser clergy can be explained as much by their role as writing clerks rather than as priests, keeping accounts, copying contracts, writing letters, drawing up and witnessing charters and wills. Clerics negotiated with the enemy, buried the dead and organized relief for the impoverished, a

role in which Bishop Hubert Walter of Salisbury, the future archbishop of Canterbury, distinguished himself during the grim winter of
1190/91 under the walls of Acre. Some also fought, like the archetype
of the crusading priest, Adhemar of Le Puy, on the First Crusade; or,
during the Third, Hubert Walter, Ralph Hauterive, archdeacon of
Colchester and the 'armed clerk' Hugh de la Mare, who unwisely
attempted to give Richard I military advice; or, on the Fourth, Robert
of Clari's brother, the priest Aleaumes, 'first in every assault where he
was present'.[57] As ecclesiastical fashion changed, fewer crusading
prelates imitated Bishop Adhemar, a noted horseman who cam-
paigned with his own military household. Later prelates tended more
to be administrators, such as Hubert Walter or the Spanish Cardinal
Pelagius, the domineering papal legate on the Fifth Crusade, or refined
scholarly preachers and politicians such as James of Vitry or Odo of
Châteauroux, papal legate to Louis IX's first crusade of 1248–54.

This did not preclude energetic clerical leadership. Bishop Albert of
Riga personally orchestrated the wars of conquest in Livonia in the
first quarter of the thirteenth century, accompanying campaigns himself under his own banner. His predecessor, Berthold, had been killed
in battle.[58] If fighting clerics were increasingly frowned upon, supporting roles were still possible. In a famous instance, Oliver of
Paderborn, Paris-trained academic *scholasticus* or schoolmaster in the
diocese of Cologne and future cardinal, preacher and recruiter for the
Cross in 1213–17, accompanied his Cologne contingent on the invasion of Egypt, about which he wrote a detailed account and apologia,
completed by 1222 and partly based on his letters home. Oliver
proved to be more than a diligent pastor. At a crucial moment in the
siege of Damietta on the Nile in August 1218, he designed a floating
siege tower that helped reduce a vital strategic point in the city's
defences. Oliver's account of this incident (which modestly avoids
revealing his own role) encouraged the English chronicler Matthew
Paris (d.1259) to commemorate it in one of his lively drawn illustrations to his great *Chronica Majora*.[59]

The most actively involved group of professed religious were the
members of the military orders, the knights, sergeants and priests of
the Templars, Hospitallers, Teutonic Knights, Sword Brothers of Livonia and the rest. From the 1140s, they played increasingly important

roles as professional, disciplined, experienced troops; as strategists with local knowledge; as international and local bankers; and as providers of a range of logistical support, including shipping. Their unique commitment to holy war lent them especial prominence. Templars and Hospitallers were recruited to help assess and levy the Saladin Tithe of 1188 in the lands of Henry II of England, one English Templar being caught embezzling the proceeds on a large scale.[60] From the later twelfth century they appeared to enjoy legal and fiscal immunities similar to crusaders'. Their role in recruitment and propaganda stemmed from their status as permanent *milites Christi*, veterans of holy wars and, individually and corporately, prominent figures and features in the social and physical landscape of western Europe, magnets for lavish lay endowment. In some regions, family patronage and association with military orders were closely associated with habits of taking the Cross. Although members of the military orders were not technically *crucesignati*, they provided a constant resource of devotion and practical assistance in any crusade plan.[61]

Criminals were also attracted to crusading. As well as facilitating clerical and lay involvement, the crusade privileges of legal exemption and protection supplied an attractive option to those seeking to escape or evade justice or punishment. This went beyond the use of the crusader's right to delay civil litigation. The most complete secular legal records for the period in western Europe, those of the English royal courts, supply numerous examples of people absconding to the Holy Land before they could be arraigned or tried for alleged offences.[62] The crusade also acted as a punishment in its own right. The export of undesirables to serve a good cause possessed a history as old as the crusades themselves. James of Vitry may have deplored the criminous riff-raff he encountered in Acre in 1217, but penitential exile, formally imposed or as an act of convenient desertion, sprang from the very roots of the crusade's penitential purpose, closely paralleling the imposition of penitential pilgrimages. Expiation of moral not necessarily criminal guilt could also act as a spur. According to the well-connected Matthew Paris, Simon of Montfort and his wife Eleanor took the Cross in 1248 to assuage their consciences over their marriage: Eleanor had previously sworn an oath of chastity. Certain convicted felons were sentenced to depart on crusade without the option, a procedure reflected in the probably legendary story of the punishment meted out to the murderers of Thomas Becket.[63] A penitential crusade could be used to signal the resolution of disputes or a commitment to new obedience. Repentant heretics were sentenced by the Inquisition to serve on crusade to defend the Latin empire of Constantinople in the 1230s and 1240s, including a professional juggler, an unlikely crusader and even more unlikely adherent of puritanical Catharism. Louis IX tried to secure the service of former heretics and their sympathizers in the 1240s, with mixed success.[64] While reformed heretics may not necessarily have harboured a taste for holy war, those previously engaged in violent crime possibly suited the life only too well. Enforced crusading might seem to contradict fundamental principles of an enterprise which rested on the concept of voluntary conversion and commitment. In reality, the crusades were sustained by a dependence culture within a social hierarchy in which very few possessed even modest free choice.

WOMEN

This applied most to women. It is a myth, a male myth, that medieval women lacked agency or social presence. Until the early thirteenth century, a wife's permission was required for a married male crusader to sign up. Even then accounts of crusade preaching are littered with misogynist stories of obstructive wives, backhanded testimony to their domestic power and tacit recognition that the attendant risks of crusading could be as high for dependants as for the crusaders themselves. Women left behind faced legal and more than occasional physical threats to their property, status or person, not least as they were often left in temporary charge of crusaders' estates. Wives, mothers and daughters held recognized stakes in the assets crusaders used, a role attested in numerous charter witness lists. However, Church authorities and military recruiters alike exhibited a distinctly equivocal attitude to women. In theory, crusading was open to all the faithful as a penitential exercise. But holy war required soldiers, an occupation culturally deemed unsuited to women. Even though, reluctantly, wives were allowed to accompany husbands, the spectre of sex, even conjugal sex, disturbed the ecclesiastical vision of a morally pure enterprise, the ideal *crucesignatus* abstaining from carnal acts (except killing).[65]

Such inhibitions failed to prevent women's participation. Many crusaders travelled with their wives and families, recognized by the inclusion of wives and children in John of Tolve's list of beneficiaries from the loot of Damietta in 1219.[66] Wives, daughters and other women were present on all crusades, many not just as licit or illicit appendages but as *crucesignatae* in their own right. It is clear that both higher clergy and parish priests, the latter entrusted by Urban II with granting permission for their parishioners to take the Cross, acquiesced. The catalogue of queens, princesses, wives of nobles and other members of the elites taking the Cross and going on crusade is extensive from the First Crusade onwards. On the Second Crusade, for example, Queen Eleanor of France was joined by the countesses of Flanders and Toulouse. By the thirteenth and fourteenth centuries it was commonplace for wives of crusading nobles to take the Cross; three of Louis IX's children were born on crusade between 1250 and 1253. Not all joined up simply to keep partners company. Ida, widow of the margrave of Austria, led her own armed contingent on crusade in 1101. A century later, Innocent III recognized that wealthy women could lead armed troops on crusade. In Genoa in 1216, rich *crucesignatae* persuaded their spouses to enlist.[67]

The habits of the grand were replicated lower down the social hierarchy. The crusade confraternity established at Dartmouth in 1147 assumed the participation of women. In a list of forty-seven Cornish crusaders of *c.*1200, four, possibly five, were women. Of 342 commoner crusaders on board the ship *St Victor* seeking to join Louis IX in the east in 1250, 42 were women, 22 of them unchaperoned. At Marseilles in 1224, women proved integral to the recruiting process.[68] Chroniclers, including the Greek Anna Comnena, noted substantial numbers of women in crusade armies and as camp followers.[69] They figure in varieties of necessary, chiefly domestic or commercial, roles, such as nursing, washing, de-lousing, prostitution, organizing markets, grinding corn, supplying and occasionally helping frontline troops. Some were remembered for their independent spirit, such as the mortally wounded wife at the siege of Acre who begged her husband to use her corpse to help fill the moat.[70] Others were held up for moral censure, such as the nun from Trier rescued from her Turkish captors at the siege of Nicaea in 1097 who subsequently returned to the Muslim lover who had allegedly ravished her in captivity.[71] Most *crucesignatae* pursued less colourful careers. Like the Parisian Jeanne Crest, who took the Cross with her husband Renard in 1224–5, women crusaders, whether in a family group or not, unsurprisingly came from the same propertied social *milieux* as male crusaders.[72] Those of humbler backgrounds only went as servants and more menial workers.

Recruiters' appeal to women and their responses were inevitably complicated. However, their presence, prominence even, at all levels cannot be doubted. In April 1250, a woman from Paris, possibly a professional physician, cradled the head of the sick Louis IX as he awaited capture at Sharamshah in the Nile Delta after the defeat at Mansourah. Meanwhile, down river at Damietta, Louis's heavily pregnant wife, Margaret, soon to give birth to a son, was trying to hold the Christian garrison together at the same time as arranging details of the king's ransom.[73] Crusader women's resourcefulness was the match of anyone's. The recruitment of women exposes a tracery of informal, sometimes intimate bonds of association, ties of family, neighbourhood, affection even, that paralleled and supported the more apparent structures of lordship, pay and finance. On board the *St Victor* in 1250 were lords and knights with their retinues, Templars, Hospitallers, seven clerics, family groups of husbands and wives, sons and brothers, servants and artisans, solitary male and female travellers, and those who were described as being linked in some way as companions (*socii*). Among these were two women, Guillelma de la Lande and Bernarda, '*sua socia*'. Was Bernarda Guillelma's business associate, servant, companion, friend, or partner?[74]

COMMUNAL ASSOCIATION

Such ambiguity nicely reflects the variety of incentives for recruits of either sex. As already sketched, tied up in motives to take the Cross and in how subsequently to run a crusade were considerations of kinship, shared location and communal action. The networks of allegiances and command of the First Crusade rested on cat's cradles of blood and marriage connections. The brothers Godfrey of Bouillon, Eustace and Baldwin of Boulogne and the brothers-in-law Robert of Normandy and Stephen of Blois are well known. Robert of Flanders was first cousin to Robert of Normandy and Stephen of Blois's wife but also the brother-in-law to Bohemund of Taranto's half-brother, Roger Borsa. Kindred links did not necessarily promote unity. Raymond of Toulouse had been married to the daughter of Roger I of Sicily, Bohemund's uncle and, like Roger Borsa, his political opponent. The Fourth Crusade lacked royal leadership but instead was initiated by a closely associated and related group of northern French counts who, like their predecessors of the 1090s, provided markedly resilient and cohesive leadership. Webs of kindred characterized recruitment for every crusade at all levels, travelling with relatives being a natural option, like living with them.

Shared locality also influenced recruitment and campaign arrangements, from great magnates to humbler gangs clustered around communal camp fires. In the camp at Acre in 1190–91, the English royal clerk and chronicler Roger of Howden, parson of a town in east Yorkshire, witnessed a charter of a local Yorkshire landowner, John of Hessle, and, in listing the English dead, gave especial attention to those far-from-grand casualties from his own neighbourhood: Richard and John of Legsby; the parson of Croxby; Robert the Huntsman of Pontefract.[75] They may have been known to him, friends or companions. Equivalent attention to known local associates, lords, relatives and friends is shown by Robert of Clari's praise for fellow Picards on the Fourth Crusade, not least his brother Aleaumes, the fighting priest.[76] Recruited together, they probably travelled together, like the Londoners who hired their own ships in 1147, 1189 and 1190. Such was almost certainly the experience of the knights and priests from the Chalons-sur-Saône region who messed together on the Fourth Crusade.[77]

Many of these regional groups formalized their association. Setting out on the Second Crusade, Milo, lord of Evry-le-Châtel in southern Champagne, and his knights swore mutual oaths of unity, 'se federaverunt juramentis'. English bands of crusaders in 1190 were described as bound together by oaths, coniurati.[78] The role of formal sworn confraternities had been exploited more than once during the First Crusade to pool resources into centrally controlled funds, as at the sieges of Nicaea and Antioch. The leaders of the Fourth Crusade pooled their authority in licensing representatives jointly to secure a transport contract with an Italian shipper. Communal arrangements became staple accompaniments to crusading, complementing or substituting for lordship: the common poor relief fund at Acre in 1190–91 or the common chest of funds at Damietta in 1219.[79] Despite modern stereotypes, medieval society was as familiar with horizontal bonds of social cohesion as with lordly hierarchies: monastic communities; religious confraternities; military orders; universities; secular saints' and trade guilds; and the more obvious political and urban communes that sprang up in western Europe in the eleventh and twelfth centuries. The communal model was not narrowly civic. It was ubiquitous across the Church and prominent in elite politics, witnessed in ideas such as the thirteenth-century English constitutional notion of the 'community of the realm' or the nobles' anti-royalist 'Commune of England' of 1258.[80]

Crusading, ostensibly a gathering of equal and independent souls freely committed to a common cause, offered a receptive setting for communal bonds of association, particularly where traditional secular lordship was either attenuated or irrelevant. Communal agreements confirmed by oaths were widespread. Louis VII's disciplinary ordinances of 1147 were agreed by mutual oaths as, more effectively, were those of Frederick Barbarossa in 1189; those of Richard I in 1190 were reached by 'common consent'. The polyglot fleet assembled at Dartmouth in 1147 agreed to a sworn association to guarantee peace and friendship between the disparate groups – a *coniuratio* or *societas coniurata*, a commune.[81] Many townsmen involved from around the North Sea region would have been familiar with this sort of association, not least those from London where collective corporate action was becoming increasingly apparent in the 1130s and 1140s. The 1147 Dartmouth commune encompassed civil and criminal justice, sumptuary rules, the conduct of women, the competitive hiring of servants, collective decision making, religious worship, distribution of money and arbitration between members.[82] Tactical and strategic decisions were reached collectively, a model replicated in the spring of 1189 by the fleet from London and other North Sea ports gathered at Dartmouth in May and by the crusade flotilla from Bremen in the same year, which also appears to have run itself on communal lines. Similar models of organization were adopted by other English ships in 1189 and 1190 and by the large fleet from the Netherlands, Frisia and the Rhineland in 1217.[83] While some of these communes may have been thrown together by the circumstances of travel or campaigning, others clearly operated from the start of recruitment and planning, such as the Châteaudun confraternity of 1247 or the *societas peregrinorum* in Florence or that of Pistoia during the Third Crusade or the Parisian *confrarie* of the Holy Sepulchre of 1317.[84] In 1210 Bishop Fulk of Toulouse instituted the so-called White Confraternity in the city whose members received the Cross and crusade indulgences. Chiefly active in condemning usury, members nonetheless assisted in the crusaders' attack on Lavaur in southern France in 1211.[85]

Acquaintance with communal structures of association and decision-making emerged on campaigns. During the First Crusade stay in Syria and Palestine, an active collective role was taken by the *populus*, a collective noun suggesting a recognized system of assembly politics within the army that involved the commoners as well as the knights and nobles. In similar fashion, the Fourth Crusade acted as a commune, the leadership consulting the 'commons of the host' and holding *parlements* at moments of peril, urgency or dissent.[86] Even the forceful Richard I was compelled to concede a second attack on Jerusalem in May 1192 through organized insistence by the commons in the army, cleverly manipulated by his critics.[87] Consensual corporate institutions were familiar to crusaders from public law courts to agrarian management. Propagandists' parallels of a crusader 'army of God' with the scriptural collectives of the Israelites or the Maccabees were appropriate. The ubiquity of communal management helps explain the remarkable cohesion within large crusader armies rarely bound together under unified lordship.

THE 'POOR'

The accumulated evidence for recruitment and service seemingly excludes a category dear to many medieval and modern commentators, the poor. It is clear that crusading was chiefly the preserve of some, not all, sections of society, of the free and those with access to material surplus. For them, the costs of individual crusade travel may not have been prohibitively exorbitant. In the 1240s, a third-class berth from Marseilles to Acre might have cost a third of a year's wages for a posh Parisian cook, or a full year's wages for a specialist Parisian tailor.[88] However, with food expensive, even without the inflation-ridden campaign markets, and war materials costly and easily depreciated, either credit or accumulated capital were essential. For the nobility, crusading, whether by land or sea, has been estimated to cost four or more times an individual's annual income.[89] For the less elevated, similar scales of cost were likely, although rulers with access to extraordinary taxation, such as Louis IX, might hope to break even. The introduction of vow redemptions for the 'debiles et inopes' ('feeble and poor'), as Innocent III put it, confirmed active crusading as a socially elite, niche activity, in many ways no different from other expressions of medieval religious devotion and charity such as alms-giving, donations to religious corporations, or pilgrimages with which crusading was culturally so closely linked.[90]

What of that other constant presence on crusade, the crowds described as the poor, the *pauperes*? Chroniclers employed a variety of blanket terms, often more literary and rhetorical than sociological, blurring social and functional distinctions between infantry, non-combatants, camp-followers, civilian providers of necessary support services and the destitute. The comparative or absolute social or economic status of *plebs*, *pauperes*, *peregrini* and *mediocres* lacked definition. For example, the 'poor' are regularly depicted as fighters. Recruits such as the *menu peuple* who rioted at Aigues Mortes in 1270 were armed and capable of mounting a violent contest.[91] Similarly, non-combatants were frequently performing tasks essential to the military effort. The *populus* of the First Crusade or the 'commons of the host' of the Fourth comprised fighting men with a collective and personal stake in the direction of operations. *Crucesignati* had to be free, to take the voluntary vow and enjoy the temporal privileges. Legally, unfree serfs taking the Cross were *ipso facto* manumitted. Of course, the incidence of freedom and servility, in law and in fact, var-ied across Europe. Technically, German *ministeriales*, conspicuous in German crusade armies, were unfree. But they represented a very unusual elite class of bondmen, culturally and economically the peers of knights. Social exclusivity in recruitment and arms merely acknowledged contemporary twelfth-century practice in raising armies. Henry II of England's Assize of Arms (1181), applicable in Henry's continental as well as insular possessions, contemplated only arming freemen, a measure copied by the king of France and the count of Flanders.[92] Obligation was extended in the following century to the unfree. Volunteer serfs illicitly left their fields to fight in the English civil wars in the 1260s.[93]

Taken with the so-called Children's Crusade of 1212, the Shepherds' Crusades of 1251 and 1320 and the popular response to the crusade in 1309, this exposes a level of conscious, independent political awareness and involvement among the mass agrarian workforce. However, such demonstrations were largely unauthorized and unwelcome to the elites that organized crusading. Servile peasants did not formally become regular members of levied armies until the Anglo-French wars of Edward I and Philip IV in the 1290s.[94] The absence of agricultural labourers on crusade as much as that of farmers sabotaged Louis IX's scheme to colonize Egypt in 1248–50.[95] Of course, legal status may not have excluded those on crusade who had not taken the Cross. Not all those who went on crusade were *crucesignati*, as revealed in Cardinal Ugolino's register of north Italian recruits for the Fifth Crusade. Standing professional garrisons were established from the mid-thirteenth century in the remaining Christian mainland outposts in the Holy Land. In the early fourteenth century, the Venetian writer Marino Sanudo Torsello advocated preliminary crusade campaigns to attack and blockade Egypt explicitly manned by non-*crucesignati*, a gesture towards professionalism rather than class.[96] However, in each of these cases, the non-*crucesignati* were to be paid – far from the individualist crusading peasantry imagined by some chroniclers and subsequently by modern historians seeking evidence of mass belief, populist action or democratic agency.

The masses of 'poor' who colour narrative accounts of crusading resist clear identification. Were they the indigent or merely the unrich? Preachers and chroniclers employed poverty almost indiscriminately to describe social status, economic condition or moral standing; a synonym variously for non-nobles, infantry, the newly impoverished, non-combatants or even, in quasi-monastic terms, all *crucesignati*. It is sometimes argued that the overt apocalyptic strand in crusade commentary, particularly associated with the First Crusade, reflected the emotions of the populace, the non-elite *crucesignati*.[97] Why the less-educated and socially disadvantaged should be more susceptible to intimations of the Last Judgment than those in the educated elites who promoted its imminence in the first place is unclear. The susceptibility to rumour and mass enthusiasm attested by witnesses to preaching campaigns in 1095–6, 1188–90 or 1213–17 was hardly the preserve of the socially marginal, as preachers' accounts show. When observers such as Guibert of Nogent cast lofty aspersions on the rabble, as he saw it, who answered the call of the Cross in 1095–6, his targets were not necessarily paupers but rather the ignorant or those lacking aristocratic lay or ecclesiastical guidance and control. Guibert's gibes at the woman and the credulous band which traipsed behind her special goose revealed that even this eccentric example of crusade enthusiasm exhibited a degree of cohesive social structure.[98] The poor harvests and economic depression of the early 1090s may have rendered the escapist prospect of a gilded Jerusalem more alluring, but primarily to those whose livelihoods had been undermined, whose expectations had been reduced or narrowed – the impoverished, not the poor. For them, the crusade may have offered material as well as spiritual relief, not a mass exodus of serfs from the fields.

Crusades, especially those travelling by land, attracted non-combatant pilgrims, eager to enjoy the protection and camaraderie of the military expedition. The camp followers, *ribaldi*, and local peasantry who joined the Albigensian Crusades against heretics in Languedoc from 1209 may have been drawn by the hope of gain as much as religious paranoia.[99] On eastern expeditions, some pilgrims may have hoped to rely on charity rather than their own resources. If they did, they soon fell by the wayside, gave up or were forced to seek patronage, subsidy or employment within the army. The same fate descended on armed crusaders, such as the archers described by one eyewitness as *plebs*, who failed to secure lordly patronage at Bari late in 1096 and so were forced to abandon the expedition. Joining any crusade, at any level, in any capacity was determined by the imperative of funds.[100] The corporate treasuries established during crusade campaigns from Nicaea in 1097 onwards were for those who lost employment, service or lordship, or who had run out of money. Their existence did not necessarily indicate legions of poor present from the outset. Most of the legends of the Children's Crusade of 1212 emphasize that the so-called *pueri* who joined the mass penitential marches in the Low Countries, the Rhineland and northern France were drawn from the social and economic margins of society: the young, adolescents, the unmarried, the old and the rootless; shepherds, ploughmen, carters, farm workers and artisans. Their failure to make it beyond the ports of France and Italy underscored the financial, hierarchical and structural requirements of crusading.[101] Recruits from equivalent social groups did travel on campaigns, but only as part of organized and funded contingents. Crusade recruiters did not want or seek the materially poor, and never said they did.

Even the mass enthusiasm for the First Crusade was not indiscriminate or wholly inclusive. The first wave of crusaders under Peter the Hermit in 1096 was distinguished by its ultimate failure and the relative dearth of major nobles taking part, rather than its lowly social or economic status. Famously, Walter sans Avoir was not 'Penniless'; Boissy-sans-Avoir is a place in the Île de France of which Walter was lord. The nickname 'the Carpenter' applied to another commander in Peter's army, Count William of Melun, referred to his method of despatching his opponents in battle rather than to any useful profession. Peter's army held together and defended itself for hundreds of miles through unfriendly territory, conducted effective sieges of cities, and possessed a central treasury. Its main force reached Asia intact, defeat by the Turks being the result of immediate indiscipline and bad tactical leadership, phenomena not reserved to this crusade army. The denigrating identification with 'peasants' or the poor owed most to its disastrous fate and the inherent cultural snobbery of contemporary commentators, not to any especial social disadvantage or indigence.[102]

The appearance of the poor on crusade may not be what it seems. Some called poor, such as Innocent III's *inopes*, evidently took the Cross. However, these may have been those with inadequate funds, rather than none at all, hence the progressively standardized offers of partial crusade privileges culminating in the fully-fledged system of redemptions after 1213.[103] Equally obvious from Innocent's and others' remarks – active crusaders required material means. The poor in chronicle accounts do not contradict this. The legends of the cannibalistic poor Tafurs on the First Crusade describe their leader as a Norman knight fallen on hard times. Describing the Second Crusade, Odo of Deuil appears to include in the crowd of 'poor' those with funds to try to buy provisions, later swelled by the 'paupers since yesterday' and 'seasoned youths' adept with bows. Elsewhere, the term 'poor' is used relatively, as in Robert of Clari's inclusion of knights of local prominence in his list of 'poor' crusaders from Picardy, Artois and Flanders. At Venice, Robert claimed, the 'poor' celebrated the news that the Venetians were going to transport the expedition by fixing torches to the ends of their lances. Like the *plebs* on the First Crusade who reached Antioch with rusty weapons, these 'poor' were fighters with equipment.[104] Commentators exposed selective views of what they meant by poor. The English historian Henry of Huntingdon celebrated the capture of Lisbon in 1147 as a triumph of the poor, a distinctly misleading description of the count of Aerschot, Hervey of Glanvill and the other commanders. Henry was drawing a dramatic moral contrast with the failure of the campaigns led by the grander crusaders Louis VII and Conrad III.[105]

This metaphorical use of poverty was shared by commentators and propagandists alike. In an increasingly prosperous society dominated by the power of wealth, Christian teaching on poverty acted as a vehicle for moral not social reform. While the virtue of moderation and sobriety in dress and behaviour were staples of puritanical crusade preachers, the poverty they lauded was not necessarily, or even usually, that of Francis of Assisi or the Lincolnshire failed crusaders in the 1190s designated as *pauperissimi*.[106] Material poverty was not the issue; indeed in crusade recruitment it would have been self-defeating. As already discussed, Alan of Lille's crusade sermon designed for the Feast of the Exaltation of the Cross (14 September) emphasized how the spiritually poor received Christ's especial favour, the humble, not the economically destitute, citing Matthew's version of the Sermon on the Mount – 'blessed are the poor in spirit', '*beati pauperes spiritu*' (Matthew 5:3) – not the potentially more socially radical Luke 6:20 that omits the spirit or Luke 6:21 that blesses the hungry.[107] Crusade recruiters urged poverty of spirit on prosperous audiences, poverty movements being aimed at moral regeneration not social reform or the redistribution of wealth.

However, the preachers' sophistical appeal to the doctrine of Christian poverty could backfire, misconstrued as a literal elevation of the efficacy of the indigent over the propertied. If the poor were uniquely chosen as the vehicles of God's purpose, why were the only poor recruited for the crusades dependants of the wealthy? Where did that leave those poor excluded from the pale of active crusading? As the preserve of the rich, successive crusades had failed to receive God's complete favour. Perhaps the two were connected? With crusade promoters around 1200 increasingly employing crusading as a general model for Christian devotion, this tension became institutionalized in the system of partial donations and vow redemptions which privileged the well-to-do. If fighting for the Cross was the pinnacle of penitential devotion, recognized as such by the uniquely generous indulgence, the system of vow redemptions implied and imposed exclusion, a segregation compounded by the redemptions' monetization of commitment. The eruptions of popular impatience such as the Children's and Shepherds' crusades exposed the discrimination in crusade recruitment. The eruptions of 1212, 1251, 1309 and 1320 each constituted a response to heightened crusade awareness: the threat of heresy in France and Muslims in Palestine and Spain in 1212; the defeat of Louis IX in Egypt in 1250; the publicity for a Hospitaller crusade in 1309; and the prominent but abortive attempts in France to reignite a crusade to recover the Holy Land in 1320. Each followed extensive crusade propagandizing that created a perception of danger, a sense of duty and a collective fear deep in society which then fused with specific anxiety and anger at the failures of the traditional social elites. Exclusion, made easier by the near-universal use of sea travel for crusaders after 1190, exacerbated frustration which, ironically, was fuelled by the very authorities whose inadequacies had been exposed by events. Striking features of these popular demonstrations lay in their understanding of crusade evangelism and, certainly in 1251, 1309 and 1320, their direct if fleeting contacts with potential crusade planners. These crusade enthusiasts were not revolutionaries.[108] Neither were they those wanted by planners as active crusaders. Despite the rhetoric of poverty, in real life the poor do not inherit the earth; nor did the indigent go on crusade. The image of hordes of peasants spontaneously abandoning their fields in sporadic outbreaks of inchoate mass hysteria to travel to the furthest ends of the known world relying on nothing but God and charity is a myth.

santaceno₂ pplè ptituus
ram multi reliquenit. 6
de pplò ꞇ duntus ipà po

Finance

7

Costs of a Crusade

In one of his pamphlets encouraging urgency in preparations for the Third Crusade, Peter of Blois declared that 'often experience teaches that it is not money or a mass of armed troops or the virtue of warriors that gives victory to Christ's soldiers but the virtue of the virtuous Lord'.[1] Fortunately for crusade planners, such corrosive optimism in divine agency failed to distract them from paying serious attention to material practicalities. Central to these was finance. Odo of Châteauroux, veteran crusade preacher and legate, could talk of the transcendence of 'the pay (*stipendia*) of the Lord' for the 'stipendiary (*stipendiarius*) of God' in the knowledge that his audience would have the comparison with temporal wages before them.[2] One of the four prerequisites for a crusade to the Holy Land proposed by the Armenian Hetoum in 1307 was prior consideration of whether planners possessed adequate funds and other logistic necessities. Another early fourteenth-century theorist urged organizers to calculate whether any such expedition would be able to cover its costs. A third spent much time outlining a possible budget for a blockade of Egypt. The preaching guru Humbert of Romans blithely assumed not only that Christendom could readily support long-term wages for crusaders and fund more permanent garrisons in the Near East but, if need be, ecclesiastical resources alone would suffice for this 'perpetual project'.[3] These writers were not just reacting to recent failure. In 1148, the battered Louis VII of France remarked 'there is no way we can prosecute the business of Christ without many expenses and much labour'.[4]

BUDGETS

Explicit evidence of crusade budgets dates from the Third Crusade. However, earlier expeditions exhibited no less concern in estimates of cost. During the First Crusade, one crusader recalled, departing husbands assured their wives of their return within three years. Others recognized the value (and hence price) of pack-animals over horses and the importance of wagons, essential for carrying food, arms, equipment and treasure.[5] Although no army took all its materiel with it from the outset, relying on re-supplying and re-endowment en route, initial costs of wages and provisions required access to liquid capital in the form of precious metal, predominantly silver, in coins, ingots or plate. Peter the Hermit carried his treasure in a cart; Richard I distributed his aboard his commissioned fleet. Godfrey of Bouillon apparently minted a special issue of coins before embarking.[6] Images of cash-rich crusaders recur: William Longspee's saddle bags packed with silver in 1248; Otto of Grandson from Savoy setting out with as much as 20,500 gold florins in 1312; the £17 18s 10d in cash recovered from the bodies of a group of crusaders who had drowned when the bridge at Ferrybridge in Yorkshire collapsed in 1228.[7]

Understanding war expenditure was ingrained. Costs provided a running theme within narratives of crusading and dominate surviving archival records, the magnitude of expenses well appreciated. Even the letter sent to the west by the victorious commanders of the First Crusade in September 1099 included precise – if incredible – cash prices for sheep and cattle.[8] Provisioning, pay and markets feature prominently in veterans' accounts and memories: those of Raymond of Aguilers or the stories told to Albert of Aachen of the First Crusade; Odo of Deuil's and the author of the account of the capture of Lisbon on the Second Crusade; the descriptions of the Third Crusade by Roger of Howden, Ambroise and the writers collated in the *Historia de expeditione* of Frederick Barbarossa and the *Itinerarium Ricardi Regis*; the memoirs of the Fourth Crusade by Geoffrey of Villehardouin and Robert of Clari; James of Vitry's observations on the Fourth and Fifth Crusades; and John of Joinville's memories of Louis IX's first crusade. Requirements of payment and supplies resound through the charters and letters from the First and Second Crusades. They echo in the provisions for the Saladin Tithe of 1188; the German crusade planning in 1188–9, 1195 and 1227–8; the English Exchequer and other royal departmental records from the Third Crusade; Innocent III's plans for the Fourth and Fifth Crusades in 1199–1200 and 1213–16; the 1201 treaty of Venice; the instigation of taxes on Church revenues in 1199 and 1215; and the extension of crusade privileges to those who redeemed their vows after 1213. The debates over how to revivify crusading in the later thirteenth and early fourteenth centuries were laden with schemes of tax and spend, how best to raise and distribute the necessary money.[9]

Planners juggled with costs and how to cover or mitigate them. Louis VII initiated extensive diplomatic efforts in 1146 to establish prospects for transport and supplies, as did Henry II of England in 1188.[10] English preparations for the Third Crusade included hiring ships and men; laying in supplies (horseshoes, cured pigs' carcasses, cheese, beans, arrows and crossbow-bolts); and budgeting for future wages. Costs were discounted in advance. A yearly tariff was set of 2d a day for soldiers and sailors and 4d for steersmen in Richard I's fleet. By calculating future outlays, officials could provide the sums required for a year's wages. Thus £2,402 18s 4d were accounted for at the Exchequer in 1190 to cover the future cost of 790 soldiers to be transported in 33 ships from the Cinque Ports of Kent and Sussex. Elsewhere, the forward wages for forty-five ships' companies came to £3,338 2s 6d.[11] Richard was thus able to assess in advance, if only in very general terms, how much parts of his campaign would cost. While the English royal archives and administration may have been exceptional in bureaucratic detail, similar procedures necessarily informed most crusade preparations. Some sort of budget established Philip II's treaty with Genoa in 1190 to ship and supply his military household. In Germany in 1188–9, Frederick Barbarossa's officials calculated the minimum cost of two years' crusade expenses per person – three marks of silver. In 1195, Frederick's son, Henry VI, costed a force of 1,500 knights and 1,500 sergeants at respectively 30 ounces and 10 ounces of gold each for one year's service, as well as adequate grain rations for them and 3,000 *servientes* accompanying the knights, presumably to make bread or dry biscuits, a staple of travelling crusaders. During preparations for the Fourth Crusade, according to Robert of Clari, in 1201 Count Theobald of Champagne bequeathed 50,000 *livres* to pay for crusaders. Half of this was later given to the leadership of the crusade, enough for an army of some thousands.[12]

The infamous Treaty of Venice in 1201 was not randomly devised. Envoys sent by the crusade leadership carried a broad budget of numbers and costs sufficiently clear to deter the Pisans from bidding for the contract. The final deal struck with Venice was fatally precise even if based on guesswork and wishful thinking. The treaty stipulated that, in return for 85,000 marks payable in four instalments between August 1201 and April 1202, Venice would provide specialist transport vessels and large passenger ships for an army of 33,500, including 4,500 knights, 9,000 squires and 20,000 paid sergeants, along with provisions – water, wine, wheat, flour, fruit, vegetables, etc. – for the men and for 4,500 horses for up to a year. The costs were itemized at 4 marks per horse and 2 marks per man, sums comparable with previous contracts such as that between Philip II and Genoa in 1190. Individual crusaders seemed to be able to raise significant amounts to meet such costs; in one deal alone the bishop of Halberstadt received 550 marks, enough of itself to ship scores of knights and horses. Other arrangements involved many hundreds of *livres* at a time. Although the exaggerated optimism of the numbers agreed in the 1201 treaty proved a devastating encumbrance (leading to the diversion of the crusade to Constantinople), the actual sum raised – 51,000 marks – suggests that the Venetian deal foundered on inadequate muster not poverty.[13]

Later thirteenth-century crusades confirm the appetite for set tariffs and budgets. Louis VIII of France paid followers on his campaigns in Languedoc in 1226 and the rate for a knight serving against the Cathars in 1244 seems to have been set at the high level of 10 *sous tournois* a day. On his first crusade, Louis IX fixed rates for his knights at 7s 6d a day, less for mounted and infantry crossbowmen and sergeants. The knightly rate was roughly the same as John of Joinville was paying his knights (*c.*140 *l.* p.a. compared with Joinville's 120 *l.* p.a.).[14] The rates of pay for nobles were greater, perhaps 40s a day plus travel, and, as in the 1226 Albigensian war, compensation for loss of horses, with free board if required. This level of remuneration, according to the agreement reached in June 1249 between the count of Angoulême and Alphonse, count of Poitiers, the king's brother, was calculated 'on the basis that is paid to a noble of this status by our dearest lord the king and his brothers overseas'; in other words a standard rate.[15] The same system operated during recruitment for Louis IX's second crusade in 1270, when the viscount of Narbonne and his son provided the wages (*vadia*) for Bernard of Durban (near Auch) and two of his knights on the same terms as the king had provided for the viscount, his followers 'and other stipendiaries'.[16] The core contingent of the future Edward I of England on crusade in 1270–72 was contracted to serve for 100 marks each a year plus travel. In 1323 the French prince of the blood, Charles, count of Valois, offered crusaders 20s for a knight banneret; 10s for other knights; 7s 6d for squires and 2s for an infantryman; a decade later his son, Philip VI, followed suit, although he was marginally meaner to squires by offering only 5s. Although neither of the Valois actually embarked, King Philip's offers, at least, were accepted.[17]

PAID CRUSADERS

Every crusade, including the First, relied upon paid troops. Crusaders' board and wages represented a prime factor in fundraising before departure as well as in the search for further endowment during campaigns: the First Crusade in 1097 or Conrad III in 1148 at Constantinople; northern European fleets' repeated sallies en route east against the ports of Muslim Spain in 1147, 1189, 1190 and 1217; Frederick Barbarossa in Thrace and at Iconium in 1189–90; Richard I at Messina and in Cyprus in 1190–91; the Fourth Crusaders at Zara and Constantinople in 1202–4. Two instances from the First Crusade expose the importance of the ability to pay and be paid. Bohemund of Taranto threatened to withdraw from the army outside Antioch in 1098, so an admittedly hostile witness recorded, because he claimed he lacked adequate funds to provide for his followers, his *familia*. At the same time, further down the social ladder, Archdeacon Louis of Toul, probably in the train of Count Rainald of Toul, was forced by the lack of pay (*'defectione sui stipendii compulsus'*) to seek food away from the camp, losing his life when his foraging party fell into a Turkish ambush.[18] Lords' responsibility for pay is everywhere apparent during the First Crusade. Both Stephen of Blois and Godfrey of Bouillon passed on to their retinues the bullion and coin given them by the Greek emperor Alexius I at Constantinople in 1096–7.[19] Paying troops reinforced moral as well as material lordship. The near-contemporary legend of the heroic death of Anselm of Ribemont at Arqa in February 1099 showed the pious knight, on receiving a vision predicting his impending death, clearing his temporal as well as spiritual debts by confessing his sins, performing penance, receiving the Eucharist and finally, before returning to the frontline to meet his fate, paying 'the wages (*stipendia*) owed his servants and fellow soldiers'. The role of pay in the balance sheet of divine as well as military account could hardly be more obvious.[20]

No less prominent, throughout the First Crusade, was the extensive use of contracts for pay which revolved around estimated costs. Ralph of Caen's early twelfth-century biography of Tancred of Lecce showed him as perennially concerned with the needs of his paid followers, providing them with wages, equipment, horses and mules. He was described as taking out loans to cover the wage bill; accepting a contract of paid service with another commander, Raymond of Toulouse; and bartering seventy severed Turkish heads for 70 marks to pay off money (*pecuniam*) he owed his troops. Plunder, such as the 7,000 marks' worth of silver he allegedly stripped off the Dome of the Rock, was channelled to arming his own knights and recruiting more. The size of Tancred's retinue varied from a few dozen to eighty to a hundred men, depending on his own wealth or the higher patronage he had managed to wangle. Lords expected to pay their household troops and to use cash incentives to attract others.[21]

The armies of the First Crusade operated as marketplaces for fighting men as well as for equipment, provisions, relics and prostitutes. Chroniclers recorded special payments to reward or attract followers and for specific services, such as the 15 *livres* demanded by the entrepreneurial Lombard siege engineer at Nicaea in 1097.[22] Tancred was promised 400 marks to pay his men for garrison duties at the siege of Antioch in 1098. Raymond of Toulouse expected to offer wages to those manning a siege tower at Antioch or filling the ditch before the walls of Jerusalem. Crusaders were paid on retainer, for example the members of Raymond Pilet's raiding party towards Aleppo in the summer of 1098; or the knights who accompanied Baldwin of Boulogne to Edessa. Recognizing the structural imperatives of the expedition, the high command issued an open offer of paid employment – in cash – to leaderless troops after the capture of Antioch in June 1098.[23] Individual settlements were unlikely to have been arbitrary any more than Raymond of Toulouse's offer to hire his fellow commanders for huge cash sums in January 1099. Such arrangements sat easily in the commerce of warfare familiar alike in southern France, Norman Italy, Normandy and the German empire. Of the leading commanders, Hugh of Vermandois, Godfrey of Bouillon and Robert of Flanders each had experience of being hired by even grander lords to fight or provide paid troops.[24] Such deals transcended campaign expedients. A lord or knight travelled with his *familia*, clients and dependants who expected the rewards of service and companionship, board and pay from the outset. One contemporary commentator noted that the first crusaders embarked only if supported by funds (*'stipendiorum facultas'*). Another described how Bohemund lavishly subsidized his followers.[25] These paymasters' requirements were further signalled by a ubiquitous concern for coin and plate.

Chains of payment continued to bind the great and the least alike, lord, knight, sergeant, servant, infantryman, merchant, artisan, priest, laundress and whore. On the Second Crusade, Louis VII of France was burdened not only with the cost of his own household and retinue, but also the demands of those, nobles included, who ran out of their own supply of cash. It was as much his inability to extend payment to the infantry as the absence of adequate shipping that forced Louis to abandon most of them at Adalia on the southern coast of Asia Minor in March 1148. Summing up the debacle, Louis's chaplain pointedly remarked that 'a king should not only be pious but also without any fear of poverty', a moral remark crafted in material observation.[26] Louis's need for ready money for daily necessities, as he described it to his regent in France, Abbot Suger of St Denis, suffused his letters home. Like Tancred of Lecce on the First Crusade, Louis was forced to borrow from fellow crusaders, in his case Bishop Arnulf of Lisieux. Once in the Holy Land, he also took out substantial loans from the resident military orders, the Templars and Hospitallers.[27] Yet Louis had been far from improvident, extracting levies on churches and probably a tax on royal lands before departure.[28] He and his advisers knew that extraordinary sums of money were needed, even if the actual amounts possibly dwarfed expectations. Cash similarly dominated the German armies. Like the First Crusade, the German march across Asia Minor left a trail of coins, some deposited in hoards. When he arrived at Acre in the spring of 1148, Conrad III assembled what he called a 'new army' with, a companion recalled, 'a lavish expenditure of money'.[29] Money, retaining troops and fighting for pay similarly provided a running theme in the description of the crusaders' attack on Lisbon in 1147.[30] Payment was an assumed feature of the enterprise and did not of itself contradict fighting for faith. The simultaneous development of crusade privileges acknowledged the crucial role of money in allowing *crucesignati* freer access to cash funds (through sales, mortgages, loans, etc.): Mammon in the service of God.

With the Third Crusade, the use of stipendiary crusaders, the provision of supplies and materiel, the deployment of subsidized or hired fleets and the scale of costs come into clearer focus. Expanding bureaucracies of written record-keeping apparent across western Europe may have helped planning become more informed now that copies of commonplace written communications by rulers, traders and property owners began to be kept more systematically. As has been seen, English official records allow for the first time direct, if incomplete, access to the range of material and financial preparations. Much even here is left unknown: the total expenditure of Richard I's crusade, let alone the full costs to his followers; a reliable total for income from the Saladin Tithe; details of the construction of the prefabricated castle Richard took from Messina to Acre or of the numerous trebuchets carried to the Holy Land by French and English nobles. While it is possible from chroniclers' remarks and comparative non-crusading accounts to reconstruct a rough budget for the German crusade, no administrative documents on the matter survive, if any existed. The French crusade may have stimulated a subsequent archival transformation in royal government, but left few administrative documents of its own, although what survives confirms the burden of fundraising.

While observers noted the especially lavish financial provision made by the English king, all crusade leaders faced similar demands and exploited the opportunities wealth afforded. Philip II strengthened his hold over largely independent nobles and their disparate contingents on campaign by providing them with hefty subsidies in Sicily.[31] In his targeted largesse, Richard I was characteristically extravagant or astute, depending on how his personality and abilities are assessed. On top of paying for his own army of perhaps 2,500 to 3,000, he helped fit out a fleet of possibly around 100 ships potentially carrying another 8,000 men. He retained more troops at Marseilles, outbid Philip II in hiring knights at Acre and later brought all the archers there into his paid service.[32] Inevitably, his entourage was (and expected to be) paid; Gerald of Wales certainly did, before he slid out of his commitment.[33] Lesser magnates faced the same requirements. Archbishop Baldwin of Canterbury led a paid force of 200 knights and 300 sergeants under the distinctive banner of Thomas Becket.[34] Paid troops satisfied the logic of command and the structures of power without escaping potentially corrosive financial constraints.

Famously, nowhere did these constraints play a larger role than in the course of the Fourth Crusade and the diversion of the main army to Zara and Constantinople in 1202–3. Coming after a decade and a half during which funding of paid crusaders had become a central planning issue, the new crusade after 1198 built on the experiences of the Third Crusade and Henry VI of Germany's crusade scheme of 1195. Preliminary arrangements unambiguously recognized the requirement of large-scale, organized and, to a degree, centralized financial planning. Innocent III floated the idea of a Church tax to pay crusaders. A lay and ecclesiastical tax of a fortieth was suggested by the kings of England and France in 1201. Fulk of Neuilly's preaching was combined with raising money for soldiers. The need for and demands of paid troops dictated Theobald of Champagne's legacy and its division as well as the provisions for 20,000 sergeants in the Treaty of Venice. Baldwin of Flanders imitated Richard I in sending troops and provisions in his own ships in the summer of 1202. To cover costs he tried to tax his subjects, with their lords' permission. The precise use of funds is suggested by the arrangements of Hilduin of Villemoyenne, in Champagne, who raised at least 280 *livres* from property transactions, 200 of which came in the form of 48,000 pennies, convenient to pay for supplies and wages.[35]

The Fifth Crusade witnessed the start of a revolution in crusade finance driven by the need of pay: redemption of vows for cash from 1213; regular Church taxation from 1215; plus the development of a more regularized system of gifts, legacies, donations and ceremonial and pastoral fundraising opportunities, such as frequent preaching tours, processions and special church liturgies and services. National or seigneurial lay taxation for crusades was politically more contentious, but became a formally accepted obligation of faith or allegiance, akin to levies for a lord's ransom, the knighting of an heir or the marriage of an eldest daughter. In step with such expanded revenue gathering, crusade commanders perfected contracts of paid service and methods to channel donations and Church taxes towards supporting lay crusaders.[36] Crusade finance became big business for Church and state alike, dominating practical discussions of defending or recovering the Holy Land in the century following Louis IX's definitive Egyptian defeat in 1250. In the crush of literary and expert advice, financial issues could be treated in very general terms, as by the Armenian Hetoum or Humbert of Romans, almost as if the will to crusade alone would somehow conjure up the necessary resources. Yet there emerged the almost universal understanding that only professional navies and armies would prove effective if new bridgeheads on the mainland of the Levant were to be secured. Experience of the previous two centuries counted for something, a pragmatic by-product of the obsessive historicism of crusade debates and rhetoric. A mass crusade on the model of the first three major eastern expeditions tended to be deprecated as too unwieldy, costly and amateur.[37] The Venetian Marino Sanudo Torsello (d.1343) typified contemporary opinion. Combining his practical proposals with an exhaustive account of crusade history, Sanudo argued at length for a professional naval blockade of Egypt followed by a similarly organized preliminary land invasion (known as a *passagium particulare*) that explicitly excluded independent, volunteer *crucesignati*, even though such come-as-you-please expeditions had relied on organized, waged crusaders.[38] The myth of spontaneity was hard to erase, but increasingly discounted.

ACCOUNTS

Sanudo, unlike some fellow crusade propagandists and theorists, displayed an acute and detailed awareness of costs. However, the accounting mentality was far from the exclusive preserve of armchair pundits or Italian merchants. It pervaded the warrior elites of western Europe. Payment of knights, household officials and servants as well as estate management required accounts, some of which demanded physical record in the form of tally sticks, parchment rolls, charters or land-surveys. Armies, like estates or governments, ran on networks of mundane instructions, commands and requests. Extrapolating from early thirteenth-century formulary collections (i.e. models or forms of letters used to teach letter writing and account keeping), it is clear that some, perhaps many, administrative communications were customarily in writing, and probably had been for generations.[39] Bohemund's written contracts and accounts at Antioch in 1098 were cases in point.[40] Crusade financial records, although not surviving independently until the Third Crusade, stalk the extant chronicles and documentary evidence from the 1090s. Mainly dealing with transient expenses, such as contracts, audits or tax demands, unless they were of future use financial accounts were rarely kept or cherished except by corporations or regimes needing long reach and longer memory. Yet the extending prevalence of payment required their use. In 1099, Tancred broke with his allegiance to Raymond of Toulouse because he claimed the latter had reneged on his 'contract of shillings and bezants', of which some record existed; Raymond's chaplain preserved its details.[41]

That a clerk in the count of Toulouse's entourage recorded such arrangements further shows how, as already noted, the lords and knights of the First Crusade inhabited a world of functional as well as academic literacy and numeracy.[42] Bohemund was raised in the literate culture of southern Italy. Robert of Normandy had enjoyed a high-powered academic training as a youth and later composed poetry. Knights dictated letters or collaborated in compiling chronicles.[43] Each lived in households that employed literacy in business, administration, worship and entertainment. Crusading too was a written enterprise. As already noted, the seeming ubiquity of lesser clergy on crusade may be explained by the need for clerks as well as priests, to keep accounts, copy contracts, write letters or collect material to be spun into acceptable literary narratives, figures such as Raymond of Aguilers or Fulcher of Chartres on the First Crusade; Odo of Deuil on the Second; Roger of Howden on the Third; Oliver of Paderborn on the Fifth; Peter of les Vaux de Cernay in Languedoc; or Henry of Livonia in the north-east Baltic. Some may have been hired, like Gerald of Wales, as campaign chroniclers.[44] Most shared an interest in finance and accounting. Literacy acted not merely as an adornment of a noble life but as an essential to its success. Effective administration of property, no less than war, required knowledge, intellect, practical learning and experience. From housekeeping to raising troops, basic numeracy was assumed and necessary for paymaster and payee alike. Literacy and numeracy combined in estate surveys, tax assessments, even military summonses sent in writing. Even if not an active participant in compiling accounts, any property owner wholly ignorant or indifferent of the process risked fraud and impoverishment. The image of a ruler shut up with his financial officials was familiar from twelfth-century literature and twelfth-century fact.[45] The powerful Anglo-Norman magnate Robert of Meulan, father, grandfather and great-grandfather of crusaders, possessed his own exchequer; one of his sons, Robert, earl of Leicester, became justiciar of England, heading a very literate royal administration. One of his sucessors, Ranulf Glanvill, son of a veteran of the Second Crusade, went on the Third Crusade.[46] Even the literary Geoffrey of Villehardouin and Robert of Clari displayed keen understanding of money and finance. Writing, reading, listening and dictating permeated knightly culture; so did keeping accounts.

Details of household finance, obligations and rewards survive from secular as well as ecclesiastical households from the mid-twelfth century.[47] The English litigant Richard of Anstey compiled meticulous detailed accounts of his costs trying to extract judgment from Henry II between 1158 and 1163, recording a huge total sum of £344 6s 4d, itself tribute to the extensive varieties of credit available in the mid-twelfth century.[48] In the eleventh century and beyond, behind any grant of land, rents or fiscal demand lay accounts of estate renders and income, from Catalonia to England.[49] The same was true of crusading. Crusaders' charters precisely identified property and income to be transferred, this aspect of the knightly life as much part of their culture as religious observance or spiritual anxiety. Experience of legal procedures, increasingly involving writing, and claims to land, rights or obligations enveloped the propertied – from princes to free peasants – in a culture of accounting. So, too, did the obsessive and iconic aristocratic indulgence in tournaments. By the 1170s and 1180s detailed lists of participants were being compiled, some of which were preserved for decades. More immediate to the tournaments and the knights themselves, written accounts (*acontes*) of winnings were recorded by household clerks, and also archived for future reference. In both cases, practical accountancy and chivalric memorialization served each other's purpose: profit and fame. By the early thirteenth century, Gerald of Wales was comparing European nations according to their rulers' incomes.[50] Over a century earlier, the world of the First Crusade was that of payments to knights and fundraising; the world of the English king's contracts to retain for pay the service and soldiers of Hugh of Vermandois and Robert of Flanders in the 1080s and 1090s; the world of the accounting abacus of the English Exchequer; the world of Domesday Book. Bohemund's *compotus* at Antioch spoke not of an eccentric exception but of a pervasive mentality of calculation.

Thus, the financial records of the Third Crusade operated in a wider tradition of written recording. To make sure *crucesignati* were held to their vows or were able to enjoy their privileges, as well as to aid military planning, preachers kept lists of those who had taken the Cross. Agents of secular rulers equally required such information in order to assess tax liability or exemptions, as for the Saladin Tithe or other taxation. The papacy and its legates retained careful records of recruits and money, a requirement of tax collection, the offer of vow redemptions for cash and solicited donations. Innocent III made this plain in his provisions for the Fourth and Fifth Crusades. As already noted, the figures contained in the Treaty of Venice, Frederick Barbarossa's estimate of a crusader's costs or his son's 1195 offer to his knights were not random guesswork, any more than John of Joinville's wages bill or the calculations of a Bavarian knight who, in 1147, collected funds 'to maintain knights serving God'.[51] Richard I's accounts for his fleet survive in part. There is no reason to suppose that Baldwin IX of Flanders' investment in the 1202 Flemish fleet or, on less lavish scales, those in the 1140s or 1190s by citizens of Cologne, London, Bristol, Boulogne, Southampton and Ipswich, or in Genoa, Pisa and Venice from the 1090s were any less rationally considered. Shipping costs determined the prosperity of maritime and riparian commercial cities. The prospect of free sea transport, if actually made, constituted the most attractive and generous element in Roger II of Sicily's offer to Louis VII in 1146.[52] For landlubbers, wage bills were not arbitrary. Even if quartermasters of the eleventh and twelfth centuries did not carry around with them written ledgers of the sort Ramon Muntaner used when running the mercenary Catalan Company in Greece in the early fourteenth century, and there is nothing to suggest they did not, budgets and balance sheets were clearly employed, if only to record debts.[53] Louis VII was able to repay his crusade loans in detail. Either he or his creditors, the Templars, kept account, as they were to do for Louis's successors on a more general basis. The royal instructions to those charged with securing these repayments, laymen included, were presumably based on some sort of invoices.

COSTS

Budgets and accounts exposed the scale of costs. Crusading to the eastern Mediterranean got more expensive in real terms in the centuries after the 1090s. Yet it was obvious from the beginning that the initial capital outlays dwarfed usual, local military expenses and were potentially prohibitive without subsidy or clever management of converting fixed assets into cash. The more detailed and sophisticated the budgets, the more apparent became the financial challenge. However, rather than the budget determining action, policy dictated costs: 'how much?' rather than 'can I afford it?' This is a common feature of warfare. To supporters, crusades were not optional. They were seen as necessary protection of Christendom's vital temporal and transcendent interests, to be paid for however high the price. This could be spectacular. Louis IX's crusade cost upwards of 1,537,570 *livres tournois* between 1247 and 1257, or perhaps five times annual royal revenues.[54] Marino Sanudo's credible estimates in the 1320s of the cost of a preliminary crusade of 900 cavalry and 15,000 infantry for three years to secure the coast of Egypt came to well over two million florins, or about ten times annual papal income. Sanudo further suggested that a subsequent general crusade to conquer Egypt would take two years and cost five million florins. A French scheme of 1323 was carefully costed by the French government: 26 ships, 4,800 crew and 3,000 crossbowmen at a cost of 300,000 *livres parisis*. The ordinary annual income of the French king between 1322 and 1325 varied from 213,000 to 242,000 *l.p.*; with clerical taxes, loans, fines, profits from currency manipulation, etc., his total annual receipts in these years came to between 477,000 and 610,000 *l.p.*[55] The accounts of Louis IX's first crusade survive because they were copied in the royal archives by officials under Philip VI when he was proposing a crusade in the 1330s. They showed Philip he could not afford a crusade without massive subsidy from the Church, which his great-grandfather Louis had enjoyed. Louis's total expenses of the equivalent of over 1 million *livres parisis* (1.5 million *livres tournois*), coupled with detailed accounts of 1250–53 of between 600,000 and 700,000 *l.p.* (1,053, 476 *l.t.*), sat uncomfortably with Philip's total annual receipts in the 1330s, even ignoring currency depreciation and devaluation in the interim decades.[56]

The burden of investment obviously depended on the number of followers being supported. The artisan crusaders on the *St Victor* stranded at Messina in 1250 who paid for themselves or, at most, very small retinues, would have been faced with basic charges for transport, food and water that might have equated to a third of the annual income of a smart tailor or a month's income of a celebrity chef.[57] For leaders of more substantial retinues, costs could reach multiples of disposable annual revenues, added incentive to seek even grander paymasters.[58] Capital costs were considerable: armour, weapons, mules, horses, harness, horseshoes and domestic utensils, as well as cash, in coin, ingots or plate. However, equipment was more within the financial compass of ordinary members of the military or even artisan classes than open-ended provision for food and wages. Even though the rich in the Middle Ages could be spectacularly wealthy, especially in comparison with the rest of society, crusade expenses could appear gargantuan. Yet, to perhaps a surprisingly large extent, they were covered.

The financial cost of the First Crusade is incalculable. It has been estimated that a knight might have required 144 silver shillings a year; a non-combatant perhaps around 18 shillings. So even a modest retinue, such as Tancred of Lecce's that hovered between 40 and 100 knights, might have cost anything between 300 and 700 pounds a year, hundreds of times an ordinary knight's landed or waged income.[59] If, as is likely, there were some thousands of knights and many thousands of others – one recent informed guess proposed c.7,000 nobles and knights and c.20,000 support troops – the costs can be imagined rather than computed.[60] These figures are highly speculative, useful only as an indication of the scale of expense. Another recent estimate suggests that Godfrey of Bouillon, from a variety of sources, could have raised 1,875 pounds in cash. Robert of Normandy raised the equivalent of £6,600 sterling from pledging his duchy in 1096. Yet these leaders required further regular windfalls en route, from Byzantine largesse, booty, plunder, tribute or protection money. In January 1099, Raymond of Toulouse offered Godfrey and Robert of Normandy 10,000 shillings each, i.e. 500 pounds, perhaps reflecting retinues of about 100 knights. Although substantial, such sums point to short-term contracts only, to cover the final march to Jerusalem.[61] Much more impressive, if Raymond's chaplain can be credited, were the 15,000 gold pieces (apparently at a conversion rate of one gold piece to eight or nine shillings) and the 5,000 gold pieces provided by the emirs of Tripoli and Jabala respectively to buy the crusaders off a few weeks later, amounting on the chronicler's figures to 8–9,000 pounds.[62] If any of these figures are remotely accurate, the total bill for just the first year for a force of tens of thousands easily dwarfed the combined royal revenues of the kings of the regions from which the crusaders were chiefly drawn. Even given that funding was a joint enterprise, spread across half a continent and shared between separate leaders, lords and men, freelancers and others, these are daunting sums, anticipated or not.

Cost helped fatally undermine the prospects for the Second Crusade. In debt himself, as the campaign progressed Louis VII was forced to bail out his leading followers as well as pay for his own troops. He had prepared for heavy expenses, his fiscal expedients including taxes, loans and extortion. Evidence survives for loans of perhaps as much as 7,500–10,000 *livres tournois*, at a time when ordinary revenues from the royal demesne ran at perhaps no more than 20,000 *l.t.*[63] From his begging letters to his regents at home, Louis's shortage of ready cash was apparent even by the time his army reached Hungary, only a few weeks into the march east.[64] It was to get worse. Witnesses' memories confirm that the plight of followers matched that of the leaders. The absence of Byzantine subsidies comparable to those offered in 1096 further stretched the crusaders' resources regardless of the free access granted to Greek markets. Military failures in Asia Minor prevented the seizure of booty and plunder. Although each contingent of the Franco-German forces carried stores of coin and precious metal, the increasing shortage of funds led to the division and dismemberment of the French army at Adalia in March 1148. The financial woes of the Second Crusade may have taken a secondary place to moral invectives in the laments over the expedition's dismal failure in Syria and Palestine, yet they were not forgotten by crusade planners. From the 1160s onwards, any scheme for campaigns in the eastern Mediterranean by western rulers would be prefaced by proposals for taxation, as in 1166 and 1185 and, most famously, with the Saladin Tithe in 1188. The inability to cover costs during the Second Crusade bequeathed a lasting legacy. Failure bred realism.

The Third Crusade confirmed the scale of expense. The records of English royal administration suggest the main costs were in wages. On figures derived from Exchequer accounts for the English fleet of 1190, these could comprise as much as two-thirds the total, although this includes payment for crew which a land-based army, such as the German one of 1188–9, would have avoided. Again precise figures remain speculative, although not to those doing the calculations in

1190. On a reasoned estimate of the size of Richard I's fleet of just over 100 vessels, annual wages might have reached c.£8,700, with ship-hire costing a further £5,700 – wages therefore reaching 60 per cent of the total £14,400, in line with a two-thirds ratio.[65] While many proppertied *crucesignati* paid for themselves, such as the Londoners who commissioned their own vessel to carry eighty well-equipped troops, the crown provided many others with the means of transport; the king even donated a ship to the Hospitallers, hardly among the destitute or dependent of his realm.[66] Wages and ship-hire constituted only part of the cost. Richard's ships, as well as crew and soldiers, like those of Baldwin of Flanders in 1202, carried military equipment – arms, armour, clothing, etc. – and food. One commentator alleged horses were shipped as well, despite the long passage around Iberia to the Mediterranean.[67]

The Exchequer accounts also show heavy royal investment in horse-shoes (almost £50 for at least 60,000 in 1190), arrows, crossbow-bolts, cheeses from Essex (£31 5s), beans from Cambridgeshire, Gloucester-shire and Hampshire (£15 4s 8d), and over 14,000 cured pigs' carcasses from Lincolnshire, Essex and Hampshire (£101 7s 11d). (A labourer at the time might earn 1d a day, and a very comfortable annual income for a knight might be between £10 and £20.) The sheriff of Hamp-shire's expenses for crusade provisions in 1190 display the range of necessary preparations: almost £58 for bacon, 20 shillings for beans; just over £14 for 10,000 horseshoes; just under £20 for a hundred-weight of cheese; over £25 towards eight ships; and £12 2s 1d for cartage and storage of supplies and treasure.[68] Food and money were currencies of patronage too. At Acre in 1191 Richard apparently gained the allegiance of the count of Champagne with 4,000 meas-ures of wheat, 4,000 sides of bacon and £4,000 of silver, a deal paralleled by the gold and grain contracts offered by Henry VI to his crusading retinue in 1195.[69] To the costs of Richard's 1190 fleet, pos-sibly upwards of £14,000, had to be added those of Richard's own force which he led overland through France to the Mediterranean – perhaps as many as 3,000 strong. Moreover, these sums only covered the initial outlay and expenses for no more (and in many instances probably considerably less) than the first year of service. To put this expenditure in context, ordinary royal revenues accounted at the

Exchequer between 1187 and 1190 hovered around £25,000. This excluded additional levies on Jews, crusade taxes, fines or other extra-ordinary receipts, but also discounted extraordinary expenses such as the 24,000 marks possibly paid as a relief or entry fine to Philip II of France for Richard's French lands.[70] Effectively, just the initial outlay and projected costs for the first year of the king's crusade consumed the equivalent of a year's worth of actual ordinary royal income.

Although details of French royal finances are vestigial by compari-son, Philip II's expenses were of the same order. He paid the Genoese 5,850 marks to ship 650 knights and 1,300 squires and their horses, with food for eight months and wine for four (presumably it went off after that). If a knight cost twice as much as a squire, this would work out at 4½ marks per knight, or the equivalent of a modest annual income. However, for the crown, the cost may have been anything but modest. The Genoese deal may have represented as much as 60 per cent of the crown's ordinary income. Add to this Philip's spending spree in Sicily to bail out some of his leading magnates which, according to a well-informed royal eulogist, amounted to 2,800 marks (c.5,600 *livres parisis*) plus 400 gold ounces, a combined sum equivalent to perhaps a quarter of ordinary royal revenue.[71] Small wonder Philip had been eager to extract a share of Sicilian debts owed to Richard; he got a third of the 40,000 gold ounces handed over. Of course, the French and English kings were better off than many of their followers. They enjoyed access to large quantities of cash beyond ordinary income from their estates; they were committing at most only one as opposed to many years' income and employed officials experienced in financial administration. The kings adopted leading roles in subsidiz-ing all aspects and every level of participant. Crusading had always been a rich man's adventure. Only the resources of the richest could hope to sustain such long-distance military and naval enterprises.

The lessons of the twelfth century encouraged the financial expedients of the thirteenth. Levels of expenditure continued to rise, a conse-quence of inflation and the near-universal use of sea-transport. Of the major thirteenth-century crusade commanders, only King Andrew of Hungary chanced the roads and hostility of Asia Minor, and then only on his return journey from a brief stay at Acre in the winter of 1217/18.[72] The dominance of naval travel reduced the number of unsought non-combatants while at the same time adding to immediate costs. On shore, an army could forage and even re-endow itself, almost pay for itself as it went. By sea, shippers required pre-payment and provisions had to be secured before departure. The compensation for organizers was the time and hence overall expenses saved. The twelfth-century trend towards higher costs and greater dependence on central command was thus accelerated. Henry VI of Germany's paid retinue of 500 knights and 500 sergeants planned in 1195 was costed at 2,000 gold ounces. In 1201, the extremely wealthy count of Champagne set aside in his will the huge sum of 50,000 *livres* to pay crusaders, and, as already seen, the Treaty of Venice envisaged a cost of 85,000 marks, perhaps 170,000 *livres parisis,* equivalent to well over the then annual revenues of the French king, and about twice as much as Philip II had available in 1202 for his war with King John of England.[73] Even though they defaulted on the total amount, the crusaders did raise over 50,000 marks, a sign that they had individually equipped themselves with adequate funds – the problem was there were too few of them. In retrospect, the failure of Innocent III's proposed Church tax of 1199 proved crucial.

Costs also fell on the shippers. It has recently been calculated that, to carry the crusade host in 1201, Venice was committed to supply perhaps over 200 ships of various sorts – war galleys, horse transports and sailing troop- and cargo-carriers – crewed by over 30,000 men. On top of that, the city promised to provide a fleet of 50 galleys of its own, crewed by perhaps as many as 7,600.[74] According to Robert of Clari, a form of conscription by lots had to be introduced to compel sufficient Venetian recruitment. Additionally, in order to construct such an armada, all other commerce was suspended. Venice's capital investment was therefore considerable.[75] While the 1201 treaty may have been the highest value single shipping deal, the same constraints and problems attended all such arrangements from the Mediterranean to the North Sea. As with many commercial transactions, benefits and risks were mutual. Venice found itself massively out of pocket when the crusaders failed to honour their bargain. This could cut both ways. Shippers were liable to complaints, even litigation, if they reneged on their obligations, as the owners of the *St Victor* in 1250 discovered to their cost when sued by disgruntled crusading passengers at Messina.[76]

One solution to the added premium on sea travel was provided by the ecclesiastical tax agreed at the Fourth Lateran Council in 1215, which supported recruitment and the lengthy amphibious campaigns in Egypt between 1217 and 1221. Again, figures were impressive. One account of money spent recruiting knights just in one region of northern Italy came to 7,730 marks. Papal accounts of income and expenditure of 1220 recorded crusade expenses of more than 775,461 marks (or perhaps over one and a half million *livres parisis*).[77] The expectation of expense became settled opinion. Philip II of France's will of 1221 bequeathed 300,000 *livres parisis* for the crusade. In 1223 Frederick II promised – fancifully perhaps – that he would deposit 100,000 gold ounces (perhaps worth two and a half million *livres*) for the crusade with bankers at Acre to guarantee his planned crusade.[78]

Such huge reported sums can be tested against the fullest surviving records of thirteenth-century crusade expenses, those for Louis IX's crusade of 1248–54, preserved as part of a budgeting process in the 1330s. As already noted, Louis's expenses between 1247 and 1257 were recorded as 1,538,570 *livres tournois*, about five times the customary royal revenue of the period. Wages comprised a major item. From a more detailed account of Louis IX's costs in maintaining himself in the Holy Land between 1250 and 1253, 23 per cent went on wages for knights alone: 243,128*l.* 4*s.* out of a total spent of 1,053,476*l.* 17*s.* 3*d.* While shipping costs in this period were only 32,000 *livres*, the previous costs of transporting the crusaders – perhaps numbering 15,000 in all – were far greater. The cost of hiring dozens of vessels from Marseilles, Aigues Mortes and Genoa probably ran into hundreds of thousands of *livres*. The largest ships cost Louis 7,000 *l.t.* each. Even before embarkation, food for the crews came to nearly 2,000 *l.t.* and one bill for additional naval equipment (canvas, rope, spars, rudders, etc.) reached around 4,500 *l.t.* (5,926 *livres viennois*). One year's provision of food (1251–2) cost 31,595 *livres tournois*. Modern estimates of Louis's daily expenses on his army vary from 700,000 to 2 million *livres* for two years; one calculation suggests a mean daily cost of 1,000 *livres*.[79] Similar charges fell on lesser lords and knights. During less than one year, 1250, Louis's brother Alphonse of Poitiers spent more than 6,000 *livres* on ships and sailors' wages, not counting pay for his contracted troops. In the event, like Joinville, Alphonse needed bailing out by the king who, by the time the crusade landed in Egypt, may have been subsidizing most of the contingents in his host.[80] Although possibly exceptional in extent, Louis's largesse was far from novel, following a long tradition: Raymond of Toulouse in 1099; Conrad III at Acre in 1148; Richard I at Acre in 1191; Cardinal Pelagius at Damietta in 1219–21.

Twenty years later, Louis's financial clout was even more persuasive. For his second crusade, in 1269, he loaned Edward of England and Gaston of Béarn 70,000 *livres* to hire knights at a rate, in Edward's case, of 200 *livres* or 100 marks each. Ships were commissioned, a fleet of forty new vessels costing perhaps as much as 280,000 *livres*.[81] Again the totals spiral, with wages (of troops and crewmen) accounting for the bulk of running costs on top of the capital expense of shipping, which itself included, as had the 1201 Treaty of Venice, an element of sailors' pay. While overall figures are absent for the 1270 crusade, the sums raised in England and France to cover costs suggest the usual high expenses, especially in the now clearly regulated system of contracted soldiery. Paid crusaders have often been regarded as a feature of the more professional, centrally directed recruitment of the thirteenth century or as adjuncts to armies acquired once they had reached the eastern Mediterranean. Yet, being a 'stipendiary in the army of God', as William of Newburgh drily described Leopold V of Austria, was probably the case for the majority of fighting crusaders on campaign from the outset.[82] Whether in Europe, Africa or the Levant, that was how all Christendom's wars were conducted (the Latin word *conduco* in its medieval sense could mean 'I hire').

This was the world from which Marino Sanudo derived his estimates. However, despite their scale it should be noted that the costs of Louis IX's crusades and Edward of England's expenses were largely covered by a variety of fundraising expedients. The biggest spenders appeared to be the most immune from long-term financial damage. The Second Crusade did not bankrupt Louis VII, neither did the Third wreck the acquisitive potential of Philip II or Richard I's ability to raise a ransom or fight a five-year war in France. This capacity to absorb crusade costs was not restricted to kings or popes. The resources of Peter des Roches, bishop of Winchester, were hardly stretched by his crusade expenditure in the 1220s.[83] Of course, Winchester was one of the richest dioceses in western Christendom and des Roches an experienced and effective administrator, so perhaps his case was exceptional. Nonetheless, especially as institutional ways of subsidizing crusaders increased in scope and value, it is hard to find many great lords made destitute after a crusade, however much of a strain finding the capital had been beforehand. Many appeared wealthy enough afterwards to lavishly memorialize their deeds.

One obvious reason for this is that many crusaders were habituated to war, their normal revenues usually directed to pursuing it. The calculation that Philip II in 1202–3 could have drawn on a war chest of some 90,000 *livres parisis* for his confrontation with King John of England puts the count of Champagne's legacy of 50,000 *livres* and the Treaty of Venice's stipulation for 85,000 marks (or c.170,000 *livres parisis*) into perspective.[84] Despite his notorious spending on the crusade in 1189–90, much of Richard I's ransom in 1194 of £100,000 was met; the king was still thereafter able to tax his realm and even pay £11,000 (or c.30,000 *livres parisis*) on building one castle, Château Gaillard.[85] A century later, the costs of Edward I's crusade paled into insignificance compared with the huge sums spent on conquering and subduing Wales, fighting the Scots or defending Gascony.[86] French kings also had many other wars to fight or plan. French knights in the mid-thirteenth century, on crusade or not, earned c.160–200 *livres tournois* a year, slightly more than Louis's crusade daily rate of 7s. 6d., although this excluded food, horses, etc., which would have made the total reward much the same.[87] In sum and in detail crusading should not be seen as operating outside its leaders' and participants' military or financial experience or assumptions. A French scheme to invade England drawn up in 1295 envisaged a fleet of about 50 ships carrying a force of about 10,000 at a monthly cost, in wages and food, of 11,900 *livres tournois*, or, for a year, almost 143,000 *l.t.* Two centuries earlier, William of Normandy successfully invaded England in 1066 with possibly a similarly large force at, contemporaries agreed, huge cost.[88] The heavy expenses of war were not unique to crusading. They were what royal, lordly or knightly income was for.

8

Paying For a Crusade

There were six basic ways of paying for a crusade open to an individual: sale of assets; mortgage (pledged property acting as security for a loan that involved payment of interest) or, more common, vifgage (where the income from the pledged property covers the gift or loan advanced), both frequently masquerading as mutual gifts; credit via simple loans; receiving money for domestic or commercial services performed during the crusade (e.g. blacksmithing); employment by another crusader; or subsidy from some common pool of crusade funds, such as redemption money or Church taxes. Given the limits of coin in circulation, very few possessed enough ready cash without resort to one or a combination of these expedients. Arranging and co-ordinating them required ingenuity, skill, patience and luck. Additionally, for knights, lords, princes or kings, exploitation of rights over people as well as property, over tenants or subjects, offered a further source of income. As already seen, the privileges granted by the Church, and largely recognized by secular authorities, provided a *crucesignatus* with a special financial status within a framework of ecclesiastical and legal protection.

PAYING WITH PRIVILEGES

As developed by the 1140s, special ecclesiastically sanctioned privileges protected a crusader's property from civil litigation (important if the property was being offered as security for loans); immunity from repayment of past interest and current credit on debts; and freedom to raise money by pledging possessions, even those held in tenancy to the Church, clerics or other Christians, with relatives or lords merely having to be informed, not give their permission.[1] As a further incentive, by the end of the twelfth century *crucesignati* enjoyed certain tax exemptions, a very successful lure to joining up when the Saladin Tithe was being collected. In England immunity from secular taxation was upheld by royal officials, even though crusaders were regarded as defaulters quit of their obligation by a generous government rather than being legally exempt.[2] By the early thirteenth century, individual ecclesiastical offices and property were also allowed to be used to support cleric crusaders in addition to the general Church taxes. Ostensibly radical in setting aside conventions of finance and hierarchy, the crusade privileges operated as both symptom and stimulant in an increasingly open land market. This was driven largely by increased profitability of agrarian land consequent on rising population, consumption and urbanization, not least in regions where crusading became popular.

Inevitably, as the privileges concerned property, complications arose. To protect the lending and justice systems and their own interests, rulers sought to define and contain crusade privileges. The French government did so in 1188 and 1215. In England, the legally accepted chronological extent of the privilege, the so-called crusaders' term, was set at three years in 1188, but varied in subsequent case law to five years or more.[3] More generally, the legal anomalies and cultural queasiness over selling property outright encouraged euphemistic fictions of reciprocal gift-giving between crusader and purchaser, especially when the buyer was a church or monastery. Similar charades were performed over mortgages and vifgages. Negotiations between crusaders and religious houses could be complex and lengthy, often very far from relaxed, enthusiastic concurrences of altruism and generosity. Individual and kindred status and identity were closely bound up in property as well as income. Families, landlords, neighbours and governments could be concerned if crusader privileges rendered them technically powerless to prevent land being alienated to the Church and so withdrawn from family control, the land market or fiscal obligations. Anxiety at the open disposal of land found expression in England, for example, in a number of statutes under Edward I, including *Mortmain* (1279, 1290), which limited grants to the Church, one of a long line of laws that tried to limit tax evasion.

The prohibition on crusaders using Jews for credit, later refined into remission from all Jewish credit, posed further problems and was frequently honoured in the breach, if regular injunctions to police this ban are any guide. While Jewish credit facilities eased the finances of some monastic lenders, such as those of the Cistercians in England, this once-removed connection was overshadowed by regular, direct appropriation of Jewish assets in the interests of crusades through tallages (a form of irregular, non-consensual tax) and confiscations. While the limit on Jewish creditors forced crusaders to look elsewhere, comprehensive debt exemption potentially scuppered their prospects of raising money. The privileges' moratorium on existing debts and ban on honouring any new interest payments for the duration of the crusade vow may have protected property values and a crusader's moral standing, but they simultaneously risked sabotaging his credit rating and thus his ability to fulfil that vow. Facing a stubborn credit market, some thirteenth-century crusaders were reduced to waiving their debt exemption, presumably so that they could more easily or cheaply borrow money.[4]

A cynic might suppose the system was designed to force crusaders into the arms of ecclesiastical institutions only too happy to extend their property portfolios under the guise of charitable assistance to those bearing the Cross of Christ. Clergy touting for crusaders' business were far from unknown. During preparations for the First Crusade, Marmoutier Abbey near Tours in the Loire valley showed initiative. One monk sought out his crusader nephew to persuade him to direct his charity towards the abbey, while the abbot trawled Brittany and Anjou to elicit gifts and pledges.[5] Before his departure, Hugh of Toucy in Burgundy, later a deserter from the First Crusade, gave land to the abbey of Molesme to build a church 'inspired by divine grace and also by the exhortation of one of our brothers, the monk John'. In return, Hugh received 30 shillings and a valuable mule.[6] Three or so generations later, Canon Godfrey of Southwark Priory near London appeared at the time Theobald of Scalers took the Cross at Longstowe in Cambridgeshire and persuaded the new *crucesignatus* to donate land to the priory in return for ('in charity') 3 silver marks and a 20s palfrey (a horse for riding as opposed to a war horse, a destrier).[7] Benefits were mutual. The religious house gained endowment and patronage. The crusader and his family could expect, on top of any capital gain, the spiritual insurance of good works, the monks' prayers, and an extension or confirmation of patterns of religious investment. Moreover, such deals represented public assertion and acceptance of the donor's title to the property, the charter transferring rights or income demonstrating publicly the legitimacy of his possession of those rights in the first place.[8] In the fissile, litigious and contested landed economy of the period, such recognition was worth the premium. Once again God and Mammon were partners in a severely practical enterprise. In *Quantum praedecessores*, where the temporal privileges were first spelt out, Pope Eugenius III condemned wasteful expenditure on luxurious clothes, popular as ever among social elites as visible, assertive signs of wealth and status, arguing that the money was better spent on arms, horses and other necessary military equipment. He added that without the right to raise funds freely on their property the faithful 'will not want or have the means to go'.[9]

REALIZING ASSETS

The First Crusaders took often drastic measures to cover estimated expenses, selling, donating or vifgaging swathes of property, lucrative rights of jurisdiction or other valuables.[10] The religious corporations acted as chief creditors and beneficiaries because they possessed accessible reserves of coin, plate, or even surplus livestock – horses, mules, etc. Handing over cash or precious objects was not without corporate risk, but this was offset by the advantages of expanded possessions and patronage. By emphasizing the spiritual imperatives and benefits of the material exchanges, the clergy, who wrote the charters recording the transactions, sought to highlight awareness of religious community that bound all degrees in society, a community of which crusading acted as a manifest symbol. In reality, the key to the relationship with donors lay in cash. Later ordinances relating to assessment of Church taxes excluded religious houses' plate and metal ornaments. Some crusaders preferred to deal with fellow laity, frequently close relations, women as well as men, who shared a stake in the property being negotiated. Robert of Normandy's pledge of his duchy to his brother William II of England, in return for 10,000 marks, merely represented the largest single such deal.[11] The First Crusade established a pattern for both individual and lordly fundraising. Even though crusaders regularly ran out of money and equipment, they took due financial precautions and appeared rapid learners. While taxes, loans and common funds featured in the 1090s, over time they assumed greater prominence. Specific national and ecclesiastical crusade treasuries were created, fed by taxation, gifts, proxy contributions and redemption payments. In the thirteenth century, the Church became a universal paymaster.

Before this institutionalization of crusade finance, the classic example of the eclectic search for money is provided by the remarkable fundraising antics of Richard I of England for his crusade in 1189–90, stamped with opportunism, bullying, thuggery and recklessness of a scale unavailable to less powerful *crucesignati*.[12] In the eighteen months between taking the Cross in January 1188 and his death in July 1189, Richard's father Henry II had shown himself no fiscal slouch. Besides starting to levy the Saladin Tithe, Henry tallaged the Jews for 10,000 marks and sequestered the profits enjoyed by the monks of Canterbury from the lucrative pilgrim traffic to the shrine of Thomas Becket. The tithe raised many tens of thousands of pounds. A clerical court official alleged that on his death Henry left a treasure worth 100,000 marks, two to three times normal annual royal revenues at the time.[13] On his accession, Richard, recognizing this was insufficient for his grand crusade, embarked on an almost unprecedented spree of state venality. The same court official, himself a crusader, remembered: 'he put up for sale all that he had, offices, lordships, earldoms, sherriffdoms, castles, towns, lands, everything.'[14] Richard supposedly quipped to friends that he would have been prepared to sell London if he had found a buyer.[15] Other towns were forced to pay for new charters. Sheriffs were dismissed and their jobs auctioned. Important civil servants, having taken the Cross at Henry II's bidding, now paid the king to be relieved of the obligation. The sacked justiciar, Ranulf Glanvill, paid a massive fine. His successor, for a half share of the job and exemption from his crusade vow, paid 1,000 marks, as well as buying an earldom for another 2,000 marks and royal lands for a further 600 marks, a total sum nearing a tenth of normal annual royal revenues. An additional tallage of 2,000 marks was imposed on the Jews and the king accepted the reversions of the property of those killed in the Jewish massacres in London and York in 1189 and 1190, of which he formally disapproved. A number of strategic border castles were handed back to the king of Scots for 10,000 marks. Valuable forest rights were sold. Vacant bishoprics were filled for a price. The only expedient not obviously exploited was credit. There may have been no lenders with large enough coffers or, as king, Richard hardly needed to borrow; he preferred to sell. No less striking than its extent, his profligacy, in the short term at least, failed to bankrupt him or his realm. However, not content with the loot of England, Richard sought further bonanzas during his crusade, extracting 40,000 gold ounces from the king of Sicily, plundering Cyprus and then selling it to the Templars for 40,000 gold bezants.[16] However politically myopic, Richard's spendthrift grand bazaar paid handsome dividends. His example of translating wealth into effective campaign command supplied a lesson not lost on those who came after.

For individuals, the bedrock of crusade finance remained realizing cash or equipment on their own property, rights and possessions. The fiction of mutual gifts with the Church could disguise complex deals and lucrative profits. In 1147 the Norfolk landowner Philip Basset of Postwick, near Norwich, gave to the local abbey of St Benet, Holme, a marsh and a flock of 300 sheep. In return the abbey promised to pay 15 marks immediately and then a rent of 5 marks a year, the first seven years of which were to be remitted. Even on the possibly unlikely assumption that the 5 marks' rent reflected the full value, quit of 35 marks' worth of rent for a payment of 15 marks, the abbey was making a profit from the vifgage of 133 per cent over seven years, or 19 per cent a year.[17] Provided interest was concealed, scruples over usury or crusaders' immunities could conveniently be avoided. The involvement of religious houses in funding crusades coincided and was closely associated with the explosion of their popularity in the century and a half after 1050. Bonds of finance were integral to this, as the pious sought religious solace in founding, endowing or joining cloistered communities. Crusading added a reciprocal dimension in which each party could be both patron and lender.

This did not preclude deals between laypeople, such as the 500 marks the count of Meulan gave to Ivo of Grandmesnil in 1101 on a pledge of all Ivo's lands for fifteen years and a marriage alliance between Ivo's heir and the count's niece; Ivo, out of favour with the count's master, Henry I of England, was clearly not expected to return. Clerics were not the only ones to take material advantage of the crusade financial market.[18] Diffident about going on crusade himself, in 1177 Henry II of England was content, in return for the county of La Marche, to grant its count, Adalbert V, 6,000 marks, 20 mules and 20 palfreys. The same year he subsidized the count of Flanders' crusade to the Holy Land, a total of 1,500 marks for an unknown *quid pro quo.* In 1183, Henry secured the sworn loyalty of William Marshal with a subvention of 100 Angevin *livres.*[19] Whether because of the growing habit of secular record-keeping or a shift in habits, the proportion of lay land deals appears to increase in the thirteenth century, a sign of the widening scope of the land market. Equally, for the very wealthy at least, the fictions of concealed credit gave way to direct loans. These could come from wealthier lords or the military religious orders, but increasingly, as in domestic war finance, they came from Italian bankers. In 1253, for example, Louis IX borrowed 100,000 pounds, mainly from the Genoese. On crusade in 1270–72, Edward of England relied heavily on the Ricciardi bankers of Lucca.[20]

The role of the Church also changed. The prominence of monasteries and other regular religious houses was overtaken by the system of Church taxation and custody of lay donations and redemptions. The relationship of money and churchmen came under closer scrutiny in the reformist atmosphere of the early thirteenth-century Church. This did not prevent crusaders from copying their predecessors in dealing with favourite local religious houses. However, from the 1230s, the custodians of ecclesiastical efforts to promote crusading passed decisively from monastic orders, notably the Cistercians, and university-trained secular clergy, academics, lawyers and bureaucrats, to the friars, professed religious and increasingly also university trained.[21] Crusade preachers now habitually collected alms, vow redemptions and tax. As the leading agents in this, the friars, mendicants in theory, unable to deal directly with money, risked charges of hypocrisy and duplicity. Nevertheless, their role became pivotal in a centralized system of crusade finance. While pledges to laymen and religious houses, sales of lands, rights or fixed assets like forests persisted, by the mid-thirteenth century, at least for those responsible for large retinues, finance revolved more closely around international treasuries of donations, legacies, vow redemptions and tax.

As noted, one potential source of funds proved contentious. The robustly anti-Semitic abbot of Cluny, Peter the Venerable (d.1156), argued that Jews should be despoiled on behalf of the crusade. However, given conflicting ecclesiastical opinion and papal prohibitions on using Jewish bankers, individual crusaders tended to be chary of direct dealings with Jewish financiers.[22] Royal rights over Jewish property opened a different avenue of exploitation. Henry II of England's tallage of the Jews for 10,000 marks in 1188 started a close association of crusade finance with the exploitation of English Jewry. Richard I added another 2,000 marks in 1190. Further English tallages, property taxes which were in effect expropriations or protection money, followed in 1237, when Henry II's grandson Earl Richard of Cornwall was granted 3,000 marks for his crusade; in 1251; and in 1269–70, which realized perhaps 4,000 marks although assessed at 6,000 marks. Such sums were insignificant if set against total crusade expenditure (the 4,000 marks in 1270 compared with the 22,500 marks paid out in knights' contracts), but acted as financial reinforcement to the popular discriminatory intolerance inherent in the crusade ideal.[23] In line with papal policy since Innocent III, the First Council of Lyons (1245) picked up on this confluence of prejudice and convenience by encouraging rulers to seize Jewish profits from interest payments. Louis IX, a vigorous opponent of Jews and Jewry, exploited this decree by expelling Jewish moneylenders and confiscating their assets to be used for his crusade.[24] Much of Louis's saintly reputation rested on this skill of cloaking self-interest with morality. Nonetheless, for the ordinary crusader, Jewish bankers were usually out of bounds, except through violence, murder and grand larceny of the sort demonstrated in the Rhineland in 1096 and 1147, England in 1190 or France in the late 1240s.

Into a gap this opened in the market stepped the newly founded military orders of the Hospitallers and Templars. Both were based in Palestine, were dedicated to the same objectives as crusaders, and possessed lands and members in western Europe as well as the Levant. Within a generation of the founding of the Templars (c.1120) and with the creeping militarization of the Hospitallers, these orders were involved in banking and supplying credit to complement their military assistance. Louis VII turned to them during his cash-strapped expedition in 1147–8. It was for their financial not military experience that planners used members of the orders to supervise the collection of the Saladin Tithe in 1188 and the Church crusade tax of 1215 and to transport funds to the Fifth Crusade. In the Holy Land before 1187, the masters of the two orders held the keys to the treasure deposited in Jerusalem on behalf of Henry II of England. The master of the newer Teutonic Knights was recruited to play a similar role for his friend Frederick II in 1225.[25] Richard of Cornwall employed the Hospitallers to send £1,000 to the Holy Land to support the 1248–50 crusade. His nephew, the future Edward I, employed Templars in the financial management of his 1270 crusade.[26] Others also used the military orders as banks. An unreleased *crucesignatus* from the Third Crusade, the veteran English royal administrator William Brewer, deposited 4,000 marks with the Templars which he left in his will for the use of his nephew and namesake, the bishop of Exeter, who went on crusade in 1227.[27]

A specific advantage of the military orders may have been their access to gold, the main large-denomination currency of the eastern Mediterranean. If silver coin was in short supply in twelfth-century Europe, gold was scarcer and none of it in regular minted coin. It is unusual to get a clear indication of the complete finance of any single crusader, but the Englishman Robert of Marsh may be an exception. Going on crusade as his father's proxy in 1201, Robert received from him 20 silver marks, 22 gold bezants, one gold ring, one horse, one helmet, one sword and a cloak of scarlet, the last presumably available to be sold for cash en route.[28] The substantial element of gold was uncommon in northern Europe but was recognized as useful by crusade organizers, wary of the capricious exchange rates encountered by crusaders as they travelled eastwards. In the 1260s, Hugh Neville was paying his own entourage in silver but local tradesmen in Acre in gold.[29] Godfrey of Bouillon took only a tiny quantity of gold (perhaps 3 marks), along with 1,300 marks of silver from his sale of his estate of Bouillon in 1096. Peter the Hermit apparently carried gold as well as silver in his treasure wagon. Louis VII received some of his levy on churches in gold, such as the 500 bezants from the abbey of Fleury.[30]

Before the widespread availability of the international banking facilities of the military orders, western European crusaders had chiefly to rely on the chance of obtaining gold plate or the services of goldsmiths. These were useful travelling companions as well. One of them, Geoffrey the Goldsmith, helped lead a contingent of Londoners to the Holy Land in 1190.[31] One attraction of booty and tribute in the Mediterranean was the availability of gold. Philip II of France used his windfall of Sicilian tribute to pay followers in gold ounces.[32] Rulers of Sicily such as Henry VI of Germany after 1194 and his son Frederick II exploited their lordship over an economy that sustained gold as a currency. Henry offered gold to pay his crusaders in 1195; Frederick not only promised 100,000 gold ounces for his crusade but actively accumulated a gold crusade treasure in the mid-1220s, with taxes on religious houses and fiefs payable in gold.[33] Building up gold reserves became a familiar accompaniment to any decision to embark on crusade. After taking the Cross in 1250, Henry III of England hoarded gold at an annual rate equivalent to 5,880 silver marks, sums in the event used in part on a campaign in Gascony in 1253–4. One of Henry's early ministers, Peter des Roches, bishop of Winchester, similarly bought gold in the years before his crusade in 1227.[34] Importantly for the running of the Fifth Crusade, significant amounts of the money from Church taxation sent to the papal legate Pelagius in Damietta came in gold, more than 25,000 ounces.[35] In many of these transactions, the military orders, particularly the Templars, played important roles as collectors, supervisors, shippers or bankers, keeping accounts and probably managing money-changing.

REDEMPTIONS AND CENTRAL FUNDING

Among novel funding strategies, the ability of *crucesignati* to redeem and satisfy their vows in return for material compensation became ubiquitous and, in some quarters, controversial. Together with official encouragement of gifts and legacies, these formed part of a general policy of extending access to the crusade's spiritual privileges. Cash redemptions and donations ultimately bled into an elaborate system of selling crusade indulgences outright. Redemptions originally addressed two long-standing complaints of crusade organizers: non-performance of vows and unsuitable recruits. The first issue was raised prominently by the leadership of the First Crusade. Backsliders were threatened with excommunication and attracted social opprobrium, helping to inspire a second wave of armies in 1101.[36] However, purist canon-law penalties failed to accommodate the reality of human behaviour, of vows taken in enthusiastic haste or good faith but subsequently repented at leisure or rendered impossible by circumstance, such as poverty. Ill-health or, in the case of Earl William of Aumale before 1150, obesity, could attract absolution, in return for substituting a suitably pious alternative – in William's case founding a monastery.[37] Excommunication or other ecclesiastical penalties did little to harness contributions from the defaulters. Parallel to the non-fulfilment of vows sat the opposite difficulty of the unsuitability of many recruits who actually did participate, a problem that drew dry commentary from close chronicle witnesses to both the First and Second Crusades. Although a screening system by local clergy had been envisaged by Urban II and, ostensibly, tests for capacity and means continued for a century thereafter, the thrust of recruiting rhetoric hardly discouraged anyone from volunteering.[38]

By the later twelfth century, vow non-fulfilment, unsuitability, the search for additional funds and the belief that, as the crusade was a model of Christian life, its privileges should be available to all, began to coalesce into measures to allow redemption of vows and reward donations. The universal obligation to defend the Holy Places, so vigorously promoted after 1187, inevitably elicited different scales of contributions. Whatever the spiritual advantages, the material incentives were obvious and recognized. Enthusiasm, regretted or not, could be exploited for material gain separate from active service. Matters came to a head during the massive and indiscriminate response to the Third Crusade. A cluster of eminent royal officials and prelates working for the English king managed to obtain papal absolution from their vows in 1189, although there seemed to be some confusion whether this was permanent discharge or temporary delay. One, Willam Brewer, ultimately paid for his nephew the bishop of Exeter to fulfil his vow by proxy. Another, Ranulf Glanvill, paid for redemption but subsequently resumed his vow, dying at Acre in 1190. The archbishop of Rouen and the bishop of Durham redeemed their vows with substantial payments (1,000 marks in the latter's case) to the king. Clearly, money could be extracted from such high-powered people.[39] Pope Clement III expressed wider anxieties. In an encyclical of February 1188, he encouraged bishops to extend a share in the crusade indulgence to those who sent aid or a proxy to defend the Holy Land.[40] Passive assistance could be just as useful as joining up.

As the tide of the Third Crusade ebbed, probably thousands of unpretentious *crucesignati* found themselves in theory facing excommunication, even if their unfulfilled vows had been caused by infirmity or poverty. Pope Celestine III (1191–8), befitting a curial veteran in his mid-nineties, relied on traditional formulae of anathema, delay or proxy. Awkward pastoral problems arose as canon law on absolving crusade vows was far from clear. Ad hoc papal dispensations were available but only at a price. Cardinals as well as popes appeared to be cashing in. The market for apostolic absolutions risked descending into a racket as little scrutiny was applied to test claims of legitimate impediments. Yet few could afford curial dispensations, corrupt or otherwise, while the options of conditional delay or forced service under pain of excommunication failed to match individual circumstances or military needs.[41]

Innocent III developed a more coherent policy. During preparations for the Fourth Crusade, while retaining the customary expedients of compulsion, delay and proxy, he allowed local diocesans to grant dispensations to those with lasting impediments, allowing them to redeem their vows according to their means. Incapacity to fight was included alongside infirmity and poverty as acceptable impediments where money not service was a better bet.[42] Redemptions became a crusading equivalent to English scutage, where a levy of money replaced a lord or knight's service to the king. Innocent went further. In his bull *Quia Maior* of 1213, he dispensed with the suitability and means tests, inviting 'anyone who wishes' to take the Cross in order for the vow to be commuted, redeemed or deferred. Although this radical provision was subsequently dropped from the crusade decree of the 1215 Fourth Lateran Council, *Ad Liberandam*, Innocent's shift to all-embracing indulgences and the creation of a universal crusade treasury including redemption money soon became integral to crusade recruitment and finance.[43]

This reached a logical conclusion in Gregory IX's bull of 1234, *Rachel suum videns*.[44] Sweeping away the hesitancy of 1215 and legalistic category distinctions, Gregory reiterated *Quia Maior*'s blanket invitation to all-comers to take the Cross in order to redeem their vow for money. Tied to this were legacies, often in lieu of unredeemed vows. These measures extracted funds from one set of the less wealthy to provide for another set of less wealthy to go on crusade, thereby involving broader sections of society in the spiritual benefits by means of their material contributions. The operation was to be run by the mendicant orders of Franciscans and Dominicans. They were to preach the Cross and collect redemptions and donations (this dual role opening them to familiar accusations of hypocrisy, conflict of interest and peculation). Once collected, money was channelled through the great lords who had taken the Cross – hardly the indigent – with little oversight or accountability as to its actual use. The *crucesignatus* Earl Richard of Cornwall was assigned vow redemptions as well as crusade taxes and legacies from England in 1238. He happened to be fabulously wealthy already, thanks to his estates as brother of King Henry III and his profits from Cornish tin mining. Collection and audit proved cumbersome. Undeniably lucrative in total, individual amounts given notionally matched ability to pay and so could run to as little as a few shillings. By contrast, Count Hugh of Lusignan left 5,000 *livres* to cover his unfulfilled vow in 1248.[45] In Earl Richard's case, one English diocese generated crusade funds of almost £90 in 1244, and an archdeaconry apparently produced 600 marks in 1247.[46] Payments were still being handed over to the earl almost twenty years after his crusade, arousing understandable accusations that the money was not being spent on its original purpose. The memory of the offerings of the old, the sick, the feeble of mind and body, women and children providing a regular pension for Earl Richard, one of the richest men in Europe, stuck in some observers' craws. In fact, Gregory IX's scheme generally was notable as much for muddled and sclerotic administration as for insider preference, funds regularly being assigned to two different crusaders at once or redirected from one to another. Later grants encountered similar problems.[47]

Gregory IX pressed ahead with this system of crosses for cash, extending it to other theatres of crusading such as his wars against Frederick II.[48] Redemptions became habitual tools of Church finance and pastoral authority. Crosses were imposed and redeemed for behaviour and aspirations far beyond any obvious desire to assist in the *negotium sanctum*, anything from crimes of violence or sexual transgression to commuting vows of pilgrimage. Critics accused preachers of extortion, bullying the vulnerable to redeem vows for exorbitant sums by threats of excommunication. Fears of forced redemptions were voiced at the highest levels in the 1240s and 1250s. The English monk Matthew Paris, no friend to ultramontane initiatives, suspected peculation and papal cupidity.[49] Handing over redemption money to the rich and powerful hardly reduced suspicions. The Franciscan Gilbert of Tournai reported to Pope Gregory X at the Second Council of Lyons (1274) that abuse of redemptions undermined the credibility of crusade preaching in general: 'if they preached the indulgence of the cross anew, it is not certain that they would make progress; but it is certain that they would suffer various insults'.[50] From this perspective, an innovation of religious democracy had become a financial scam.

Nonetheless, legacies, donations and redemptions on deposit in dioceses across Europe were welcomed by crusaders, even if some lower down the social hierarchy felt cheated. Redemptions contributed significantly to the crusades of 1239–41 and the finances of Louis IX and his magnates in the late 1240s.[51] A whiff of corruption continued to hang over the exercise, as friars competed over collection rights or illicitly posed as collectors to line their own pockets. Innocent IV, alarmed by evidence of the profligate sale of redemptions on the cheap, established a form of audit to tighten accountability.[52] As a means of raising money, the system was too profitable and popular with crusade leaders to be abandoned. The proceeds compared well with other sources of support. Two English crusaders in 1270 received 600 marks each from the central fund, the same as they got from the crown.[53] Despite vulnerability to abuse and knotted bureaucracy, as a means of tapping enthusiasm, spreading the benefits of the indulgence, directing the widest range of laity to a popular religious exercise as well as addressing the financial shortfalls of crusade expenses, the redemption system was neat, logical and lucrative. So successful was it that by the early fourteenth century, while not abandoned, redemptions were being simplified and superseded by a system of direct selling of indulgences, customized to suit the buyer's circumstances and pocket.[54]

TAX

The most striking and effective financial expedient was taxation.[55] Tax is distinguished from theft by the assertion or acceptance of obligation. Consent by the taxed eased collection, a fact recognized across medieval western Europe, but obligation, invariably defined by the imposer, lent taxation social, even moral, respectability. This could be contested, but even clauses 12 and 14 of Magna Carta recognized the king's right to tax subjects, only insisting on a consensual process of establishing the necessity and legitimacy of his doing so. Both customary practice and Roman Law insisted that subjects were bound to support lords who protected them, especially when that lordship faced threat or emergency. Equally, emerging concepts of community implied an individual's public duty of aid. By no great extension, duty to lords or communities formed twin pillars of justifications for crusade taxes. The demands of Christian fraternity had been evident from the earliest preaching of the First Crusade. To this was added the common complicity of all Christians for the sins that imperilled the Holy Land, a point made explicit in Gregory VIII's *Audita Tremendi* and in the explanation for the Saladin Tithe. Gregory IX wrote of the Holy Land as all Christians' homeland – a prominent propaganda motif.[56] If all Christians were responsible for the fate of Jerusalem, so all shared in the penitential duty to take the Cross or subsidize those who did.

Christocentric rhetoric from the Third Crusade insisted that God's lordship demanded service. Offering promise and threat, Christ as Lord was presented as providing infinite charity with inescapable judgment. As Innocent III put it in 1198:

Who, then, in a case of such great emergency shall refuse to pay obedience to Jesus Christ? When he comes to stand before Christ's tribunal to be judged, what answer will he be able to make to him in defence of himself? If God has submitted himself to death for man, is man to hesitate to submit to death for God? ... Shall then the servant deny temporal riches to his lord when his lord bestows on the servant riches that are eternal?[57]

The imperative of service in an emergency was contrasted with the stigma of failure to help the crusade. In *Quia Maior* Innocent was blunt:

If some temporal king was delivered of his kingdom by his enemies, if his vassals do not only sacrifice their property but also their persons, would he not when he recovered his lost kingdom condemn them as unfaithful ... Thus the King of kings, our Lord Jesus Christ, who brought body and soul and other goods to you, will condemn you for the vice of ingratitude and the crime of infidelity if you should fail to aid him with the result that he lost his kingdom that he bought with the price of his blood.[58]

This secular regal parallel was a common theme in crusade sermons. To the clergy he wanted to tax in 1199, Innocent, using a favourite authoritarian text, sketched the alternatives: 'For even though obedience to divine service ought to be voluntary, nevertheless we read in the Gospel that those invited to the Lord's wedding feast should be compelled to enter.'[59]

The failure of Innocent III's 1199 tax exposed inevitable resistance. For all the talk of Christian obligation, Louis VII struggled with his levy on the Church in 1146–7; the monks at Fleury, for instance, robustly negotiated a reduction of almost two-thirds on the king's initial demand.[60] Both the French and Scottish baronage refused to accept the Saladin Tithe. Frederick Barbarossa's public glamour and grandeur failed to allow him to tax beyond his own tenants.[61] Reluctance to contribute to a forced tax became standard. Frederick II faced hostility against his crusade imposts in southern Italy and Sicily in the 1220s. Experience as a tax collector in 1221 may have helped Gregory IX decide to exploit redemptions instead in 1234. Louis IX managed to create a positive atmosphere for redemptions and crusade-giving only through a concerted programme of reform perceived as providing greater equity in royal administration. It took the English government two years to persuade parliamentary representatives of the shires and boroughs to agree a crusade subsidy in 1270. Successive French monarchs in the early fourteenth century were unsuccessful in persuading their subjects of the need for crusade subsidies.[62]

Clerical opposition was not confined to the innovation of 1199. The suggestion in *Quia Maior* for a voluntary levy was similarly ignored. The French clergy were distinctly unenthusiastic about Honorius III's clerical tenth for the Albigensian Crusade in 1226. Local churches could be as jealous of their autonomy and property as their lay neighbours. Both the purposes and principles of taxation could be challenged, as by the rectors of Berkshire who objected to the papal levy to fight a crusade against Frederick II in 1240.[63] Matthew Paris was not alone in his criticisms. Similar and more sweeping objections to papal crusade taxes were voiced by the French bishops in 1262. Such opposition to crusade taxation featured prominently on the agenda of the Second Council of Lyons in 1274 and in the various reports submitted to it.[64] Goodwill or papal diktat were insufficient to overturn custom, allay suspicions, or challenge self-interest. Instigators of taxation were forced to demonstrate active endeavour through visible preparations for crusade or, as with popes after Innocent III, personal financial commitment to the cause. Even then collectors faced an uphill task.

Crusade taxation presented at least two paradoxes: the concentration on money while proclaiming the virtuous necessity of poverty; and seeking consent to a transcendent religious duty, to help Christ, his Holy Land and his Church. Reactions to crusade taxation were no different from those to any other sort; nor were techniques of authorization, persuasion or collection. Crusade taxation assumed a prominent place in the general development of extraordinary taxation across western Europe. The earliest taxes on surplus income were those agreed by the kings of England and France on behalf of the Holy Land in 1166, 1185 and 1188. The first two were presented as alms for the Holy Land rather than funds for crusaders. However, all three were publicized as having been agreed after consultation with

the great of the realm, in recognition of their novelty rather than their
piety. The Saladin Tithe became a model for future parliamentary taxation in England.[65] The important innovation of the tax on a twentieth
of the receipts from clerical incomes in 1215 only secured compliance
because of the express approval of the assembled clergy at the Fourth
Lateran Council. To underline this point, every letter sent to the tax
collectors included the formula '*sacro concilio approbante*': 'with the
holy council's approval'.[66] While other fiscal expedients and more
localized ecclesiastical levies relied on papal prerogative power, general Church taxation required the formal imprimatur of universal
consent through a general council: the Lateran in 1215; Lyons in
1245 and 1274; Vienne in 1312. Exceptionally, the loss of Acre in
1291 provoked a general Church tax from Pope Nicholas IV. Only
protracted and often heated negotiations persuaded an old and obstinate John XXII to accede to a French request for a new general tax in
1333, aborted when the crusade it was designed to fund was cancelled
in 1336. Although by 1274 administration was well honed, with
Christendom divided into twenty-six regions or collectories with clear
local bureaucratic mechanisms, this ultimate fiscal weapon only operated for less than half a century, the Vienne tax of 1312 being the last
to be raised in full, between 1313 and 1319. The magnitude of income
generated ensured the tax's demise: too onerous for churchmen; too
tempting for laymen.[67]

For secular rulers, crusading provided new opportunities to tap the
wealth of subjects, many of whom traditionally recognized no such
fiscal obligation. The Saladin Tithe fell on clergy and laity alike, the
distinction in status so fiercely contested in law and politics blurred
by the common responsibility for Christ's heritage. By the early
fourteenth century, suggestions even circulated for the enforced disen-
dowment of the Church for the crusade and lay control of clerical
profits. The first lay crusade tax was William II's levy on his English
subjects to pay his brother Robert the 10,000 marks vifgage for the
duchy of Normandy in 1096. A land tax, in a century-old English
tradition, it fell on clergy and laity alike, although the personal
demesne lands of the king's tenants-in-chief were exempt (an obvious
sweetener as they oversaw collection). Subsequent taxes were more
direct. Kings authorized taxes on all their subjects, as in 1188; or on

the laity alone, as with the levy of a fortieth agreed by the kings of France and England in 1201, Frederick II's impost of 8 ounces of gold per fief in Sicily in 1228, or the English parliamentary tax of 1270.[68] Voluntary lay contributions formed a regular part of papal appeals.

While general taxation raised sensitive issues of custom, precedent, power and constitutional propriety, monarchs could additionally exploit regalian jurisdictions over churches within their patronage, royal estates, Jews and towns. Although Louis VII of France was reported as conducting a general census in 1146 – a *descriptio generalis* – his effective fiscal reach probably did not extend far beyond churches under royal patronage, certain towns and his own demesne.[69] Frederick Barbarossa, similarly constrained in Germany, reportedly levied a hearth tax of one penny on his own lands in 1188, in noted contrast with the income-based Saladin Tithe in England and France.[70] Towns, which often sat outside, even in opposition to, local aristocratic control and so were more dependent on distant royal or princely patronage to secure their liberties, offered a distinct target, identified in successive papal decrees. In the fundraising for the Fifth Crusade, towns and cities were requested to provide either fully equipped soldiers or tax. Lucca levied a fortieth. In 1221 Siena provided 6 shillings for local crusaders, although insisting on the commune's free consent, and Florence levied a hearth tax of 20s per knight and 10s per infantryman.[71] It has been calculated that Louis IX raised 275,000 *l.t.* through notional 'gifts' from towns for his first crusade in the 1240s.[72]

Individual lords could extract funds from their tenants. In 1188, Leopold V of Austria supervised the disposal of property by his *ministeriales*. The same year the count of Nevers imposed a 12*d.* hearth tax in his county on both church and lay property, perhaps as a politically more palatable alternative to the Saladin Tithe that the French nobility forced Philip II to cancel in 1189. In 1202, Count Baldwin IX of Flanders sought subsidies from his subjects with the permission of their overlords. As part of the tax levied for the Albigensian crusade in 1221, the countess of Champagne, regent for the youthful count, exacted a twentieth from her revenues. Louis IX's brother, Alphonse of Poitiers, imposed a hearth tax on his lands '*in subsidium Terrae Sanctae*' in 1261.[73] These regional taxes were extensions of lordship rights, but over people as well as objects. Flexibility and expediency marked the whole process. Thus a subsidy for the Holy Land in England in 1222–3 was framed as a poll tax, with a sliding scale of minimum payments according to status: 3 marks for an earl; 1 mark for a baron; 12d for a knight; 1d for a free tenant.[74]

The great fiscal innovation of crusade taxation lay in its introduction of surplus moveable wealth as a basis of assessment, the first income taxes. Initially, in 1166 and 1185, the rates agreed were marginal: $1/120^{th}$ for one year then $1/240^{th}$ for four subsequent years in 1166; $1/100^{th}$ followed by $1/240^{th}$ for the next three years in 1185. Even so, it has been argued that the sums raised could have reached tens of thousands of marks.[75] The Saladin Tithe, designed to be levied in the lands of the kings of England and France and the count of Flanders, potentially offered massive receipts, being assessed on a tenth of the income and moveables of non-*crucesignati*, excluding all jewels and knights' arms, horses or clothing and clerics' horses, clothes, books and church vestments and furniture. Although no full accounts survive from England it is possible that a contemporary estimate of a yield of £70,000 may not be entirely incredible or out of step with similar national taxes and tallages of the period. At least some money appears to have reached the royal Exchequer in 1188–90, although the tax was dealt with by a separate department established in Salisbury and so was not necessarily recorded elsewhere in government; 2,700 marks went from Salisbury to Bristol (for ships?) and to Gloucester (for iron or horseshoes?). It is possible the 25,000 marks (i.e. £16,666) despatched to the king in 1190 included some tithe receipts.[76] Whatever the yield, people took the Cross in droves – in town and country, clergy and laity – to avoid payment and allow them – in theory at least – access to their non-*crucesignati* neighbours' contributions.[77] The formula of the Saladin Tithe thus foreshadowed the later choice of money or service. It also created the precedent for Innocent III's clerical fortieth of 1199 and the subsequent ecclesiastical twentieths and tenths. The ability to tap growing moveable wealth, i.e. profits, was clearly attractive, even if, in the twelfth century at least, there remained a persistent shortage of actual coin with which to pay these levies. Employing such devices, crusade planners stood in the vanguard of fiscal and economic exploitation. Zealots they may have been; blinkered they were not.

THE BALANCE SHEET

Taxation allowed large-scale crusading to survive. The Saladin Tithe, even if frittered away on domestic wars, provided at least a financial platform for Richard I's orgy of fundraising in 1189–90. The Fifth Crusade was bankrolled by the 1215 Church tax. The central fund of redemptions and legacies provided a standing treasury, but taxation met the needs of the increasing costs for great amphibious campaigns across the Mediterranean. A 1220 papal account of the proceeds of the 1215 tax sent to Cardinal Pelagius at Damietta itemized over 35,000 silver marks (alone perhaps 150 per cent of the ordinary annual income from the king of France's demesne and half the total revenues of the kings of France and England) and 25,000 gold ounces. In 1221, Cardinal Ugolino, the future Pope Gregory IX, was able to subsidize about 450 northern Italian crusaders out of the Church tax he was simultaneously collecting to the tune of over 7,730 marks. The Church tax of 1245 provided Louis IX with 950,000 l.t., which, with the 'gifts' from towns of 250,000 l.t., the confiscation of Jewish assets and a tightening of government financial management, went a long way to covering the costs of his hugely expensive crusade. Judging by Tuscan returns, the proceeds from the 1274 tax were equally substantial.[78] The potency of tax, both lay and clerical, meant it was applied to the Albigensian crusades in 1209 and 1221, as well as to the wars against the Hohenstaufen from the late 1230s.[79] The status of the early thirteenth-century holy wars in the Baltic may be judged by the sight of the new colonial church of Livonia paying the crusade twentieth for the Holy Land to support the Fifth Crusade despite the effort of the bishop of Riga to get his wars in the region recognized as equivalent to those in the eastern Mediterranean.[80] The lack of this fiscal weapon may have added to the incentive to devolve the whole northern enterprise to the knights of the Teutonic Order from the mid-thirteenth century.

The availability of large sums of Church receipts as well as the central treasury of redemptions, legacies and donations altered the dynamics of crusade organization. Great lords competed for these funds that were not available simply to anyone who happened to apply. Alphonse of Poitiers's variety of financial resources for his crusade in 1249 gives some idea of the range of funds available to a great magnate: the Church tax, legacies, redemptions, confiscated property of heretics, profits of illicit usury, a hearth tax, protection money from Jews and loans from his brother, Louis IX.[81] The greater the lord the greater their scope for access to subsidy, increasing the premium on *crucesignati* to be associated with a co-ordinated lordship or communal command. Rather than constituting a denial of crusade enthusiasm, centralized funding reflected a sustained, possibly desperate, seriousness in planning for success. The growth in financial clout enhanced the authority, control and responsibility of lay and ecclesiastical leaders. This in turn complicated crusade recruitment and propaganda, seeming to exclude ordinary people of faith not just from money and decisions but from active participation as well. The organized reality increasingly grated against the democratic rhetoric, potentially inspiring popular resentment if things went wrong, as witnessed during the Shepherds' Crusade of 1251 in France.[82] The concentration on raising money evident from papal encyclicals, preachers soliciting redemptions and the chests placed in parish churches to receive donations, aroused anxieties, especially when the destination of the funds either appeared unclear or proved unpopular, as with attempts to re-direct Holy Land crusade funds to wars to prop up the Latin empire of Constantinople or to fight the Hohenstaufen.

Nonetheless, such methods of funding were part of a clear-headed understanding of the practical problems of crusading which stimulated proposals for further reform that revolved around finance, not faith. By 1274, *soi disant* experts, even friar preachers such as Gilbert of Tournai and Humbert of Romans, were arguing that crusading required a professional basis and a permanent garrison of paid troops in the Holy Land funded by western subsidies. The creation of a crusader force paid by the contributions of those who stayed at home had been most clearly floated by Gregory IX in 1234.[83] The extension to the establishment of a paid garrison was made possible by tax and the central fund. The kings of France and England commissioned just such garrison regiments at Acre after 1250.[84] Inevitably, such schemes questioned the role of the existing permanent fighting forces of the military orders. In colonial Prussia and Livonia, the Teutonic Order had taken over the entire operation of holy war, including recruitment of western crusaders.[85] However, the politics of Outremer hardly allowed for such a wholesale transfer of power. Instead a growing orthodoxy developed in the late thirteenth century for the military orders to combine, their joint resources providing for the desired standing professional crusade army. A more radical alternative, self-servingly fashionable around the French court in the early fourteenth century, was to expropriate the resources of the military orders, and perhaps other religious corporations, to support a new pan-European crusade initiative under secular, not papal, control, commanded by a secular chief, a *Bellator Rex*.[86]

The road from Clermont was long and expensive, but one not travelled without calculation, vision and ingenuity. The financial expedients of individual crusaders and the fiscal innovations of rulers and the Church, though complex and frequently messy, stand comparison in variety and sophistication with the most imaginative and lasting administrative, commercial and economic developments of the period. Crusade finance contributed to the freeing of the land market, the opening of international credit markets and the creation of novel fiscal techniques. Some crusade planners and thinkers, such as the early fourteenth-century Norman lawyer Peter Dubois, or Marino Sanudo, even indulged in demographic and economic theory, the one concerned with how to people the Levant with good Catholics; the other keen to show how to undermine Egyptian commercial power with the power of market forces: 'for just as water will naturally flow into valleys, so goods will be attracted to places where they are most required'.[87] Domestically, the crusades provided models of financial exploitation copied by western European rulers. The existence of regional treasuries of Church crusade funds and the abiding options for ecclesiastical taxation inevitably and contentiously attracted the avarice of lay rulers, refuelling and recalibrating tensions between Church and state. More generally, crusade taxes revealed the same tensions of authority, obligation, legitimacy and consent that accompanied their secular equivalents. The contrasting fiscal experiences of different regions of western Europe presaged divergent future histories of central or national taxation. The wholly different responses to the Saladin Tithe in England (collected), France (cancelled) and Germany (not adopted) spoke eloquently of contrasting polities. The ecclesiastical crusade taxes and sales of redemptions and indulgences helped propel the Church as a whole – and the papacy in particular – towards becoming the bureaucratic fiscal leviathan familiar to the later Middle Ages. The demands of finance transformed not just crusading but its financiers too.

However, such financial expedients also made crusading, if not individual crusaders, potentially solvent. Marino Sanudo's daunting figures may have been, and may have been designed to be, off-putting in their honesty.[88] Yet his contemporaries continued to draw up budgets and calculate how to meet the costs. They had the example of Louis IX before them. If the most striking fact of Louis's crusade to Egypt was its utter defeat, the next is that, up to that point, he had covered his huge costs with money to spare. He was not alone. The occupation of medieval warfare differed in its assumptions from those of modern business. Profit and gain were measured in more than crude monetary surpluses. It was expected that the wealth of a king, lord or knight existed to be expended in the pursuit of war. Money was there to be spent. Miserly monarchs earned no respect. Any appreciation of crusaders' finances must recognize, as they did, that although huge sums were spent, their purpose was achieved. Crusades were fought. The fatal paradox emerged when a ruler's greater secular resources, often bolstered by crusade taxes and treasuries, brought with them sterner domestic responsibilities. Edward I of England, lauded for his crusade by one contemporary eulogist as shining 'like a new Richard', may have had access to greater war resources than his crusading great-uncle, but with them came greater domestic political constraints.[89] Daunting costs had not previously deterred the great expeditions that punctuated western European politics in the centuries after Clermont. Expenditure did not constitute some facile barometer of piety. Rather, it reflected the values of a martial society that employed its assets to serve its ambitions. Crusade finance supplied a means to an end, one that, for all the odds against, worked.

Gir ai ita fit qd oligo 7 fu
dam ctum debilitandi fol
dam potetia babilonia. et
irmouendi a multis occasi
one pticapandi cu illis ini
mias crucis ꝫ pceptu ecclie
7 acgirendi 7 etia tenendi tʼas
scam fit pone istud opꝰ an dcm

Logistics

9

Co-ordination

Co-ordination of action across wide geographic areas distinguished crusading from its inception. By the time he preached at Clermont in 1095, Urban II had recruited the bishop of Le Puy as his legate and Count Raymond IV of Toulouse as a commander. A departure date was initially fixed for 15 August 1096, subsequently modified to fit varying regional harvests. While the main forces travelled primarily by familiar trade and pilgrim land routes, with the minimum of sea passages, for example across the Adriatic from Bari to Durazzo, first Genoa, then Pisa were encouraged by the pope to send fleets east. The widespread mobilization generated a general awareness of timing and direction. The rendezvous for the land armies was Constantinople, reached by the chief contingents in the winter and spring of 1096–7. Italian flotillas from Lucca, Genoa and Pisa coincided in the Levant with the land army's siege of Antioch in 1097–8, navies that may have included, if a letter written by Luccan crusaders at Antioch in 1098 can be believed, ships from England.[1] While it is fanciful to imagine an agreed detailed strategy to attack Syria by land and sea, the confluence of western forces at Antioch shows an awareness of the general thrust of policy and bears witness to the constant flow of information from the crusade armies as they lumbered east. Only in the orbit of Byzantine foreign policy did the First Crusaders get sucked into what might properly be described as strategic policy and planning.

Just as Pope Urban held a series of conferences during his French tour in 1095–6, recruits also consulted widely, as shown by the witnesses to their charters. Gatherings to hear sermons and take the Cross could translate into wider discussions of plans and logistics. King Philip of France hosted a meeting of crusaders from his dominions at Paris in

February 1096 at a time, Guibert of Nogent remarked, when the details of how to organize the expedition were engrossing those who had signed up.[2] Regional musters were agreed, at traditional centres of lordship or commerce, such as Troyes, Dijon, Poitiers, St Gilles, Lille, Rheims, Rouen and Chartres. Advance muster points may also have been arranged, such as Godfrey of Bouillon's at Tulln on the Danube near Vienna where he assessed news of Peter the Hermit's passage on the same route a few months earlier.[3] These plans clearly worked. French, German and Italian forces coincided with Peter the Hermit at Constantinople in the late summer of 1096. The contingents that followed coalesced into larger forces, which then joined others to form the very large armies that finally assembled in a combined host of scores of thousands at the siege of Nicaea in the spring of 1097. A pattern of merging has been posited for Robert of Normandy's contingent. Gathered probably at Rouen, it then combined with Stephen of Blois's force, possibly at Chartres. Together they joined Robert of Flanders, perhaps at Besançon, before crossing the Alps into Italy and dividing once more at Bari to cross the Adriatic.[4]

The movement of such large armies presented significant problems of supplies. Lack of prior negotiation over access to markets could jeopardize the survival of any army on a long-distance march. Peter the Hermit secured licence to trade from rulers in Hungary and Bulgaria before commercial tensions and indiscipline exploded into violence. Albert of Aachen's detailed description of Godfrey of Bouillon's market negotiations with King Coloman of Hungary for the survival and safe passage of his army reflected their importance; leaving such matters to chance courted disaster.[5] Although details of the diplomatic exchanges between crusade leaders and Emperor Alexius of Byzantium have largely vanished, the appearance of imperial agents at key moments during the marches of western forces, and the ability of the Greeks to cope with the massive influx of western troops, suggests close prior contact, even if arrangements on the ground proved inadequate or contested. Both the pope and the eastern emperor kept tabs on the crusade armies as they advanced eastwards and, it must be assumed, on each other.[6] Once at Constantinople and with Nicaea taken, Byzantine military advice was sought and given.

The First Crusade, and its successor expeditions of 1100–1101, showed how thousands of individual and group decisions could combine in a coherent military enterprise. Channels of communication were extensive, in lordship and kinship networks, shared locality and economic exchange. The expansion of local, inter-regional and international trade provided a vital grounding for mass crusading, as demonstrated, during the Second Crusade, by the North Sea fleet that assembled at Dartmouth in May 1147.[7] Drawn mainly from Brabant, Flanders, the Rhineland, Normandy, southern and eastern England, the crusaders came from places connected by commerce: London, Bristol, Southampton, Hastings, Dover, Ipswich, Boulogne, Cologne, Rouen. The North Sea and English Channel formed a closely knit trading area bound together through fishing, mainly of herring, and wool. The translation of co-operation from trade to war exploited similar skills: in maritime technology, shared investment and, as revealed by the Dartmouth commune, social organization. For all the martial heroics of the surviving accounts of their deeds at Lisbon, the language of trade suffused the army's debates, contracts, provisioning and hard bargaining. The agreement with King Alfonso of Portugal included an exemption from customs duty not only for the crusaders' ships and goods but for those of their heirs as well, a hardly covert invitation to establish a privileged trading station in conquered Lisbon similar to those offered Italian allies of crusaders in the Levant.[8] Later North Sea fleets, in 1189 and 1217, spread the commercial net further including the Danes and ports such as Bremen as well as those in the Rhineland. Similar patterns of war running in the grooves of commerce marked crusades in the eastern Baltic, inspired by the merchants of Lübeck, and in the Mediterranean, where trading cities were involved in assaults on the Balearic islands in the early eleventh and early twelfth centuries, the Pisan raid on Tunisia in 1087 and the attacks on western Iberian ports from the early twelfth century.[9]

Long-distance crusades did not proceed at random. Outlines of direction and duration were established, based on precedents from trade, travel and previous expeditions. However, there were limits. In 1147, the German army built new bridges along the Danube to be used by the French army following behind some weeks later.[10] Yet these armies lacked coherent operational plans for Asia Minor, let alone for military targets once the crusaders reached the Holy Land in 1148. Odo of Deuil remembered that, when they met to discuss the crusade, Pope Eugenius III omitted to advise Louis VII on how to treat the schismatic Greeks.[11] The closest contemporary accounts of the crusaders' siege of Lisbon described it as an opportunist diversion, in line with earlier non-crusading forays by northern European privateers against the ports of al-Andalus and with the similar assaults by passing crusaders in 1189 and 1217.[12] All crusade forces were alert to such chances for re-endowment; Lisbon offered just such a serendipitous windfall. Nonetheless, the gathering of the coalition armada at Dartmouth was hardly coincidental. Its location, the last suitable sheltered natural harbour before the Atlantic approaches, became the customary muster port for North Sea fleets bound for the Mediterranean, in 1189, 1190 and 1217.

The Second Crusade highlighted this contrast between what might be called functional as opposed to strategic planning. Ostensibly well planned, the initial impetus came from a sequence of large assemblies in 1146–7 at Vézelay, Etampes, Speyer and Frankfurt.[13] Despite huge numbers recruited from a vast area and very different experiences en route, most of the land and sea forces bound for the Holy Land set out between April and June 1147, arriving in Palestine roughly a year later, a timescale that subsequently proved standard. Oral and written communication synchronized the preaching of Bernard of Clairvaux and the diplomacy of recruiting two European monarchs; the musters in May 1147 for the North Sea fleets at Dartmouth and the German army at Regensburg, and that for the French at Metz a month later. Subsequent rendezvous with latecomers, such as Ottokar of Styria with the Germans at Vienna in late May or June 1147 or the Anglo-Norman troops with the French at Worms in late June, or the final gathering of the French forces at Constantinople in October, when those who had split off at Worms to travel via the Adriatic and Balkans rejoined the main army, did not occur by chance.[14] If the precise mechanics of organization remain obscure, the results in terms of assembling armies were impressive. Yet, for all its co-ordination, the Second Crusade lacked practical strategy.

The preparations for the Third Crusade displayed familiar patterns. Regional assemblies to confirm commitment and agree details of finance and privileges were held between December 1187 and March

1188 at Strasburg, Gisors, Geddington, Mainz and Paris. Diplomacy of internal peace-making and foreign alliances secured recruits, provisions and passage. Preaching was centrally inspired but locally managed. If his fellow crusader, the English civil servant and chronicler Roger of Howden, is to be believed, Frederick Barbarossa was typical in his consulting the best military experts in his lands.[15] Frederick, a veteran of the Second Crusade, knew the importance of adequate preparations and a coherent plan of march. He stamped his authority on attempts by the bishop of Würzburg to break ranks and travel by sea. Unity and control were features of Frederick's leadership in 1188–90. Deciding to follow the familiar Danube land route, Frederick sent ambassadors to Hungary, Serbia, Byzantium and even to the sultan of Iconium, at the time a German ally, and received their embassies in return. He may even have attempted to open diplomatic channels with Saladin despite a reputation for being determined, in Howden's words, to 'destroy the enemies of the Cross of Christ'. The muster at Regensberg in April 1189, set a year earlier at Mainz, was highly effective, attracting about 70 great nobles, including 12 bishops, 2 dukes, 2 margraves and 26 counts, not all of them close associates of the emperor.[16] A year to prepare a substantial land army mirrored the timing of the 1147 campaigns and allowed for another year for the army to reach the Holy Land, as in 1147–8. This followed even earlier precedent. Most of the leaders of the First Crusade had set out in the autumn of 1096, nine or ten months after Clermont; they reached the outskirts of Antioch a year later, in late October 1097. On the march in 1189–90, Frederick's expedition remained characterized by decisive control, particularly impressive given the German emperor's uneven domestic political power and lack of centralized administration. Yet Frederick's expedition also presents the planning paradox at its most extreme. Despite meticulous arrangements and decisive leadership, when Frederick unexpectedly died on reaching Cilicia in June 1190, the German crusade imploded and disintegrated.

The organizers of the Third Crusade did not lack information. Even though many of the surviving letters purporting to be eyewitness reports of the disasters of 1187 were probably doctored to suit recruiting propaganda, knowledge of events in the east was plentiful, perhaps

too much so. Guy of Bazoches, a cantor of Châlons-sur-Marne, travelled to Palestine with Count Henry of Champagne and the French
advance-guard of 1190. In a letter sent from Marseilles before he
embarked, Guy warned his nephews not to believe rumours about
the fate of the '*milicia Christiana*' and the Holy Land unless proven
by weight of testimony or evidence.[17] Just such scepticism had
helped prevent western rulers sending effective aid to the kingdom of
Jerusalem before 1187. However, crusade planners sought their own
intelligence gleaned from ambassadors and agents (or spies) such as
Godfrey of Wiesenbach and Henry of Dietz, sent by Frederick Barbarossa to Kilij Arslan II of Iconium and Saladin, or Henry II's envoy
Richard Barre, despatched to eastern Europe with a roving brief in
1188 to scout prospects for a land-based Angevin campaign.[18]

Information flowed two ways. The arrival of western relief for the
beleaguered Frankish outposts in Outremer in 1188–9 may have helped
determine the timing of subsequent aid and the start of the siege of
Acre in 1189. Winds, weather and currents imposed a twice-yearly
rhythm of arrivals and departures from Syria and Palestine. However,
while the Germans could not hope to arrive by land before 1190 and
a succession crisis in the Angevin empire delayed the Anglo-French
monarchs' expeditions for at least a year to 1190, the needs of Outremer met more immediate responses. News around the Mediterranean
could travel quite rapidly, especially in summer: in 1190 Guy of
Bazoches sighted Syria thirty-five days after leaving Marseilles; Archbishop Baldwin of Canterbury and Ranulf Glanvill made landfall at
Acre on 21 September 1190 after a voyage (also from Marseilles) of
two months; news of Frederick Barbarossa's departure from Germany
in May 1189 took five months to reach Saladin's court via Byzantium
and Aleppo.[19] Guy of Lusignan's decision to besiege Acre in the summer of 1189 may have been encouraged by news brought by a Pisan
fleet that arrived at Tyre in April of further reinforcements. Guy
pitched his camp before Acre on 28 August 1189; within a month he
had been joined by substantial fleets from Denmark, Frisia, Germany,
Flanders and England and a French army commanded by James of
Avesnes, who had taken the Cross with the kings of France and England at Gisors in January 1188. That is not to say that Guy summoned
these forces, each of which assembled through a dynamic of its own.

However, James of Avesnes may have been aware of the plans of the monarchs of the west; others who arrived certainly were, such as Philip II's cousins Robert of Dreux and the bellicose Bishop Philip of Beauvais, or Frederick Barbarossa's nephew Landgrave Louis II of Thuringia.[20] Once established, the siege of Acre attracted what appear to have been concerted reinforcements encouraged if not sponsored by the kings of France and England: Count Henry of Champagne, nephew to both the kings, arrived at Acre in July 1190 with some of the most powerful lords from northern France and, it was recalled later, elements of Philip II's armoury. He was promptly accepted as commander of the crusaders in the Christian camp.[21] The siege of Acre may not have been planned from a distance but its relief was.

The Third Crusade also provided the most remarkable example of co-ordinated crusading in the twelfth century. Richard I's government made provision to pay the sailors and troops on board the crusade fleet for a year from, at the latest, June 1190; the king landed at Acre on 8 June 1191, on schedule despite the capture of Messina, wintering in Sicily, a serious storm in April and the conquest of Cyprus in May, of which only the stay in Sicily to refit and extort more funds could have been anticipated. Luck combined with design. The timings of Richard's land and naval forces indicated a concerted plan informed by detailed knowledge of conditions. The Angevin fleet comprised three squadrons. One left Dartmouth in late March and April 1190; another embarked from the Loire in June; the third from the island of Oléron further south in July. The fleet was bound by a central command; disciplinary ordinances, issued by Richard at Chinon in June; and, for the English element at least, a stated pay structure. The full fleet mustered at the mouth of the Tagus in late July, pausing only to allow its members to entertain themselves in alcohol-fuelled mayhem at the expense of the Jewish, Muslim and Christian inhabitants of Lisbon. The next rendezvous was with Richard's land army at Marseilles in early August, with a final muster, agreed earlier by Richard and Philip II, at Messina in Sicily.

The two kings had carefully synchronized their preparations. The date of 24 June, the Feast of the Nativity of John the Baptist, a suitably preparatory intercessor for the restoration of Christ's heritage, had been set as the formal date of the start of their crusades. On that day, the kings simultaneously received the scrip and staff of pilgrimage, Richard at Tours and Philip at St Denis. In an orchestrated ritual of departure, they met, as arranged, at Vézelay on 2 July and set out together two days later on 4 July, the third anniversary of the battle of Hattin. While Philip aimed for Genoa and the shipping he had hired, Richard made for Marseilles, arriving in late July to find his fleet was not there. After waiting a couple of weeks, impatient to press on to Sicily, he hired twenty galleys and ten cargo vessels and left on 7 August, although some detachments were still embarking over a week later. Yet the main fleet only missed him by a matter of days, reaching Marseilles on 22 August, a remarkably close-run thing. There the fleet would have learnt of Messina as the next destination if it had not already been agreed. The choreography maintained its shape. The main fleet put in at Messina on 14 September; Philip II arrived on the 16th; Richard, after an unhurried cruise down the Italian coast, made his ostentatious entry into Messina on the 23rd.[22] However, this image of efficiency should be set against the incidences of accident and muddle. The collapse of the bridge at Lyons in 1190 under the weight of crusaders from the Angevin and French armies became notorious.[23] Away from the influence of kings and great lords, crusaders made their own dispositions and found their own ways east, always a complicated and often messy process.

Carefully laid schemes did not necessarily translate into effective action. The Fourth Crusade presents the classic example, exposing the limits of planning and leadership in the face of exaggerated ambition and adverse circumstances. This was not due to lack of preparation or understanding of the problems but, if anything, the opposite. The leaders of the Fourth Crusade were precisely aware of how their plans were unravelling and why. In the absence of kings, the commanders quickly organized themselves into a formal collective leadership, holding regular meetings and deciding issues of strategic importance in apparently open debates, for example at gatherings during the summer of 1200 at Soissons and Compiègne. Cohesion was helped by the early leaders, the counts of Champagne, Flanders and Blois, coming from neighbouring regions, surrounded by interlaced political and dynastic circles crowded with crusade veterans and saturated in memories of past crusading heroics. This collective leadership proved impressively united and resilient, or, alternatively, its critics might have said, purblind, self-interested and obstinate.

At an initial conference at Soissons, the leaders decided there were too few crusade barons present to make sensible strategic decisions. A fuller meeting at Compiègne held a lively discussion about objectives and transport, finally agreeing to send an embassy to scout for a contract with an Italian port. Given that this embassy negotiated a deal to target Egypt, the destination may have been decided at Compiègne. Beneath the appearance of frank and easy collegiality, the major decisions rested with the counts of Champagne, Flanders and Blois. They chose the six plenipotentiary envoys to Italy who went on to agree the Venetian treaty. On the count of Champagne's death in 1201, Champenois associates such as Geoffrey of Villehardouin and Geoffrey of Joinville (uncle of the companion of Louis IX) played significant backstage roles in seeking a new leader. An inner circle, including figures such as Count Hugh of St Pol, made most of the running, notably in the choice, after refusals by the duke of Burgundy and the count of Bar, of the Italian Marquis Boniface of Montferrat to assume overall command, although his authority was to be more *primus inter pares* than absolute. More conferences were held at Soissons in the summer of 1201 to approve the choice of Boniface and receive him as leader, with another formal assembly at the annual Cistercian general chapter at Cîteaux. Despite this public show of open debate, strategic planning rested with the inner coterie. The bulk of crusaders were kept in the dark over the decision to target Egypt. This concentration of executive power invited a damaging contradiction when openness proved a sham, leading to the bruising confrontations with representatives of the bulk of the army. These had to be consulted because they formed much of the army's fighting power and had earlier been called upon to subsidize the shortfall in the debt owing to the Venetians. The Venice debacle exposed the leadership's inability to impose their will on those beyond their own retinues or the paid sergeants identified in the Venice treaty.[24]

For all that, this harried high command did steer a large, disparate, amphibious force to a series of astounding victories at Constantinople in 1203–4. From the perspectives of Geoffrey of Villehardouin, Robert of Clari and many others across western Christendom, this was a glorious achievement. Before the lurid denouement of the main campaign at Constantinople, the Fourth Crusade followed the example of its predecessors: orchestrated acceptances of the Cross; well-publicized assemblies of planning and commitment; secured transport on precise terms; extensive preparatory diplomacy; a clear – at least to the high command – ultimate target; a willingness to take the opportunity for re-endowment en route. The planning still came unstuck. The count of Flanders was one of the wealthiest princes in Europe. His lands boasted an unsurpassed crusading pedigree. Yet the contrast between the fate of his crusade fleet and Richard I's a dozen years earlier is telling. The fleet that sailed from Flanders in the summer of 1202 was a coalition, part the count's ships and men, part independent allies, such as the governor of Bruges, who had sworn to obey the count's orders, although not in his pay or control. They failed to reach Venice, if that had ever been the plan, wintering in Marseilles. From there they sent to the count, now in Zara, asking where they should rendezvous. Count Baldwin suggested Modon, on the southern tip of the Peloponnese. Whether it missed its aim, failed to coincide or preferred to sail to the Holy Land, perhaps wholly unaware of the Constantinople démarche, Baldwin and his fleet never met.[25]

Ability to plan international enterprises was exactly what Innocent III in his frequent expansive moods thought he possessed. The Fourth Crusade was not alone in proving him wrong. He effectively lost control over the course of Simon of Montfort's conquest of Languedoc after the initial successes of the Albigensian crusade. His refusal to afford full Holy Land crusade status to German annexation of Livonia by the bishop of Riga, the merchants of Lübeck and the Cistercians failed to deter them from assuming it.[26] Undaunted, Innocent not only rebranded the ideas, image and finances of crusading but reordered how they were planned. The experience of the Fourth Crusade seems to have persuaded Innocent to usurp some of the co-ordinating roles previously taken by secular leaders, including strategy. A general Church Council, attended by numerous secular ambassadors, observers and petitioners as well as by hundreds of clerical representatives from across western Europe, for the first time provided the administrative and political focus of crusade planning, a model copied in 1245 and 1274. In 1215 the Fourth Lateran Council

not only agreed to the crusade Church tax but fixed a muster date –
1 June 1217 – and embarkation points – Brindisi and Messina and
their neighbouring ports. The pope promised that he would be in
attendance to deliver his benediction. For those determined to travel
by land, Innocent offered advice and a papal legate.[27] The overarching
ecclesiastical direction was unequivocal. Oliver of Paderborn even
suggested that the Lateran Council had decided on Egypt as the crusade's target.[28] Papal agents combined preaching, tax collection and
recruitment more systematically over far more territory than officials
of any individual ruler could manage. Great men still took the Cross
and gathered assemblies. People enlisted and raised private funds in
much the same way as had their predecessors, although the balance of
administrative support had tilted towards the Church. Clearly this
was achieved with a degree of lay support; the choice of the ports of
southern Italy and Sicily spoke of the alliance between the pope and
his then-protégé Frederick II, king of Sicily as well as Germany, who,
like King John of England, took the Cross in 1215 before the Lateran
Council met. Although the preaching campaign went badly in France,
the French king had probably been involved in negotiations allowing
him to publish restrictions on the use of crusaders' privileges six
months before the council met. To underline the genesis of his plans,
Innocent even cheekily suggested to the Venetians that they might
wish finally to fulfil their crusade vow of 1202.[29]

Innocent's grand scheme did not die with him in 1216. Many of
the initial musters conformed to the established timetable even if
not the location of departure. Fleets from Frisia, the Netherlands and
the Rhineland set out in late May and early June 1217; Oliver of
Paderborn left Marseilles on 1 June, exactly on schedule; the muster
of the armies of Leopold VI of Austria and King Andrew of Hungary gathered at Split in August, the Hungarians having mustered a
month earlier.[30] Once again, the dynamic of constructing a crusade
army or navy imposed its own rhythm. However, linking the practical
mechanics of action with conciliar decrees could misfire. In 1216
papal recruiters in France ran into trouble with nobles unable to meet
the June 1217 deadline. They were worried lest by missing the departure date they would be in breach of their vow and have their privileges
cancelled. Similarly, there was concern that the same penalties would

apply to poorer *crucesignati* who were ready but who could not set out because they lacked adequate additional funds promised by the council or knightly leaders.[31] Increased bureaucracy and legal precision did not always reap anticipated benefits.

In many ways, the Fifth Crusade was a success. Egypt was invaded; a bridgehead was maintained for three years; during this time recruits came and went in large numbers, drawn from most parts of western Christendom; a major Nile port, Damietta, was occupied for twenty-two months; and money continued to flow east from Church taxes and crusade donations. The Fifth Crusade's failures did not appear to lie in its preparations or on the home front. Yet, as the French episode indicated, papal oversight risked falling out of step with local opinion and increasing the complexity of arrangements. The more crusading became integrated into immediate papal politics, the more it could be operationally disadvantaged. In the preparations for the so-called Barons' Crusade of 1239–41, Pope Gregory IX not only failed to co-ordinate the expeditions to Palestine of the count of Champagne and the earl of Cornwall, but irritated and confused actual and putative *crucesignati* by his attempts to divert Holy Land recruits to other papal pet projects such as the defence of Latin Constantinople or the defence of Rome from Frederick II, which were also given the status of crusades.[32] While legally sound (Gregory was a canon lawyer), this made little political or operational sense. Popes could facilitate diplomacy, collect information, offer the necessary privileges, and supervise preaching and fundraising. However, the evidence of crusading in the first half of the thirteenth century demonstrated that effective crusading required the political capital and material clout of the secular powers to take the lead. Unless allied with local partisan factions, as against the Hohenstaufen in Italy and Germany, popes were ineffectual. Gregory X and Nicholas IV discovered this after 1274 and 1291 respectively. Crusades away from the Holy Land were delegated, to the local Christian kings in Iberia and, after 1218, Languedoc; to the Teutonic Knights in the Baltic; or to local Church and lay authorities in the English civil war of 1264–5 or the squalid persecution of Frisian and Netherlandish peasants in the 1230s. After 1240, realization of the limits to ecclesiastical administration of Outremer crusades confirmed the need to harness the material and political strengths of monarchs, most obviously – but not exclusively – the king of France.

The administration of Louis IX's crusades, especially his first, can be studied in detail, showing advances in record-keeping, fundraising and techniques of hiring troops. However, a comparison with Richard I's preparations gives pause to easy assumptions of qualitative novelty.[33] Both kings established political consensus through assemblies and networks of kindred, lordship and patronage, backed by financial subsidy. Both relied on taxation and the exploitation of often predatory regalian fiscal rights, including extortion of Jewish communities. Both hired their own fleets and lavished funds on acquiring and transporting necessary war materials. Both fixed on a forward Mediterranean muster point, Messina in Sicily for Richard; Limassol on Cyprus for Louis. Before setting out, both indulged in elaborate rituals of departure focused on the receipt of the insignia of a pilgrim. Both assumed the presence alongside their own troops of forces raised by other magnates but both reinforced their authority on campaign by bailing them out. Neither ran out of funds. The size of the forces Richard led to Acre and Louis to Damietta may have been roughly equivalent, perhaps over 10,000 strong. Both adopted a measured approach to preparations, Richard arriving on station in the Levant three and a half years after taking the Cross; Louis after four and a half.

However, significant differences emerge. The Church in the 1240s played a more central role in raising and conveying funds and managing privileges. Under Richard the clergy lacked the corporate bureaucratic and institutional identity that constituted Innocent III's legacy. This should not be exaggerated; the French clergy was subservient to their pious monarch in the 1240s, the friars in particular providing a moral dimension to the king's pre-crusade programme of domestic reform.[34] The bulk of Louis's additional revenue for the crusade derived from Church taxation granted by the general Council at Lyons in 1245 and from ecclesiastically administered redemptions and donations, obviating the need to copy Richard's profligate auctioneering. Louis's propaganda portrayed him as a devout penitent, the king dressing as a pilgrim on his progress south to the Mediterranean. While Louis prayed to the relics of the Passion, Richard had carried the sword Excalibur. More concretely, although Richard had loaded his ships with necessary provisions and later transported with him siege engines and a prefabricated castle, Louis stockpiled vast dumps of food and wine in Cyprus over the two years before he arrived and prepared for the settlement of a conquered Egypt by carrying agricultural as well as war equipment in his ships.

For his fleet, Richard relied on commandeering and hiring ships in ports within his own realm, often as part-shareholder with existing owners. Through detailed and precise contracts, Louis hired ships as sole leaseholder of complete and fully equipped vessels from Genoa and Marseilles, more akin to the 1201 Venetian contracts. Richard appears to have paid below the market price for his ships; Louis may well have been exploited on costs, and probably outfitting as well, although the Genoese connection served him well when he needed credit after paying his ransom from Egyptian captivity in 1250. Most obviously, Richard was fortunate in ruling the coastline of southern Britain and western France, providing him with ports, shipbuilders, merchant vessels and seamen within his own realms. Louis lacked this luxury so, to avoid reliance on other powers or self-serving urban patriciates, he built his own port, at Aigues Mortes in the Rhône delta. This served as the first muster point (Cyprus being the second) and all hired vessels were to be delivered there. Despite its shallow harbour, prone to silting up, and tricky channel to the Mediterranean, the construction of Aigues Mortes symbolized Louis's determination to control all aspects of preparation, a policy dictated by the lessons of the past, and the implementation of a broad understanding of logistics. Louis's arrangements tried to narrow the scope or need for the expensive improvisations that marked Richard's flashy crusade career. Louis IX's crusade plans (his second of 1267–70 mirrored his first in its administrative intensity) reacted to past failures and present obstacles with sense and initiative. Men, money and materiel were carefully and smoothly co-ordinated. Louis's first crusade had been prepared with enormous thoroughness, the best-funded, most proficiently organized large crusade of all. Louis had shown how best to plan a successful crusade. The conundrum for later observers was that it had also been a disaster.

10

Health and Safety

No less important than muster rolls, balance sheets, high politics, diplomacy and the paraphernalia of war sat the personal welfare of crusaders: security of property and family left at home; discipline and rules of conduct on campaign; and their physical health in transit or in action. While it would be too glib to argue that a happy crusader made a successful crusade, this may not be too far from what contemporaries imagined. Happiness did not mean easy contentment. Stories of crusaders deliberately lingering over taking leave of their children to heighten the agony of departure, or others pointedly refusing emotional final views of the familiar landscapes of home, were designed to emphasize the element of sacrifice.[1] The pain of separation acted as a form of strenuous devotional exercise that produced its own spiritual endorphins. Such emotions differed from anxiety about the safety of those people and places left behind or concerns about the conduct or well-being of fellow crusaders.

The defenders of Lisbon in 1147 apparently taunted crusaders that their wives at home were probably being unfaithful and their possessions plundered.[2] While such fears operated as cultural clichés, they were nonetheless grounded in fact. Concern for security of property and those left behind is etched in crusaders' charters and underpins central features of crusader privileges. The novelty of Urban II's offer of Church protection for *crucesignati* initially generated some confusion. After pressure from ecclesiastical and secular lawyers, no doubt reflecting the demands of anxious and/or litigious crusaders, in 1123 the First Lateran Council confirmed that crusaders' houses, families and possessions enjoyed papal and ecclesiastical protection on pain of excommunication for those who threatened them.[3] Even if frequently honoured in the breach, the privilege addressed a central impediment to recruitment. Elaborate schemes were hatched to protect the integrity of estates during a crusader's absence or in the event of his death. These provisions tended to include the explicit involvement and agreement of relatives, if only as witnesses. Kinsmen often provided the main threat to such arrangements, for instance over provisions regarding dower lands, which explained why many charters received the explicit approval of the crusader's wife, some of whom were left legally (and sometimes administratively) in charge of their husbands' estates. The records of English courts from the thirteenth century are littered with cases where wives sought to protect their dower rights as well as defending against wider encroachments on family property. Changes of ownership were regularly challenged by returned crusaders, or, if they had died, their heirs.[4]

Crusading added to the uncertainty of land holding within an increasingly competitive market. Dependants were left at material and physical risk. They could be stranded with inadequate funds in the face of creditors or even made destitute. In 1192, in an unlikely spasm of generosity, the English government bailed out two crusaders' wives from Gloucestershire with 100 and 130 shillings respectively to support them in their husbands' absence.[5] Widows (occasionally unwittingly bogus as their supposedly dead husbands subsequently turned up alive) and heiresses suffered disparagement and forced marriages. Crusaders' wives risked assault or worse. A number were murdered, for their possessions probably more often than for sexual motives. Henry III of England acknowledged the problem in 1252 when he secured Pope Innocent IV's reiteration of the privilege of papal protection for crusaders' wives against molestation.[6] If the chroniclers' scenes of distressed families bidding lachrymose farewell to crusaders are sentimental, those weeping had something to cry about. Despite the condescension of misogynist preachers castigating obstructive wives, these women in real life could encounter genuine hardship, a plight not improved by Innocent III's relaxation of Urban II's insistence that young married crusaders must obtain their spouse's consent. Until then conjugal rights in law had been mutual, their unilateral denial frowned upon.[7] However, the effectiveness of Church protection was contingent on the co-operation of interested parties and lay authorities. Occasionally these failed spectacularly, never more so than in the detention of Richard I in Germany while his lands were annexed by his enemies in France.

Even if reassured that provisions for the home front were adequate, the crusader confronted another threat to individual well-being and the cohesion of the whole enterprise. The coalitions that gathered under the banners of the Cross were potentially lawless, literally so, lacking a common legal system or unitary ties of lordship. Crusade planners appeared sensitive to the problem. The collective leadership of the First Crusade developed a collegial process of making decisions, pooling finance and dispensing justice, often in consultation with the wider crusade community, the *populus* as one veteran dubbed it.[8] At one stage, before the siege of Antioch, the high command appointed a *ductor*, Stephen of Blois, perhaps a sort of chief executive. However, these arrangements emerged from the circumstances of the campaign. There is little sign, beyond the appointment of Bishop Adhemar of Le Puy as the pope's representative, of prior arrangements for a shared command or regulations of conduct between the various contingents.[9] The experience of the First Crusade may have stimulated subsequent crusade organizers to pre-emptive action. Regulations governing everything from clothes, discipline and personal conduct to the sharing of booty became habitual accompaniments to Holy Land crusades, not just for those polyglot forces that constituted themselves as formal communes but also in the armies of great lords and monarchs. For an activity that stressed the link between the behaviour and morality of the fighters with military success, this was, perhaps, not unexpected.

In *Quantum praedecessores*, Eugenius III reiterated the Church's protection of crusaders' families and possessions. He emphasized the spiritual commitment required of crusaders, specifically enjoining against luxury in dress or behaviour.[10] The regulations governing the commune sworn at Dartmouth in 1147 included a similar sumptuary injunction, but concentrated on settlement of disputes and criminal offences, imposing '*leges severissimas*': 'a life for a life, a tooth for a tooth'.[11] A formal peace (i.e. an agreed ad hoc set of binding laws which if broken invoked penalties) among the army was established, with injuries and offences covered by the commune agreement to be punished. Prostitution was outlawed. Poaching the services of sailors and servants was forbidden. A system of communal meetings was instituted; justice was to be in the hands of constables who would bring cases to elected judges, or *conjurati*, two per thousand men. These elected officials were also to control the distribution of money, which included the sharing of booty and plunder, an obvious and perennial source of friction (as it proved when, after the fall of Lisbon, crusaders from Flanders and Cologne ignored this provision). The Dartmouth ordinances tackled the most prominent internal threats to an army's effectiveness: order, discipline, justice and the division of spoils. As events during the voyage showed, the security of the system of resolving conflicts, not least the accountability and sustained collegial process of reaching decisions, prevented the expedition from falling apart. The failure of Louis VII to implement similar sworn ordinances, 'laws of peace and other useful things necessary on the journey', may have played a part in his army's near-disintegration in Asia Minor, rescued only by the imposition of military discipline by the Templars, an enforced 'unity of spirit' which, an eyewitness argued, compensated for hunger and low morale.[12]

Whatever Louis VII's regulations contained, those promulgated by Frederick Barbarossa on 28 May 1189 at the Virfelt plain on the Danube near modern Bratislava echoed the Dartmouth ordinances. From chronicle descriptions Frederick, with the agreement of his magnates, imposed a formal peace throughout the army, applicable to all regardless of status. Especial attention seems to have been paid to theft, cheating, fraud and violence. Penalties were draconian: assault punishable by the loss of a hand; breaking market regulations by beheading. Special judges were appointed to enforce these rules, obedience to which was sworn by everyone in the army, oaths being taken 'in every tent' as one account put it. While the accompanying vision of an army replete with almost edenic honesty may be rose-tinted, the German crusade was notable for its cohesion and effectiveness until Frederick's death in Cilicia. The imposition of sworn obedience to laws, supported by the consent of the expedition's leaders, compensated for the loose political allegiances within the German army, offering a common guarantee of security, equality and fair treatment across ranks and regional origins.[13]

The Angevin provisions for the Third Crusade, which survive in more detail, served a similar function, directed as much to the security of the crusaders as to the convenience of their commanders. They shared features with both the German and the Dartmouth ordinances. In February 1188, at a council held at Geddington in Northamptonshire, Henry II issued decrees for the Saladin Tithe, the implementation of the crusaders' temporal privileges and for the conduct of *crucesignati*, banning extravagant dress, swearing, gambling and unattached women, except for respectable (i.e. aged) laundresses (who on campaign in Palestine doubled as de-lousers). These decrees represented what might be seen as the moral stage of crusade preparations, suitably elevated statements of intent to suit the propaganda campaign launched at the same time. To underline this, one decree determined that any money left by a crusader who died during the expedition would be divided between the army's general fund, alms for poor crusaders and support of the deceased's own followers. This provision effectively dispensed with customary testamentary conventions, further emphasizing the special status and unique commitment of those taking the Cross.[14]

Further detailed ordinances were issued for conduct on campaign, some of which may simply have reflected wider contemporary military conventions, such as Richard I's command before the storming of Messina in October 1190 that commoner deserters should lose a foot and knights be stripped of their belts, i.e. their status of knighthood, claiming this was the law.[15] The ordinance for the Angevin crusade fleet in the summer of 1190, again promulgated with explicit consent of clerical and lay magnates, addressed discipline. Order was to be maintained by constables and marshals, with justiciars appointed with authority to enforce laws over the whole fleet, 'English, Norman, Poitevin and Breton', their judgments taking precedence over any regional legal customs. Murderers were to be thrown into the sea or buried alive on land. Assaults that drew blood would be punishable by mutilation; affrays that stopped short of bloodshed by keelhauling. Swearing would attract fines.[16]

At Messina in October 1190, faced with the behaviour of an actual rather than putative army, the Geddington decrees on gambling, debt exemption and legacies were modified. Recognizing the habits of the noble classes, knights and clerics were permitted to gamble, but only up to a limit of losses of 20 shillings a day, which implicitly curtailed winnings as well; any debts beyond that incurred a fine of 100 shillings per 20 shillings over the limit. Tellingly, kings and magnates were now exempted from all restrictions and their household servants permitted the same licence as clerics and knights, presumably so that their masters always had someone to gamble with. Punishments for illicit gambling by ordinary soldiers and sailors were savage – keel-hauling for seamen; three days' whipping for the rest. All gambling debts as well as others incurred during the crusade were to be paid, regardless of the general crusaders' immunity. Fights over wagers and gambling posed an obvious threat to morale, especially among possibly competitive groups of strangers gathered in crusading armies. The Geddington testamentary decree was also altered in the interests of wealthy crusaders whose patronage would be expected to extend even beyond death. Now crusaders were allowed freely to dispose by will of arms, horses and clothing, along with half of the other goods they had with them, the other half to be reserved, as before, for general purposes.[17] It says much for the probity of Archbishop Baldwin and his executors that, on his death at Acre in November 1190, his money was divided, as he had wished, between paying for knights and sergeants on sentry duty and helping the poor, more or less in accord with the Geddington decrees.[18] As with the other restrictions that challenged aristocratic habits, on clothing and gambling, attempts to control legacies proved short-lived; no such restrictions seemed to inhibit crusaders in the following century. Further measures proposed at Messina suffered similarly mixed fortune. While repeating the Dartmouth ban on poaching servants, other potential sources of friction were tackled by the attempt to regulate the internal markets for bread, wine and meat, their price, quality and profit margins. In support, a fixed exchange rate between the Angevin and English currencies was established. None of this, of course, prevented hoarding, profiteering and the inflation caused by too much money pursuing too few supplies in the cash-rich camp outside Acre.[19]

The Angevin ordinances fitted a pattern. Although most do not survive, similar ordinances governing law, justice and maintaining peace were common necessary accompaniments to crusades. In 1217, the fleet of Rhinelanders, Frisians and other Netherlanders under the count of Holland mustered once more at Dartmouth, where they too agreed to 'laws and new rules (*iura*) establishing peace'. These included procedures for taking and sharing plunder.[20] Few crusades passed without some arguments or violence over the distribution of spoils. These could involve high politics, as in the rows between Richard I, Philip II and Leopold of Austria during the Third Crusade; the rivalries and jealousies of national and regional contingents, as at Lisbon in 1147; the greed of individuals, as at Alcazar in 1217; or feelings of betrayal by a manipulative high command expressed by Robert of Clari over the fate of the plunder of Constantinople in 1204, speaking for perhaps the majority of crusading footsloggers who felt cheated by their commanders – a familiar complaint from the First Crusade onwards.[21] Disciplinary ordinances demonstrated awareness of coalition armies' requirements for unitary discipline and mitigation of perennial causes of friction, social, recreational and commercial as well as criminal. The harshness of punishments was bolstered by the degree of prior consent and sense of community on which the viability of these temporary legal systems rested, stitched together in rational, deliberate responses to specific problems of mixed crusade armies. Their effectiveness can be seen where they worked – at Lisbon in 1147, in the armies of Frederick Barbarossa and Richard I – and where they did not – in the French forces in Asia Minor in 1147–8. Commenting on the sworn ordinances, 'laws of peace', at Metz, Odo of Deuil concluded caustically: 'because they did not observe them well, I have not preserved them either'.[22]

The corporate health sought by such regulations was of little consequence if an army lacked the bodily equivalent. Medical practice in medieval western Europe has often been seen as operating on different academic and practical levels – the educated physician and the artisan surgeon – with assumptions that neither was particularly rational nor effective. Recent research has cast doubt on many of these assumptions, with theoreticians observed as practitioners and not all medical interventions being useless or harmful.[23] Warfare inevitably generated intense demand for effective surgery, the treatment of infection and nursing. The Mediterranean crusades not only provided extensive empirical evidence but also contact with other medical traditions. It is clear from western medical treatises that by the fourteenth century, to a limited degree, theory had embraced experience. Given that most non-surgical medicine before the nineteenth century dealt with alleviation not cure, the record of medieval physicians may not have been quite as dire as their stereotype insists. With battlefield injuries, they achieved some effectiveness. However, most medical care remained largely palliative, with the emphasis on nursing rather than intervention, although one could lead to or combine with the other.

From the start, crusaders took their doctors with them. At least one of them was a laywoman, Louis IX's *physica* in 1248–50, *Magistra* Hersende, possibly the Parisian woman (*'une bourjoise de Paris'*) John of Joinville recorded (without acknowledging her professional status) as cradling the sick king when he was captured (he was suffering from dysentery). Louis took a clutch of medical advisers with him to Egypt, both physicians and surgeons.[24] He was following long precedent. When Godfrey of Bouillon badly wounded himself in fighting a bear during the march across Asia Minor in 1097, doctors (*medicos*) were on hand to treat him, almost certainly by cauterizing what seems to have been a serious arterial wound.[25] Western medics appear in Outremer from the earliest days of the Frankish settlement, and can be traced on almost all the major eastern crusades thereafter, usually associated with a great lord or specific regional contingent, although some physicians and surgeon-barbers probably travelled as entrepreneurial freelancers hoping, with some certainty, that their skills might find employment. Medical support on the battlefield and on the march was not restricted to the personal physicians of the great. Italian cities employed doctors to travel with their armies and navies. Bologna employed Hugh of Lucca and a Master Robert to attend the city's troops at Damietta during the Fifth Crusade. Hugh had been retained for 600 Bolognese lire a year; Robert was on contract for 50 gold bezants for the first year and 100 each year thereafter. Both were evidently smart, academically trained physicians, the top consultants of their day. Hugh later contributed to a *Chirurgia*, a surgical textbook by one of his pupils, Theodoric Borgognoni, that contained advice on treating weapon injuries of the sort Hugh would have seen on crusade.[26]

Crusade armies provided some communal nursing facilities. With typical thoroughness, in 1189 Frederick Barbarossa prepared ambulance wagons (*vehicula*) 'for sick travellers so that the infirm should not delay the healthy and the crowd of sick and destitute should not perish on the way'.[27] At the siege of Acre, crusaders from Lübeck, Hamburg and Bremen built a field hospital out of wood and canvas salvaged from breaking up the ships they had arrived in. Dedicated to St Mary, this improvised medical centre developed in a few years into the Teutonic Order, which, like its model the Hospitaller Order of St John, combined nursing and military functions.[28] A similar field hospice dedicated to Thomas Becket was established by English crusaders, probably Londoners, inspired by a clergyman, William, chaplain to the dean of St Paul's. During a storm on the way east, he swore a vow to found a chapel in honour of St Thomas if he managed to reach the Holy Land safely. (The horror of seasickness for landlubber crusaders should not be underestimated; both James of Vitry and John of Joinville left vivid, agonized accounts of their sufferings; chaplain William's was far from the only storm-driven plea for heavenly intervention.) At Acre, William buried the dead and nursed the sick, his chapel evolving quickly into a formal religious hospitaller institution, later also becoming militarized.[29] These initially ad hoc arrangements contrast with the more considered preparations of Italian cities and secular lords.

Crusade armies did not habitually leave their wounded or infirm behind; it would be bad for morale even though coping with them could slow down progress, exposing nursing columns to enemy attack. Like Frederick Barbarossa, Richard I provided for the wounded and sick beyond his immediate entourage, regarding it as part of a commander's duty. During his stay in Palestine he apparently set up a form of hospice at Ramla in 1191–2. In battle he provided shelter for the wounded at his so-called 'Standard', a sort of fortified cart, heavily armed, defended by a company of crack troops, surmounted by the royal banner fixed, for ease of identification, to a very long pole, probably a recycled ship's mast.[30] These expedients raise the question of the role of the Hospitallers of St John, whose great hospital in Jerusalem would have been familiar to all twelfth-century visitors to the Holy City before 1187. The order also operated field hospitals for the armies of the Franks on Outremer. There are hints of institutional protectionism that encouraged the formation of the new national nursing stations by visiting crusaders.[31] More likely, sheer numbers overwhelmed local resources. The Hospitallers' main medical function was nursing, providing the sick and needy, including pregnant women, with shelter, accommodation, food and basic hygiene. However, they and crusade doctors did essay some active treatments.

The fatality rate among the knights on long crusades, such as the First, Third or Fifth, has been estimated at between 25 and 35 per cent, the causes more or less equally divided between injuries and disease or malnutrition. The overall rate and the preponderance of disease over injury were probably higher for the lower ranks.[32] Disease was an endemic problem of military camp life, some conditions, like scurvy, linked to diet; others to insanitary conditions. Interest in the causes of infection can be found in Joinville's detailed description of the malady that struck the French army in the Nile Delta in 1250, which he ascribed, not unreasonably, to eating eels that had feasted on putrid corpses (in fact it was most probably scurvy).[33] Diet was of especial interest to physicians and nurses, detailed prohibitions and prescriptions appearing in twelfth-century Hospitaller statutes, including advice to eat quantities of fruit but not pulses or cheese. More active intervention was common. Trepanning, with an apparently acceptable survival rate; basic surgery to remove arrows; more skilled operations to extract broken bone fragments, again with an assumption of competence and success; bloodletting for crush wounds; the setting of broken bones; and washing wounds with wine or vinegar all feature in anecdotes or textbooks based on medical practice. Some empirical medical experimentation was possible. An autopsy was conducted on a slaughtered dancing bear to help determine the best treatment for a deep wound suffered by the ex-crusader Baldwin I of Jerusalem. This persuaded the doctors not to bandage or cover the wound, allowing the infected pus to drain out. Baldwin survived.[34] Archaeology has shown that medieval warriors could overcome serious fractures and other wounds; sawbones were not invariably killers, although Richard I's death in 1199 from gangrene after a botched attempt to remove a crossbow bolt should dispel too positive a view of medieval surgical prowess.

Crusade organizers took medical and nursing provision seriously. When preparing what transpired to be an aborted crusade in the 1330s, Philip VI of France received a treatise devoted to two apparently incompatible, but in practice proximate, features of crusade warfare. Physician to the great, Guy of Vigevano's *Texaurus Regis Francie* (1335) advised the king on the best diet, how to avoid poisoning, and on the health of ears, eyes and teeth. Additionally, Guy described, with detailed illustrations, a number of elaborate if improbable war machines: prefabricated moveable siege engines; devices for getting horses across water; and wind-propelled vehicles for desert use.[35] Crusading was ever father to ingenuity. Guy's coupling of medicine (he was at the time the queen of France's doctor) with military hardware reflected an obvious truth. The most effective preventatives of harm, injury, disease or death on crusade were food and drink, but also arms and armaments.

11

Supplies

The Bayeux Tapestry is the most famous misnomer in English history, being stitched embroidery not woven tapestry. In describing the fateful and fatal events surrounding the successful invasion of England in 1066 by Duke William of Normandy, the story is framed by epic, romance and homily to construct a personal drama from the narrative of high politics and war. Within this, the Tapestry reveals the prosaic mechanics behind the invasion. The story is punctuated by the transit of messengers, scouts or spies. Before action, both in Normandy and on arrival in England, William is shown taking advice with his close councillors. Space is lavished on the details of shipbuilding, from tree felling to carpenters fitting planks and the completed vessels being dragged by pulleys to the shore to be launched. Before embarkation, the necessary provisions and equipment are paraded in detail. Men and carts are shown bearing coats of mail, swords, helmets and spears (shields seemingly were brought by the cavalrymen themselves) along with wine barrels and wineskins. Across the Tapestry events are accompanied by the particulars of war: armour, swords, spears, lances, maces, axes, bows, arrows, horses and their harness, and, not least, the supply and consumption of food. Just as the final scenes before departure from France concern logistics of supplies and transport, so the first images following the landings at Pevensey depict the invaders foraging, cooking, baking and feasting, all before they build a wooden fort for protection, in a loud pre-echo of Napoleon's famous clichéd dictum.[1]

Such seemingly mundane details contribute to the tightening of dramatic tension, building towards the final confrontation at Hastings. They also resonated with an audience of military aristocrats, lay and clerical.

Even where inaccurate or distorted by artistic design, the inclusion of these images point to their importance. The pictures in the Bayeux Tapestry open a window onto the world of the First Crusade a generation later, an adventure on which one of the heroes of the Tapestry, and possible patron of its creation, William's brother Bishop Odo of Bayeux, died. Portrayed as a distinctly military churchman, Odo's is perhaps the earliest surviving visual portrait of a future *crucesignatus* (plate 20).[2] The Tapestry's far from incidental evidence of preparations, logistics and military domestic life is paralleled in details of crusaders' preparations and equipment in charters and from the narratives of chroniclers and poets. These interests remained central both to the practical consideration of warfare and how it was perceived. Three centuries later, in the glowing illuminations in the fourteenth-century manuscript statutes of the Neapolitan chivalric Order of the Knot (1352), details of embarkation on crusade find a similarly prominent place.[3] Once again victuals, military equipment and horses feature beside various classes of oared galleys and a sailing cargo vessel. Crusade planners required a cause, money, men, information, organization and a plan of action. They also needed supplies: food, arms, horses, ships, fortifications and siege engines.

Organizers left as little as possible to chance, with extensive systems for collecting war materiel stretched by the demands of long-distance crusading. Technical details were carefully considered before a step was taken. Whether these were influenced by theoretical manuals is debatable. Contemporary compilations such as the *Mappae Clavicula* (*A Little Key to the World*) contain seemingly relevant recipes for incendiary devices, flaming arrows and fire-resistant battering rams that on inspection prove unscientific, obscure and impractical.[4] More soundly based treatises held mixed usefulness.[5] The practical aspects of warfare attracted some academics, like Oliver of Paderborn, grounded in the mathematics of the classical curriculum. The standing of engineers, architects and master carpenters during the twelfth century elevated some of them to professional status, able to command professional fees.[6] Nevertheless, such skills remained rooted in artisan pragmatism, stimulated by immediate needs of the march, siege or battlefield, not contemplation in a cloistered study. Count Geoffrey of Anjou may have consulted the Roman Vegetius's manual on warfare, and earned a reputation for carpentry and engineering, even devising a bomb, but as a commander rather than practitioner. Henry I of England showed practical enthusiasm rather than expertise at the siege of Pont Audemer in Normandy in 1123 when he encouraged his team of carpenters to build a 24-foot-high moveable siege tower. Henry and Geoffrey may have been intelligent, observant and well educated with a natural interest in all aspects of military enterprise, but that does not necessarily mean they were expert technical engineers, any more than Gaston IV of Béarn, who led siege operations on one section of the walls of Jerusalem in 1099 and went on to act in a similar role at the siege of Zaragoza in 1118 where, it was said, he had experts working under him. The Lombard engineer who sold his skills dearly at Nicaea operated as overseer of a team.[7]

Improvisation, specialization, command and co-operation braided together in every aspect of supplies and materiel. Some strategic thinking was evident. Carpentry and weaponry, along with shipping and maritime trade, provided the crusaders with some of the few areas in which they could compete, or even claim an advantage over their opponents in the Near East. The basic raw materials of wood and iron were in theory jealously protected; trading these commodities with Muslim powers was outlawed by the Third Lateran Council in 1179 on pain of excommunication, deprivation of property and reduction to the status of a slave. The ban, which extended to weaponry, navigational aid and military intelligence, was repeated at the Fourth Lateran Council and subsequent papal crusade appeals. In the same vein, pirates and anyone trading with them were repeatedly condemned as preying on the vital supply lines to the eastern Mediterranean.[8] Economic warfare was well understood, even if largely incapable of being effectively pursued, given that policing the seas was impossible. The gathering of provisions and materiel, by contrast, relying on long experience of war and logistics, was more firmly grounded in effective practice.

FOOD

Food and drink determined the course of crusades, through the need for markets, foraging or plunder for land armies, or through the rate of consumption of prepared supplies by forces transported by ship. Behind these logistics lay the varying regional levels of domestic agricultural production and the ability to exploit them. Statistics are impossible, yet in general terms crusading depended on the expanding productivity of rural Europe as it did on the consequent increased intensity of commerce. It has been suggested that while it took the labour of nine workers to feed one horse for a year in eleventh-century Europe, two hundred years later it only demanded two or three.[9] Adequate provisioning was central from the outset. The timing of local harvests, even when not abundant, necessarily ordered the timing of the departures of the land contingents on the First, Second and Third Crusades. Similarly, the requirement for winter bases to refit and restock shaped successive crusades: Constantinople in 1096–7, for the Germans in 1147–8 and the Fourth Crusade in 1203–4; Frederick Barbarossa's occupation of Thrace in 1189–90; Richard I and Philip II in Sicily in 1190–91; the Flemish fleet at Marseilles in 1202–3; in 1217–18 the Netherlanders and Rhinelanders at Lisbon and Alcazar and the Frisians at Civitavecchia; the musters at Acre in 1217–18 and Cyprus in 1248–9. The tensions surrounding access to markets and fair prices provided a leitmotif in all eastern crusading, both in transit to and on arrival in the Holy Land.

The search for secure supply chains was constant: the markets of the Danube Basin and the north Balkans in 1096–7, 1147–8 and 1189; Cyprus or the fertile regions of northern Syria during and after the siege of Antioch in 1097–8; Byzantine markets in Asia Minor in 1147–8; Cyprus after its seizure by Richard I in 1191. Given the hostile hinterlands, supplying the many thousands camped at Acre in 1189–91 or Damietta in 1218–21 demanded sourcing provisions from across the eastern Mediterranean, and possibly beyond, unless there was a greater degree of commercial exchange between the competing armies than appears in the sources. These, at least for the Third Crusade, suggest little more than fraternizing for paid sex.[10] Some staples, such as salted pork, would have been largely unobtainable from Muslim regions. Louis IX's agents were active in Cyprus for two years before his crusade arrived in 1248, building up stores of grain and wine, a precedent followed by his brother Alphonse of Poitiers in buying up provisions in Apulia and Sicily in 1269. Louis may have taken salt pork or bacon with him from France, as Richard I did from England in 1190.[11] On campaign, the imperatives of supply provoked risky and often disastrous forays beyond crusader lines, whether outside Antioch in 1098 or from Damietta in 1220.[12] Before any crusade embarked, markets and supplies framed diplomacy, particularly in the first three great eastern campaigns with the Hungarians and Greeks, and shipping treaties, such as those with Genoa in 1190 and Venice in 1201. Failure to secure basic logistics could shatter or twist the best-laid plans: the German and French expeditions' lack of adequate markets in Asia Minor in 1147–8; or the crusaders in Venice in 1202 consuming supplies intended for the future campaign.[13]

A fundamental difficulty concerned the need to carry victuals set against their weight and bulk, a problem on land and sea. It has been estimated by modern scholars that the daily food consumption for a man on board a crusade ship (which presumably would not radically differ from the amount needed for a footslogger on land) was 1.3 kilos, made up chiefly of grain or flour (which weighed less) to make bread or biscuit; small amounts of cheese; salted meat, ubiquitously pork, and dried legumes. To drink, crusaders' daily intake of liquid may have come to between 3 and 4 litres a day for inactive seaborne troops, but 8 litres for those on moderate active duty short of fighting.[14] In the Mediterranean, drink could comprise wine of varying amounts, possible between 1 and 2 litres a day (remember the wineskins and hogsheads of the Bayeux Tapestry, suggesting wine not just for the bosses). Notoriously, the Norwegians underestimated the strength of the retsina they quaffed at Constantinople in 1110, with disastrous consequences.[15] Additionally, horses, even on land and used to being stall fed, required 5 kilos of grain, 5 of hay and 32 litres of water each, ten times the weight of a man's daily diet.[16] This presented organizers with a dual problem: cartage and restocking. On land, a military column's capacity to carry its own supplies was limited by the number of food wagons required and their drag on the speed of march. At sea, the conundrum revolved around the clashing imperatives of space, given the bulkiness of liquids, and the need for fresh water, for cooking and, especially, horses that obviously could not drink wine. For land crusaders such conflicts were tackled by frequent recourse to local markets or, in hostile territory, foraging; and, at sea, by frequent landfalls to replenish water supplies. Such enforced strategies involved either diplomatic finesse or military risk, or both.

Most of these calculations of amounts of food and drink rest on contemporary estimates: the Genoa treaty of 1190; the Venice treaty of 1201; Louis IX's contracts with the Venetians in 1268; crusade advice provided by Marseilles in 1318; or Marino Sanudo's detailed analysis of the practical requirements of crusading naval blockades. To this list, which excludes non-crusade quartermasters' calculations, could be added Emperor Henry VI's 1195 offer of grain to his paid crusader knights and sergeants.[17] Contracts contained detailed and exact provisions for supplying men and horses. The Venetian treaty of 1201 specified provisions for up to a year, i.e. during a year not necessarily for a whole year. The amounts for each man within the contract are precisely configured: six *sextaria* (*c*.400 kilos) of bread, flour, grain and legumes (perhaps enough for ten months) and half an amphora (perhaps 340 litres) of wine (just over a litre a day if spread over ten months). The horses were to be provided with three *modia* of grains, about a cubic metre or *c*.800 kilos, enough for a year, but omitting the necessary supplement of hay or grazing which constituted about three-quarters of a horse's food diet. This omission implied either that hay and/or pasture were expected to be readily available at Venice or at the necessarily frequent watering stops en route east. Similarly, an unspecified sufficiency of water was also included in the terms of the treaty.[18] This Venetian thoroughness was mirrored just over a century later by Marino Sanudo. Besides exhaustive details of geography, tactics, manning, shipping (down to the best season to cut timber), weaponry and wages, Sanudo provided extraordinarily precise estimates for the consumption of biscuits, wine, meat, cheese and beans for 1 day, 30 days, 12 months and 5¼ days (a working week?) for one man, then for ten, a hundred, one thousand, ten thousand and one hundred thousand men.[19]

Comparable attention to provisioning is evident from earlier campaigns. Albert of Aachen described the carts of food supplies that accompanied Peter the Hermit's march down the Danube, the often rapacious search for new provisions and the hardship suffered in Bulgaria 'because they had lost over two thousand wagons and carts which were carrying corn, barley, and meat'. Peter's forces were reduced to roasting ears of newly ripened corn (it was July) to survive, a suggestion that came from Peter's advisers. The example of the collapse of Peter's provisioning into desperate chaotic hand-to-mouth larceny led Godfrey of Bouillon, a few months later, to negotiate a detailed trading agreement with the king of Hungary.[20] The importance of crusaders' victuals dominate passages of veterans' accounts of later expeditions, the cliché of it being a matter of life or death for once being literally true. The problems were most agonizing, protracted and dangerous for land armies, problems well anticipated judging by the exhaustive preparatory diplomatic negotiations to secure markets and equitable trading conditions in 1096, 1146–7 and 1188–9. Odo of Deuil claimed to have included so much topographical detail in his account of the march of the French army in 1147 in order to advise and warn successors of the difficulties in securing provisions. He also described how progress of the French march was severely impeded by slow-moving packhorses and carts clogging up the roads.[21] Foraging for food presented problems of discipline as well as organization. As the German host trundled through Bulgaria in late July 1189, the servants and other youths who had been detailed to collect grain, honey and vegetables began to indulge themselves in wholesale theft. Although they and their knightly masters were severely taken to task by the high command, their freelance robberies stand as reminders of the difficulties and temptations but, above all, of the natural human dimensions in these vast undertakings that no amount of pious gloss could wholly conceal.[22]

Sea passage in some respects made the difficulties more predictable and contained, especially if the crusade leadership furnished its own carrying fleet. The contrast between the fortunes of Philip II and Richard I is revealing. While Richard provisioned his own fleet, Philip had to negotiate supplies, '*victui necessaria*' as the chronicler Rigord commented, from the Genoese, which were to last only eight months. Consequently, before securing a share in Richard's Sicilian windfall, at Messina in the winter of 1190–91, Philip had to cast about for ways to supply his forces on the next leg of the journey. Clearly toying with a land route, which he may have calculated would be cheaper and offered easier provisioning, Philip approached the king and queen of Hungary, asking for help with food supplies ('*ut sibi subvenirent in victualibus*'), and the Byzantine emperor, requesting safe passage, implicitly seeking guaranteed access to markets.[23]

Richard's position was quite different. From the start his officials exerted a degree of direct control over provisioning. He committed to providing food for a year for the knights, infantrymen, sailors and horses in his fleet, which, on the evidence of one observer, Richard of Devizes, could have numbered 100 vessels, carrying 80 men and 40 horses, with another 14 ships carrying 160 men and 80 horses.[24] On these figures, Richard was providing for about 10,000 men and 5,000 horses. If the scale of his preparations and the survival of record evidence stand out, in essence Richard's problems and solutions mirrored the general crusader's condition, in this case the need for non-perishable food and other essentials. For once evidence is not reliant solely on admiring chronicle descriptions of military preparations. The accounts of the English Exchequer, recorded on the Pipe Rolls, chart some of the collection of food supplies for Richard's crusade fleet. From Essex and Hertfordshire came 140 cheeses, clearly, at almost 4s 6d each, quite substantial ones, and 300 bacon carcasses; from Hampshire 800 bacon carcasses, 100 cheeses (6d cheaper than those from Essex and Hertfordshire); 20 measures of beans at 1s each, and 10,000 horseshoes with nails; from Cambridgeshire and Huntingdonshire 100 measures of beans at 1s 3d each; from Lincolnshire 300 bacons at 1s 5d each; from Gloucestershire, with its iron works in the Forest of Dean, 50,000 horseshoes and nails, an additional supply of iron worth £100, and 276 measures of dried beans; from the Tower of London, the armoury of the capital, came crossbow bolts and 3,600 crossbow arrowheads.[25]

Some important requirements are missing from the Pipe Roll accounts: grain, wine, hay for horses and armour for the hired soldiers being transported by sea or those following Richard overland to Marseilles. What seem to be noted were the secondary necessities for which the king had made himself responsible, including for horses, which traditionally fell to lords and commanders to support and even supply replacements. Even here, the Pipe Roll listing of 60,000 horseshoes would only serve an active cavalry force of 5,000 for perhaps three months.[26] Armour was probably the responsibility of each soldier; certainly knights and their *équipes* would have provided their own. The crossbowmen's equipment indicated that they were in the king's employ; at Acre he was to offer to take all the crusade host's archers into his paid service.[27] In general, although the Pipe Roll evidence is indicative rather than comprehensive, representing only a fraction of his total supply of victuals and equipment, Richard's provisions reflected the standard requirements for crusade leaders and led. Scales might differ, with the involvement of private commercial entrepreneurs more or less prominent, and the extent of dispositions of individual crusaders, as opposed to collective leaderships, variable. However, the model of what was required and prepared remained consistent. The quartermaster stood behind events, one of the great missing presences in crusade narratives.

HORSES

Horses were central to western European military tactics and culture. Unsurprisingly, horses feature in two-thirds of the Bayeux Tapestry, by no means all in scenes of battle. Military effectiveness and social status alike relied on the possession of horses. The reality that much crusade warfare actually revolved around sieges – Nicaea, Antioch, Jerusalem, Lisbon, Damascus, Acre, Zara, Constantinople, Toulouse, Damietta – did nothing to diminish their importance. Providing mounts, replacements or compensation for their loss formed a part of lordship's patronage of knights.[28] A central task for planners was to ensure a continuous supply. Land armies needed to carry or acquire grain as well as hay and to provide regular pasturage, which could divert the route, riskily break the column or delay the march. The need for re-shoeing demanded the employment of regiments of blacksmiths, although their expertise could also assist in constructing siege engines or mending and replacing weaponry. The loss of horses and the necessity to replenish stocks influenced the course of campaigns, as on the First Crusade. Strategically, horses limited how crusades were planned. Until technology and naval engineering allowed for their long-distance transport by sea, in the first half of the twelfth century, war horses had to go by land, with only short sea journeys, such as those of the Norman armies across the English Channel in 1066, the straits of Messina in 1061 and, more riskily, the Adriatic in the Normano-Byzantine wars of the 1080s; or the Pisan attack on Mahdia in 1087.[29] Mounted contingents on the First and Second crusades were therefore forced to travel by land, with restricted ferry crossings of the Adriatic or Bosporus.[30] The great northern coalition fleet that assembled at Dartmouth and attacked Lisbon in 1147 did not carry horses, the knights on board presumably intending to acquire mounts once they reached the Holy Land – a feasible policy as Palestine was largely in friendly hands, unlike fifty years earlier. The siege of Lisbon was an infantry affair.[31] A resident in Jerusalem commented that the new Frankish kingdom had been in peril in 1101 partly because reinforcements by sea were unable to bring horses with them.[32] This changed. The lead was taken in the south. Horses were shipped long distances during campaigns in the western Mediterranean in 1114–15. The Venetian crusade of 1122 was supposed to have embarked with 15,000 fighting men and 300 horses.[33] The history of Mediterranean crusading was transformed.

The logistics of transporting horses by sea presented acute challenges. Horses occupied considerable space, as did their feed. They needed regular supplies of fresh water, hay or pasturage, which may explain the frequent stops and leisurely progress of the Venetian fleet from the lagoon to the Levant between August 1122 and May 1123 and of other crusade fleets recorded by veterans of sea passages. Each day, a well-nourished horse could produce c.25 kilos of faeces and as much as 36 litres of urine.[34] Successful carriage by sea required purpose-built or modified ships and specialist skills. The weight of the necessary iron had to be considered as well. A horseshoe might weigh between 280 and 425 grams; Richard's 60,000 could therefore have weighed between 16 and 25.5 tonnes. A single set of six nails per shoe might weigh a further 84 grams (14 grams each), which would add another 5 tonnes; the Pipe Rolls suggest two sets were taken, which meant 10 tonnes for the nails. Small wonder Frederick Barbarossa was deterred from essaying the sea route by the size of his army, perhaps 10–12,000 men, with 3,000 knights – and their horses.[35] Whether or not Richard of Devizes' figures for the 1190 Angevin fleet are correct, in particular for the number of horses, the attendant problems are clear; so, too, the success in dealing with them. Richard may have taken far fewer than the 5,000 horses of Richard of Devizes' description. However, Philip II's contract with Genoa specified 1,300 horses (albeit with a get-out clause stipulating the need for new terms for shipping without horses) and the Venice treaty of 1201, 4,500. Shipping contracts for Louis IX's first crusade included precise details of horse transport and cost.[36] By 1248, as for the previous assault on Damietta in 1218 or the crusade of 1202–4, it was assumed that crusaders would sail with their horses.

SHIPPING

One of the few clear advantages possessed by crusaders over their enemies lay in shipping and the ability to sail and row long distances. They were well aware of it. Crusade ships were blessed on departure; Cross-giving liturgies included prayers for their safe return.[37] During the eleventh and twelfth centuries, maritime technology allowed Latin Christians to dominate trade across the Mediterranean; to seize ports around the Iberian coast, invade the Balearic Islands, Sicily, the Adriatic coast of the Balkans, Tunisia, Cyprus and the coastal lands of the north and eastern Baltic; and to supply the new settlements in the Levant with colonists, tourists, raw materials and commerce. The ability to transport horses by sea immeasurably advanced Latin power on all fronts of political expansion. To landlubbers, this could appear wondrous. John of Joinville, from a family steeped in generations of crusade service, remembered seeing his horses loaded onto a ship at Marseilles in August 1248:

> the port of the ship [i.e. a door in the stern] was opened, and all the horses we wanted to take to Outremer with us were put inside and then the door was closed again and plugged well, as when a cask is caulked, because when the ship is on the high sea, the whole door is under water.[38]

In fact, these hatches were probably only completely covered sporadically, when the ship rolled in the sea swell.

As the detailed contracts Louis IX and his followers secured with Genoa and Marseilles demonstrated, planners paid close attention to precise details of ship construction to obtain suitable vessels. There was even talk – possibly garbled – of the count of St Pol in 1248 having to source a suitable vessel from as far away as Inverness. The

Genoese contracts itemized the exact dimensions of keel, decks, bulwarks, forecastles, sterncastles and masts (two, fore and midships).[39] Accommodation for horses formed just one aspect of the rapid development of the types of ships used by crusaders: cargo carriers, troop ships, landing craft, sailing vessels and oared galleys. Technologies of form and construction differed locally between northern Europe and the Mediterranean. Oars and sail were combined in both. Single-masted, open, half-decked oared ships, such as the Norse *knerrir* and larger *snekkjur*, or open lateen-rigged sailing transports familiar from ships of the Viking age and the Bayeux Tapestry, or the Mediterranean equivalent *naves*, were gradually supplanted by multi-decked sailing vessels of the sort described in the Genoese contracts and large adapted cargo ships. Ocean-going round-hulled cogs of northern Europe appeared on crusade in the later twelfth century, becoming familiar carriers in the Mediterranean in the thirteenth. Bireme oared galleys, powered by two (or later three) men per bench, were joined by oared triremes; as early as 1189 Clement III was writing of the departure of fifty Danish and twelve Frisian armed triremes.[40]

Dimensions varied. Richard I commanded at least one sixty-oared *esnecca* (literally 'snake') that made the trip from England to Syria.[41] Clear distinctions were made by planners and hirers between types of vessel, even if their exact characteristics now remain unclear. Richard of Devizes distinguished between busses, with twice the capacity of the *naves*, in 1190 and noted that the armada Richard led from Sicily comprised 156 *naves*, 24 busses and 39 galleys. At Marseilles Richard had hired ten busses and twenty galleys.[42] His own accounts point to different sized vessels. His officials trawled the ports of southern England commandeering vessels, usually for two-thirds of their full value, at an average of £50 per ship. Their variety can be judged from the different sizes of crews (between twenty-one and sixty-one on the Pipe Rolls, echoed by Richard of Devizes' figures of between thirty and sixty). It has been estimated that the fleet that sailed from Venice in 1202 comprised a few grand sailing vessels for the high command, 150 horse transports and 50 galleys (provided by the Venetian war fleet), assuming ship's companies of 600 passengers. Crewmen were required, possibly in numbers not far short of the soldiers they were transporting.[43] Accounts of veterans distinguish between a parade of vessels, even though the language was usually more literary than technical and precise characteristics are elusive: barges, cogs, dromons (an oared vessel), galleys with two or single banks of oars, longships, skiffs, rowing boats or just generic *naves*, ships. The choice of vessel was not neutral. The presence of specialist horse-carrying galleys in the 1201 Venetian contract might indicate the goal of the fleet was not a port but beaches – Egypt not Acre.[44]

Greater clarity of function appeared in shipping contracts. The Treaty of Venice specified specialist horse-carrying transport galleys, *uissiers*, as well as *naves* for the bulk of troops. These horse transports, also known as *taridae*, were fitted with stern ports for embarking and disembarking horses, used effectively before the walls of Constantinople.[45] Frederick II planned to take fifty such vessels on crusade in the 1220s, each capable of holding forty horses.[46] In 1246, Louis IX ordered twelve *taridae* from the Genoese, with capacity for twenty horses each. He also commissioned further horse transports and landing craft in Cyprus.[47] Not all these schemes worked as intended. Although a local Outremer lord, the count of Jaffa, seems to have successfully beached his landing craft at Damietta in 1249, most of the French, having disembarked from large ships to small ones, still had to wade ashore in the face of enemy fire, the king included; another classic case of the limits of planning.[48]

The restriction of numbers of horses per horse-transport ship, between twenty and forty seeming to be the usual range in the mid-thirteenth century, raised the costs of crusading. It also reflected the greater care afforded the animals, each held upright in individual stalls by a form of cradle that prevented them falling over because of the sea's swell or in storms. Horses were high value items of military equipment needing careful handling and protection at sea as on land. Such specialist vessels lay at the top end of the market, luxury military equipment subject to high price contracts, as in 1201 (each *uissier* perhaps with a capacity of thirty horses) or 1246. The large converted cargo vessels, such as cogs, could, ad hoc, carry far more: eighty in Richard I's busses, according to Richard of Devizes; accommodation for sixty horses in addition to passengers in a Marseilles lease of a ship to the count of Forez for his voyage to Cyprus in 1248; a hundred on the lowest deck in a Marseilles contract for Louis IX's second crusade of 1268.[49] Conditions below decks can hardly have been anything but primitive and grim: the Marseilles contract implied stowage for men and horses indiscriminately.

The treatment of the crusaders on board ship was not neglected. The increase in cabin space and decking spared passengers exposure to the elements. The numbers carried varied. The company on board the *St Victor* from Marseilles in 1250, excluding crew, numbered 453. Louis IX's flagship on his return from Acre in 1254 held over 500. In the thirteenth century Marseilles legislated for complements of 500 to 550 passengers in ships bound for the Levant. Some transport vessels apparently held a greater capacity, over 1,000 in the case of one Genoese ship in 1248. The 80 to 160 on Richard I's ships in 1190 was on the low side, reflecting perhaps the horses and amount of materiel taken with them, although one ship in the fleet, hired by Londoners, also carried between 80 and 100 people. The English chronicler Ralph of Diceto, with close contacts with some of the crusaders involved, estimated that 37 ships in 1189 from England, Denmark and Flanders carried 3,500 passengers between them.[50] Some vessels may have been much smaller, at least on the Mediterranean leg. By contrast, the great northern cogs and Mediterranean passenger carriers, many, if not all, like Richard I's fleet, adapted from cargo ships, encouraged the formation of substantial temporary communities, adopting their own patron saints, as did the Londoners in 1189–90, or, like the passengers on the *St Victor* in 1250, acting together in a lawsuit. Floating communes were not the prerogative of crusaders. The pirate flotilla from northern Europe that apparently put in at Tarsus in the autumn of 1097 was described as a sworn association.[51]

Such arrangements did not eradicate social distinctions. Grandees like James of Vitry might secure more cabin space than ordinary spear carriers. The leaders of the Fourth Crusade cruised across the Adriatic and Aegean in large sailing ships with roomy upper decks, just as Louis IX did in the eastern Mediterranean, while lesser ranks squeezed into galleys.[52] Conditions were cramped but not disorderly. A form of martial law prevailed. Living accommodation was regulated. Every ordinary passenger, at least on thirteenth-century Marseilles ships, who might be paying up to 25 shillings each, was given a parchment ticket with his name and number and instructions on which crew member he was to mess with. Scribes kept copies of each crusader's name and a record of cargo and horses. It was a business, with crusaders eager and, occasionally, vulnerable clients. The Marseilles rules forbad ships' masters from being in business with the providers of food, the latter having to accompany the voyage, a potentially rather effective disincentive to fraud. Bribing scribes, presumably in the hope of preferential treatment or a better berth, was outlawed. Such anxieties were not new. The 1190 Genoa contract included a fair-dealing clause.[53] Crusaders were men of affairs no less than their entrepreneurial maritime partners.

The near-monopoly of Latin Christians in long-distance shipping was closely allied to the sophistication of carpentry across Europe. The profession of Christ, carpentry attracted a degree of social kudos for its master craftsmen directly linked to its social and economic importance. Medieval culture was largely built in wood, used for shelter, accommodation, display, building, fuel, storage, wheels, ladders, carts, boats, bridges, barrels, fishing, domestic utensils, saddles, arrows, crossbow bolts and spear shafts. The flexibility of timber technology combined with the skill of carpenters found striking confirmation during the crusades. Ships often played central roles, proving highly adaptable. The success of the assault on the walls of Constantinople in 1204, and the capture of the Tower of Chains at Damietta in 1218, depended on the conversion of transport ships into floating siege engines, a technique familiar from the siege of Lisbon.[54] For his raid into the Red Sea in 1183, Reynald of Châtillon apparently used ships that had been dismantled, carried across the desert and then reassembled.[55] More often, the timbers of crusade ships were recycled. In 1192, Richard I re-used timber from smashed cargo ships to construct new troop carriers on the coast of southern Palestine.[56] The requirements of siege engines for finished planks and beams invited cannibalizing ships' timbers if crusader forces had failed to bring ready-made materials with them. Timber from recently arrived western fleets may have been used to build siege towers at Jerusalem in 1099; certainly salvaged ropes, hammers, nails, axes, mattocks and hatchets from Genoese ships were employed.[57] The relative paucity of seasoned timber in the Near East provided one incentive, particularly when large throwing engines required long beams, for which ships' masts could be effective.

A simple fact of navigation also encouraged the re-use of ships' timbers in crusade warfare in the Levant. From 1098 onwards, fleets from northern Europe assisted in campaigns in the eastern Mediterranean, some travelling very great distances from Scandinavia, northern Germany and the British Isles. However, none returned. The Atlantic flows into the Mediterranean through the Straits of Gibraltar in a passage of $c.45$ miles, with a strong surface current from west to east of $c.6$ knots, almost impossible for a galley to row against successfully. The prevailing winds also blow west to east. Only by hugging the coast would it have been feasible to get through from east to west, but during the twelfth and thirteenth centuries all of the southern shore, and much of the northern, lay in hostile hands. Eventually, the addition of extra sails and heightened sides enabled galleys to overcome these obstacles. Yet the first recorded ship from the Mediterranean to reach northern waters via the Straits only arrived in 1277.[58] Consequently, northern crusaders who came by sea had to find a different return route, usually via the ports of Italy and southern France and then overland. For crusade leaders, this added to the complexity of their arrangements. The currents in the Straits of Gibraltar, combined with cack-handed diplomacy, forced Richard I to risk returning from Palestine via Austria and led directly to his capture by Duke Leopold, imprisonment in Germany and ransom.

Less dramatically, the ultimate redundancy of many of the cogs and other ships from the north, added to natural physical degradation of hulls and timbers and the reduction in return passenger numbers because of the casualty rate, further encouraged the re-use of materials. The flag pole of Richard I's 'Standard' was almost certainly a ship's mast. It is hard to see where else the necessary timber and parts could have been assembled from for the huge stone-throwing machines and other siege engines built after the arrival at Acre of Richard and Philip II, not least as these were in addition to the siege machinery the crusaders had brought with them. Crusaders from Lübeck, Bremen and Hamburg built their field hospital outside Acre in 1190 out of timbers and canvas from their ships, materials ubiquitous in that and all other similar crusader camps.[59] The English hospice established in the camp at Acre at the same time probably exploited the same resource. The provision of ships, therefore, involved more than a means of transport. As ready stores of vital military and domestic raw materials, spare parts and even as siege machines in their own right, ships provided a very diverse and sustained resource for any crusade army, on land as well as on the seas.

SIEGE MACHINES

It is unlikely that crusade organizers necessarily planned for the dismantling of their ships; and certainly not for those hired in the Mediterranean. However, they did prepare for siege warfare. The main siege equipment comprised means to scale walls, often wooden towers on wheels or rollers as well as ladders; to undermine walls, a process needing overhead and side protection; to batter walls, with huge throwing devices such as mangonels or trebuchets; or to break down gates with rams. Another option, used at Antioch in 1097–8 and to a more limited extent at Messina in 1190 and at Acre in 1191, were counter-forts to prevent enemy or defenders' access or egress. The First Crusade's initial siege, at Nicaea, required machines to be constructed on site, presumably with materials supplied by the Byzantines. The leaders were careful to stockpile both machines and raw materials, Albert of Aachen referring to the piles of wood, including oak beams, stored by the princes during the siege.[60] The strategy of counter-forts and subterfuge at Antioch suggest the crusaders did not take such raw materials with them on their march. The appearance of siege engines again on the march south might reflect the coincidence of the arrival of supporting Italian and northern fleets. Every crusade was accompanied by potentially expert engineers, some, like Gaston IV of Béarn on the First Crusade, or Archdeacon William of Paris during the Languedoc crusade, combining roles – in William's case with that of a recruiting preacher.[61] On at least one occasion, during the Third Crusade, crusaders recruited enemy siege experts under duress.[62]

Although most siege engines continued to be constructed on site to suit immediate demands, by the Third Crusade commanders were transporting siege weapons and construction materials from the west. In 1190 Count Henry of Champagne arrived at Acre with French siege engines, possibly including throwing machines.[63] A year later, Richard I had arranged for ships in his fleet to carry materials specifically to build siege machines, possibly alongside pre-fabricated mangonels, presumably transported in sections. The necessary technology was available. A year later he shipped his stone-throwers in sections by sea to besiege Darum in southern Palestine.[64] Possession of large stone-throwing machines acted as symbols of status and martial virility; each of the main leaders at Acre possessed their own and one was even built at the expense of the common crusade fund. Trebuchets were reputed to be capable of throwing horses and were probably able to hurl stones of between 90 and 135 kilos up to 275 metres. A not-always friendly rivalry appeared to develop around their power and effectiveness. They were given names: Bad Neighbour (*Malvoisine*) or God's Stone-thrower. How many were brought ready-made is unknowable; probably some, possibly many. In 1202, the crusader fleet that sailed from Venice to Zara took on board, so Geoffrey of Villehardouin remembered, 'more than three hundred petraries [i.e. stone-throwers of various sorts and sizes] and mangonels'.[65]

Predictably, perhaps, one of the most extravagant demonstrations of combined technology and planning was associated with Richard I. In the winter of 1190/91 he had built a wooden castle outside Messina, both as a secure headquarters and to intimidate the locals. (It was called, with typical subtlety, 'Mattegriffon', or 'Kill the Locals'.) This he dismantled, packed up in sections and took with him to Palestine, where he re-erected it outside the walls of Acre. This technology may not have been new. The mid–twelfth-century Norman historical romancer, Wace, claimed that William the Conqueror took ready-made forts with him to England in 1066. Richard's castle acted as more than a symbol of bravado. It provided both a siege fortress and secure base, far superior to the more customary corral of tents.[66] In romance and fiction, Richard was and is portrayed as the epitome of the chivalric crusade warrior and leader. In ways wholly unglamorous but more significant to the running of the wars of the Cross – in planning, strategy, logistics, administration and execution – this image stands.

12
Strategy

The crusades opened windows onto a wider world, for crusaders and their opponents alike. Pushed by economic, social, intellectual and ideological developments in western-European culture, crusaders were simultaneously attracted beyond the previous confines of Christendom by trade and competition for control of natural resources and political space. The crusades did not create these forces. A striking feature of the First Crusade were the numbers of westerners encountered as the armies marched east, some, like the Norman émigrés in Byzantium, of close acquaintance. One story described how a squadron of Flemish and Frisian pirates had been plying their business across the Mediterranean for eight years before they coincided with Baldwin of Boulogne at Tarsus in September 1097. True or not, it clearly made for a credible yarn. Even the notorious Norman murderer Hugh Bunel managed to find sanctuary in far-off Jerusalem where, no doubt to mutual surprise, he found he was joined by his duke and a Norman army in June 1099.[1] The previous and parallel engagement of Italian ports with Levantine entrepôts and trade routes provided added incentive and vital support. The growth of long-distance pilgrimage to the Holy Land lent knowledge and specific focus, reflected in the founding myth of Peter the Hermit, the returning pilgrim, the '*primus auctor*', bent on revenge.[2] The routes employed by the First Crusade armies to Constantinople displayed sound geographic knowledge, even before the acquisition of Byzantine guides. The Danube–north Balkans road, the Bari–Dyrrachium ferry crossing and the Via Egnatia were familiar from pilgrims, merchants and Norman-Italian warriors. The tortuous journey of the Provençal army through north Italy and down the Dalmatian coast, whether or not arranged with the Greek emperor, did not mean they were lost.[3] Even the gloss applied to the Danube route as following in the footsteps of Charlemagne confirmed rather than clouded practical knowledge.[4] From the start, crusade armies knew where they were going and how to get there.

KNOWING WHERE TO GO

Accurate or useful geographic knowledge in the eleventh, twelfth and thirteenth centuries had to compete with theoretical, imaginative and fantasized descriptions of the world, virtual geography that mapped stories, concepts and spiritual aspiration, routes to heaven not directions on earth. Most empirical knowledge was local or partial, derived from travellers, the inherited observations of trading communities or the rounds of visitations within networks of religious houses. The internal opening up of Europe in the eleventh and twelfth centuries increased the movement of people, the transmission of information and shared knowledge of distant places. By contrast, virtual geography was backed by the authority of Scripture and tradition. When Fulcher of Chartres described the fauna of his new homeland in Palestine in the early twelfth century, he copied from the Roman author Solinus's *Collection of Memorable Things*, itself based largely on the elder Pliny's *Natural History*. So he inserted accounts of fabulous creatures such as capricorns, basilisks, dragons and chimeras. Yet Fulcher was quite able to present an observant account of his tour of the Dead Sea area in 1100, including tasting for himself the sea's salty water and speculating on the physical reasons for its high salinity.[5] This juxtaposition of objective personal observation and the dominance of received artificial wisdom was characteristic of the travelogues contained in pilgrims' accounts and veterans' chronicles. The impression of unreason is compounded by surviving cartographic depictions, particularly the so-called *mappae mundi*, maps of the world that reflected the virtual geography of Bible and fable together with remembered scraps of classical learning.

However, an image of irrational medieval fantasy combining with ignorance of how the world was configured misleads. Some general features were well understood. It was known that the world was a sphere and it was portrayed as such. The learned were acquainted with Erastosthenes' calculation of the earth's circumference, at *c.*25,000 miles. The St Albans monk Matthew Paris (d.1259) knew that there was a place where the sun stood directly overhead twice a year, the equator.[6] Although realistic knowledge of Central Asia and the Far East came only with diplomatic, commercial and missionary contact with the Mongol empire and China in the thirteenth and four-teenth centuries, the tripartite division of the known world into the three continents of Europe, Asia and Africa, in roughly accurate if formalized alignment, was standard. In any case, most elite accounts of the geography of the physical world did not intend to provide travel advice. They were produced to entertain, edify, explain and enlighten, to instruct and guide the mind, spirit or imagination, not the body. Their readers and listeners understood this. If they had not, such works would have been both pointless and redundant. Those, including crusade veterans, who sought to describe actual travel employed prose rather than pictures in defining precise linear routes, written equivalents to modern satellite navigational devices fitted in motor cars. Cartography, as it developed in the thirteenth century, expressed a variety of objects. Although most maps of the time were useless for the purpose of accurately charting the physical world, many were diagrammatically indicative, in the way the London Underground map is indicative rather than accurate. Despite the sup-posedly limiting religious, theoretical and imaginative frame in which the natural world was conceived, travellers displayed alert, clear-eyed awareness of the physical features, landscapes and places they encoun-tered. Perceptions of geography were thus bifurcated, the imagined and the observed complementing not contradicting each other in search of a vision of an ordered world. Crusade planners resource-fully charted their way along both paths.

Information on suitable routes for crusade armies took three forms: oral; literary; and visual. Although, unlike in modern travel, the third was perhaps the least important, all three combined to provide useful, not merely figurative, representations of routes, places, distances, top-ography and winds. The presence of merchants and former pilgrims on the First Crusade, and crusade veterans, such as Conrad III or

15 and 16. The logistics of medieval warfare: shipbuilding.

17 and 18. The logistics of medieval warfare: arms and supplies. (*See p. 256.*)

19. The logistics of medieval warfare: food. (*See p. 256.*)

20. One of the first crusaders: Odo of Bayeux in armour at the battle of Hastings. (*See p. 273.*)

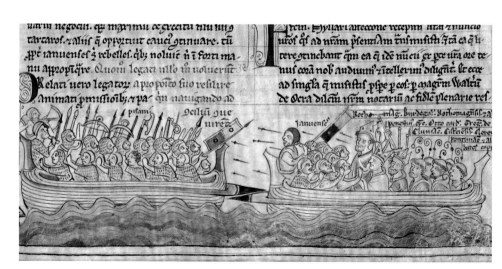

21. Naval warfare, with attendant priests: a battle between Pisans and Genoese.

22. Building a battlefield fort.

23. A thirteenth-century Englishman's view of the Holy Land. (*See p. 280.*)

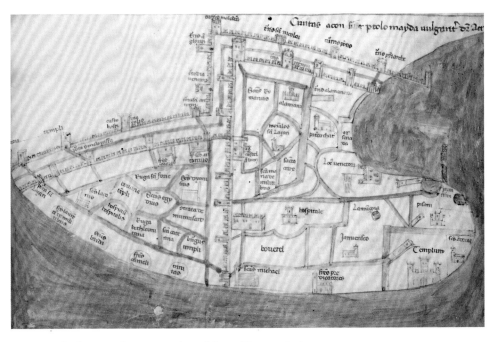

24. An early fourteenth-century plan of Acre. (*See p. 282.*)

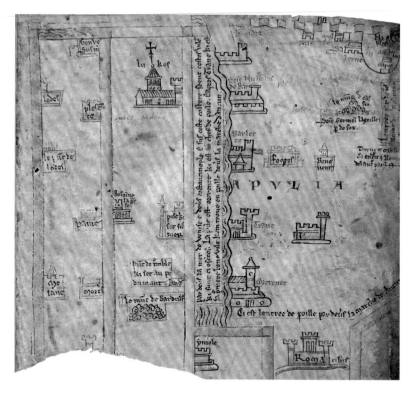

25. Knowing where to go: from a thirteenth-century itinerary from London to southern Italy.

26. Knowing where to go: an early fourteenth-century chart of the Near East.

27. How to influence people: Marino Sanudo Torsello presenting copies of his treatise on how to recover the Holy Land to Pope John XXII in 1321. (*See p. 282.*)

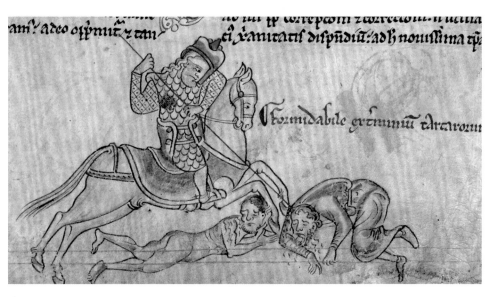

28. New strategic threats: the Mongol invasion of eastern Europe.

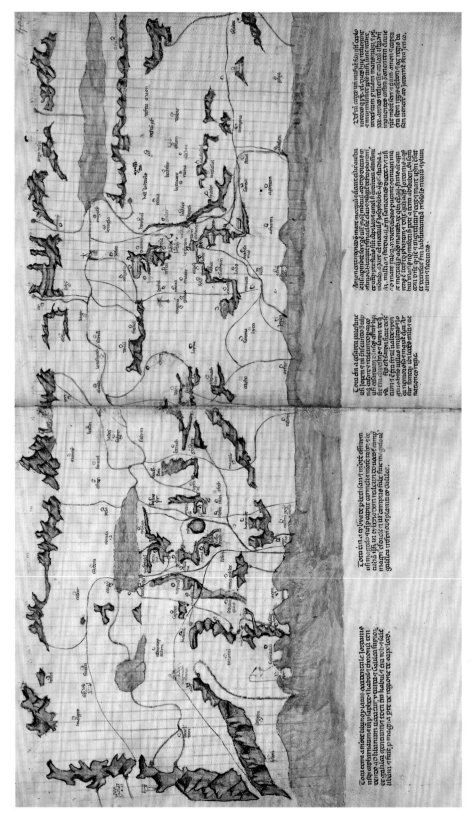

29. Knowing what to find: a grid map of the Holy Land. (*See p. 282.*)

Frederick Barbarossa, on all subsequent expeditions, provided a ready stock of relevant knowledge and experience. Some crusaders used letters home to convey useful information very similar to the kind found in veterans' chronicles. In 1190, Guy of Bazoches's letters to his nephews contained detailed descriptions, first of his journey to Marseilles, and then of his voyage from there to Syria (it took him thirty-five days via Sicily, Crete and Cyprus), accounts full of local colour, anecdote and historical background, such as Sicily's lurid history being one of tyranny and rebellion since Classical times. Guy may have been writing for the benefit of posterity as well as his relations. The author of a book 'on the regions of the world', he clearly held an especial geographical interest.[7] He was not alone. The author of a late twelfth-century Pisan nautical handbook, *On the existence of the coasts and form of our Mediterranean sea*, consulted navigational maps and sailors for his descriptions of winds, ports and the distances between them, calculations strikingly similar to other contemporary estimates by both Latin and Arabic writers. The book exhibited practical purpose and reasonable method, *'rationabiliter'* being a key word, and chimed with a commercial society boasting permanent trading posts across the Mediterranean and North Africa.[8] The appetite and market for such accurate information was evident in the urgent appeals of planners such as Innocent III, Gregory X and Nicholas IV, and was implicit in all preparatory diplomacy. Direct advice and news from the east were commonplace in crusade planning. Papal crusade appeals were loaded with scare stories of events in the Holy Land, often in some detail. Although only one letter, from Acre to the count of Champagne in 1240, survives suggesting a particular itinerary to a crusader about to depart (advice the count rejected), it is unlikely to have been unique.[9]

By the late thirteenth and early fourteenth centuries, when plans for the defence or re-conquest of the Holy Land were most urgent, an avalanche of detailed advice on routes and strategy, some solicited, some not, survives, much of it tinged with ulterior religious, missionary, political or commercial motives. Authors included kings of Aragon, Cyprus and Sicily, Hospitallers and Templars, Franciscans and Dominicans, professional polemicists, merchants, bishops, pilgrims, politicians, maritime corporations and an Armenian prince.

Information came from direct experience of the eastern Mediterranean, intelligence sources behind enemy lines, observations of captives, wishful thinking, self-interest and prejudice.[10] The Mongol invasions of western Asia, first rumoured during the Fifth Crusade, followed by their invasions of eastern Europe in the 1240s and Iraq and Syria in the 1250s, tore open western eyes to see a wider global panorama. Basic geographical information, while varying greatly in extent and usefulness, underpinned most of the proposals on how best to attack the Muslim rulers of the Near East. Yet appreciation of the wider world long pre-dated this, enhanced by two centuries of crusade experience.

From the earliest campaigns, participants' literary accounts used geographical information. Itineraries and topography provided readers or listeners with more than a convenient narrative skeleton. Setting action in vivid, identifiable, three-dimensional scenes enhanced credibility. This was Albert of Aachen's technique in weaving together veterans' stories of the First Crusade. Fulcher of Chartres, revealing or revelling in his posh academic credentials, provided precise itineraries, including times for crossing the Adriatic and the lengths of stay at bivouacs along the road to Constantinople, adding a detailed list of places passed between Thessalonica and the imperial capital. Fulcher maintained this close attention to places, dates and times when recounting his subsequent journey across Anatolia and beyond to Edessa with Baldwin of Boulogne.[11] The tradition of incorporating travellers' guides into crusade histories became firmly established. Odo of Deuil, wishing to inform those who might follow, listed the towns and the times taken between them from Metz to Branitz, and sketched the pros and cons of the three different routes across Anatolia to Antioch in Syria.[12] The author of the main account of the siege of Lisbon, with no such obvious advisory intent, was equally meticulous in charting the crusade fleet's progress from Dartmouth, across the stormy Bay of Biscay and down the Atlantic seaboard to Oporto, and then on to Lisbon.[13] Similar maritime itineraries, often spiced with digressions on topography and local legends, appeared regularly in subsequent veterans' reports: the account of the Bremen fleet that attacked Silves in 1189; Roger of Howden's extremely detailed description of his voyage around Spain to Marseilles and Messina in

1190 and his return trip with Philip II from Tyre and Beirut to Italy via the Greek archipelagos; the narratives of the Rhineland fleet in 1217.[14]

Parts of these may have been based on written nautical manuals or seamen's experiences. Around the middle of the twelfth century, the much-travelled Genoese grandee Caffaro seems to have provided, from memory we are told, a detailed description of the coastline of the Levant from Antioch to Jaffa and Ascalon, complete with precise and largely accurate distances. Intriguingly, Caffaro's calculations matched closely those in the Pisan *On the existence of the coasts*, which in turn contained distances comparable in a few places with those provided by the North African and Sicilian geographer al-Idrisi (d.1165) and the Andalusian traveller Ibn Jubayr, who undertook the haj in 1183–5.[15] Roger of Howden went beyond simply recounting the places he passed on his voyages out to Palestine and back. He mentioned prevailing winds and provided a somewhat schematic overview of Mediterranean sea-lanes: Rhodes was a third of the 1,600 *milliaria* (miles) between Acre and Brindisi; the distances from Marseilles and Sicily and Sicily and Acre were similarly 1,600 miles each, with, respectively, Sardinia and Crete halfway between. Such symmetry hints at sight of a diagrammatic map.[16]

It has been argued that, besides his chronicles containing these crusade itineraries, on his return from the Third Crusade Howden himself compiled a maritime geographical guide, *De viis maris* (*Sea Journeys*). Written between 1191 and 1193, this traced in detail the coasts of eastern England and the Atlantic seaboard to the Mediterranean and, apparently using the work of the Sicilian admiral Margaret, beyond to India; the empirical leading to the fanciful. Howden may also have composed a study of world maps and a *Liber nautarum* (*Book of mariners*) based on Isidore of Seville. The latter belied its academic provenance by concluding pragmatically that any ship's company needed to employ a *conductor*, expert in sea routes.[17] Whether or not Roger of Howden compiled these tracts, whatever their inspiration or sources, whether personal observations, nautical manuals, geographic treatises or what has been called 'sailors' common knowledge', these varied texts show how detailed geographic knowledge of the coasts and seas was readily available to those planning a crusade. It may be significant that in the late twelfth century the Pisan handbook on the Mediterranean was copied at Winchester, a centre of preparations for the Third Crusade.[18]

By the thirteenth century, the opening of the eastern Mediterranean to western European settlers, crusaders, merchants and pilgrims produced a growing variety of detailed accounts of the lands visited or occupied. Some were derivative, formulaic pilgrim manuals designed to stimulate travel of the soul. Others supplied topographical, social, ethnographic, cultural and even political detail. This range of geographic writing contributed to a radical change in visual representations. The few surviving late twelfth-century maps of the eastern Mediterranean were derived from the imaginative *mappae mundi* or were highly schematic, with little accuracy or helpful detail, even where broad physical outlines are recognizable. Not working maps, they illustrate scripture or history. Subsequent increased sophistication of charting and mapping the world went beyond this desire to illustrate the message of the Bible to cater for the requirements of trade, travel and the curiosity of travellers. The visual remained integrated into the literary. Maps of the Holy Land or the world, such as those by Matthew Paris, were festooned with text. Paris also produced a detailed pictorial itinerary of the pilgrimage route from London to Apulia, a visual partner to the familiar written itineraries.[19] Maps became increasingly common adjuncts to texts as well as vice versa. Most influential, perhaps, the Dominican Burchard of Mount Sion wrote a detailed description of the Holy Land between 1274 and 1285. Packed with geographical information, at least one version was accompanied with a map, Burchard sending it to a friend in Magdeburg: 'so that all things can be the better pictured, I am sending you with this a sheet of parchment on which they are all set out visually'.[20] More generally, Burchard's highly popular *Descriptio* supplied the inspiration and basis for a whole cartographical tradition which seems to have begun with the author himself.

Parallel and in contrast to such aids to pilgrimage and religious devotion, nautical maps were developed. These chiefly took the form of 'portolan' charts, showing coastlines, ports, harbours and the distances between them, with directional gridlines drawn from a number of different fixed points on the maps. While these had probably existed since the twelfth century, the earliest surviving examples date from a century later, at the start of the fourteenth century, and derive from the commercial world of Italian maritime cities. Some of the earliest were produced between 1310 and the early 1330s by a Genoese cartographer, Pietro Vesconte, working in Venice. These portolan charts, based on regional maps and the experience of sailors, were practical tools as medieval sea journeys tended to hug coastlines and hop between islands to maintain access to fresh water and other supplies. These charts were not necessarily based on compass bearings. While the compass was known to western European sailors and intellectuals at least from the late twelfth century, its use appears to have been limited to times when the sun, moon or stars were not visible.[21]

With the portolan charts comes direct evidence of crusade planners' engagement with maps. This may be assumed for earlier periods. It has been suggested that *mappae mundi* may have supplied the most basic of geographic knowledge to crusade commanders as early as the First Crusade.[22] The habit of consulting maps, as well as oral expertise and listening to written texts, followed in the wake of the expanding culture of writing and record-keeping, the visual supplementing the aural. The increased numbers of surviving maps and related written geographical works around the period of the Third Crusade might support this. However, the first reported instance of a crusade leader consulting a map dates from 1270, when Louis IX is described as being shown a chart, misleadingly called a *mappa mundi*, by Genoese sea captains during the stormy passage from Aigues Mortes to Sardinia. It showed details of the site and port of Cagliari and was almost certainly a portolan chart. Louis's extreme piety accommodated a strong desire for efficiency.[23] A generation later, the propagandizing efforts of Marino Sanudo demonstrated how geographic culture could be harnessed by crusade planners in general. His use of maps to support his encyclopaedic written advice also revealed the adaptable nature of the medium, simultaneously practical and prophetic.

Other crusade polemicists such as Fidenzio of Padua and Galvano of Levanto in the late thirteenth century had supported their crusade proposals with maps of the eastern Mediterranean and the Holy Land, although more by way of decorative illustration than practical geographical primer. Sanudo's purpose was different. A writer with experience of Venetian commerce and of Outremer before 1291, Sanudo regarded maps and charts as weapons, deployed alongside his texts to explain and inform as well as to illustrate.[24] He commissioned, from Vesconte and others, a portfolio of maps and charts. They formed an integral part of the campaign of persuasion and explanation Sanudo pursued at close quarters with crusade planners in France and Italy for two decades or more. At Avignon in 1321, together with two copies of his exhaustive *Secreta Fidelium Crucis*, Sanudo presented Pope John XXII with an atlas including a world map, maps of the eastern Mediterranean and Asia, and of Palestine, plans of Acre and Jerusalem, and five portolans of the Mediterranean and Black Sea. Some of these were cross-referenced in the text of the *Secreta*. The map of Palestine, planned on a grid and drawn to scale, precisely illustrated the relevant descriptive passage in the *Secreta* (plate 29).[25] Subsequently, Sanudo hawked his book and maps around the leading figures in plans to re-launch a Holy Land crusade in France and Italy. Some would have been receptive. In 1323, in Paris, Sanudo 'hurried to the house of lord Louis, count of Clermont giving him maps and some other items concerning these affairs'. Count Louis, the appointed leader of French crusade planning, already possessed a copy of the *Secreta*; he had also, off his own bat, in 1322, bought a map of Outremer for 30 *sous*. A decade later, in 1332, Sanudo similarly pressed the usefulness of his maps on Philip VI.[26]

Yet, in common with the rest of Sanudo's enterprise, not all was dry pragmatism. The portolans may have represented the latest in nautical chart-making, but the maps reflected a more static, idealized vision of the world. Sanudo's grid map of Palestine was based on Burchard's *Descriptio* and the plethora of maps derived for his didactic travelogue, a mixture of Biblical past and territorial present. The map of Acre recalled the days before its loss and destruction in 1291. The plan of Jerusalem mapped the city's defences and water supplies but also the sites of Holy Week, the Passion, Crucifixion and Resurrection.[27] In the poignancy of contrast between the known desolation of the fourteenth-century Judean city and the unsullied image of Holy Places lay the crusade's inspiration, paradox and ultimate futility.

GRAND STRATEGY?

'This is a mighty affair. Great forces have passed thither long ago on various occasions. I will tell you what this is like; it is like the little dog barking at the great big one, who takes no heed of him.'[28] So Erard de Valéry summed up two centuries of crusading to the Holy Land. A veteran of Louis IX's crusades and Outremer garrisons, he was speaking at the Second General Council of Lyons called by Pope Gregory X in 1274 to consider future crusade strategy. The pope had already received extensive written submissions which provided a rather discouraging range of evidence and opinion. An uneven orthodoxy was emerging. In place of a single mass military and naval assault, the Christian advantage in sea power should be exploited by launching an economic blockade on Egypt, followed by a preliminary attack by professional forces to secure bridgeheads prior to any general crusade. Behind the usual revivalist rhetoric, the tone of the discussions at Lyons echoed Erard's sobering realism. If not exactly defeatist, the submitted evidence and the council's deliberations confronted the inescapable and severe challenges faced by any scheme to reverse the tide of retreat and loss in Palestine. The view from Lyons stretched from the Atlantic to Central Asia, seen not as some fictive *mappa mundi* but more as a portolan of problems. In seeking adequate responses, the pope and council were forced to consider the holy war in its widest contexts: selling the crusade within Christendom; international economics and logistics; the new political configurations in the Near East following the stemming of the Mongol advance to the Mediterranean and the consolidation of the Mamluk empire of Egypt; and even the clash of global religions, expressed in pipe-dreams of the implosion of Islam. In the event, what emerged from Lyons was chiefly hot air.

However, the Lyons Council confirmed that crusade organizers were not innocent of the world around them or of the potential international impact of their plans. It also exposed fundamental problems in translating spiritual objectives into terrestrial facts. How limited were the physical and political goals of crusading? Should strategic aims be universal or immediate? Some were defined by existing local circumstances: the conquests in Iberia; the German annexation of Prussia and the eastern Baltic; the suppression of local dissidents in Languedoc or elsewhere in Christendom; the competition for power in Italy or Germany; the defence of eastern Europe from Mongols or, later, the Ottomans; the maintenance of western European outposts in Greece or the Aegean. Although the same might be said to have been true for Outremer once it had been established, the nature of the Palestine wars differed. Jerusalem offered no material advantages. There were no obvious or compelling economic or political reasons for soldiers and settlers from western Europe to contest for power and land in Syria and Palestine. Did eccentricity of religious motive and absence of material incentive fatally compromise their continued occupation? Were crusader leaders aware of any narrowness in their strategic vision? Did the crusades to the Holy Land possess any credible temporal strategy at all? A universal strategy would include the elimination of Islam by force or conversion. A less ambitious approach might address more mundane but always more urgent schemes to re-order the political geography of the Near East. The former remained largely the preserve of propaganda, theory and romantic literature; the latter of generals in armchairs, council chambers and battlefields.

Whether Urban II's and the Council of Clermont's combination of assistance for the eastern Church and the liberation of Jerusalem represented nuanced bipartite policy or jumbled portmanteau rhetoric cannot now be discerned. In common with Muslim observers in the Near East, Urban II grasped the significance of Christian rulers' advances in Spain and Sicily. He regarded these providentially and practically, offering a chance to restore the boundaries of late Roman Christendom and revive the faith. He and his immediate predecessors had helped sponsor wars against Islamic al-Andalus and Sicily.[29] However, his propagandist focus on Jerusalem might appear to have precluded larger concepts of the eradication of Islam. Later memories attributed to Urban and the Council of Clermont a policy of elimination of non-Christian religious rites, but only in conquered territory.[30] Limited objectives certainly proved to be the reality of the First Crusade and the subsequent settlements. The crusade was a war of faith but not necessarily an open-ended war between faiths. Nonetheless, some observers inevitably extrapolated grander schemes as the scare stories generated somewhat undifferentiated Islamophobia, fuelled by the attitudes popular in vernacular literature, such as the famous apostrophe in the *Song of Roland*: 'Pagans are wrong and Christians are right'. Although veterans' chronicles managed to distinguish between their enemies, even affording them admiration for fighting skills, they included references to forced conversion and one likened the crusaders to the Apostles. Resident in Jerusalem, Fulcher of Chartres claimed Muslim women converted to marry Latin settlers. However, this was hardly a war aim.[31]

The theme of a clash of civilizations never entirely took root, not least because of an asymmetry of understanding. In western Europe 'Saracens' were rarely afforded genuine autonomy, regarded more usually as inhabiting a sort of perverted version of Christendom. Not until the thirteenth century did academic interest and the missionary projects of the friars stimulate a more accurate western image of Islam, if not of Muslims. One apparent contradiction suffused crusading, summed up by Odo of Deuil: 'we are to visit the Holy Sepulchre . . . to wipe out our sins with the blood or the conversion of the infidels'.[32] One problem lay in the canonical illegality of forced conversion. However, many crusade enthusiasts, such as Abbot Peter the Venerable of Cluny or James of Vitry, also promoted conversion. By the thirteenth century, an influential body of academic opinion came to regard crusading and the conquest of Muslim lands as necessary prerequisites to conversion. Others, however, such as the friars William of Tripoli or Roger Bacon, took a more fancifully pacific stance, looking to the internal decay and disintegration of Islam, a process they saw as impeded by Christian attacks that shored up Muslim resistance.[33]

Beside academic posturing, the enemies of the Cross tended to be cast as barbaric or inhuman, views sustained by demotic preaching and vernacular literature, the lurid bogeymen of the chansons, the crusades as a 'tournament between Heaven and Hell'.[34] Such emotions helped recruitment but hardly determined planning. Ideas of cosmic conflict were (and are) intrinsically awkward to realize in military strategy. Crusading may have tapped wells of apocalyptic anxiety or eschatological enthusiasm, but these provided feeble sustenance for a temporal war plan. The Baltic wars stood as part exceptions to this, configured in Livonia and Prussia as existential struggles against primitives, apostasy and Evil. Bernard of Clairvaux's incautious advocacy of religious extermination in 1147 became the effective reality a century later.[35] In the culturally sophisticated and diverse Levant, such confident racism was harder to maintain. In any case, the eastern crusades' essential focus on Jerusalem and the Holy Places physically defined the inter-faith contest in very narrow terms. Thirteenth-century lawyers rejected blanket justifications for annexation of non-Christian lands that had never been part of Christendom.[36] Ideas for a general conquest of the Muslim world, as opposed to the lands adjacent to the Holy Places, are hard to find. Some over-excited crusaders at Constantinople in 1101 were reported to have toyed with an attack on Iraq and Baghdad, but such bravado, if genuine, soon ended in the harsh reality of defeat and death.[37] The excitement of 1099 never wholly dissipated in the imaginations of western European believers. Yet, for commanders, the failed crusades in Anatolia in 1101 or the Balkans in 1107, let alone the laborious capture and defence of Syrian and Palestinian ports and hinterland, lowered sights and tempered ambitions. Strategies launched in the name of universal providence could only be realized in operations of immediate contingency.

The absence of plans to reshape Eurasia did not prevent strategic thought. While they understood where and why they were going, the extent of the crusaders' prior knowledge of the political situation in the Levant in 1096 is unknowable, but possibly minimal. However, Byzantine briefing altered that, suggesting routes and local alliances to be secured and drawing the western leaders into negotiations with the Fatimids of Egypt with whom they shared a common enemy, the Seljuk Turks. Initiated in the summer of 1097 after the capture of Nicaea, these were pursued in earnest from early 1098, lasting until a few weeks before the siege of Jerusalem in June and July 1099.[38] Discussions with the Greeks may also have influenced the crusaders' plans for their conquests. Urban II's plans for the future are unknown, except that he seems to have envisaged a role for a papal legate. Predictably, after the capture of Jerusalem and the installation of a Latin ruler, talk circulated about the re-creation of the kingdom of Judea, a pleasingly fitting scriptural anachronism for a venture that framed its actions so tightly within biblical exegesis. There survives a later, possibly misleading hint that, as early as 1098, thought had been given by Adhemar of Le Puy to a bipartite division of Syria and Palestine along a frontier similar to that between Byzantines and Fatimids a century earlier. Discussions between Emperor Alexius I and Bohemund in Constantinople may have revolved around the re-creation of a pre-1085 Byzantine province around Antioch.[39] It is unlikely that such plans had been proposed before the crusaders left western Europe, owing their thrust and content primarily to Greek imperial policy which never lost sight of strategy at its grandest. However, once installed in Syria and Palestine, certain basic strategies proved inescapable: the need to conquer the coastal ports to secure lifelines to the west and prevent an Egyptian re-conquest; the desirability to push frontiers to the surrounding deserts for military protection and commercial hegemony, a policy that led to unsuccessful attacks on Damascus in the 1120s and 1148; or, failing that, the requirement to forge alliances for mutual benefit with local rulers, Muslim or not.[40] The First Crusade leaders had been adept at acquiring strategies as they went along. So were their successors.

Two recurrent issues cast deep shadows over the next three centuries: what to do about Byzantium and Egypt. Both were constant factors in any Near Eastern policy: one a putative but equivocal ally; the other a permanent threat. Despite the determinism of hindsight and the neurosis of certain Greek intellectuals, no consistent crusading policy towards Byzantium existed. The closeness and mutual dependence of the relationship produced a sequence of fluid, often contradictory, responses. Western commanders wanted Greek material and logistical assistance: access to markets and guides for land armies; naval help and money for sea-borne expeditions; and additional manpower for both. When co-operation faltered, as it often did, seizure of Greek assets or territory was repeatedly canvassed, often justified under the guise of disciplining Christian schismatics or enforcing obedience to Rome. Violence erupted over food supplies during the First Crusade's passage to Asia in 1096–7. Apparently serious debates were held over the justice of an attack on Constantinople within the French high command in 1147. In the winter of 1189/90 Frederick Barbarossa occupied Thrace to ensure adequate supplies. The Fourth Crusade went further and annexed the imperial capital, ostensibly in its search of promised Greek wealth and assistance.[41] Yet in none of these cases had an assault on Byzantium featured as a strategic objective at the start of the campaigns, unlike the Norman invasions of the Balkans in 1107 or 1185. By contrast, in 1195 Frederick Barbarossa's son, Henry VI, now ruler of Sicily and heir of Norman Mediterranean ambitions, explicitly incorporated extravagant demands for Byzantine assistance in his crusade plans, demanding protection money from the emperor under the threat of invasion. Henry's imperial schemes also included patronage of the new kingdoms of Cyprus and Cilician Armenia. Such strategic pan-Mediterranean policies were pursued by his son, Frederick II, who sought to combine his rule of Germany and Sicily with the kingdom of Jerusalem, and by the Hohenstaufen nemesis, Charles of Anjou, whose international aspirations following his conquest of Sicily in 1266 embraced the restored Byzantine Empire as well as Outremer. The Latin conquest of significant tracts of Greece after 1204 imposed its own line in western strategic thinking, although, judged by the modest popularity of crusades to defend them, a minority interest.[42]

The permanent engagement of transalpine western Europeans in Mediterranean politics, of which the crusades formed one part, encouraged expansive outlooks in which Egypt could not be ignored. Crusaders confronted a wealthy, interconnected, well-populated and urbanized environment where powers competed fiercely for restricted natural resources and control of mouth-wateringly lucrative trades in luxury textiles, spices and rare dyes, as well as in foodstuffs and slaves. Egypt provided a main commercial hub for goods from further east as well as enjoying its own rich agricultural base. Economically, Egypt dominated the Mediterranean end of the Fertile Crescent that stretched from the Persian Gulf to the Nile; politically too, if and when its rulers enjoyed internal order and external security. In Egypt lay the power to dominate the Levant. Crusaders were immediately aware of this and the threat a hostile Egypt posed to any Latin conquests in Palestine. One veteran recalled a debate at Ramla in June 1099, when a direct attack on Egypt was proposed: 'if through God's grace we could conquer the kingdom of Egypt, we would not only acquire Jerusalem but also Alexandria, Cairo and many kingdoms'. Against this was argued that the expedition lacked adequate numbers to invade Egypt with any chance of lasting success; the Egyptian diversion was rejected.[43] The Ramla debate presciently set the tone for centuries of strategic contemplation and action. The Latin kings of Jerusalem competed with the rulers of Syria for tribute and then control of Egypt in the 1160s and 1170s, a conflict that drew in Byzantium in the 1170s. The implications of the Latins' failure and the consequent unification of Egypt with Syria under Saladin were well appreciated. William of Tyre, watching these developments at close quarters, noted how Saladin drew huge quantities of gold from Egypt which allowed him to recruit vast companies of troops from his other domains. William's model of Outremer's encirclement funded by Egypt soon entered western strategic orthodoxy, not least through the various vernacular translations and continuations of his work circulated in the west over the following century.[44]

The military challenge of Egypt was taken up by Richard I when he floated the idea of an invasion during the Palestine war of 1191–2. His plan was to hire (at 50 per cent of cost) a Genoese fleet to join his troops on an assault on the Nile in the summer of 1192. Supported by local veterans, Richard seemed aware of the strategic and practical difficulties of holding Jerusalem, unashamedly pointing this out to his more Jerusalem-fixated followers, a contest of reason and faith that neither side won. Richard's opponents could equally reasonably enquire what was he in the Holy Land for, and why he had laboriously toiled through the Judean hills in the dying days of 1191 if not for Jerusalem.[45] After 1192, and the temporary agreement to a two-state solution in Palestine, an invasion of Egypt became seen as less as an alternative to a direct assault on Jerusalem and increasingly as a prerequisite. The Nile was to have been the destination for the Fourth Crusade and was the target for invasions in 1218 and 1249. At a council of war at Cagliari in 1270, Louis IX even portrayed his planned attack on Tunis as a blow against the power of Egypt.[46] Much of the energy of the writers of crusade proposals between 1270 and 1336 was spent on explaining the need and the method to crush the economic and military power of Egypt as the key to Palestine. Without a friendly or neutral Egypt, no tenure of the Holy Land could be secure. While patently true and demonstrated by events, this realization opened up wider considerations of the reasons for the weakness and failure of the Latin settlements in Outremer: lack of numbers and inadequacy of resources, points made potently in works as different as Peter Dubois's expansive *Recovery of the Holy Land* (c.1306) and Marino Sanudo's pragmatic-seeming *Secreta*.[47]

However, the apparent realism of the lawyer's study or merchant's office did not entirely circumvent the inherent self-deception in crusade strategy, in which such writers were complicit. Western Europeans seeking Jerusalem represented a strategic nonsense. Only as a religious exercise could it be justified. This exposed confusion of policy. During the Fifth Crusade, to remove the crusaders from the Nile Delta the sultan offered to cede back the lost lands of the kingdom of Jerusalem. This was refused; it would still have left the Latin occupation vulnerable. However, refusal implied that only regime change in Egypt would allow for the safe return of Jerusalem, that, or a diplomatic volte face. The latter occurred briefly when Frederick II took advantage of the political rivalries among local Muslim rulers and negotiated the return of a demilitarized, shared Jerusalem in 1229, a fragile arrangement that ended in 1244. Louis IX recognized the essentials of the problem. He prepared for an outright conquest, settlement and conversion of Egypt, a policy that dictated his aggressive and fatal tactics in the Nile Delta in 1249–50. Yet, he apparently recognized that 'he had not enough people to guard and inhabit the territory in Egypt which he had already occupied and was about to seize'. The crusaders' Egyptian strategy was fantasy.[48] They never possessed the resources for a blanket conquest, there or anywhere else in the mainland of the Levant. The long-term Latin rule in Cyprus relied on it being an island with an indigenous Christian population. The demographic and economic deficits were tackled by the theorists such as Dubois, but his remedies, such as insinuating well-educated Christian women as fifth columnists into Muslim harems, stretch (and probably stretched) credulity.[49] Sanudo's and others' blueprints for economic warfare showed a stronger grasp of the strategic problems, and perhaps a greater practicality in assessing the international context and possibilities.[50] Yet, while insisting on gritty pragmatism, they nonetheless dealt in theories that paid more than lip-service to optimistic assumptions of providential favour.

Along with the contributors to the debates at Lyons in 1274, the authors of such crusade proposals revealed a corpus of theoretical grand strategy to keep planners well occupied. Yet the main driver of strategic thought remained events. These conspired to strip crusaders and their plans of both credibility and importance. In December 1248, while Louis IX was gathering his forces and war materials in Cyprus, he received an embassy from the Mongol general in Persia, ostensibly willing to negotiate over the plight of eastern Christians in the Levant. The mirage of an alliance between Latin Christendom and a non-Muslim or even Christian empire in Asia had teased western strategists since the 1140s when garbled stories of a Seljuk defeat by the non-Muslim Kara-Khitan khanate near Samarkand reached Europe. Legends of Prester John, a Christian priest and monarch, were circulated, a mixture of scriptural fantasies derived from tales of the mysterious Magi and distorted snippets of news from the now dimly perceived vastness of Central Asia. These stories appeared to receive support when rumours of Genghis Khan's victories in Central Asia filtered through to the crusaders at Damietta during the Fifth Crusade. The existence of a non-Muslim power to the east that tolerated and employed local Christians seemed to offer the chance of opening a second front against the Muslim dominance of the Near East. This proved a dangerous fallacy. Successive western embassies confirmed intransigent Mongol supremacist insistence on world domination. No general Mongol conversion to Christianity occurred. Instead, the Mongols invaded Christendom itself in 1241–2, when they devastated eastern Europe and even reached the Adriatic.[51]

Nonetheless, to the alarm and astonishment of those on the frontline, like King Béla IV of Hungary, the focus of Christendom's official foreign policy, while acknowledging the Mongol threat, remained trapped, glued to the priority of the Holy Land.[52] The break-up of the Mongol empire in the later thirteenth century and the continued battle over Syria between the Mongol Il-Khanate of Persia and the Mamluks of Egypt stimulated further contacts between the Il-Khans, popes and the kings of France and England into the early fourteenth century. In 1299–1300, Ghazan of Persia's failed invasion of Syria generated wildly over-optimistic, if evanescent, expectations in the west. Writers with accurate and detailed knowledge of the Mongols' place in Near Eastern politics, such as Prince Hetoum of Armenia or the widely travelled Dominican William Adam, still fashioned their evidence to suit a policy of co-operation with the Il-Khans, a project to which even Sanudo subscribed although by the time he had completed his *Secreta* the Il-Khan and the Mamluks were about to conclude peace.[53] The irony lay in the contrast between an unchanging strategic objective and new understanding of the actual Near East, with Adam advocating a blockade of the Persian Gulf, Sanudo and Hetoum an anti-Egyptian alliance with the Nubians, and Hetoum providing a history of the Mongols and a gazetteer of Asiatic realms from China to Turkey.[54] The Mongol dimension helped extend the practical horizons of crusade strategists without dislodging their conceptual blinkers that prevented them accepting the practical irrelevance of their doomed ambition.

This was not a failure of ingenuity, of information or even, within its traditional solipsist boundaries, of reason. The conquest of Cyprus, occupation of regions of the mainland Levant and the invasions of Egypt were objectively remarkable achievements, not essayed again by western Europeans in the region for half a millennium. Crusaders deployed their constrained resources so effectively as to conceal the precariousness of their aspirations for more than two centuries; but not for ever. The abiding flaw in crusade strategy remained the impossible legacy of 1099, a cultural imperative in the end lacking adequate material reserves to be sustained, relying on an ideology that limited the necessary pragmatic accommodation to local conditions to succeed; Erard of Valéry's lapdog yapping at a mastiff.

Conclusion

This book began by insisting on rationality in the crusading enterprise and ended by observing its unreasonable objectives. The paradox was inherent in transcendent conviction seeking expression in temporal practice. The premise of the Jerusalem war and its surrogates insisted that extreme physical action could redeem dutiful Christians and restore order to a divinely created world forced out of joint by sin. God's immanence was assumed, not conditioned by intuitive caprice but explored through empirical reasoning in attempts to understand not just what but why natural phenomena were as they were. What might appear to some modern eyes a sequence of category confusions struck crusaders as no such thing. Faith was manifest, not abstract in a religious culture dominated by concrete expressions of belief: in stone and glass, liturgies, rituals, alms-giving, charitable patronage, commitment to the cloister, convent and friary, fasting, sexual abstinence or pilgrimage. A system of penitential mitigation was developed that offered believers the chance to improve their prospects of salvation through accessible and comprehensible temporal exercises: physical hardship, material charity, oral confession, receiving the sacraments, buying remissions of sins. Crusading occupied an iconic position in this relay of spiritual obligations, bargains and balance sheets. Unique in scope and ambition, crusades were represented as religious precept made flesh. In the twenty-first century violent political enterprises framed by religious and secular ideology may not appear alien or incomprehensible.

The crusades can be dismissed as bullying, destructive, wasteful, unnecessary, paranoid, indulgent, and, in most theatres of action, ultimately ephemeral except for the scars left on popular memory.

They can also be explained as expressions of idealism, earnest devotion and practical intelligence, products of a society of increasing material wealth and cultural self-confidence. Perspectives are as numerous as observers and there is evidence for all of these views. Historical assessment need not require moral judgment. Were crusades successful; or, a rather different question, was crusading successful? Answering the former involves arguments centred on politics; the latter, consideration of theology, culture or psychology.

A different lens of scrutiny is provided here. By studying their preparation and realization, crusade schemes are revealed as functionally effective, grounded in practical programmes of promotion, recruitment, planning and finance, less Don Quixote, more Dwight Eisenhower. Whatever their outcome, long-distance campaigns of the Cross reached battlefields across Europe, North Africa and western Asia, from Damascus to the Algarve, the Nile to the Gulf of Finland. Those planned predominantly from Europe west of a line from the Elbe to the Adriatic achieved striking success in reshaping the territories they invaded. In Prussia, Livonia and al-Andalus, their impact permanently redirected social as well as political developments. While internal crusades, in France, Italy or Germany for example, reflected more obviously local habits of organizing and conducting war, their propaganda and funding devices borrowed directly from those aimed beyond Christendom. The projected re-ordering of the Mediterranean, the chief focus of this book, was only imperfectly realized, as ambition outran resources. Yet, regarded away from a crude model of impermeable contest, there too crusades exerted lasting influence. Within a wider process of expanding commercial markets, political diversification, social co-operation and cultural exchange, the contribution of crusades in channelling western European interest, resources, men and treasure cannot be ignored.

Practical achievements were many, even on crusaders' terms. Cyprus was pulled into the orbit of western Christendom for four centuries. Venetian colonies were established that lasted even longer. The Latin Christian presence in the Aegean persisted into the sixteenth century, securing western investment, however modest, on the frontline against the Ottoman advance. Crusading forced the politics of the eastern Mediterranean and Levant into the consciousness and actions of western Europeans. Some of this would have occurred with or without crusading. Besides conflict came accommodation, in trade, diplomacy, shared space. The transmission of information about different and distant people and places was accelerated. None of this should be accepted as 'good' or 'bad', nor as the exclusive consequence of crusading. The crusades did not create the wars of Christian conquest in Spain or the Baltic. They complemented rather than caused the commercial penetration of western traders into the eastern Mediterranean. Jacques le Goff's famous quip that the crusades produced nothing for western Europe except the apricot had the virtue of locating the enterprise in a context of exchange and contact, not just of ideology and war.

Viewed objectively, the ambition for western Europeans to occupy Palestine and rule Jerusalem defied political, military and financial sense, a dream from an imagined world. Except it worked. The capture of Antioch and Jerusalem in 1098–9 might have owed much to luck, as do most successful military campaigns. The presence of the Christian army and the subsequent conquests in Palestine and Syria did not. The failures of 1148, 1191–2, 1221 or 1250 belied the complexity and sophistication of preparations but do not invalidate them. Neither was the idealism behind the projects necessarily irrational. To cohere, ideology requires reasoned argument, its implementation rational behaviour. Wars attract idealism, spontaneous, confected or a combination of both. Yet rational engagement with the practical problems of men, treasure, supplies and strategy was necessary for them to be fought at all. These efforts in turn stimulated innovation and enquiry, from geography to income tax.

If this book has shown anything, it is that those who planned crusades knew what they wished to achieve and devised pragmatic ways to achieve it. Crusaders may in the elevated gaze of retrospect appear as bigots, their value system possibly alien in its insouciant sadism, elitism, exclusivity and self-righteousness, although such a view itself seems tinged with not-a-little modern self-satisfaction. However, those who planned and fought crusades were neither ignorant nor idiotic. As the First Crusade veteran William Grassegals urged Louis VII to do in studying the collection of crusade chronicles he had given the king in 1137, they regarded holy war 'with the eye of reason'. Disbelief, disapproval or disgust at either the inspiration or performance of crusading should not admit accusations of unreason. The *miles Christi* that emerges from this study, zealot, professional or waged drudge, was not, just by virtue of his calling, especially irrational, a dolt, foolish, reckless, misguided or uninformed. Crusade commanders and knights were men of affairs, literate or surrounded by literacy and numeracy in business, law, religion, entertainment and the profession of arms. A crusader's terms of reference were of his time, not ours. Violence operated as a cultural norm and signifier, from public and private warfare to draconian legal punishments. For adherents, God's wars may have appeared more rational than any other. In pursuing the ideal, even if simply following orders, crusaders displayed ingenuity, invention and an unsentimental grasp of the practical essentials of politics, propaganda, finance, logistics and war. Reason made religious war possible, a conclusion that might give anyone pause in the twenty-first century.

Notes

ABBREVIATIONS

MGH   Monumenta Germaniae Historica

MGHS   *Monumenta Germaniae Historica Scriptores*, ed. G. H. Pertz
           et al. (Hanover and Leipzig, 1826–)

ODNB   *Oxford Dictionary of National Biography*, ed. C. Matthew et
           al. (Oxford, 2004–)

RHC   *Recueil des historiens des croisades*

RHC Occ.   *Recueil des historiens des croisades. Historiens Occidentaux*
           (Paris, 1844–95)

RHF   *Recueil des historiens des Gaules et de la France*, ed. M. Bou-
           quet et al. (Paris, 1738–1876)

INTRODUCTION

1. E. Barker, *The Crusades* (London, 1923), p. 104.

2. Raymond of Aguilers, *Historia Francorum qui ceperunt Iherusalem*, trans. J. H. Hill and L. L. Hill (Philadelphia, 1968), Introduction, p. 14.

3. William of Tyre, *Historia*, ed. R. B. C. Huygens (Turnhout, 1986), bk XIX, ch. 3, pp. 867–8.

4. D. D'Avray, *Medieval Religious Rationalities* (Cambridge, 2010), pp. 37–42.

5. The third-century BC Alexandrian librarian Eratosthenes' calculation – c.25–30,000 miles – was widely known through Pliny the Elder and the textbook of John of Sacrobosco, *De Spera* (c.1230–45), see P. Biller, *The Measure of Multitude* (Oxford, 2000), p. 218; L. Thorndyke, *The Sphere of Sacrobosco and its Commentators* (Chicago, 1949). This was much more accurate than Ptolemy of Alexandria's c.20,000 miles that

became fashionable in the fifteenth century and probably influenced Columbus.

6. M. Prestwich, *Armies and Warfare in the Middle Ages: The English Experience* (New Haven and London, 1996), pp. 341–2; G. Parker, *The Military Revolution* (Cambridge, 1988), p. 64.

7. *Itinerarium Ricardi Regis*, ed. W. Stubbs (London, 1864), pp. 168, 172–3, 214, 353, trans. H. Nicholson, *The Chronicle of the Third Crusade* (Aldershot, 1997), pp. 167, 171, 204, 316–17.

8. J. France, *Victory in the East* (Cambridge, 1994); J. M. Powell, *Anatomy of a Crusade 1213–1221* (Philadelphia, 1986); W. C. Jordan, *Louis IX and the Challenge of the Crusade* (Princeton, 1979); A. Murray, 'The Army of Godfrey of Bouillon', *Revue belge de philologie et d'histoire*, 70 (1992), pp. 301–29; idem, 'Money and Logistics in the First Crusade', in *Logistics of Warfare in the Age of the Crusades*, ed. J. H. Pryor (Aldershot, 2006), pp. 229–50 and passim; J. H. Pryor, *Geography, Technology and War* (Cambridge, 1988); P. Mitchell, *Medicine in the Crusades* (Cambridge, 2004).

9. A. Leopold, *How to Recover the Holy Land* (Aldershot, 2000).

10. J. Gillingham, 'Roger of Howden on Crusade', *Medieval Historical Writing in the Christian and Islamic Worlds*, ed. D. O. Morgan (London, 1982), pp. 60–75.

11. Geoffrey of Villehardouin, *La Conquête de Constantinople*, ed. and French trans. E. Faral (Paris, 1938–9), trans. M. R. B. Shaw, *Chronicles of the Crusades* (London, 1963); Robert of Clari, *The Conquest of Constantinople*, ed. and trans. E. H. McNeal (repr. New York, 1966).

12. Archives Nationales de France, MS J 456 no. 36; the changes are on folio 36-ii.

13. For the Catalan *computa*, T. N. Bisson, *The Fiscal Accounts of Catalonia under the Early Count-Kings (1151–1213)* (Berkeley, Los Angeles, London, 1984).

14. *The Bayeux Tapestry*, ed. F. M. Stenton (London, 1957), esp. plates 37–42, and above, plates 15–19.

15. Hayton, *La Flor des estoires de la Terre Sainte*, *RHC Documents Arméniens* (Paris, 1869–1906), vol. ii, p. 220.

I. IMAGES OF REASON

1. In general see C. Tyerman, *The Debate on the Crusades* (Manchester, 2011).

2. *Gesta Francorum at aliorum Hierosolimitanum*, ed. and trans. R. Hill (London, 1962), p. 36 where Bohemund is praised for being '*sapiens et prudens*'.

3. E. Grant, *God and Reason in the Middle Ages* (Cambridge, 2001), p. 364.

4. D. D'Avray, *Medieval Religious Rationalities* (Cambridge, 2010), esp. pp. 17–30.

5. A. Murray, *Reason and Society in the Middle Ages* (Oxford, 1978). For a sane, lively popular interpretation, see J. Hannam, *God's Philosophers* (London, 2009).

6. Grant, *God and Reason*, p. 9.

7. R. Bartlett, *The Natural and the Supernatural in the Middle Ages* (Cambridge, 2008), pp. 12–17; D'Avray, *Medieval Religious Rationalities*, pp. 15, 36–41.

8. Anselm, *Prayers and Meditations of St Anselm with the Proslogion*, trans. B. Ward (London, 1973).

9. Peter Abelard, *Sic et Non: A Critical Edition*, ed. B. B. Bryer and R. McKeon (Chicago, 1976–7), pp. 103, 113. In general, see M. Clanchy, *Abelard: A Medieval Life* (Oxford, 1997).

10. Murray, *Reason and Society*, pp. 132–6 and generally pp. 130–37.

11. C. Morris, 'Policy and visions: the case of the holy lance at Antioch', in *War and Government in the Middle Ages*, ed. J. Gillingham and J. C. Holt (Woodbridge, 1984), pp. 33–45; the most partisan account in favour of the lance's authenticity is Raymond of Aguilers, *Historia Francorum qui ceperunt Iherusalem*, *RHC Occ.*, vol. iii, pp. 253–61, 279–88; trans. J. H. Hill and L. L. Hill (Philadelphia, 1968), pp. 51–64, 93–108; the most hostile, Ralph of Caen, *Gesta Tancredi in expeditione Hierosolymitana*, *RHC Occ.*, vol. iii, pp. 676–9, 682–3, trans. B. Bachrach and D. S. Bachrach, *The Gesta Tancredi of Ralph of Caen* (Aldershot, 2005), pp. 118–21, 126–7.

12. M. Angold, *The Fourth Crusade* (Harlow, 2003), pp. 227–47; in general, P. J. Geary, *Furta Scara. Theft of Relics in the Central Middle Ages* (Princeton, 1978). For Guibert of Nogent's *On the Relics of Saints* (*c.*1120) see Guibert of Nogent, *Monodies and On the Relics of Saints*, trans. J. McAlhany and J. Rubinstein (London, 2011).

13. P. Riant, *Exuviae sacrae constantinopolitanae* (Geneva, 1876–7), pp. xcv, xcvii, 127–40.

14. *Decrees of the Ecumenical Councils*, trans. N. P. Tanner (London and Washington, 1990), Lateran IV, canon 62, pp. 263–4.

15. M. Clanchy, *From Memory to Written Record* (London, 1979), but cf. M. Carlin and D. Crouch, *Lost Letters of Medieval Life* (Philadelphia, 2013).

16. Richard FitzNeal, *The Dialogue of the Exchequer*, ed. C. Johnson (London, 1950).

17. Roger of Wendover, *Flores historiarum*, ed. H. G. Hewlett (London, 1886–9), vol. ii, p. 323 for Master Hubert's roll of English crusaders in 1227; *Registro del Cardinale Ugolino d'Ostia*, ed. G. Levi (Rome, 1890), pp. 128–33 for lists of Italian recruits in 1221.

18. *Gesta Francorum*, p. 75 describes how at Antioch in the autumn of 1098, Bohemund showed his fellow leaders his written account of expenses ('*suumque ostendit compotum*').

19. See the incident of Baldwin I of Jerusalem and the autopsy on a dancing bear, fully discussed in the pioneering work by P. Mitchell, *Medicine in the Crusades* (Cambridge, 2004), pp. 159–63 and below pp. 251–5.

20. Caesarius of Heisterbach, *Dialogus Miraculorum*, ed. J. Strange (Cologne, 1851), vol. i, p. 212: bk IV, ch. 44; S. Flanagan, *Doubt in an Age of Faith: Uncertainty in the Long Twelfth Century* (Turnhout, 2008), p. 69.

21. Theophilus, *De Diversis Artibus*, ed. and trans. C. R. Dodwell (Oxford, 1986), pp. 64–5, 71 and 142–58.

22. Albert of Aachen, *Historia Ierosolimitana*, ed. and trans. S. Edgington (Oxford, 2007), pp. 120–23.

23. *Lettres de Jacques de Vitry*, ed. R. B. C. Huygens (Leiden, 1960), p. 106; cf. Oliver of Paderborn, *The Capture of Damietta*, trans. E. Peters in *Christian Society and the Crusades 1198–1221* (Philadelphia, 1971), p. 65 where Oliver himself modestly conceals his identity.

24. Gervase of Canterbury, *Opera historica*, ed. W. Stubbs (London, 1879–80), vol. i, pp. 6 and 19–21.

25. J. H. Harvey, *English Medieval Architects* (London, 1987), p. 202.

26. E.g. the frequently reproduced National Library of Austria, Vienna, Cod. 2554, fol. iv from the mid-thirteenth century, see J. H. Harvey, *The Master Builders: Architecture in the Middle Ages* (London, 1971), p. 49.

27. Anna Abulafia, *Christians and Jews in the Twelfth Century Renaissance* (London, 1995); eadem, *Christians and Jews in Dispute 1000–1150* (Aldershot, 1998).

28. Clanchy, *Abelard*, pp. 288–321.

29. J. Thijssen, *Censure and Heresy at the University of Paris 1200–1400* (Philadelphia, 1998).

30. C. Burnett, ed. *Adelard of Bath* (London, 1987) and idem, 'Adelard of Bath', *ODNB*.

31. Baldwin of Forde, *De commendatione fidei*, ed. D. H. Bell (Turnhout, 1991), ch. lxxxv, pp. 433–4; cf. Flanagan, *Doubt*, p. 45; see C. Holdsworth's *ODNB* entry on Baldwin.

32. Gerald of Wales, *Journey through Wales*, trans. L. Thorpe (London, 1978), p. 184.

33. Isidore of Seville, *Etymologia*, ed. W. M. Lindsay (Oxford, 1911), bk X, ch. 11; *Chanson de Roland*, ed. J. Dufornet (Paris, 1973), v. 1093; *Gesta Francorum*, pp. 6, 10, 13, 14, 18, 19, 20, 21, 25, 28, 32, 35, 36, 61, 63 and p. xviii for Hill's dismissal of these epithets having any precise meaning.

34. Robert of Rheims, *Historia Iherosolimitana*, *RHC Occ.*, vol. iii, pp. 741, 745, 760, 780, 799.

35. Baldric of Bourgueil, *Historia Jerosolimitana*, *RHC Occ.*, vol. iv, p. 23; for date, see *The* Historia Jerosolimitana *of Baldric of Bourgueil*, ed. S. Biddlecombe (Woodbridge, 2014), pp. xxiv–xxx.

36. For example in Albert of Aachen, *Historia*, pp. 94–5 (Bohemund), 96–7 (Warner of Grez).

37. William of Tyre, *Historia*, p. 453, trans. E. Babcock and A. Krey in *A History of the Deeds done beyond the Sea* (repr. New York, 1976), vol. i, p. 415.

38. P. van Luyn, 'Les milites dans la France du XIe siècle', *Le Moyen Age*, 77 (1971), pp. 5–51, 193–235, esp. tables pp. 234–6.

39. Ralph of Caen, *Gesta Tancredi*, *RHC Occ.*, vol. iii, p. 605; trans. p. 22.

40. W. L. Warren, *Henry II* (London, 1977), p. 208 and n. 3 for refs. to three contemporary commentators.

41. Murray, *Reason and Society*, pp. 376–80.

42. In general, M. Keen, *Chivalry* (New Haven, 1984); G. Duby, *The Chivalrous Society* (London, 1977); J. Flori, *L'Essor de Chevalerie xie–xiie siècles* (Geneva, 1986); D. Crouch, *The English Aristocracy 1070–1272. A Social Transformation* (New Haven, 2011).

43. Guibert of Nogent, *Gesta Dei per Francos*, *RHC Occ.*, vol. iv, p. 219; Raymond of Aguilers, *Historia*, *RHC Occ.*, vol. iii, p. 235; for translations of Anselm's letters, see E. Peters, ed., *The First Crusade* (Philadelphia, 1998), pp. 284–7, 289–91.

44. Eadmer, *Historia Novorum*, ed. M. Rule (London, 1884), pp. 179–81; Orderic Vitalis, *Ecclesiastical History*, ed. and trans. M. Chibnall (Oxford, 1969–80), vol. v, pp. 170–73; J. Shepard, 'When Greek meets

Greek: Alexius Comnenus and Bohemund in 1097–8', *Byzantine and Modern Greek Studies*, 12 (1988), pp. 185–277; *Canso d'Antioca*, ed. and trans. C. Sweetenham and L. M. Paterson (Aldershot, 2003), pp. 5–6; Walter Map, *De Nugis Curialium*, ed. and trans. M. R. James et al. (Oxford, 1983), pp. 476–7.

45. In general, V. H. Galbraith, 'The Literacy of Medieval English Kings', *Proceedings of the British Academy*, 21 (1935), pp. 201–38; J. T. Rosenthal, 'The Education of the Early Capetians', *Traditio*, 25 (1969), pp. 366–76; R. V. Turner, 'The *Miles Literatus* in Twelfth and Thirteenth Century England: How Rare a Phenomenon?', *American Historical Review*, 83 (1978), pp. 928–45 (p. 931 for 'pragmatic readers'); J. W. Thompson, *The Literacy of the Laity in the Middle Ages* (New York, 1960); Clanchy, *From Memory to Written Record*; M. Aurell, *Le chevalier lettré: Savoir et conduit de l'aristocracie au xiie et xiiie siècle* (Paris, 2011). For Stephen of Blois's mother, see Guibert of Nogent, *Gesta, RHC Occ.*, vol. iv, p. 147; for his wife, the formidable Adela, see L. Huneycutt's *ODNB* article; for the final comment, N. Orme, *Medieval Children* (New Haven, 2001), p. 240.

46. D. Crouch, *The Beaumont Twins* (Cambridge, 1986), pp. 7, 207–11.

47. Riant, *Exuviae sacrae constantinopolitanae*, p. 133.

48. Walter Map, *De Nugis Curialium*, pp. 12–13.

49. Galbraith, 'Literacy', pp. 212–23 for refs.

50. Otto of Freising, *The Deeds of Frederick Barbarossa*, trans. C. C. Mierow (New York, 1966), p. 333; Gerald of Wales, *De Invectionibus*, i, *Opera Omnia*, ed. J. Brewer et al. (London, 1861–91), vol. iii, p. 30.

51. Fulk le Réchin, *Fragmentum historiae Andegavensis*, ed. L. Halphen and R. Poupardin, *Chroniques des comtes d'Anjou et des seigneurs d'Amboise* (Paris, 1913), pp. 206–45.

52. William of Tyre, *Historia*, p. 631, trans. Babcock and Krey, *History*, vol. ii, p. 47.

53. John of Marmoutier, *Historia Gaufredi, Chroniques des comtes d'Anjou*, pp. 176, 218; cf. similar eulogizing remarks by Stephen of Rouen, *Draco Normannicus*, ed. R. Howlett, *Chronicles of the Reigns of Stephen, Henry II and Richard I*, vol. ii (London, 1885), pp. 772–3.

54. Warren, *Henry II*, pp. 38–9.

55. William of Tyre, *Historia*, pp. 714–15, 864–5, 867–8; R. Huygens, 'Guillaume de Tyre étudiant. Un chapître (xix.12) de son "Historie" retrouvé', *Latomus*, 31 (1962), pp. 811–29; P. Edbury and J. G. Rowe, *William of Tyre* (Cambridge, 1988), p. 17 and n. 17 and passim.

56. Warren, *Henry II*, p. 208.

57. *Itinerarium Ricardi Regis*, p. 143, trans. Nicholson, *Chronicle*, p. 146 (cf. the Nestor epithet used for James of Avesnes, another Third Crusade commander, *Itinerarium*, p. 63, trans. Nicholson, *Chronicle*, p.74); J. Gillingham, *Richard I* (New Haven and London, 1999), pp. 254–61.

58. D. M. Stenton, 'King John and the Courts of Justice', *Proceedings of the British Academy*, 44 (1958), pp. 103–28; M. Lovatt's *ODNB* article on Geoffrey.

59. France, *Victory in the East*, pp. 45–6 and passim.

60. Gerald of Wales, *De Principis Instructione*, *Opera*, vol. viii, pp. 39–43; R. Bartlett, *Gerald of Wales* (Oxford, 1982), pp. 69–71.

61. See M. Gabriele, *An Empire of Memory. The Legend of Charlemagne, the Franks, and Jerusalem before the First Crusade* (Oxford, 2011); cf. *Gesta Francorum*, p. 2 etc.

2. ESTABLISHING A CASE FOR WAR

1. The literature on Urban's speech is vast. As a start, see J. Riley-Smith, *The First Crusade and the Idea of Crusading* (London, 1986), esp. chs. 1, 4 and 6; C. Tyerman, *God's War: A New History of the Crusades* (London, 2006), chs. 1 and 2.

2. Guibert of Nogent, *Gesta Dei per Francos*, *RHC Occ.*, vol. iv, p. 124.

3. Sigebert of Gembloux, *Chronica*, *MGHS*, vol. vi, p. 367.

4. Robert of Rheims, *Historia Iherosolimitana*, *RHC Occ.*, vol. iii, p. 729, trans. C. Sweetenham, *Robert the Monk's History of the First Crusade* (Farnham, 2006), p. 81; for the crusade decree, R. Somerville, *The Councils of Urban II*, vol. i, *Decreta Claromontensia*, Annuarium Historiae Conciliorum: Supplementum, i (Amsterdam, 1972), p. 74.

5. W. Wiederhold, 'Papsturkunden in Florenz', *Nachrichten von der Gesellschaft der Wissenschaften zu Göttingen*, Phil.-Hist. Kl (Göttingen, 1901), p. 313, trans. J. Riley-Smith and L. Riley-Smith, *The Crusades: Idea and Reality* (London, 1981), p. 39.

6. *Gesta Francorum at aliorum Hierosolimitanum*, ed. and trans. R. Hill (London, 1962), p. 1; J. Riley-Smith, *The First Crusaders* (Cambridge, 1997), pp. 62–3; for an early use of *'pugnatores Dei'*, see Fulcher of Chartres, *Historia Hierosolymitana*, *RHC Occ.*, vol. iii, p. 325; similar formulae saturate the letters of crusaders themselves and contemporary commentators' accounts.

7. Wiederhold, 'Papsturkunden in Florenz', p. 313; H. Hagenmeyer, *Die Kreuzzugsbriefe aus den Jahren 1088–1100* (Innsbruck, 1901), pp. 137–8 (Urban to his supporters in Bologna, Sept. 1096); P. Kehr,

Papsturkunden in Spanien, vol. i, *Katalonien* (Berlin, 1926), pp. 287–8, trans. Riley-Smith and Riley-Smith, *Crusades: Idea and Reality*, pp. 39–40. On representing the crusade as Christian charity, see J. Riley-Smith, 'Crusading as an Act of Love', *History*, 75 (1980), pp. 177–92.

8. Ralph Glaber, *Opera*, ed. J. France et al. (Oxford, 1989), pp. 200–201; in general, C. Morris, *The Holy Sepulchre and the Medieval West* (Oxford, 2005).

9. Albert of Aachen, *Historia Ierosolimitana*, ed. S. Edgington (Oxford, 2007), pp. 2–9; Guibert of Nogent, *Gesta Dei per Francos*, *RHC Occ.*, vol. iv, pp. 142–3; E. O. Blake and C. Morris, 'A Hermit Goes to War: Peter and the Origins of the First Crusade', in *Monks, Hermits and the Ascetic Tradition*, ed. W. J. Shields, Studies in Church History, vol. 22 (Oxford, 1985), pp. 79–109; J. Flori, *Pierre L'Ermite et la première croisade* (Paris, 1999); Tyerman, *God's War*, pp. 65–6, 72–4.

10. On the origins, see in general C. Erdmann, *The Origin of the Idea of Crusade*, trans. M. W. Baldwin and W. Goffart (Princeton, 1977); for critiques see C. Tyerman, *The Debate on the Crusades* (Manchester, 2011), pp. 183–92; cf. Tyerman, *God's War*, pp. 27–57.

11. H. E. J. Cowdrey, 'Pope Gregory VII's "Crusading" Plans of 1074', in *Outremer*, ed. B. Z. Kedar et al. (Jerusalem, 1982), pp. 27–40; *The Register of Pope Gregory VII 1072–1085*, trans. H. E. J. Cowdrey (Oxford, 2002), pp. 50–51, 122–4, 127–8; for Byzantine contacts with the west, see P. Frankopan, *The First Crusade: The Call from the East* (London, 2012), esp. pp. 57–100.

12. Guibert of Nogent, *Gesta Dei per Francos*, *RHC Occ.*, vol. iv, p. 124.

13. Hagenmeyer, *Kreuzzusbriefe*, p. 136, trans. Riley-Smith and Riley-Smith, *Crusades: Idea and Reality*, p. 38.

14. Bernold of St Blasien, *Chronicon*, *MGHS*, vol. v, p. 462.

15. For example Raymond of Aguilers' *Historia Francorum*, *RHC Occ.*, vol. iii or the *Chanson d'Antioche*, ed. S. Duparc-Quioc (Paris, 1977).

16. *Gesta Francorum*, p. 1; cf. Guibert of Nogent, *Gesta Dei per Francos*, *RHC Occ.*, vol. iv, p. 140.

17. *Vita Altmanni episcopi Pataviensis*, *MGHS*, vol. xii, p. 230 for the 1064 pilgrimage.

18. See Tyerman, *God's War*, pp. 607–11, 802–4, 875–81.

19. Ibid., pp. 100–106 and 282–6; cf. Riley-Smith, *The First Crusade*, pp. 50–57; R. Chazan, *European Jewry and the First Crusade* (London, 1987), pp. 50–136; S. Eidelberg, *The Jews and the Crusaders* (London, 1977).

20. Hayton, *La Flor des estoires de la Terre Sainte, RHC Documents Arméniens*(Paris, 1869–1906), vol. ii, p. 220; above p. 7.

21. As in Urban's letter to the monks of Vallombrosa, near Florence, Wiederhold, 'Papstkurkunden in Florenz', p. 313.

22. A. Wauters, *Table Chronologique des Chartes et Diplômes Imprimés concernant l'histoire de la Belgique*, vol. iii (Brussels, 1871), p. 74; M. Purcell, *Papal Crusading Policy 1244–91* (Leiden, 1975), pp. 200–201.

23. H. E. J. Cowdrey, 'Christianity and the Morality of Warfare During the First Century of Crusading', in *The Experience of Crusading*, vol. i, *Western Approaches*, ed. M. Bull and N. Housley (Cambridge, 2003), pp. 175–92; idem, 'Pope Gregory VII and the Bearing of Arms', in *Montjoie*, ed. B. Z. Kedar et al. (Aldershot, 1997), pp. 21–35; in general, F. H. Russell, *The Just War in the Middle Ages* (Cambridge, 1977).

24. Bernard of Clairvaux, *Letters*, trans. B. S. James (Stroud, 1998), no. 394, p. 467.

25. Gratian, *Decretum*, ed. A. Frieberg, *Corpus Iuris Canonici*, vol. i (Leipzig, 1879), Causa XXIII; cf. E.-D. Hehl, *Kirche und Krieg im 12 Jahrhundert* (Stuttgart, 1980); J. A. Brundage, *Medieval Canon Law and the Crusade* (Madison, 1969), pp. 39–45; Russell, *Just War*, pp. 55–85.

26. William of Tyre, *Chronicon*, ed. R. B. C. Huygens (Turnhout, 1986); Russell, *Just War*, pp. 86–126; Riley-Smith and Riley-Smith, *Crusades: Idea and Reality*, p. 120.

27. *The Chronicle of Henry of Livonia*, trans. J. A. Brundage (New York, 2003); C. Tyerman, 'Henry of Livonia and the Ideology of Crusading', in *Crusading and Chronicle Writing on the Medieval Baltic Frontier*, ed. M. Tamm et al. (Farnham, 2011), pp. 23–44.

28. For what follows, see J. Muldoon, *Popes, Lawyers and Infidels* (Liverpool, 1979), pp. 1–71.

29. Tyerman, *God's War*, p. 585.

30. Muldoon, *Popes, Lawyers and Infidels*, pp. 6–7.

31. Ibid, esp. pp. 15–17; M. Villey, *La Croisade: essai sur la formation d'une théorie juridique* (Paris, 1942).

32. Sigebert of Gembloux, *Chronica*, p. 367.

33. Riley-Smith and Riley-Smith, *Crusades: Idea and Reality*, p. 120 (*Quia Maior* 1213); Albert of Aachen, *Historia*, pp. 4–7; in general, see S. Throop, *Crusading as an Act of Vengeance 1095–1216* (Farnham, 2011).

34. Bernard of Clairvaux, *Letters*, no. 391, p. 462. Cf. *Chanson d'Antioche*, ll. 39, 99, 173, 207, in general pp. 20–25; C. Morris, 'Propaganda for War. The Dissemination of the Crusading Ideal in the Twelfth Century',

in *Studies in Church History*, ed. W. Shields, vol. xx (Oxford, 1983), esp. pp. 94–101; W. Jordan, 'The Representations of the Crusade in the Songs Attributed to Thibaud, Count Palatine of Champagne', *Journal of Medieval History*, 25 (1999), pp. 27–34; for trans., by M. Routledge, see *An Eyewitness History of the Crusades*, ed. C. Tyerman (London, 2004), vol. iv, pp. 268–73; and notes 27 above and 36 below.

35. Riley-Smith and Riley-Smith, *Crusades: Idea and Reality*, pp. 57–9, 64–7 for the bulls.

36. J. P. Migne, *Patrologia Latina* (Paris, 1844–64), vol. cciv, cols. 249–52, 350–61; *Actes des comtes de Namur 946–1196*, ed. F. Rousseau (Brussels, 1936), no. 28, pp. 61–4 (Othon de Trazegnies).

37. Russell, *Just War*, pp. 98, 100; Throop, *Crusading as an Act of Vengeance*, pp. 76, 83, 131; Bernard of Clairvaux, *De laude novae militiae*, trans. M. Barber and K. Bate, *The Templars* (Manchester, 2002), p. 219. For papal acceptance of revenue, see the constitution *Zelus fidei* of Gregory X's Second Council of Lyons, 1274, in N. P. Tanner, *Decrees of the Ecumenical Councils* (London and Washington, 1990), vol. i, p. 309.

38. Ralph of Caen, *Gesta Tancredi*, *RHC Occ.*, vol. iii, p. 606, trans. B. Bachrach and D. S. Bachrach, *The* Gesta Tancredi *of Ralph of Caen* (Aldershot, 2005), p. 22.

39. Bonizo of Sutri, *Liver de Vita Christiana*, ed. E. Perels (Berlin, 1930), pp. 35, 56, 101, 248–9; on chivalry in general, M. Keen, *Chivalry* (New Haven, 1984).

40. Ralph of Caen, *Gesta Tancredi*, *RHC Occ.*, vol. iii, p. 606, trans. Bachrach and Bachrach, p. 22.

41. Bernard of Clairvaux, *De laude novae militia*, p. 218. For the western tradition, see Tyerman, *God's War*, pp. 38–57; for Byzantine holy war in the seventh century, see P. Sarris, *Empires of Faith* (Oxford, 2011), pp. 250–53, 258, 266–7.

42. H. W. C. Davis, 'Henry of Blois and Brian FitzCount', *English Historical Review*, 25 (1910), pp. 301–3; cf. E. King, 'The Memory of Brian Fitz-Count', *Haskins Society Journal*, 13 (2004), pp. 89–90; Riley-Smith and Riley-Smith, *Crusade: Idea and Reality*, p. 57.

43. Bernard of Clairvaux, *Letters*, pp. 461–2, no. 391.

44. Riley-Smith and Riley-Smith, *Crusade: Idea and Reality*, p. 128; Keen, *Chivalry*, pp. 96–8.

45. Robert of Rheims, *Historia*, *RHC Occ.*, vol. iii, p. 728, trans. Sweetenham, *Robert the Monk's History*, p. 80.

46. *Canso d'Antioca*, ed. and trans. L. M. Patterson and C. Sweetenham (Aldershot, 2003); Albert of Aachen, *Historia*, p. 514 and books i–vii,

passim; William of Malmesbury, *De Gestis Regum Anglorum*, ed. W. Stubbs, Rolls Series (London, 1887–9), vol. ii, pp. 460–61; Geffrei Gaimar, *Estoire des Engleis*, ed. and trans. I. Short (Oxford, 2009), l. 5750, p. 312; cf. Tyerman, *Debate*, pp. 12–15.

47. *De expugnatione Lyxbonensi*, ed. and trans. C. W. David (New York, 1976), pp. 104–7.

48. *De profectione Danorum in Hierosolymam*, ed. M. C. Gertz, *Scriptores Minores Historie Danicae* (Copenhagen, 1970), vol. ii, pp. 465–7.

49. *Chevalier, Mult Estes Guarez*, ed. J. Bédier, *Les chansons de croisade* (Paris, 1909), p. 10; *Chronica regia Coloniensis*, ed. G. Waitz, *MGHS*, vol. xviii, pp. 203–8, trans. A. J. Andrea, *Contemporary Sources for the Fourth Crusade* (Leiden, 2000), p. 201.

50. Ambroise, *Estoire de la guerre sainte*, trans. as *The Crusade of Richard Lionheart* by M. J. Hubert (New York, 1941 repr. 1976), ll. 4,665–6, p. 198; *Itinerarium peregrinorum et gesta regis Ricardi*, ed. W. Stubbs (London, 1864) passim and, for Roland and Oliver, pp. 143, 216 and 422, trans. H. Nicholson, *The Chronicle of the Third Crusade* (Aldershot, 1997), pp. 145, 206, 367.

51. Geoffrey of Villehardouin, *La Conquête de Constantinople*, ed. E. Faral (Paris, 1938–9), trans. M. R. B. Shaw, *Chronicles of the Crusades* (London, 1963); Robert of Clari, *La Conquête de Constantinople*, ed. P. Lauer (Paris, 1924), trans. E. H. McNeal (New York, 1936 repr. 1966); John of Joinville, *Histoire de Saint Louis*, ed. N. de Wailly (Paris, 1874), trans. Shaw, *Chronicles of the Crusades*.

52. Trans. by M. Routledge, in ed. Tyerman, *Eyewitness History of the Crusades*, vol. iii, pp. 12–13.

53. *Itinerarium peregrinorum regis Ricardi*, p. 33, trans. Nicholson, *Chronicle*, p. 48.

54. Rutebeuf, *La desputizons dou croisié et dou descroisié*, *Onze poems concernant la croisade*, ed. J. Bastin and E. Faral (Paris, 1946), pp. 84–94; C. Tyerman, *The Invention of the Crusades* (Basingstoke, 1998), p. 53.

55. Archives nationales de France, JJ 59, no. 76; re-registered JJ 60, no. 100.

56. *Ordinatio de predicatione S. Crucis in Angliae*, *Quinti Belli Sacri Scriptores Minores*, ed. R. Röhricht, *Société de l'Orient Latin*, vol. ii (Geneva, 1879), pp. 1–26, esp. p. 20.

57. J. B. Pitra, *Analecta Novissima* (Paris, 1885–8), vol. ii, Sermon XI, pp. 328–31.

58. *Gesta Francorum*, p. 20. For the Clermont decree, Somerville, *Councils of Urban II*, *Decreta Claromontensia*, p.74 and for *honor*, see *Mediae*

Latinitatis Lexicon Minus, ed. J. F. Niermeyer et al. (Leiden, 1984), cols. 495–8.

59. Fulcher of Chartres, *Historia, RHC Occ.*, vol. iii, p. 324, trans. F. R. Ryan and H. Fink, *A History of the Expedition to Jerusalem* (Knoxville, 1969), p. 67; Baldric of Bourgueil, *Historia Jerosolimitana, RHC Occ.*, vol. iv, p. 15, trans. Riley-Smith and Riley-Smith, *Crusades: Idea and Reality*, p. 52; *Canso d'Antioca*, pp. 5–6, 201, 217, 229; Robert of Rheims, *Historia, RHC Occ.*, vol. iii, p. 728, trans. Sweetenham, *Robert the Monk's History*, p. 81; see below ch. 5, pp. 138–49.

60. Ekkehard of Aura, *Hierosolymita, RHC Occ.*, vol. v, p. 17.

61. Gunther of Pairis, *The Capture of Constantinople*, ed. and trans. A. Andrea (Philadelphia, 1997), p.71

62. For the material privileges in general, see Brundage, *Medieval Canon Law and the Crusader*, pp. 159–90; for women taking the Cross as early as 1096, Riley-Smith, *The First Crusade*, p. 35, cf. idem, *First Crusaders*, pp. 198, 204, 205, 210 and 213. See below ch.10, pp. 245–7.

63. Riley-Smith and Riley-Smith, *Crusade: Idea and Reality*, pp. 58–9.

64. Ibid, pp. 121–2.

65. Tyerman, *Invention*, pp. 55–62 for a brief general survey.

66. Migne, *Patrologia Latina*, vol. clxxx, col. 1063; *Constitutiones Concilii quarti Lateranensis una cum Commentariis glossatorum*, ed. A. Garcià y Garcià (Vatican City, 1981), p. 113; for a fuller discussion, see below ch. 8 pp. 204–7.

67. In general, Brundage, *Medieval Canon Law and the Crusader*, pp. 139–58.

68. Bernard of Clairvaux, *Letters*, pp. 462, 467, Fulcher of Chartres, *Historia, RHC Occ.*, vol. iii, p. 325, trans. Ryan and Fink, *History of the Expedition*, p. 68; Tyerman, *Invention*, pp. 81–3.

69. Villehardouin, *La Conquête*, vol. i, p. 4; Brundage, *Medieval Canon Law and the Crusader*, pp. 146–50 and p. 148 n. 33.

70. For 1198 bull, *Die Register Innocenz' III*, ed. O. Hageneder et al. (Graz, Cologne, Rome and Vatican City, 1964–), vol. i, no. 336; Roger of Howden, *Chronica*, ed. W. Stubbs, Rolls Series (London, 1868–71), vol. iv, pp. 70–75; Tyerman, *Invention*, p. 58 and refs.; for Languedoc, Peter of Les Vaux-de-Cernay, *Historia Albigensis*, trans. as *The History of the Albigensian Crusade* by W. A. Sibly and M. D. Sibly (Woodbridge, 1998), p. 97; for one year qualification in the Baltic in 1230, see Gregory IX, *Registres*, ed. L. Auvray (Paris, 1890–1955), no. 493.

71. Brundage, *Medieval Canon Law*, pp. 158–90; Tyerman, *Invention*, pp. 55–62.

72. E. Christiansen, *The Northern Crusades* (London, 1997), pp. 79–80, 98–100; Tyerman, 'Henry of Livonia and the Ideology of Crusading'.

73. R. C. Smail, 'Latin Syria and the West, 1149–87', *Transactions of the Royal Historical Society*, 5th series, 19 (1969), pp. 1–20.

74. *Register Innocenz' III*, vol. i, no. 336; Riley-Smith and Riley-Smith, *Crusades: Idea and Reality*, pp. 120–21.

75. D. E. Queller and T. F. Madden, *The Fourth Crusade* (Philadelphia, 1997), p. 16 and n. 54 and passim. In retrospect, Robert of Clari made clear the high command's preference for the Egyptian strategy – *La Conquête*, trans. McNeal, pp. 36, 37.

76. Riley-Smith and Riley-Smith, *Crusades: Idea and Reality*, pp. 64–7.

77. See, for example, Peter of Blois's *Passio Reginaldi*, in Migne, *Patrologia Latina*, vol. ccvii, cols. 957–76.

78. Baha al-Din Ibn Shaddad, *The Rare and Excellent History of Saladin*, trans. D. S. Richards (Aldershot, 2001), p. 125.

79. Used, e.g., in the conciliar decree *Ad Liberandam* of 1215, Riley-Smith and Riley-Smith, *Crusades: Idea and Reality*, p. 128.

80. Ibid, p. 120.

81. Oliver of Paderborn, *Historia Damiatina*, trans. J. J. Gavigan, in *Christian Society and the Crusades 1198–1229*, ed. E. Peters (Philadelphia, 1971), pp. 89–91, 112–14; James of Vitry, *Lettres*, ed. R. B. C. Huygens (Leiden, 1960), pp. 141–53.

82. E. R. David, 'Apocalyptic Conversion: The Joachite Alternative to the Crusades', *Traditio*, 125 (1969), pp. 127–54; B. Z. Kedar, *Crusade and Mission* (Princeton, 1984), pp. 112–16, 219–23.

83. Riley-Smith and Riley-Smith, *Crusades: Idea and Reality*, p. 122; Tyerman, *God's War*, pp. 596–9.

84. On Gregory's crusade schemes, see M. Lower, *The Barons' Crusade: A Call to Arms and its Consequences* (Philadelphia, 2005).

85. Matthew Paris, *Chronica Majora*, ed. H. R. Luard, Rolls Series (London, 1872–84), vol. iii, p. 620; Tyerman, *God's War*, pp. 762–3 and refs.

86. T. Rymer, *Foedera*, 3rd edn (London, 1745), 1, i, pp. 148–9, new edn (London, 1816), 1, i, pp. 258–9.

87. Matthew Paris, *Chronica Majora*, vol. v, pp. 521–2, 526, 532–3, 536; C. Tyerman, *England and the Crusades* (Chicago, 1988), pp. 120–23.

88. In general, W. Jordan, *Louis IX and the Challenge of the Crusade* (Princeton, 1979).

89. For a discussion of papal policy, C. T. Maier, *Preaching the Crusades* (Cambridge, 1994), pp. 52–6, 58–9 and refs.

90. For partial coverage, N. Housley, *The Italian Crusades* (Oxford, 1982); idem, *The Avignon Papacy and the Crusades 1305–78* (Oxford, 1986).

91. J. F. O'Callaghan, *Reconquest and Crusade in Medieval Spain* (Philadelphia, 2003), pp. 62–4, 88–9 and passim.

92. In general, Christiansen, *Northern Crusades*, passim.

93. Tyerman, 'Henry of Livonia and Crusading Ideology', pp. 32–3; in general, I. Fonnesberg-Schmidt, *The Popes and the Baltic Crusades 1147–1254* (Leiden, 2007).

94. Christiansen, *Northern Crusades*, p. 152 and refs.

95. Above note 90.

96. Innocent IV, *Registres*, ed. E. Berger (Paris, 1884–1921), no. 2945.

97. Ibid., nos. 1981, 1986, 1987, 2487, 2572, 2878, 2883, 2945, 2956, 3812, 3842, 4062, 4094, 4681, 5083, 5279, 5336, 5345.

98. Riley-Smith and Riley-Smith, *Crusade: Idea and Reality*, pp. 86–9; cf. Urban IV, *Registres*, ed. J. Guiraud (Paris, 1899–1958), nos. 809, 817.

99. Above note 87; H. E. Mayer, *The Crusades*, 2nd edn (Oxford, 1988), pp. 320–21.

100. P. Throop, *Criticism of the Crusade* (Amsterdam, 1940), esp. pp. 69–213, 229–32; Tanner, *Decrees of the Ecumenical Councils*, vol. i, pp. 304, 309–14; and below pp. 283–5.

101. *Albert von Beham und Regesten Innocenz IV*, ed. C. Hofler (Stuttgart, 1847), pp. 16–17; S. Lloyd, 'Political Crusades in England', in *Crusade and Settlement*, ed. P. Edbury (Cardiff, 1985), pp. 113–20; Tyerman, *England and the Crusades*, pp. 133–51.

102. Kedar, *Crusade and Mission*, pp. 177–83.

3. PUBLICITY

1. The literature on the First Crusade is vast. See, on planning, C. Tyerman, *God's War: A New History of the Crusades* (London, 2006), pp. 58–89; J. Riley-Smith, *The First Crusaders* (Cambridge, 1997), pp. 7–22, 53–143.

2. R. Somerville, 'The Council of Clermont', in *Papacy, Councils and Canon Law* (London, 1990), vol. vii, p. 58 and passim; Guibert of Nogent, *Gesta Dei per Francos*, *RHC Occ.*, vol. iv, p. 149.

3. For a short survey, T. Reuter, 'Assembly Politics in Western Europe from the Eighth to the Twelfth Centuries', in *The Medieval World*, ed. P. Linehan and J. Nelson (London, 2001), pp. 432–50.

4. Tyerman, *God's War*, pp. 276, 278–81, 286–8, 377–8, 381, 387, 392, 394, 499, 502–4 and refs.; C. Tyerman, *England and the Crusades*

(Chicago, 1988), pp. 59–61, 75–6 and refs.; J. R. Sweeny, 'Hungary in the Crusades 1169–1218', *International History Review*, 3 (1981), pp. 475–6; Geoffrey of Villehardouin, *La Conquête de Constantinople*, ed. E. Faral (Paris, 1938–9), trans. M. R. B. Shaw, *Chronicles of the Crusade* (London, 1963), pp. 29–31, 37–9; A. Andrea, *Contemporary Sources for the Fourth Crusade* (Leiden, 2000), pp. 279–80.

5. *Ad Liberandam*, decree no. 71 of Fourth Lateran Council, trans. N. P. Tanner, *Decrees of the Ecumenical Councils* (London and Washington, 1990), pp. 267–71; *Recueil des actes de Philippe Auguste*, ed. H.-F. Delaborde et al. (Paris, 1916–79), no. 1360; C. T. Maier, *Preaching the Crusades. Mendicant Friars and the Cross in the Thirteenth Century* (Cambridge, 1994), pp. 32–95; Tyerman, *God's War*, pp. 772–4, 778–9, 785, 814–16 and refs.; N. Housley, *The Later Crusades. From Lyons to Alcazar* (Oxford, 1992), pp. 10–15, 28–30 and refs.; J. Maddicott, 'The Crusade Taxation of 1268–70 and the Development of Parliament', *Thirteenth Century England*, 2 (1988), pp. 93–117; idem, *The Origins of the English Parliament 924–1327* (Oxford, 2010), pp. 266–72.

6. Tyerman, *God's War*, pp. 829–32, 865–6, 870 and refs.; for a detailed analysis of the 1313 festival, see E. A. R. Brown and N. F. Regalado, 'La grant feste', in *City and Spectacle in Medieval Europe*, eds. B. A. Hanawalt and K. L. Reyerson (Minneapolis, 1994), pp. 56–86.

7. Humbert of Romans, *Treatise on Preaching*, trans. W. M. Conlon (London, 1955), p. 74; *Historical Papers and Letters from the Northern Registers*, ed. J. Raine, Rolls Series (London, 1873), pp. 93–6.

8. Landulph of St Paul, *Liber Hystoriarum Mediolanensis Urbis*, ed. C. Castiglioni (Bologna, 1935), pp. 4–5; in general, J. Richard, 'La papauté et la direction de la première croisade', *Journal des savants* (1960), pp. 49–59.

9. Baldric of Bourgueil, *Historia Jerosolimitana*, *RHC Occ.*, vol. iv, p. 15; Urban II's letter to the Flemish, December 1095, H. Hagenmeyer, *Die Kreuzzugsbriefe aus den Jahren 1088–1100* (Innsbruck, 1901), pp. 136–7, trans. E. Peters, *The First Crusade* (Philadelphia, 1998), p. 42.

10. Richard, 'La papauté et la direction', pp. 54–5, but Fulcher of Chartres is less specific, *Historia Hierosolymitana*, *RHC Occ.*, vol. iii, p. 329 about Urban's approval: 'from whom we received a blessing'.

11. In general see J. Phillips, *The Second Crusade* (New Haven, 2007), pp. 37–8, 39–41, 97 for a positive view of Eugenius's role; for gossip about the legates and the French bishops, see John of Salisbury, *Historia Pontificalis* (London, 1962), pp. 54–6.

12. Tyerman, *God's War*, p. 282; Bernard of Clairvaux, *Letters*, trans. B. S. James (Stroud, 1998), letter no. 393, pp. 465–6.

13. For examples, see Maier, *Preaching the Crusades*, pp. 51–2, 88–9, 137–41.

14. For the Third Crusade preparations, see Tyerman, *God's War*, pp. 374–99; for the role of bishops, *Itinerarium Ricardi Regis*, trans. H. Nicholson, *The Chronicle of the Third Crusade* (Aldershot, 1997), pp. 48, 142.

15. Gerald of Wales, *Journey through Wales*, trans. L. Thorpe (London, 1978), p. 200; M. C. Gaposchkin, 'The Pilgrimage and Cross-blessings in the Roman Pontificals of the Twelfth and Thirteenth Centuries', *Medieval Studies*, 73 (2011), pp. 261–86, esp. p. 279 and refs.; J. A. Brundage, 'Cruce Signari: The Rite For Taking The Cross in England', *Traditio*, 22 (1966), pp. 289–310; K. Pennington, 'The Rite For Taking The Cross in the Twelfth Century', *Traditio*, 30 (1974), pp. 429–35; for a trans. of an English example, see J. Riley-Smith and L. Riley-Smith, *The Crusades: Idea and Reality 1095–1274* (London, 1981), pp. 137–9.

16. Andrea, *Contemporary Sources for the Fourth Crusade*, pp. 10–19 (the Narbonne version of the crusade bull), 20–21 for Fulk's appointment; for Vacarius see the York version of the 1198 bull, in Roger of Howden, *Chronica*, ed. W. Stubbs (London, 1868–71), vol. iv, pp. 70–75.

17. Gunther of Pairis, *The Capture of Constantinople*, ed. and trans. A. Andrea (Philadelphia, 1997), pp. 68–71.

18. James of Vitry, *Historia Occidentalis*, ed. J. F. Hinnebusch (Freiburg, 1972), p. 101.

19. J. L. Cate, 'The English Mission of Eustace of Flay', *Etudes d'histoire dédiées à la mémoire de Henri Pirenne* (Brussels, 1937), pp. 67–89; Roger of Howden, *Chronica*, vol. iv, pp. 123–4, 167–72.

20. *Pium et sanctum*, trans. J. Bird, E. Peters and J. M. Powell, in *Crusade and Christendom* (Philadelphia, 2013), p. 113; cf. Riley-Smith and Riley-Smith, *Crusades: Idea and Reality*, pp. 130–31.

21. Humbert of Romans, *Treatise on Preaching*, p. 38; Thomas of Chobham, *Summa de Arte Praedicandi*, ed. F. Morenzoni (Turnholt, 1988), pp. 69–70.

22. Andrea, *Contemporary Sources for the Fourth Crusade*, pp. 39–52, 72–3, 128, 152, 163–8, 171–6, 250–51; Gunther of Pairis, *Capture of Constantinople*, pp. 78–9.

23. G. Dickson, *The Children's Crusade* (Basingstoke, 2008), esp. chs. 2–5.

24. J. M. Powell, *Anatomy of a Crusade 1213–1221* (Philadelphia, 1986), pp. 15–50; for trans. of *Quia Maior* and the instructions to preachers, *Pium et sanctum*, Bird et al., *Crusade and Christendom*, pp. 106–13; Riley-Smith and Riley-Smith, *Crusades: Idea and Reality*, pp. 129–33.

25. *Registri dei Cardinali Ugolino d'Ostia e Ottaviano degli Ubaldini*, ed. G. Levi (Rome, 1890); for the intellectual background, see J. W. Baldwin, *Masters, Princes and Merchants: The Social Views of Peter the Chanter and His Circle* (Princeton, 1970).

26. For an introduction to this see H. E. J. Cowdrey, 'Christianity and the Morality of Warfare During the First Century of Crusading', in *The Experience of Crusading*, ed. M. Bull and N. Housley (Cambridge, 2003), vol. i, pp. 175–92; J. Muldoon, *Popes, Lawyers and Infidels* (Liverpool, 1979).

27. Bird et al., *Crusade and Christendom*, p. 140; ibid., p. 135 for the Parisian academics and, generally, pp. 119–20, 135–41; for later laments, see the works of Thomas of Chobham and Humbert of Romans, notes 7 and 21 above.

28. E. Baratier, 'Une prédication de la croisade à Marseille en 1224', *Economies et sociétés au moyen âge: Mélanges offerts à Edouard Perroy* (Paris, 1973), pp. 690–99, trans. Bird et al., *Crusade and Christendom*, pp. 232–5; Powell, *Anatomy*, esp. ch. 4.

29. Pay: Riley-Smith and Riley-Smith, *Crusades: Idea and Reality*, p. 133 (Innocent III to the bishop of Regensberg, 10 Sept. 1213); for English examples from 1252, 1254 and 1290, *Calendar of Patent Rolls 1247–58*, pp. 168, 370; *Register of Archbishop J. Le Romeyn*, vol. ii, ed. W. Brown, Surtees Society (Durham, 1916), p. 93. Seals: Maier, *Preaching the Crusades*, p. 100 and n. 23, p.106 and n. 56.

30. Maier, *Preaching the Crusades*, pp. 8–19 and passim for the friars' role in general.

31. Maier, *Preaching the Crusades*, esp. pp. 20–31.

32. Matthew Paris, *Chronica Majora*, ed. H. R. Luard, Rolls Series (London, 1872–84), vol. iv, p. 256.

33. *Calendar of Close Rolls 1251–53*, pp. 201–2.

34. *Historical Papers from Northern Registers*, pp. 93–6; for Humbert's treatise, above note 7; for the 1265 gourmands, Borelli de Serres, 'Compte d'une mission de prédication pour secours à la Terre Sainte', *Mémoires de la Société de l'histoire de Paris et de l'Île de France*, 30 (1903), pp. 243–61, and generally pp. 243–80.

35. Orderic Vitalis, *Ecclesiastical History*, ed. and trans. M. Chibnall (Oxford, 1969–80), vol. vi, pp. 68–73, esp. 68–71; M. Barber, *The New Knighthood* (Cambridge, 1994), pp. 12–18; *De profectione Danorum in Hierosoymam*, ed. M. C. Gertz, *Scriptores Minores Historiae Danicae* (Copenhagen, repr. 1970), vol. ii, pp. 465–7.

36. Thomas of Chobham, *Summa de Arte Praedicandi*, p. 54; Humbert of Romans, *Treatise on Preaching*, p. 47; for his insistence on extended learning by crusade preachers, see K. Michel, *Das Opus Tripartitum des Humbertus de Romans OP* (Graz, 1926), pp. 14–16; A. Lecoy de la Marche, 'La prédication de la croisade au treizième siècle', *Revue des questions historiques*, 48 (1890), pp. 15–18.

37. Orderic Vitalis, *Ecclesiastical History*, vol. v, p. 324; for official misogyny (in this case Innocent III's), Bird et al., *Crusade and Christendom*, p. 120; for a short summary and useful bibliography, see N. Hodgson, 'Women', in *The Crusades: An Encyclopedia*, ed. A. V. Murray (Santa Barbara, 2006), pp. 1285–91.

38. Ch. 20 of Humbert of Romans' *De predicatione s. crucis*, in Michel, *Opus Tripartitum*, pp. 14–16; Lecoy de la Marche, 'La prédication', p. 15; J. P. Migne, *Patrologia Latina* (Paris, 1844–64), vol. ccxvi, col. 1262; ibid, vol. cxcvii, cols. 187–8. See on various aspects, S. Edgington and S. Lambert, *Gendering the Crusades* (New York, 2002), esp. chs.1, 3, 6, 11.

39. R. Somerville, *The Councils of Urban II. Decreta Claromontensia* (Amsterdam, 1972), p. 74 and passim; Hagenmeyer, *Kreuzzugsbriefe*, pp. 136–7 (NB: *relatum* means written record); see also P. Frankopan, *The First Crusade: The Call from the East* (London, 2012), pp. 60–61, 87–100 and refs.; in general M. Aurell, *Le chevalier lettré: Savoir et conduit de l'aristocracie au xiie et xiiie siècle* (Paris, 2011); M. Clanchy, *From Memory to Written Record* (London, 1979) and above pp. 20–27.

40. Hagenmeyer, *Kreuzzugsbriefe*, pp. 140, 149.

41. Bohemund, *Gesta Francorum*, ed. and trans. R. Hill (London, 1962), p. 75.

42. E. van Houts, *The Normans in Europe* (Manchester, 2000), pp. 130–31; M. Hagger, 'A Pipe Roll for 25 Henry I', *English Historical Review*, 122 (2007), pp. 133–40.

43. Albert of Aachen, *Historia Ierosolimitana*, ed. and trans. S. Edgington (Oxford, 2007), pp. 6–7; Hagenmeyer, *Kreuzzugsbriefe*, pp. 144–6, 155–6, 175–6; Guibert of Nogent, *Gesta Dei per Francos*, *RHC Occ.*, vol. iv, p. 219; Peters, *First Crusade*, pp. 284–7, 289–91, 292–7.

44. *Chronicon S. Andreae in Castro Cameracesii*, ed. L. C. Bethmann (Hanover, 1846), pp. 544–6; in general, C. Tyerman, *The Debate on the Crusades* (Manchester, 2011), esp. pp. 7–25 and pp. 32–3, nn. 1–15.

45. Trans. Peters, *First Crusade*, pp. 293–6.

46. N. L. Paul, 'A Warlord's Wisdom: Literacy and Propaganda at the Time of the First Crusade', *Speculum*, 85 (2010), pp. 534–66; see also N. L. Paul, *To Follow in Their Footsteps* (Ithaca, 2012).

47. E.g. Robert of Rheims, *Historia Iherosolimitana*, ed. D. Kempf and M. G. Bull (Woodbridge, 2013), pp. xlii–xlvii; cf. J. Flori, *Chroniqueurs et propagandists: Introduction critique aux sources de la première croisade* (Geneva, 2010).

48. *Monitum Willelmi Grassegals militis ad historias belli sacri, RHC Occ.*, vol. iii, pp. 317–18, trans. J. Rubinstein, 'Fitting History to Use: Three Crusade Chronicles in Context', *Viator*, 35 (2004), pp. 132–68, at p. 134.

49. J. Phillips, 'Odo of Deuil's *De profectione* as a source', in *Experience of Crusading*, ed. Bull and Housley, vol. i, pp. 83–4 and nn. 18 and 23.

50. Robert of Rheims, above note 47, Introduction passim esp. pp. xlv–xlvi for the luxury illustrated ms; *Quantum praedecessores*, trans. Riley-Smith and Riley-Smith, *Crusades: Idea and Reality*, pp. 57–9.

51. James of Vitry, *Lettres*, ed. R. B. C. Huygens (Leiden, 1960), pp. 135, 139; cf. William of Tyre's *Historia*, ed. R. B. C. Huygens (Turnholt, 1986), bk v ch. 10.

52. Lecoy de la Marche, 'La prédication', pp. 15–18.

53. C. Tyerman, *The Invention of the Crusades* (Basingstoke, 1998), pp. 14, 36–7; Migne, *Patrologia Latina*, vol. cc, cols. 1294–6, vol. ccxvi, col. 822.

54. Riley-Smith and Riley-Smith, *Crusades: Idea and Reality*, pp. 131–3; F. Kempf, 'Das Rommersdorfer Briefbuch des 13 Jahrhunderts', *Mitteilungen des Österreichischen Instituts für Geschichtsforschung, Erganzungsband*, 12 (1933), pp. 502–71.

55. Maier, *Preaching the Crusades*, pp. 101–3.

56. Above ch. 1 note 50.

57. For Ilger Bigod, Orderic Vitalis, *Ecclesiastical History*, vol. v, pp. 170–72; Eadmer, *Historia novorum*, ed. M. Rule, Rolls Series (London, 1884), pp. 179–81; for Pons of Balazun, see above p. 21 and *RHC Occ.*, vol. iii, p. 235; for Anselm of Ribemont, Hagenmeyer, *Kreuzzugsbriefe*, pp. 144–6, 155–6.

58. Aurell, *Le chevalier lettré*, pp. 28–9 and passim.

59. D. Crouch, *Beaumont Twins* (Cambridge, 1986), pp. 7, 207–11; John Hudson, 'Ranulf Glanvill', *ODNB*.

60. *Canso d'Antiocha*, ed. L. M. Paterson and C. Sweetenham (Aldershot, 2003), pp. 5–17, 34–40; Aurell, *Le chevalier lettré*, p. 195.

61. William of Tyre, *Historia*, bk 14 ch. 21

62. See Bernard's letter to the duke of Bohemia which he hopes the bishop of Moravia will explain, Bernard of Clairvaux, *Opera*, vol. viii, *Epistolae*, ed. J. Leclerq and H. Rochais (Rome, 1977), no. 458, pp. 436–7 (B. S. James's trans., *Letters* n. 392, p. 464, is highly misleading); Otto of Freising, *The Deeds of Frederick Barbarossa*, trans. C. C. Mierow (New York, 1966), p. 75; in general Phillips, *Second Crusade*, pp. 69–77.

63. See for a discussion, J. H. Pryor, 'Two *excitationes* for the Third Crusade', *Mediterranean Historical Review*, 25 (2010), pp. 147–68, esp. pp. 152–7, 163, n. 163.

64. For his three crusade pamphlets, *De Hierosolymitana peregrinatione acceleranda*; its associated *Dialogus inter regem Henricum secundum et abbatem Bonnevallensem*; and the hagiographical *Passio Reginaldi*, see Migne, *Patrologia Latina*, vol. ccvii cols. 957–75, 976–88 and 1058–70; Tyerman, *Invention*, pp. 26–9; R. W. Southern, 'Peter of Blois', *ODNB*.

65. Gerald of Wales, *Opera*, ed. J. S. Brewer, Rolls Series (London, 1861–91), vol. i, p. 79, trans. *The Autobiography of Giraldus Cambriensis*, ed. H. E. Butler (London, 1937), p. 104.

66. Ambroise, *Estoire de la guerre sainte*, trans. M. J. Hubert (New York, 1976); *Ordinatio de predicatione s. crucis in Angliae*, in ed. R. Röhricht, *Quinti Belli Sacri Scriptores Minores, Société de l'Orient Latin*, vol. ii (Geneva, 1879), p. 20; for Villehardouin's vernacular, *La Conquête de Constantinople*, ed. E. Faral (Paris, 1938–9); *La Chanson de la croisade albigeoise*, ed. E. Martin-Chabot (Paris, 1931–61); Peter of les Vaux-de-Vernay, *Hystoria albigensis*, ed. P. Guébin and E. Lyon (Paris, 1926–39); trans. of Oliver of Paderborn, by J. J. Gavigan, is reproduced in Bird et al., *Crusade and Christendom*, pp. 159–225.

67. U. Berlière, 'A propos de Jacques de Vitry', *Revue Bénédictine*, 27 (1910), pp. 521–4; Riley-Smith and Riley-Smith, *Crusades: Idea and Reality*, pp. 135–6; for Roger of Wendover and Oliver's chronicle version, Bird et al., *Crusade and Christendom*, pp. 132, 166; Caesarius of Heisterbach, *Dialogus miraculorum*, ed. J. Strange (Cologne, Bonn and Brussels, 1851), vol. ii, p. 245; for Oliver's texts in general, *Schriften*, ed. H. Hoogeweg (Tübingen, 1894).

68. *Regestri del Cardinale Ugolino*, pp.7–153; *Epistolae selectae saeculi XIII*, ed. C. Rodenberg (Berlin, 1883–94), vol. i, pp. 89–91, no. 124, tabulated in Powell, *Anatomy*, pp. 100–101.

69. *Gesta Francorum*, p. 75.

70. Tyerman, *England and the Crusades*, pp. 16–17, 78–81; idem, *God's War*, pp. 276–7, 389–91. See below pp. 197–9.

71. *De expugnatione Lyxbonensi*, ed. and trans. C. W. David (New York, 1976), pp. 56–7.

72. Ilger Bigod, see above note 57; for legal impact, see Tyerman, *Invention*, pp. 55–62.

73. Tyerman, *England and the Crusades*, pp. 66, 70–71, 169–72.

74. Roger of Wendover, *Flores historiarum*, ed. H. G. Hewlett, Rolls Series (London, 1884–9), vol. ii, p. 297; Berlière, 'A propos', pp. 522–4; Riley-Smith and Riley-Smith, *Crusades: Idea and Reality*, pp. 135–6; *Testimonia Minora de Quinto Bello Sacro*, ed. R. Röhricht (Geneva, 1882), p. 177.

75. Tyerman, *England and the Crusades*, p. 80 and below ch. 10.

76. *Ordinatio de predicatione s. crucis in Angliae*, p. 22; M. Purcell, *Papal Crusading Policy 1244–91* (Leiden, 1975), p. 200.

77. S. Lloyd, *English Society and the Crusade 1216–1307* (Oxford, 1988), pp. 80, 81, 106– 7, 115– 23, 134– 8, 144– 5 and Appendix 5.

78. Cf. Maier, *Preaching the Crusades*, p. 106.

4. PERSUASION

1. Gerald of Wales, *Journey through Wales*, trans. L. Thorpe (London, 1978), passim; idem, *Opera*, ed. J. S. Brewer, Rolls Series (London, 1861–91), vol. i, pp. 75, 77–8; Caesarius of Heisterbach, *Dialogus miraculorum*, ed. J. Strange (Cologne, Bonn and Brussels, 1851), vol. i, pp. 70–72, vol. ii, pp. 234–5, 332–5; *Testimonia Minora de Quinto Bello Sacro*, ed. R. Röhricht (Geneva, 1882), p. 178.

2. Oliver, above p. 82; James of Vitry, *Lettres*, ed. R. B. C. Huygens (Leiden, 1960), p. 77; J. Bird, E. Peters and J. M. Powell, *Crusade and Christendom* (Philadelphia, 2013), pp. 232–5.

3. G. R. Owst, *Preaching in Medieval England* (Cambridge, 1926), pp. 56–7, citing the *Speculum Laicorum*.

4. Gerald of Wales, *Opera*, vol. i, p. 75.

5. Caesarius of Heisterbach, *Dialogus*, vol. i, p. 205; *Ordinatio de predicatione s.Crucis in Angliae*, ed. R. Röhricht, *Quinti Belli Sacri Scriptores Minores*, Société de l'Orient Latin, vol. ii (Geneva, 1879), p. 24.

6. For surveys in English, see P. Cole, *The Preaching of the Crusades to the Holy Land 1095–1291* (Cambridge, Mass., 1991); S. Menache, *The Vox Dei: Communication in the Middle Ages* (Oxford, 1990); C. T. Maier, *Preaching the Crusades. Mendicant Friars and the Cross in the Thirteenth Century* (Cambridge, 1994); idem, *Crusade Propaganda and Ideology: Model Sermons for the Preaching of the Cross* (Cambridge, 2000), esp. ch. 2; C. Muessig, ed., *Preacher, Sermon and Audience in the Middle Ages* (Leiden, 2002), esp. B. M. Kienzle, 'Medieval Sermons and their Performance', pp. 110–45.

7. Thomas of Chobham in R. Copeland and I. Sluiter, *Medieval Grammar and Rhetoric. Language, Arts and Literary Theory AD 300–1475* (Oxford, 2009), pp. 628, 638; cf. Thomas of Chobham, *Summa de Arte Praedicandi*, ed. F. Morenzoni (Turnholt, 1988), p. 303 and passim; Humbert of Romans, *Treatise on Preaching*, trans. W. M. Conlon (London, 1955), passim.

8. Baldwin of Forde, 'Sermo de Sancta Cruce', in *Opera: Sermones de Commendatione Fidei*, ed. D. N. Bell (Turnholt, 1991), p. 127, '*in militia vexillum, in victorie tropheum et triumphi titulum*'. C. Tyerman, *The Invention of the Crusades* (Basingstoke, 1998), p. 73 and n. 185 for mss ref.

9. Humbert of Romans, *Treatise on Preaching*, pp. 11–12.

10. A. Lecoy de la Marche, 'La prédication de la croisade au treizième siècle', *Revue des questions historiques*, 48 (1890), pp. 19–20 and passim; Cole, *Preaching*, pp. 202–17; Maier, *Preaching the Crusades*, p. 115; for Humbert's sermons, Maier, *Crusade Propaganda*, pp. 210–29.

11. Lecoy de la Marche, 'La prédication', p. 25.

12. Lecoy de la Marche, 'La prédication', pp. 15–18.

13. The text was edited by Röhricht as *Ordinatio de predicatione S.Crucis*, in *Quinti Belli Sacri Scriptores Minores* (Geneva, 1879), pp. vii–x, 1–26; cf. Cole, *Preaching*, pp. 109–26; for the context, S. Lloyd, 'Political Crusades in England', in *Crusade and Settlement*, ed. P. Edbury (Cardiff, 1985), pp. 113–20; idem, *English Society and the Crusade 1216–1307* (Oxford, 1988), pp. 66–7 and pp. 9–70 for promotion in England generally.

14. *Ordinatio*, pp. 22, 25 and generally pp.18–26; cf. T. F. Crane, *The Exempla of Jacques de Vitry* (London, 1890), p. 41 no. lxxxix.

15. Matthew Paris, *Chronica Majora*, ed. H. R. Luard, Rolls Series (London, 1872–84), vol. v, p. 101.

16. J. Riley-Smith and L. Riley-Smith, *The Crusades: Idea and Reality 1095–1274* (London, 1981), p. 136; *Testimonia Minora*, ed. Röhricht, p. 145.

17. Tyerman, *Invention*, p. 74.
18. Bird et al., *Crusade and Christendom*, p. 43 trans. from K. Pennington, 'The Rite for Taking the Cross in the Twelfth Century', *Traditio*, 30 (1974), pp. 433–5; Bernard of Clairvaux, *Letters*, trans. B. S. James (Stroud, 1998), no. 391, p. 461; Robert of Rheims, *Historia Iherososlimitana*, *RHC Occ.*, vol. iii, p. 730; Otto of Freising, *The Deeds of Frederick Barbarossa*, trans. C. C. Mierow (New York, 1966), p. 75; Gilbert of Mons, *Chronicle of Hainault*, trans. L. Naplan (Woodbridge, 2005), p. 112; Gerald of Wales, *Journey through Wales*, pp. 132, 169, 185, 200; Riley-Smith and Riley-Smith, *Crusades: Idea and Reality*, pp. 135–6.
19. Odo of Deuil, *De profectione Ludovici VII in orientem*, ed. V. G. Berry (New York, 1948), pp. 6–9.
20. Otto of Freising, *Deeds of Frederick*, p. 75.
21. Gunther of Pairis, *The Capture of Constantinople*, ed. and trans. A. Andrea (Philadelphia, 1997), p. 68, pp. 69–71 for sermon.
22. Baldric of Bourgueil's version of Urban's speech was appended to a manuscript of Humbert of Romans's treatise of crusade preaching; Gerald of Wales, *Opera*, vol. i, p. 76, cf. G. Constable, 'The Language of Preaching in the Twelfth Century', *Viator*, 25 (1994), pp. 142–51.
23. E.g. Humbert of Romans, Maier, *Preaching the Crusades*, p. 106 and n. 60.
24. C. Tyerman, *God's War: A New History of the Crusades* (London, 2006), pp. 74–5, 77–8, 94–5; Guibert of Nogent, *Gesta Dei per Francos*, *RHC Occ.*, vol. iv, p. 142.
25. For Genoa and Marseilles, above p. 71; H. C. Scheeben, *Albert der Grosse: Zur Chronologie seines Lebens* (Leipzig, 1931), ch. 9, 'Kruezzugspredigt in Deutschland (1263–1264)', pp. 72–7; H. Wilms, *Albert the Great* (London, 1933), pp. 200, 203–5.
26. Gerald of Wales, *Journey through Wales*, p. 114; Geoffrey of Villehardouin, *La Conquête de Constantinople*, ed. E. Faral (Paris, 1938–9), p. 29 (although there is no explicit mention of a sermon); Eudes of Rouen, *Register*, ed. S. Brown and J. O'Sullivan (New York and London, 1964), p. 687.
27. Clerkenwell hosted the failed sermon of Patriarch Heraclius of Jerusalem, C. Tyerman, *England and the Crusades* (Chicago, 1988), p. 51.
28. Tyerman, *God's War*, p. 74; Eudes of Rouen, *Register*, p. 687.
29. Robert of Rheims, *Historia Iherosolimitana*, *RHC Occ.*, vol. iii, p. 727.

30. *Historical Papers and Letters from the Northern Registers*, ed. J. Raine, Rolls Series (London, 1873), pp. 93–6; *Register of Archbishop J. Le Romeyn*, vol. ii, ed. W. Brown, Surtees Society (Durham, 1916), pp. 8–9 (and p. 90 n. 1), 113.

31. Bird et al., *Crusade and Christendom*, pp. 83–5 (Spain 1212) and 111 (Holy Land 1213); *Register of Bishop John de Pontissara of Winchester*, Surrey Record Society (London, 1913–24), pp. 191–4.

32. Riley-Smith and Riley-Smith, *Crusades: Idea and Reality*, pp. 135–6; *Testimonia Minora*, ed. Röhricht, p. 177; J. Hanska, 'Reconstructing the Mental Calendar of Medieval Preaching', in *Preacher, Sermon and Audience*, ed. Muessig, p. 293; Maier, *Preaching the Crusades*, p. 107 n. 62; the experienced Franciscan preacher concerned, Berthold of Regensberg, regularly preached the Cross, including with Albert the Great in 1263–4; Humbert of Romans, *Treatise on Preaching*, pp. 41–3.

33. G. Frenken, *Die Exempla des Jacob von Vitry* (Munich, 1914), p. 149.

34. J. Brundage, *Medieval Canon Law and the Crusader* (Madison, 1969), pp. 154–5; H. E. Mayer, *The Crusades*, 2nd edn (Oxford, 1988), p. 321; Bird et al., *Crusade and Christendom*, p. 456.

35. Matthew Paris, *Chronica Majora*, vol. v, pp. 73–4.

36. Arnold of Lübeck, *Chronica Slavorum*, ed. J. M. Lappenberg (Hanover, 1868), p. 215.

37. C. Tyerman, 'Who Went on Crusade to the Holy Land', in idem, *The Practices of Crusading: Image and Action from the Eleventh to the Six-teenth Centuries* (Farnham, 2013), no. XIII, esp. p. 17; Tyerman. *England and the Crusades*, pp. 170–72.

38. *Ordinatio*, p. 17; for a similar contemporary sermon use of nets as an image, see Bird et al., *Crusade and Christendom*, p. 118.

39. Alan of Lille, *Sermo de cruce domini*, in *Textes inédits*, ed. M. T. Alverny (Paris, 1952), pp. 281–2; cf. usury provisions in *Quantum praedeces-sores* and see general introductory description in Brundage, *Medieval Canon Law*, pp. 179–83.

40. Caffaro, *De liberatione civitatum orientis*, *RHC Occ.*, vol. v, p. 49 ('*de melioribus*'); James of Vitry, *Lettres*, p. 77; for occupations in gen-eral, Tyerman, 'Who Went on Crusade to the Holy Land', passim; and below ch. 6.

41. *Anecdotes historiques legendes et apologues d'Etienne de Bourbon*, ed. A Lecoy de la Marche (Paris, 1877), no. 101, pp. 91–2.

42. *Itinerarium Ricardi Regis*, ed. W. Stubbs, Rolls Series (London, 1864), p. 33, trans. H. Nicholson, *The Chronicle of the Third Crusade* (Aldershot, 1997), p. 48.

43. Gerald of Wales, *Journey through Wales*, p. 172, cf. p. 90 for Gerald's visceral misogyny; Caesarius of Heisterbach, *Dialogus*, vol. ii, p. 234; cf. J. Brundage's articles on crusaders' wives, *Studia Gratiana*, 12 (1967), pp. 425–41 and 14 (1967), pp. 241–52; Innocent III on the matter, see Bird et al., *Crusade and Christendom*, pp. 52, 120; for examples of abuse, Tyerman, *England and the Crusades*, pp. 209–11; Brundage, *Medieval Canon Law*, p. 154; Bird et al., *Crusade and Christendom*, p. 118 and n. 14.

44. Humbert of Romans, *Treatise on Preaching*, pp. 29–33, 107–8.

45. Mayer, *Crusades*, pp. 320–21.

46. Bird et al., *Crusade and Christendom*, p. 233; James of Vitry, *Lettres*, p. 86; Humbert of Romans, *Treatise on Preaching*, pp. 74, 128–30.

47. J.-L. Bataillon, 'Approaches to the Study of Medieval Sermons', *La prédication au xiiie siècle en France et Italie* (Aldershot, 1993), pp. 21–4; Maier, *Crusade Propaganda*, pp. 18–21; for examples, see Cole, *Preaching*, pp. 222–6; Bird et al., *Crusade and Christendom*, pp. 115–19.

48. Gerald of Wales, *Journey through Wales*, p. 75.

49. Robert of Rheims, *Historia Iherosolimitana*, *RHC Occ.*, vol. iii, p. 729, trans. C. Sweetenham, *Robert the Monk's History of the First Crusade* (Farnham, 2006), p. 81; Maier, *Crusade Propaganda*, pp. 64–7.

50. For processions for Spanish crusade of 1212, see Bird et al., *Crusade and Christendom*, pp. 82–5; G. Dickson, *The Children's Crusade* (Basingstoke, 2008), pp. 51–8.

51. Tyerman, *God's War*, pp. 802–4, 880–81 and refs.; *Annales Paulini*, *Chronicles of the Reigns of Edward I and II*, ed. W. Stubbs, Rolls Series (London, 1882–3), vol. i, pp. 156, 266; T. Guard, *Chivalry, Kingship and Crusade: The English Experience in the Fourteenth Century* (Woodbridge, 2013), pp. 23–4, 137–8.

52. Sigebert of Gembloux, *Chronica*, *MGHS*, vol. vi, p. 367.

53. Geoffrey of Auxerre, *S. Bernardi Vita Prima*, bk iii, in J. P. Migne, *Patrologia Latina* (Paris, 1844–64), vol. clxxxv, p. 307; Gerald of Wales, *Opera*, vol. i, p. 76; Constable, 'Language of Preaching', p. 150 and, in general, pp. 131–52.

54. Humbert of Romans, *Treatise on Preaching*, p. 32.

55. *De expugnatione Lyxbonensi*, ed. and trans. C. W. David (New York, 1976), pp. 70–71. Gerald of Wales, *Journey through Wales*, p. 126.

56. Orderic Vitalis, *Ecclesiastical History*, ed. and trans. M. Chibnall (Oxford, 1969–80), vol. vi, pp. 68–73; *De profectione Danorum in Hierosoymam*, ed. M. C. Gertz, *Scriptores Minores Historiae Danicae* (Copenhagen, repr. 1970), pp. 466–7.

57. Humbert of Romans, *Treatise on Preaching*, pp. 34–5.
58. *Chronicle of Jocelin of Brakelond*, ed. and trans. H. E. Butler (London, 1949), p. 40.
59. Humbert of Romans, *Treatise on Preaching*, p. 42; cf. Clement V's insistence on vernacular preaching of the cross in 1309, *Regestum* (Rome, 1885–92), nos. 2989, 2990.
60. For some general comments, Maier, *Preaching the Crusades*, pp. 96–7 and pp. 102–3 for the translated papal bull.
61. Gerald of Wales, *Journey through Wales*, p. 75; above note 53; *History of the Expedition of the Emperor Frederick*, trans. G. A. Loud, *The Crusade of Frederick Barbarossa* (Farnham, 2010), p. 41.
62. *Barling's Chronicle, Chronicles of the Reigns of Edward I and II*, vol. ii, p. cxvi.
63. In general, see now N. Paul, *To Follow in Their Footsteps: The Crusades and Family Memory in the High Middle Ages* (Cornell, 2012), pp. 1–203; for examples, E. A. R. Brown and M. W. Cothren, 'The Twelfth-Century Crusading Window of the Abbey of St Denis', *Journal of the Warburg and Courtauld Institutes*, 49 (1986), pp. 1–40; Tyerman, *England and the Crusades*, p. 117; F. Cardini, 'Crusade and "Presence of Jerusalem" in Medieval Florence', in *Outremer*, ed. B. Kedar et al. (Jerusalem, 1982), pp. 332–46; C. Morris, *The Sepulchre of Christ and the Medieval West* (Oxford, 2005), esp. ch. 7; D. F. Glass, *Portals, Pilgrimage and Crusade in Western Tuscany* (Princeton, 1997); A. Linder, *Raising Arms: Liturgy in the Struggle to Liberate Jerusalem in the Late Middle Ages* (Turnhout, 2003); cf. C. Morris, 'Propaganda for War. The Dissemination of the Crusading Ideal in the Twelfth Century', *Studies in Church History*, 10 (1983), pp. 79–101; idem, 'Picturing the Crusades: The Uses of Visual Propaganda', in *The Crusades and their Sources*, ed. J. France and W. G. Zajac (Aldershot, 1998), pp. 196–216.
64. For examples, see Bird et al., *Crusade and Christendom*, pp. 43–7; Riley-Smith and Riley-Smith, *Crusades: Idea and Reality*, pp. 137–9; M. Purcell, *Papal Crusading Policy 1244–91* (Leiden, 1975), pp. 200–201. In general, see Kienzle, 'Medieval Sermons and their Performance'.
65. Odo of Deuil, *De profectione*, p. 9 n. 14 ref.; Thomas of Chobham, *Summa de Arte Praedicandi*, pp. 269–303 and see trans. in Copeland and Sluiter, *Medieval Grammar*, esp. pp. 628–38; *Testimonia Minora*, ed. Röhricht, p. 146.
66. Gerald of Wales, *Opera*, vol. i. p. 75 (a hand-held cross, *crucem portatilem*); *Westminster Chronicle 1381–1394*, ed. L. C. Hector and B. F. Harvey (Oxford, 1982), pp. 32–3; H. E. J. Cowdrey, 'Pope Urban II and

the Idea of the Crusade', *Studi Medievali*, 3rd ser., 36 (1995), pp. 737–8;
De expugnatione Lyxbonensi, pp. 146–7.

67. *Winchester Annals, Annales Monastici*, ed. H. R. Luard, Rolls Series
(London, 1864–9), vol. ii, p. 38; for tattoos and reactions *RHC Occ.*,
vol. iv, pp. 182–3, 251, vol. v, p. 255; Fulcher of Chartres, *A History of
the Expedition to Jerusalem*, ed. H. Finke (Knoxville, 1969), p. 76.
68. Odo of Deuil, *De profectione*, pp. 8–9; Tyerman, *God's War*, p. 71.
69. Gerald of Wales, *Opera*, vol. i, p. 75; Lecoy de la Marche, 'La prédication', p. 25; Cole, *Preaching*, p. 203; Landulph of St Paul, *Liber
Hystoriarum Mediolanensis Urbis*, ed. C. Castiglioni (Bologna, 1935),
p. 5.
70. Mayer, *Crusades*, pp. 320–21.
71. Baha al-Din Ibn Shaddad, *The Rare and Excellent History of Saladin*,
trans. D. S. Richards (Aldershot, 2002), p. 125; Ibn al-Athir, *Chronicle
for the Crusading Period*, trans. D. S. Richards, vol. ii (Aldershot, 2007),
p. 363; in general, Morris, 'Picturing the Crusades', esp. p. 197.
72. P. Edbury, ed. and trans., *The Old French Translation of William of
Tyre, The Conquest of Jerusalem and the Third Crusade* (Aldershot,
1998), p. 73.
73. Orderic Vitalis, *Ecclesiastical History*, vol. vi, pp. 68–73; Migne, *Patrologia Latina*, vol. ccxv, cols. 1070–71; cf. J. W. Harris, *Medieval Theatre
in Context* (London, 1992), pp. 45–6.
74. *The Chronicle of Henry of Livonia*, trans. J. Brundage (New York,
2003), p. 53; N. H. Petersen, 'The Notion of a Missionary Theatre:
The *ludus magnus* of Henry of Livonia's Chronicle', in *Crusading
and Chronicle Writing on the Medieval Baltic Frontier*, ed. M. Tamm,
L. Kaljundi and C. Selch Jensen (Farnham, 2011), pp. 229–43.
75. Migne, *Patrologia Latina*, vol. clxxx, cols. 381–6.
76. For trans. of the relevant passages in Salimbene's *Chronica*, see Bird et
al., *Crusade and Christendom*, pp. 414–17.
77. Gerald of Wales, *Journey through Wales*, p. 141; Otto of Freising,
Deeds of Frederick, p. 75; Odo of Deuil, *De profectione*, pp. 8–11;
J. Phillips, *The Second Crusade* (New Haven, 2007), pp. 81, 83, 94, 97
and refs.
78. Matthew Paris, *Chronica Majora*, vol. v, p. 191; idem, *Historia Anglorum*, ed. F. Madden, Rolls Series (London, 1886–9), vol. ii, p. 297;
cf. Roger of Howden's story of Christ crucified and the Cross appearing over Dunstable in August 1188 during the preaching of the
Third Crusade, 'Benedict of Peterborough' (sic), *Gesta Regis Henrici
Secundi*, ed. W. Stubbs, Rolls Series (London, 1867), vol. ii, p. 47.

79. *Chartes et documents pour server à l'histoire de l'abbaye de Saint-Maixent*, ed. A. Richard, *Archives historiques de Poitou*, vol. xvi (Poitiers, 1886), p. 222, no. 190.

80. Guibert of Nogent, *Gesta Dei per Francos, RHC Occ.*, vol. iv, pp. 250–51.

81. Peter of les Vaux-de-Cernay, *Historia Albigensis*, trans. W. A. Sibly and M. D. Sibly, *The History of the Albigensian Crusade* (Woodbridge, 1998), p. 147.

82. *Chronica regia Colonensis*, ed. G. Waitz (Hanover, 1880), p. 281; *Anecdotes historiques d'Etienne de Bourbon*, p. 90.

83. Roger of Wendover, *Flores historiarum*, ed. H. S. Hewlett, Rolls Series (London, 1884–9), vol. ii, pp. 323–4, trans. Bird et al., *Crusade and Christendom*, pp. 239–40.

84. In general, Y. Congar, 'Henri de Marcy', *Analecta Monastica*, vol. v (*Studia Anselmiana*, fasc. 43, Rome, 1958), pp. 1–90; Cole, *Preaching*, pp. 65–71; Loud, *Crusade of Frederick Barbarossa*, pp. 41–5, 143–4; Migne, *Patrologia Latina*, vol. cciv, cols. 249–52; Gilbert of Mons, *Chronicle of Hainault*, pp. 110, 112–13.

85. The English chroniclers William of Newburgh and Roger of Howden and the German anonymous *Historia de Expeditione Friderici Imperatoris*, trans. Loud, *Crusade of Frederick Barbarossa*, pp. 37–41, 141 for preaching and writing; J. H. Pryor, 'Two *excitationes* for the Third Crusade', *Mediterranean Historical Review*, 25 (2010), p. 163, n. 163; *De profectione Danorum*, pp. 464–5.

86. Roger of Howden, *Gesta Regis Henrici Secundi*, vol. ii, pp. 26–8; J. Bédier and P. Aubry, *Les Chansons de croisade* (Paris, 1909), vol. iii, pp. 32–5.

87. Loud, *Crusade of Frederick Barbarossa*, pp. 37–43.

88. Migne, *Patrologia Latina*, vol. cciv, cols. 251–402, cols. 350–61 for Tract 13.

89. Tyerman, *God's War*, pp. 296, 381; Gerald of Wales, *Journey through Wales*, p. 178.

90. Peter of Blois, *De Hierosolymitana Peregrinatione Acceleranda*, Migne, *Patrologia Latina*, vol. ccvii, col. 1063; cf. Henry of Albano, *De peregrinante*, Migne, *Patrologia Latina*, vol. cciv, col. 352, and above p. 81.

91. Henry of Albano, *De peregrinante*, col. 355; above note 71.

92. Gilbert of Mons, *Chronicle of Hainault*, p. 112.

93. *Epistolae Cantuarienses*, ed. W. Stubbs, *Chronicles and Memorials of Richard I*, Rolls Series, vol. ii (London, 1865), nos. 158, 167; F. Opll,

Das Itinerar Kaiser Friederich Barbarossas (1152–1190) (Cologne-Graz, 1978), p. 93.

94. Gerald of Wales, *Journey through Wales*, p. 200 and passim; Tyerman, *England and the Crusades*, pp. 61, 76, 156 et seq.; P. Edbury, 'Preaching the Crusade in Wales', in *England and Germany in the High Middle Ages*, ed. A. Haverkamp and H. Vollrath (Oxford, 1996), pp. 221–34; K. Hurlock, *Wales and the Crusades c.1095–1291* (Cardiff, 2011), esp. ch. 2.

95. Gerald of Wales, *Journey through Wales*, p. 76.

96. Maelgwn ap Cadwallon, prince of Maelienydd, Gerald of Wales, *Journey through Wales*, p. 77.

97. Gerald of Wales, *Journey through Wales*, p. 185; cf. p. 164 for Baldwin's determination to say Mass in every Welsh cathedral.

98. Gerald of Wales, *Journey through Wales*, p. 75. For Gerald and his writing in general, R. Barlett, *Gerald of Wales* (Oxford, 1982).

99. Gerald of Wales, *Opera*, vol. i, p. 74

100. Gerald of Wales, *Opera*, vol. i, pp. 75–6; idem, *Journey through Wales*, p. 141.

101. Above p. 104.

102. Gerald of Wales, *Opera*, vol. i, p. 77.

103. Gerald of Wales, *Journey through Wales*, p. 172.

104. Gerald of Wales, *Opera*, vol. i, p. 79. Others who actually did compose memoires or histories of the crusade as participants included Tageno, dean of Passau, the Englishman Roger of Howden and the Norman Ambroise, who composed a verse account, and they were not alone. See Loud, *Crusade of Frederick Barbarossa*, pp. 3–5; J. Gillingham, 'Roger of Howden on Crusade', in *Medieval Historical Writing in the Christian and Islamic Worlds*, ed. D. O. Morgan (London, 1982), reprinted in J. Gillingham, *Richard Coeur de Lion* (London, 1994), pp. 141–53; P. Damian-Grint, 'Ambroise', *ODNB*.

5. RECRUITING AND REWARD

1. *Histoire générale de Languedoc*, ed. C. de Vic and J. Vaisete (Toulouse, 1872–1905), vol. viii, cols. 1402–3, cf. col. 1258 and for other examples of contracts for the 1248 crusade, cols. 1221, 1223, 1276–7.

2. *Gesta Francorum*, trans. R. Hill (London, 1962), p. 75.

3. Trans. J. Riley-Smith and L. Riley-Smith, *The Crusades: Idea and Reality* (London, 1981), pp. 119–24 at p. 121.

4. C. Tyerman, *The Practices of Crusading: Image and Action from the Eleventh to the Sixteenth Centuries* (Farnham, 2013), no. XIII, 'Who went on Crusades to the Holy Land' and no. XIV, 'Paid Crusaders'.
5. E. Siberry, 'The Crusading Counts of Nevers', *Nottingham Medieval Studies*, 34 (1990), p. 65 and n. 5; *Querimoniae Normannorum, RHF*, vol. xxiv, p. 61, n. 464.
6. Trans. A. J. Andrea, *Contemporary Sources for the Fourth Crusade* (Leiden, 2000), p. 188.
7. Trans. Riley-Smith and Riley-Smith, *Crusades: Idea and Reality*, p. 39, Urban II to the congregation of Vallambrosa, 7 Oct. 1096.
8. Ralph of Caen, *Gesta Tancredi, RHC Occ.*, vol. iii, p. 701, cf. trans. B. S. Bachrach and D. S. Bachrach, *The Gesta Tancredi of Ralph of Caen* (Aldershot, 2005), p. 152.
9. For a general account, P. Spufford, *Money and its Use in Medieval Europe* (Cambridge, 1988), and esp. chs. 4–6.
10. Raymond of Aguilers, *Historia Francorum qui ceperunt Iherusalem, RHC Occ.*, vol. iii, p. 278; cf. Albert of Aachen, *Historia Ierosolimitana*, ed. and trans. S. Edgington (Oxford, 2007), pp. 220–21, 300–301; A. V. Murray, 'Money and Logistics in the Forces of the First Crusade', in *Logistics of Warfare in the Age of the Crusades*, ed. J. H. Pryor (Aldershot, 2006), esp. pp. 235–41; Tyerman, 'Paid Crusaders' in *Practices of Crusading*, pp. 32–3.
11. Spufford, *Money*, pp. 99, 161.
12. *Select Charters*, ed. W. Stubbs, 9th edn (ed. H. W. C. Davis) (Oxford, 1921), p. 299.
13. Tyerman, 'Paid Crusaders', pp. 8–10 and refs., esp. n. 26.
14. John of Salisbury, *Policraticus*, ed. C. C. I. Webb (Oxford, 1909), vol. ii, p. 26 (bk VI, ch. X); ibid., p. 25 for quoting Luke 3:14; cf. S. Brown, 'Military Service and Monetary Reward in the 11th and 12th Centuries', *History*, 74 (1989), pp. 22–3.
15. Orderic Vitalis, *Ecclesiastical History*, ed. and trans. M. Chibnall (Oxford, 1969–80), vol. vi, pp. 348–51.
16. Galbert of Bruges, *Histoire du meutre de Charles le Bon, comte de Flandre*, ed. H. Pirenne (Paris, 1891), p. 20, trans. J. Ross, *The Murder of Charles the Good of Flanders* (New York, 1967), p. 111; E. Oksanen, 'The Anglo-Flemish Treaties and Flemish Soldiers in England 1101–1163', in *Mercenaries and Paid Men*, ed. J. France (Leiden, 2000), pp. 261–3.
17. William of Malmesbury, *Gesta Regum Anglorum*, ed. W. Stubbs (London, 1887–9), vol. ii, p. 320.

18. J. Bumke, *The Concept of Knighthood in the Middle Ages* (New York, 1982), pp. 52–3, and generally, pp. 33–4, 41–3, 47–54.

19. *Benzonis Episcopi Albanesis ad Henricum IV Imperatorem Libri VII*, *MGHS*, vol. xi, pp. 600–601; J. C. Andressohn, *The Ancestry and Life of Godfrey de Bouillon* (Bloomington, 1947), pp. 38–9 and nn. 51–3; Tyerman, 'Paid Crusaders', pp. 10–11.

20. Bumke, *Concept of Knighthood*, p. 52 and generally pp. 41–2, 48–9; for mid-twelfth-century example, *Constitutio Domus Regis*, ed. C. Johnson, *Dialogus de Scaccario* (London, 1950), pp. 133–4 and generally pp. 128–35; J. O. Prestwich, 'The Military Household of the Norman Kings', *English Historical Review*, 96 (1981), pp. 1–35.

21. H.-F. Delaborde, *Recueil des Actes de Philippe Auguste*, vol. i (Paris, 1916), no. 292; *Codice diplomatica della republica de Genova*, ed. C. Imperiale de Saint'Angelo (Genoa, 1936–42), vol. ii, pp. 366–8; *Chronica Regis Coloniensis cont. a 1195*, ed. G. Waitz (Hanover, 1880), p. 157; J. F. Böhmer, *Regesta Imperii IV, Die Regesten des Kaiserreiches unter Heinrich VI*, ed. G. Baaken (Cologne and Vienna, 1972), p. 173 no. 425.

22. B. Arnold, *German Knighthood 1050–1300* (Oxford, 1985), p. 101.

23. Richard of San Germano, *Chronica*, *MGHS*, vol. xix, pp. 343–4, 347–9; C. Tyerman, *God's War* (London, 2006), pp. 742–3; *Chronica regia Colonensis*, ed. G. Waitz (Hanover, 1880), p. 157; Otto of St Blasien, *Chronica*, *MGHS*, vol. xliv, p. 45, trans. G. Loud, *The Crusade of Frederick Barbarossa* (Farnham, 2010), p. 176; A. V. Murray, 'Finance and Logistics of the Crusade of Frederick Barbarossa', in *In Laudem Hierosolymitani*, ed. I. Shagrir et al. (Aldershot, 2007), pp. 357–68, esp. pp. 358–61.

24. L. Paterson, *The World of the Troubadours* (Cambridge, 1993), pp. 40–89; K. Bosl, *Die Reichsministerialitäder Salier und Staufer* (Stuttgart, 1950), vol. ii, p. 90 cited by J. Prestwich, *The Place of War in English History 1066–1214* (Woodbridge, 2004), p. 97 n. 83; Orderic Vitalis, *Ecclesiastical History*, vol. ii, p. 58.

25. *Dialogus de Scaccario*, pp. 40–41; William of Poitiers, *Gesta Guillelmi*, eds. R. H. C. Davis and M. Chibnall (Oxford, 1998), p. 102.

26. *RHF*, vol. x, p. 599 for 1016 evidence from Corbie in the Beauvaisis, vol. xxiii, pp. 699–700 for 40 days' service; for other refs and discussion see P. Guilhiermoz, *Essai sur l'origine de la noblesse en France au moyen âge* (Paris, 1902), pp. 273–85, esp. pp. 273 n. 51, 274–5; H. A. Haskins, *Norman Institutions* (New York, 1918), pp. 20–22; M. Chibnall, 'Military Service in Normandy before 1066', *Anglo-Norman Studies*, 5 (1982), pp. 65–77.

27. *Select Charters*, pp. 173–4, 175–8; *English Historical Documents*, vol. ii, ed. D. C. Douglas (London, 1953), pp. 447, 912 n. 228, and generally pp. 438–48, 903–15; *Liber Eliensis*, ed. E. O. Blake, Camden 3ʳᵈ Series (London, 1962), pp. 216–17. On *liberatio* meaning wages, see J. O. Prestwich, 'Mistranslations and Misinterpretations in Medieval English History', *Peritia*, 10 (1996), pp. 324–5.

28. '*Great Domesday*', fol. 56v, in *Select Charters*, p. 107; *Domesday Book*, trans. A. Williams and G. H. Martin (London, 1992), p. 136.

29. Suger, *Vie de Louis VI le Gros*, ed. H. Waquet (Paris, 1964), p. 8.

30. Suger, *Vie de Louis VI*, p. 8; *Sugerii Vita, Suger, Oeuvres*, ed. F. Gaspari (Paris, 1996–2001), vol. ii, p. 337.

31. C. Erdmann, *Die Enstehung des Kreuzzusgedankens* (Stuttgart, 1935), pp. 251–2, trans. M. W. Baldwin and W. Goffart, *The Origin of the Idea of the Crusade* (Princeton, 1977), pp. 270–71.

32. For early thirteenth-century examples see *Ordinacio de predicatione S. Crucis in Angliae*, ed. R. Röhricht, *Quinti Belli Scari Scriptores Minores, Société de l'Orient Latin*, vol. ii (Geneva, 1879), pp. 22–3; C. Maier, *Crusade Propaganda and Ideology: Model Sermons for the Preaching of the Cross* (Cambridge, 2000), pp. 87, 89, 93, 111–13 (James of Vitry); cf. Bibliothèque nationale de France MS Lat. 14525, fols. 105vb–106rb, a sermon of John the Teuton observed by Dr Jesslaynn Bird who generously provided this reference.

33. *The Letters of St Bernard*, trans. B. S. James (Stroud, 1998), p. 462; Gunther of Pairis, *Historia Constantinopolitana*, ed. P. Riant, *Exuviae Sacrae Constantinopolitanae*, vol. i (Geneva, 1877), p. 64, trans. A. Andrea, *The Capture of Constantinople* (Philadelphia, 1997), p. 71.

34. *Curia Regis Rolls Preserved in the Public Record Office* (London, 1922–), vol. viii, p. 324; in general J. Brundage, *Medieval Canon Law and the Crusader* (Madison, 1969), pp. 159–90.

35. Riley-Smith and Riley-Smith, *Crusades: Idea and Reality*, pp. 39, 58; Gunther of Pairis, *Historia*, p. 64, trans. Andrea, *Capture*, p. 71.

36. R. Somerville, *The Councils of Urban II*, vol. i, *Decreta Claromontensia* (Amsterdam, 1972), p. 74; for probable meaning of *honor*, see *Mediae Latinitatis Lexicon Minus*, ed. J. F. Niermeyer et al. (Leiden, 1984), cols. 495–8; *Dictionary of Medieval Latin from British Sources*, ed. D. R. Howlett et al. Fascicule IV (Oxford, 1989), p. 1169.

37. *Historia Peregrinorum*, ed. A. Chroust, *Quellen zur Geschichte des Kreuzzuges Kaiser Friedrichs I*, MGH (Berlin, 1928), p. 9; Riley-Smith and Riley-Smith, *Crusades: Idea and Reality*, p. 66.

38. Guibert of Nogent, *Gesta Dei per Francos*, *RHC Occ.*, vol. iv, p. 124; Ralph of Caen, *Gesta Tancredi*, *RHC Occ.*, vol. iii, p. 606; trans. Bachrach and Bachrach, *Gesta Tancredi*, p. 22.

39. Trans. and ed. E. Peters, *The First Crusade* (Philadelphia, 1998), pp. 293–6.

40. Bernard of Clairvaux, *De laude novae militiae*, trans. M. Barber and K. Bate, *The Templars* (Manchester, 2002), p. 218.

41. Above pp. 45–7 and refs.; Fulcher of Chartres, *Historia Hierosolymitana*, *RHC Occ.*, vol. iii, p. 324, trans. F. R. Ryan and H. Fink, *A History of the Expedition to Jerusalem* (Knoxville, 1969), p. 67; Robert of Rheims, *Historia Iherosolimitana*, *RHC Occ.*, vol. iii, p. 728, trans. C. Sweetenham, *Robert the Monk's History of the First Crusade* (Aldershot, 2005), p. 81; Baldric of Bourgueil, *Historia Jerosolimitana*, *RHC Occ.*, vol. iv, p. 15; cf. Riley-Smith and Riley-Smith, *Crusades: Idea and Reality*, p. 52.

42. For a recent discussion of these and the cult of memorialization, see N. I. Paul, *To Follow in their Footsteps: The Crusades and Family Memory in the High Middle Ages* (Ithaca, 2012), pp. 90–134, esp. pp. 90–95; *History of William Marshal*, ed. A. J. Holden (London, 2002–6), vol. ii, ll. 18184–5, 18216–26.

43. M. G. Bull, 'The Capetian Monarchy and the Early Crusading Movement', *Nottingham Medieval Studies*, 40 (1996), pp. 25–46.

44. Orderic Vitalis, *Ecclesiastical History*, vol. vi, p. 287; in general see Tyerman, *God's War*, ch. 8, pp. 243–67.

45. P. Edbury, *The Kingdom of Cyprus and the Crusades 1191–1374* (Cambridge, 1991), pp. 22–5; J. Riley-Smith, *The First Crusaders 1095–1131* (Cambridge, 1997), pp. 169–88; G. Perry, *John of Brienne* (Cambridge, 2013).

46. Odo of Deuil, *De profectione Ludovici VII in Orientem*, ed. V. G. Berry (New York, 1948), pp. 20–21; Otto of Freising, *The Deeds of Frederick Barbarossa*, trans. C. C. Mierow (New York, 1953), pp. 74–9.

47. C. Tyerman, *England and the Crusades* (Chicago, 1988), pp. 36–56; T. Guard, *Chivalry, Kingship and Crusade: The English Experience in the Fourteenth Century* (Woodbridge, 2013), p. 139 and n. 57.

48. For regional examples, see Tyerman, *England and the Crusades*, pp. 208–28; more widely, see C. Tyerman, *The Invention of the Crusades* (Basingstoke, 1998), esp. pp. 55–62, 'Secular Law and the Crusader'; Brundage, *Medieval Canon Law*, pp. 115–90.

49. *The Book of the Foundation of Walden Monastery*, eds. D. Greenway and L. Watkiss (Oxford, 1999), pp. 54–5.

50. *Gesta Francorum*, pp. 73–4, 83, 87–9.
51. Ralph of Caen, *Gesta Tancredi, RHC Occ.*, vol. iii, p. 644, trans. Bachrach and Bachrach, *Gesta Tancredi*, p. 77; in general, Tyerman, 'Paid Crusaders', esp. pp. 29–30, 38–40.
52. *De expugnatione Lyxbonensis*, ed. C. W. David (New York, 1976), pp. 84–5, 98–101, 110–13; *Die Urkunden Konrads III*, ed. F. Hausmann, MGH *Diplomatum Regum*, vol. ix (Vienna, 1969), p. 355; Otto of Freising, *Deeds of Frederick*, p. 102.
53. Roger of Howden, alias 'Benedict of Peterborough', *Gesta Regis Henrici Secundi*, ed. W. Stubbs (London, 1867), vol. ii, pp. 112, 186 (Howden was himself a crusader on this expedition); Ralph of Diceto, *Ymagines Historiarum, Opera Historica*, ed. W. Stubbs (London, 1876), vol. ii, p. 88; *Itinerarium Regis Ricardi*, ed. W. Stubbs (London, 1864), pp. 213–14, 225–6, trans. H. J. Nicholson, *The Chronicle of the Third Crusade* (Aldershot, 1997), pp. 204, 214.
54. *Chronica Coloniensis*, p. 157; Tyerman, 'Paid Crusaders', pp. 17–18; W. Jordan, *Louis IX and the Challenge of the Crusade* (Princeton, 1979), pp. 65–104, esp. p. 102 for figures.
55. Orderic Vitalis, *Ecclesiastical History*, vol. v, pp. 170–72; Eadmer, *Historia novorum*, ed. M. Rule (London, 1884), pp. 179–81; and above p. 21.
56. *Regesta Chartarum Pistoriensium. Canonica di S. Zenone Secolo XI*, ed. N. Rauty, *Fonti Storiche Pistoiesi*, 7 (Pistoia, 1985), nos. 297 and 298, pp. 241–3; cf. Tyerman, 'Paid Crusaders', pp. 37–8 and n. 163.
57. John of Joinville, *Histoire de Saint Louis*, ed. N. de Wailly (Paris, 1868), p. 48 and generally pp. 40–48, trans. M. R. B. Shaw, *Chronicles of the Crusades* (London, 1963), pp. 191–2, 194–8.
58. *Gesta Francorum*, pp. 19–20 and above, for material rewards, ch. 2 pp. 45–8.
59. H. Hagenmeyer, *Die Kreuzzugsbriefe aus den Jahren 1088–1100* (Innsbruck, 1902), p. 149, trans. Peters, *First Crusade*, p. 287; for details of the First Crusade campaign, J. France, *Victory in the East* (Cambridge, 1994).
60. A. Andrea, *Contemporary Sources for the Fourth Crusade* (Leiden, 2000), p. 253 and n. 57; for the other examples, France, *Victory in the East*, pp. 165, 315; *Urkunden Konrads III*, p. 355; Tyerman, *God's War*, pp. 423–7, 442–6 and refs.
61. E. Christiansen, *The Northern Crusades* (London, 1997), esp. chs. 3–5.
62. For a summary, Tyerman, *God's War*, pp. 563–605; D. Power, 'Who Went on the Albigensian Crusade?', *English Historical Review*, 128 (2013), pp. 1047–85.

63. Orderic Vitalis, *Ecclesiastical History*, vol. vi, pp. 100–101; N. L. Paul, 'A Warlord's Wisdom: Literacy and Propaganda at the Time of the First Crusade', *Speculum*, 85 (2010), pp. 534–66; Tyerman, *God's War*, pp. 261–3.

64. Ralph Niger, *De Re Militari et Triplici Via Peregrinationis*, ed. L. Schmugge (Berlin, 1977), pp. 193–4.

65. Note 21 above; G. L. Tafel and G. M. Thomas, *Urkunden zur alteren Handels- und Staatsgeschichte der Republik Venedig* (Vienna, 1856–7), vol. i, pp. 362–73; A. Jal, *Pacta Naulorum, Collection de documents inédits sur l'histoire de France* (Paris, 1841–8), vol. i, pp. 605–9, esp. p. 606 'retinere si voluerit', vol. ii, pp. 51–67; cf. *RHF*, vol. xxii, pp. 404, 513–15.

66. Caffaro, *De liberatione civitatum Orientis*, ed. L. Belgrano, *Fonti per la storia d'Italia* (Rome, 1887–1993), vol. xi, p. 111, trans. M. Hall and J. Phillips, *Caffaro, Genoa and the Twelfth Century Crusades* (Farnham, 2013), p. 117.

67. Caffaro, *De liberatione*, p. 120, trans. Hall and Phillips, *Caffaro*, p. 122; Tyerman, *God's War*, pp. 265–6 and n. 54 for refs.

68. *Chronica Coloniensis*, pp. 143, 144.

69. Ambroise, *Estoire de la guerre sainte* ed. G. Paris (Paris, 1877), trans. M. J. Hubert, *The Crusade of Richard the Lion-Heart* (New York, 1976), p. 44, ll. 365–70; cf. discussion in J. Gillingham, *Richard I* (New Haven and London, 1999), p. 128 and n. 13; Tyerman, *God's War*, esp. pp. 118–22; *De expugnatione Lyxbonensis*, pp. 56–7.

70. William of Tyre, *Historia*, trans. E. A. Babcock and A. C. Krey, *A History of Deeds Done Beyond the Sea* (New York, 1976), pp. 193–4.

71. Innocent III to the archbishop of Canterbury, in J. P. Migne, *Patrologia Latina* (Paris, 1844–64), vol. ccxvi, col. 1261; A. Leopold, *How to Recover the Holy Land: The Crusade Proposals of the Late Thirteenth and Early Fourteenth Centuries* (Aldershot, 2000); Matthew Paris, *Chronica Majora*, ed. H. R. Luard (London, 1872–84), vol. v, p. 107, vol. vi, p. 163.

6. WHO WENT ON CRUSADE?

1. Fulcher of Chartres, *Historia Hierosolymitana*, *RHC Occ.*, vol. iii, p. 333, trans. F. R. Ryan and H. Fink, *A History of the Expedition to Jerusalem* (Knoxville, 1969), p. 81; John of Tubia (or Tolve), *De Iohanne Rege Ierusalem*, ed. R. Röhricht, *Quinti Belli Sacri Scriptores Minores* (Geneva, 1879), p. 139; Roger of Howden, alias 'Benedict of

Peterborough', *Gesta Regis Henrici Secundi*, ed. W. Stubbs (London, 1867), vol. ii, pp. 30–32.

2. Urban II to supporters in Bologna, 19 Sept. 1096, trans. J. Riley-Smith and L. Riley-Smith, *The Crusades: Idea and Reality* (London, 1981), p. 39.

3. *Recueil des actes de Philippe Auguste*, ed. H.-F. Delaborde et al. (Paris, 1916–79), no. 1360.

4. J. Riley-Smith, *The First Crusaders* (Cambridge, 1997), pp. 197–226.

5. Above ch. 3, pp. 83–4; C. Tyerman, *England and the Crusades* (Chicago, 1988), pp. 168–72.

6. C. Tyerman, 'Who Went on Crusade to the Holy Land?', no. XIII in *The Practices of Crusading: Image and Action from the Eleventh to the Sixteenth Centuries* (Farnham, 2013), p. 17 and passim.

7. Tyerman, *England and the Crusades*, pp. 70–72 and refs.; in general see Tyerman, *Practices of Crusading*, nos. XIII passim and XIV ('Paid Crusaders'), pp. 15–40.

8. William of Tyre, *Chronicon*, ed. R. B. C. Huygens (Turnhout, 1986), vol. i, p. 137, trans. E. A. Babcock and A. C. Krey, *A History of Deeds Done Beyond the Sea* (New York, 1976), vol. i, p. 94.

9. *Itinerarium Ricardi Regis*, ed. W. Stubbs, Rolls Series (London, 1864), pp. 212–13, trans. H. Nicholson, *The Chronicle of the Third Crusade* (Aldershot, 1997), p. 203.

10. *Historia Peregrinorum*, ed. A. Chroust, *Quellen zur Geschichte des Kreuzzuges Kaiser Friedrichs I* (Berlin, 1928), p. 123, trans. G. Loud, *The Crusade of Frederick Barbarossa* (Farnham, 2010), p 141; cf. *Historia de Expeditione Friderici*, ed. Chroust, *Quellen*, pp. 13, 14–15, trans. Loud, *Crusade of Frederick Barbarossa*, pp. 43, 45.

11. C. Tyerman, *God's War* (London, 2006), pp. 66, 276–80, 281–2, 286–7, 288, 377–8, 417–19, 489–91,615, 740–41 and refs.

12. Tyerman, *God's War*, pp. 502–3, 618–28, 757–64, 770–83, 807–11; cf. J. M. Powell, *Anatomy of a Crusade 1213–1221* (Philadelphia, 1986), esp. pp. 67–87; M. Lower, *The Barons' Crusade* (Philadelphia, 2005); W. Jordan, *Louis IX and the Challenge of the Crusade* (Princeton, 1979), pp. 3–34.

13. See above chs. 3 and 4.

14. *De expugnatione Lyxbonensi*, ed. C. W. David (New York, 1976), pp. 160–61, cf. pp. 54–7, 100–105.

15. Caffaro, *De liberatione civitatum Orientis*, ed. L. Belgrano, *Fonti per la storia d'Italia* (Rome, 1887–1993), vol. xi, p. 102, trans. M. Hall and J. Phillips, *Caffaro, Genoa and the Twelfth Century Crusades* (Farnham, 2013), p. 110.

16. Tyerman, *England and the Crusades*, pp. 73–4, 329 and refs.; A. Forey, 'The Military Order of St Thomas of Acre', *English Historical Review*, 92 (1977), pp. 481–503; and below p. 253.

17. *Historia de Expeditione Friderici*, pp. 18–24, trans. Loud, *Crusade of Frederick Barbarossa*, pp. 47–57.

18. *Itinerarium Ricardi Regis*, pp. 217–18; trans. Nicholson, *Chronicle*, pp. 207–8 and notes; cf. Ambroise, *L'Estoire de la Guerre Sainte*, ed. G. Paris (Paris, 1877), ll. 4705–36, trans. M. J. Hubert, *The Crusade of Richard the Lion-Heart* (New York, 1976), pp. 199–201.

19. Robert of Clari, *La Conquête de Constantinople*, ed. P. Lauer (Paris, 1924), pp. 1–4, trans. E. H. McNeal, *The Conquest of Constantinople* (New York, 1966), pp. 31–4.

20. Robert of Clari, *La Conquête*, p. 4.

21. Robert of Clari, *La Conquête*, p. 10, trans. McNeal, *Conquest*, p. 40.

22. Tyerman, *Practices of Crusading*, nos. XIII and XIV, esp. pp. 16–20, 29–40; S. Lloyd, *English Society and the Crusade 1216–1307* (Oxford, 1988), esp. chs. 3 and 4; Jordan, *Louis IX and the Challenge of the Crusade*, pp. 14–34, 100–104.

23. William of Newburgh, *Historia rerum Anglicarum*, ed. R. Howlett (London, 1884–5), vol. i, pp. 360, 383; Ralph of Diceto, *Ymagines Historiarum, Opera Historica*, ed. W. Stubbs (London, 1876), vol. ii, p. 88; *Itinerarium Ricardi Regis*, pp. 213–14, 225–6, trans. Nicholson, *Chronicle*, pp. 204, 214; Roger of Howden, *Gesta Henrici Secundi*, vol. ii, p. 186.

24. Matthew Paris, *Chronica Majora*, ed. H. R. Luard (London, 1872–84), vol. iv, pp. 43–5 and esp. p. 44 n. 6; Lloyd, *English Society*, p. 136.

25. Lloyd, *English Society*, p. 281: Appendix 5.

26. For a magisterial account of the details of Edward's preparations, see Lloyd, *English Society*, pp. 113–53, esp. pp. 137–45.

27. Jordan, *Louis IX and the Challenge of the Crusade*, p. 71; Lloyd, *English Society*, pp. 135–6.

28. Tyerman, 'Paid Crusaders', *Practices of Crusading*, no. XIV, pp. 20, 21–5, 29–40; A. V. Murray, 'Finance and Logistics of the Crusade of Frederick Barbarossa', in *In Laudem Hierosolymitani*, eds. I. Shagrir et al. (Aldershot, 2007), pp. 357–68.

29. Odo of Deuil, *De profectione Ludovici VII in Orientem*, ed. V. G. Berry (New York, 1948), pp. 10–15; Tyerman, *England and the Crusades*, pp. 66, 80–83; Geoffrey of Villehardouin, *La Conquête de Constantinople*, ed. E. Faral (Paris, 1938–9), vol. i, pp. 51–2, trans. M. R. B. Shaw, *Chronicles of the Crusades* (London, 1963), pp. 40–41; Richard of San

Germano, *Chronica*, *MGHS*, vol. xix, pp. 343–4, 347–9; Tyerman, *God's War*, pp. 742–3.

30. Tyerman, *England and the Crusades*, p. 67 and refs.

31. B. Arnold, *German Knighthood 1050–1300* (Oxford, 1985), pp. 100–101; A. V. Murray, 'The Army of Godfrey de Bouillon 1096–99', *Revue belge de philologie et d'histoire*, 70 (1992), esp. pp. 302–3, 311 and refs.

32. *Historia de expeditione Friderici*, ed. Chroust, *Quellen*, pp. 96–7, trans. Loud, *Crusade of Frederick Barbarossa*, pp. 120–21.

33. *Titres de la maison ducale de Bourbon*, ed. A. Huillard-Bréholles (Paris, 1867–74), vol. i, pp. 46–7, no. 221.

34. Riley-Smith and Riley-Smith, *Crusades: Idea and Reality*, pp. 174–5.

35. M. S. Giuseppi, 'On the Testament of Sir Hugh de Nevill', *Archaeologia*, 56 (1899), pp. 352–4; Matthew Paris, *Historia Anglorum*, ed. F. Madden (London, 1866–9), vol. iii, p. 55.

36. Roger of Howden, *Gesta Henrici Secundi*, vol. ii, pp. 30–32.

37. F. M. Stenton, 'Early Manumissions at Staunton', *English Historical Review*, 26 (1911), pp. 95–6.

38. Royal Commission on Historical Manuscripts, *Report on Various Collections*, vol. i (London, 1901), pp. 235–6; Tyerman, *England and the Crusades*, p. 171.

39. J. P. Migne, *Patrologia Latina* (Paris, 1844–64), vol. ccxvi, col. 1261.

40. J. Brundage, *Medieval Canon Law and the Crusader* (Madison, 1969), pp. 176–7.

41. Tyerman, 'Who Went on Crusade?', p. 17 and n. 12.

42. Ibid, pp. 17–18 and nn. 13–14; Tyerman, *England and the Crusades*, esp. pp. 168–72.

43. Robert of Clari, *La Conquête*, p. 46, trans. McNeal, *Conquest*, p. 72; John of Joinville, *Histoire de Saint Louis*, ed. N. de Wailly (Paris, 1868), trans. M. R. B. Shaw, *Chronicles of the Crusades* (London, 1963), p. 233.

44. *Councils and Synods with other documents relating to the English Church*, ed. F. M. Powicke et al., vol. i (Oxford, 1961), pt 2, pp. 1025–9; Ambroise, *L'Estoire*, ll. 5695–8, trans. Hubert, *Crusade*, p. 233; Tyerman, *England and the Crusades*, pp. 61, 63.

45. Powell, *Anatomy of a Crusade*, pp. 208–46; Tyerman, 'Who Went on Crusade?', passim; for medics see below pp. 251–5.

46. Albert of Aachen, *Historia Ierosolimitana*, ed. and trans. S. Edgington (Oxford, 2007), pp. 120–21.

47. Raymond of Aguilers, *Historia Francorum*, *RHC Occ.*, vol. iii, p. 297, trans. J. H. Hill and L. L. Hill (Philadelphia, 1968), p. 124.

48. Ambroise, *L'Estoire*, ll. 4475–6, 4498–512, trans. Hubert, *Crusade*, pp. 189–91; *Itinerarium Ricardi Regis*, pp. 136–7; trans. Nicholson, *Chronicle*, pp. 136–7.

49. Innocent IV, *Registres*, ed. E. Berger (Paris, 1884–1921), no. 2644.

50. *A Cartulary of the Hospital of St John the Baptist*, ed. H. E. Salter, Oxford Historical Society, 68 (1915), ii, pp. 134–5; *Cartulary of St Frideswide's, Oxford*, ed. S. R. Wigram, Oxford Historical Society, 28 and 31 (1894/1896), i, p. 418, no. 594; *Eynsham Cartulary*, ed. H. E. Salter, Oxford Historical Society, 49 (1906–7), i, p. 37, no. 7; *Cartulary of Oseney Abbey*, ed. H. E. Salter, Oxford Historical Society, 89 (1929), i, p. 319 no. 363.

51. Albert of Aachen, *Historia*, pp. 22–3; *De expugnatione Lyxbonensi*, pp. 160–61; William of Newburgh, *Historia*, vol. i, pp. 308–24.

52. *Pleas before the King or his Justices 1198–1202*, ed. D. M. Stenton (London, 1948–9), vol. i, pp. 135–6; vol. ii, p. 49, no. 248; *Cartulary of Oseney Abbey*, i, p. 319, no. 363; Giuseppi, 'Testament of Sir Hugh de Nevill', p. 353.

53. Tyerman, 'Who Went on Crusade?', pp. 18–19 and n. 16.

54. Riley-Smith and Riley-Smith, *Crusades: Idea and Reality*, p. 39; Tyerman, *God's War*, pp. 277, 282, 296, 381, 499, 503–4, 588; Tyerman, *England and the Crusades*, p. 68.

55. Brundage, *Medieval Canon Law*, pp. 177–9.

56. *Layettes du Trésor des Chartes*, vol. iii, ed. J. De Laborde (Paris, 1875), p. 104a.

57. Ralph of Diceto, *Ymagines*, vol. ii, p. 88; *Itinerarium Ricardi Regis*, pp. 91, 116, 192–3, trans. Nicholson, *Chronicle*, pp. 96, 119, 186; Ambroise, *L'Estoire*, ll. 1607–16, trans. Hubert, *Crusade*, p. 90; Robert of Clari, *La Conquête*, pp. 97–8, trans. McNeal, *Conquest*, pp. 117–18.

58. *The Chronicle of Henry of Livonia*, trans. J. Brundage (New York, 2003), pp. 33, 42, 91–2, 127–31 and passim.

59. H. Kümper, 'Oliver of Paderborn', *Encyclopaedia of the Medieval Chronicle*, ed. G. Dunphy (Leiden, 2010) and refs.; J. Bird, E. Peters and J. M. Powell, *Crusade and Christendom* (Philadelphia, 2013), pp. 158–9, 169–71; Oliver as the engineer was identified by James of Vitry, *Lettres*, ed. R. B. C. Huygens (Leiden, 1960), p. 106; Matthew Paris, *Chronica Majora*, Corpus Christi College, Cambridge MS 16, fol. 55 v; see frontispiece.

60. Roger of Howden, *Gesta Henrici Secundi*, vol. ii, pp. 47–8.

61. See J. Schenk, *Templar Families* (Cambridge, 2012).

62. Otto of Freising, *The Deeds of Frederick Barbarossa*, trans. C. C. Mierow (New York, 1953), p. 76.

63. James of Vitry, *Lettres*, pp. 86–8; Matthew Paris, *Chronica Majora*, vol. v, p. 1; F. Barlow, *Thomas Becket* (London, 1986), pp. 258–9; Tyerman, *England and the Crusades*, pp. 26, 69, 98, 158, 220–21, 315, 419 n. 155.

64. Brundage, *Medieval Canon Law*, pp. 126 n. 42, 174; C. T. Maier, *Preaching the Crusades. Mendicant Friars and the Cross in the Thirteenth Century* (Cambridge, 1994), pp. 69–70 and refs.

65. Brundage, *Medieval Canon Law*, pp. 32, 44, 77; idem, 'The Crusader's Wife', *Studia Gratiana*, 12 (1967), pp. 425–42; idem, 'The Crusader's Wife Revisited', *Studia Gratiana*, 14 (1967), pp. 241–52; N. Hodgson, *Women, Crusading and the Holy Land in Historical Narrative* (Woodbridge, 2007); S. Edgington and S. Lambert, *Gendering the Crusades* (Cardiff, 2001); for protection of women see below, p. 246.

66. John of Tubia, *De Iohanne*, p. 139.

67. Migne, *Patrologia Latina*, vol. ccxvi, col. 1262; James of Vitry, *Lettres*, p. 77, this despite his characteristic preacher's misogyny; idem, *Sermones Vulgares*, ed. T. F. Crane (London, 1890), p. 56.

68. *De expugatione Lyxbonensi*, p. 57; Royal Commission on Historical Manuscripts, *Fifth Report*, Appendix (London, 1872), p. 462; *Layettes du Trésor des Chartes*, vol. iii, pp. 103a–106a, 770; B. Kedar, 'The Passenger List of a Crusader Ship', *Studi Medievali*, 13 (1972), pp. 267–79; Bird et al., *Crusade and Christendom*, p. 234.

69. Anna Komnene, *The Alexiad*, trans. E. R. A. Sewter and P. Frankopan (London, 2003), p. 275.

70. *Itinerarium Ricardi Regis*, pp. 101–2, trans. Nicholson, *Chronicle*, p. 106.

71. Albert of Aachen, *Historia*, pp. 126–9.

72. *Archives de l'Hôtel Dieu de Paris*, ed. L. Briele (Paris, 1894), no. 203, pp. 87–8.

73. Joinville, *Histoire de Saint Louis*, trans. Shaw, *Chronicles*, pp. 241, 262–3; and below p. 252.

74. Kedar, 'Passenger List', pp. 273–4 and refs.

75. D. M. Stenton, 'Roger of Howden and Benedict', *English Historical Review*, 68 (1953), pp. 576–7; Roger of Howden, *Gesta Henrici Secundi*, vol. ii, p. 149.

76. Robert of Clari, *La Conquête*, pp. 3–4, trans. McNeal, *Conquest*, pp. 33–4.

77. Tyerman, 'Who Went on Crusade?', p. 18, n. 15; P. Riant, *Exuviae Sacrae Constantinopolitana* (Geneva, 1876–7), vol. i, p. 135.

78. M. Quantin, *Cartulaire générale de l'Yonne* (Auxerre, 1854–60), vol. i, p. 437, no. 283; William of Newburgh, *Historia*, vol. i, pp. 308–24.

79. Ralph of Diceto, *Ymagines*, vol. ii, p. 88; *Itinerarium Ricardi Regis*, pp. 134–5, trans. Nicholson, *Chronicle*, pp. 135–6; Riley-Smith and Riley-Smith, *Crusades: Idea and Reality*, p. 175. Barzella Merxadrus left 1 bezant to the army's common chest at Damietta.

80. For background, see J. Maddicott, *The Origins of the English Parliament 924–1327* (Oxford, 2010), esp. pp. 139–47, 228–32; in general, see S. Reynolds, *Kingdoms and Communities in Western Europe 900–1300* (Oxford, 1997).

81. Odo of Deuil, *De profectione*, pp. 20–21; *Historia de expeditione Friderici*, ed. Chroust, *Quellen*, pp. 24–5, trans. Loud, *Crusade of Frederick Barbarossa*, pp. 57–8; Roger of Howden, *Gesta Henrici Secundi*, vol. ii, pp. 110–11; idem, *Chronica*, ed. W. Stubbs (London, 1868–71), vol. iii, p. 8; *De expugnatione Lyxbonensi*, pp. 56–7, 104–5.

82. *De expugnatione Lyxbonensi*, pp. 56–7, 100–111.

83. Ralph of Diceto, *Ymagines*, vol. ii, pp. 65–6; Roger of Howden, *Gesta Henrici Secundi*, vol. ii, pp. 116, 117–19; *Narratio de Itinere Navali Peregrinorum*, ed. Chroust, *Quellen*, pp. 188, 189, 195, cf. trans. Loud, *Crusade of Frederick Barbarrosa*, pp. 198, 201, 204, 207; *Gesta Crucigerorum Rhenanorum* and *De Itinere Frisonum*, ed. R. Röhricht, *Quinti Belli Sacri Scriptores Minores, Société de l'Orient Latin*, vol. ii (Geneva, 1879), pp. 29–56, 59–70; Oliver of Paderborn, *Capture of Damietta*, Bird et al., *Crusade and Christendom*, p. 165; and below pp. 247–8.

84. Innocent IV, *Registres*, no. 2644; F. Cardini, 'Crusade and "Presence of Jerusalem" in Medieval Florence', in *Outremer*, ed. B. Z. Kedar et al. (Jerusalem, 1982), p. 337 n. 36; C. Tyerman, 'Court, Crusade and City: The Cultural Milieu of Louis I, Duke of Bourbon', *Practices of Crusading: Image and Action from the Eleventh to the Sixteenth Centuries* (Farnham, 2013), no. IV, pp. 53–6.

85. L. W. Marvin, 'The White and Black Confraternities of Toulouse and the Albigensian Crusade 1210–11', *Viator*, 40 (2009), pp. 133–50.

86. C. Tyerman, '"Principes et Populus": Civil Society and the First Crusade', *Practices of Crusading: Image and Action from the Eleventh to the Sixteenth Centuries* (Farnham, 2013), no. XII, pp. 1–23.

87. Tyerman, *God's War*, pp. 467, 469, 510, 530–31, 547 and refs.

88. *RHF*, vol. xxi, pp. 262–3; Kedar, 'Passenger List', pp. 271–2.

89. Riley-Smith, *First Crusaders*, p. 112.

90. Migne, *Patrologia Latina*, vol. ccxvi, col. 1261.

91. Guillaume de Nangis, *Gesta Ludovici*, *RHF*, vol. xx, pp. 440–42.
92. Stubbs, *Select Charters*, pp. 183–4; trans. *English Historical Documents*, vol. ii, ed. D. C. Douglas (London, 1953), pp. 416–17; Roger of Howden, *Gesta Henrici Secundi*, vol. i, pp. 279–80.
93. D. Carpenter, 'English Peasants in Politics 1258–1267', *Past and Present*, 136 (1992), pp. 3–42; finerollshenry3.org.uk/content/month/fm-09-2010.html, accessed 31/5/2014.
94. H. S. Bennett, *Life on the English Manor* (Cambridge, 1956), pp. 118–25; for the politicized 'popular' crusades, see Tyerman, *God's War*, pp. 607–11, 802–4, 879–81; T. Guard, *Chivalry, Kingship and Crusade* (Woodbridge, 2013), pp. 23–9 and nn. 5 and 6.
95. Matthew Paris, *Chronica Majora*, vol. v, p. 107, vol. vi, p. 163.
96. *Registro del Cardinale Ugolino d'Ostia*, ed. G. Levi (Rome, 1890), *Fonti per la storia d'Italia*, vol. viii, pp. 128–33, no. cv; Marino Sanudo Torsello, *Liber Secretorum Fidelium Crucis*, ed. J. Bongars, *Gesta Dei per Francos* (Hanau, 1611), esp. bk II, pt. I, pp. 34–7.
97. E.g. P. Alphandéry, *La chrétienté et l'idée de croisade*, ed. A. Dupront (Paris, 1954–9); M. Mollat, *The Poor in the Middle Ages* (London, 1986), esp. p. 72; cf. now J. Rubinstein, *Armies of Heaven: The First Crusade and the Quest for the Apocalypse* (New York, 2011).
98. Guibert of Nogent, *Gesta Dei per Francos*, *RHC Occ.*, vol. iv, p. 251.
99. William of Puylaurens, *Chronicle*, trans. W. A. Sibly and M. D. Sibly (Woodbridge, 2003), pp. 33 n.6, 128.
100. Fulcher of Chartres, *Historia*, *RHC Occ.*, vol. iii, p. 329; trans. Ryan and Fink, *History*, pp. 75–6.
101. Tyerman, *God's War*, pp. 607–11.
102. Tyerman, *God's War*, pp. 78–81, 94–106.
103. Brundage, *Medieval Canon Law*, pp. 132–8; *Quia Maior*, 1213, trans. Riley-Smith and Riley-Smith, *Crusades: Idea and Reality*, esp. pp. 121–2; in general see refs. under 'vows, crusade, redemption of' in Bird et al., *Crusade and Christendom*, p. 508.
104. Tyerman, 'Who Went on Crusade?', p. 25 and nn. 40, 41, 42.
105. Henry of Huntingdon, *Historia Anglorum*, ed. D. Greenway (Oxford, 1996), pp. 752–3.
106. Royal Commission on Historical Manuscripts, *Report on Various Collections*, vol. i, pp. 235–6.
107. Alan of Lille, *Sermo de cruce domini*, *Textes inédits*, ed. M. T. d'Alverny, *Etudes de philosophie médiéval*, vol. 52 (Paris, 1965), pp. 281–2; and above pp. 100–101.
108. Above, note 94.

7. COSTS OF A CRUSADE

1. Peter of Blois, *De Hierosolymitana pererginatione acceleranda*, J. P. Migne, *Patrologia Latina* (Paris, 1844–64), vol. ccvii, col. 1068.

2. Odo of Châteauroux, Sermon XIV, *Analecta Novissima Spicilegii Solesmensis* (Paris, 1885–8), vol. ii, p. 332.

3. *RHC Documents Arméniens* (Paris, 1869–1906), vol. ii, pp. 340 (Hetoum), 371, 402–7 (the *Directorium*); for Sanudo, see J. Bongars, *Gesta Dei per Francos* (Hanau, 1611), vol. ii, esp. pp. 30–31; Humbert of Romans, *Opusculum tripartitum*, trans. J. Bird, E. Peters and J. M. Powell, *Crusade and Christendom* (Philadelphia, 2013), pp. 462–3.

4. *RHF*, vol. xv, p. 508.

5. Fulcher of Chartres, *Historia Hierosolymitana*, *RHC Occ.*, vol. iii, p. 328 n. 19 (refs. to two twelfth-century mss); cf. H. Hagenmeyer's edition (Heidelberg, 1913), p. 163 n. 1; for crusaders' materiel, see refs. in J. Riley-Smith, *The First Crusaders* (Cambridge, 1997), pp. 109–14.

6. Albert of Aachen, *Historia Ierosolimitana*, ed. and trans. S. Edgington (Oxford, 2007), pp. 24–5; Richard of Devizes, *Chronicle*, ed. J. T. Appleby (London, 1963), p. 15; A. V. Murray, 'Money and Logistics in the Forces of the First Crusade', in *Logistics of Warfare in the Age of the Crusades*, ed. J. H. Pryor (Aldershot, 2006), pp. 240–41.

7. Matthew Paris, *Historia Anglorum*, ed. F. Madden (London, 1866–9), vol. iii, p. 55; Clement V, *Regestum* (Rome, 1885–92), no. 8205 (unsurprisingly Otto was robbed); *Calendar of Close Rolls 1227–31*, pp. 34–5.

8. Trans. E. Peters, *The First Crusade* (Philadelphia, 1998), p. 293.

9. On these schemes see A. Leopold, *How to Recover the Holy Land* (Aldershot, 2000).

10. J. Phillips, *The Second Crusade* (New Haven, 2007), pp. 115–22; C. Tyerman, *England and the Crusades* (Chicago, 1988), p. 60; idem, *God's War* (London, 2006), p. 434.

11. Tyerman, *England and the Crusades*, pp. 80–81 and n. 121.

12. *Recueil des actes de Philippe Auguste*, ed. H.-F. Delaborde et al. (Paris, 1916–79), vol. i, no. 252; Otto of St Blasien, *Chronica*, ed. A Hofmeister (Hanover, 1912), p. 4, trans. G. Loud, *The Crusade of Frederick Barbarossa* (Farnham, 2010), p. 176; *Chronica Regis Coloniensis cont. a 1195*, ed. G. Waitz (Hanover, 1880), p. 157; Robert of Clari, *La Conquête de Constantinople*, pp. 4, 6, 8, trans. E. H. McNeal, *The Conquest of Constantinople* (New York, 1966), pp. 34, 36, 38.

13. G. L. Tafel and G. M. Thomas, *Urkunden zur alteren Handels- und Staatgeschichte der Republik Venedig* (Vienna, 1856–7), vol. i, pp. 362–73; Tyerman, *God's War*, pp. 510–14, 525–7; *The Deeds of the Bishops of Halberstadt*, trans. A. Andrea, *Contemporary Sources for the Fourth Crusade* (Leiden, 2000), p. 247.

14. *Querimoniae Normannorum*, *RHF*, vol. xxiv, p. 22, no. 157, p. 40 no. 301; C Tyerman, 'Paid Crusaders', *Practices of Crusading: Image and Action from the Eleventh to the Sixteenth Centuries* (Farnham, 2013), no. XIV, pp. 17–18 and refs.

15. Trans. P. Jackson, *The Seventh Crusade, 1244–1254* (Aldershot, 2007), pp. 34–5.

16. *Histoire générale de Languedoc*, ed. C. de Vic and J. Vaisete (Toulouse, 1872–1905), vol. viii, cols. 706–7.

17. S. Lloyd, *English Society and the Crusade 1216–1307* (Oxford, 1988), pp. 116–19; N. Housley, 'Costing the Crusade', in *The Experience of Crusading*, vol. i, *Western Approaches*, eds. M. Bull and N. Housley (Cambridge, 2003), pp. 50–51; C. Tyerman, 'Philip VI and the Recovery of the Holy Land', *English Historical Review*, 100 (1985), pp. 42–3, p. 43 n. 1.

18. Raymond of Aguilers, *Historia Francorum qui ceperunt Iherusalem*, *RHC Occ.*, vol. iii, p. 245; Albert of Aachen, *Historia*, pp. 220–23; in general see above pp. 151–8.

19. H. Hagenmeyer, *Die Kreuzzugsbriefe aus den Jahren 1088–1100* (Innsbruck, 1902), pp. 138, 140; Albert of Aachen, *Historia*, pp. 86–7, cf. pp. 72–3.

20. Ralph of Caen, *Gesta Tancredi*, *RHC Occ.*, vol. iii, pp. 680–81, trans. B. Bachrach and D. S. Bachrach, *The* Gesta Tancredi *of Ralph of Caen* (Aldershot, 2005), pp. 124–5.

21. For a discussion of these, see Tyerman, 'Paid Crusaders', pp. 38–40, cf. pp. 6, 29–30, 31, 34.

22. Albert of Aachen, *Historia*, pp. 120–23; Tyerman, 'Paid Crusaders', p. 7 n. 24.

23. *Gesta Francorum*, trans. R. Hill (London, 1962), pp. 43, 72–3, 91; Peter Tudebode, *Historia de Hierosolymitana Itinere*, *RHC Occ.*, vol. iii, p. 50; Raymond of Aguilers, *Historia Francorum*, *RHC Occ.*, vol. iii, p. 297; Albert of Aachen, *Historia*, pp. 356–7.

24. Raymond of Aguilers, *Historia Francorum*, *RHC Occ.*, vol. iii, p. 271; Tyerman, 'Paid Crusaders', pp. 10–11.

25. Baldric of Bourgueil, *Historia Jerosolimitana*, *RHC Occ.*, vol. iv, p.17; Robert of Rheims, *Historia Iherosolimitana*, *RHC Occ.*, vol. iii,

pp. 741, 744, trans. C. Sweetenham, *Robert the Monk's History of the First Crusade* (Aldershot, 2005), pp. 92, 93.

26. Odo of Deuil, *De profectione Ludovici VII in Orientem*, ed. V. G. Berry (New York, 1948), pp. 122–5, 136–7, 142–3.

27. *RHF*, vol. xv, pp. 487, 488, 495–7, 499, 500–502, 508–10, nos. xii, xiii, xxxvi, xxxvii, xxxviii, xxxix, xlv, xlviii, lii, lxvii, lxviii, lxix.

28. Ralph of Diceto, *Abbreviationes Chronicorum, Opera Historica*, ed. W. Stubbs (London, 1876), vol. i, pp. 256–7; Phillips, *Second Crusade*, pp. 107–12; Tyerman, 'Paid Crusaders', p. 27 and n. 116.

29. Otto of Freising, *Gesta Friderici*, p. 89, trans. C. C. Mierow, *The Deeds of Frederick Barbarossa* (New York, 1953), p. 102; Phillips, *Second Crusade*, p. 184.

30. *De expugnatione Lyxbonensi*, ed. C. W. David (New York, 1976), pp. 56–7, 84–5, 98–101, 104–13.

31. Rigord, *Oeuvres*, ed. H. F. Delaborde (Paris, 1882–5), vol. i, p. 106.

32. Tyerman, *England and the Crusades*, pp. 66, 80–81; Roger of Howden, alias 'Benedict of Peterborough', *Gesta Regis Henrici Secundi*, ed. W. Stubbs (London, 1867), vol. ii, pp. 112, 186; *Itinerarium Ricardi Regis*, ed. W. Stubbs, Rolls Series (London, 1864), pp. 213–14, 225–6, trans. H. Nicholson, *The Chronicle of the Third Crusade* (Aldershot, 1997), pp. 204, 214; Ralph of Diceto, *Ymagines Historiarum, Opera Historica*, ed. W. Stubbs (London, 1876), vol. ii, p. 88.

33. *Episcopal Acts and Cognate Documents Relating to Welsh Dioceses 1066–1272*, ed. J. Conway Davies (Cardiff, 1946), vol. i, p. 326.

34. *Itinerarium Ricardi Regis*, p. 116, trans. Nicholson, *Chronicle*, p. 118.

35. Roger of Howden, *Chronica*, ed. W. Stubbs (London, 1868–71), vol. iv, p. 111; Tyerman, *England and the Crusades*, pp. 96, 190; James of Vitry, *Historia Occidentalis*, ed. J. F. Hinnebusch (Freiburg, 1972); Robert of Clari, *La Conquête*, pp. 4, 6, 8, trans. McNeal, *Conquest*, pp. 34, 36, 38; Geoffrey of Villehardouin, *La Conquête de Constantinople*, ed. E. Faral (Paris, 1938–9), vol. i, pp. 51–3, 103–4, vol. ii, pp. 28–9; A. Wauters, ed., *Table chronologique des chartes et diplômes imprimés concernant l'histoire de la Belgique* (Brussels, 1866–1965), vol. iii, p. 174; *Cartulaire de Montier-le-Celle*, ed. C. Lalone (Paris-Troyes, 1882), pp. 10–11, no. 9.

36. In general, J. M. Powell, *Anatomy of a Crusade 1213–1221* (Philadelphia, 1986), esp. pp. 51–106.

37. Leopold, *How to Recover the Holy Land*, passim.

38. *Secreta Fidelium Crucis*, Bongars, *Gesta Dei per Francos*, bks 1 and 2.

39. See now M. Carlin and D. Crouch, *Lost Letters of Medieval Life* (Philadelphia, 2013), esp. pp. 1–23; cf. M. Aurell, *Le chevalier lettré* (Paris, 2011).

40. *Gesta Francorum*, p. 75.
41. Raymond of Aguilers, *Historia Francorum, RHC Occ.*, vol. iii, p. 271; Albert of Aachen, *Historia*, pp. 384–5.
42. Above, ch. 1.
43. See comments by Aurell, *Chevalier Lettré*, pp. 8–9, 19–20, 34, 39, 62–3, 64, 80–86, 195; for literate laymen and letters, see Peters, *First Crusade*, pp. 42–4, 284–9; for Robert of Normandy, see W. M. Aird, *Robert Curthose* (Woodbridge, 2008); Raymond of Aguilers, *Historia Francorum, RHC Occ.*, vol. iii, 235, 275.
44. Gerald of Wales, *De rebus a se gestis, Opera Omnia*, ed. J. S. Brewer, Rolls Series (London, 1861–91), vol. i, p. 79.
45. Wace, *Roman de Rou*, ed. A. J. Holden (Paris, 1970–73), ll. 2003–8, trans. G. Burgess, *History of the Norman People* (Woodbridge, 2004), pp. 113–14 for the story of Bernard the Philosopher and Duke Richard II presiding over the reckoning of his accounts; cf. the source, *Gesta Normannnorum Ducum*, ed. E. M. C. Van Houts (Oxford, 1992–5), pp. 30–31 where the duke's administrative task is less specific.
46. D. Crouch, *The Beaumont Twins* (Cambridge, 1986), esp. pp. 163–6; R. Mortimer, 'The Family of Ranulf de Glanville', *Bulletin of the Institute of Historical Research*, 54 (1981), pp. 1–16.
47. E.g. *Constitutio Domus Regis, c.* 1135–9, ed. with the *Dialogus de Scaccario* by C. Johnson (London, 1950), pp. 129–35; as ecclesiastical households could include or be run by laymen, the lay/cleric distinction may be artificial.
48. *English Lawsuits from William I to Richard I*, ed. R. C. Van Caenegem (London, 1990–91), vol. ii, pp. 397–404, no. 408.
49. For a Catalan agreement on estate renders of 1071, T. Bisson, ed., *Fiscal Accounts of Catalonia under the Early Count-Kings* (Berkeley and Los Angeles, 1984), vol. ii, pp. 255–6, no. 139.
50. *History of William Marshal*, ed. A. J. Holden (London, 2002–6), pp. 230–31, ll. 4538–40 for the *escrit* of the knights at the Lagny tournament in 1179 available to the Marshal's biographer in the 1220s (full list ll. 4457–780) and pp. 174–5, ll. 3414–24 for the accounts, including that for the Marshal and Roger of Jouy by the 'clerk of the kitchen', Wignant, also preserved for the Marshal's biographer's inspection. Gerald of Wales, *De Principis Instructione, Opera*, vol. viii, pp. 316–18.
51. 'Ad sustentaculum militantium deo in loco prescripti martyris', *Die Traditionem des Klosters Tegernsee 1003–1242*, ed. P. Acht (Munich, 1952), p. 189, no. 250.

52. Odo of Deuil, *De profectione*, pp. 10–11, 14–15, is the only source for these negotiations.

53. *Crònica de Ramon Muntaner*, ed. F. Soldevila (Barcelona, 2011), chs. 225, 233; I owe this reference to a forthcoming essay by Professor David Jacoby.

54. *RHF*, vol. xxii, pp. 404, 513–15; cf. W. Jordan, *Louis IX and the Challenge of the Crusade* (Princeton, 1979), pp. 78–9 and nn. 94, 95.

55. Housley, 'Costing the Crusade', pp. 47–52; F. Cardini, 'I costi della crociata', *Studi in memoria di Federigo Melis* (Naples, 1978), vol. iii, pp. 179–210; J. B. Henneman, *Royal Taxation in Fourteenth Century France: The Development of War Financing 1322–1356* (Princeton, 1971), pp. 348–9, Table 2.

56. Henneman, *Royal Taxation*, pp. 349–51 for Philip VI's income.

57. B. Kedar, 'The Passenger List of a Crusader Ship', *Studi Medievali*, 13 (1972), pp. 271–2; *RHF*, vol. xxi, pp. 262–3; above p. 171.

58. Riley-Smith, *First Crusaders*, p. 112 and generally pp. 109–35; Murray, 'Money and Logistics', pp. 230–32.

59. Figures derived from Murray, 'Money and Logistics', p. 234, who calculates in pennies, which can be divided by 12 to reach shillings; Ralph of Caen, *Gesta Tancredi*, *RHC Occ.*, vol. iii, pp. 630, 703, trans. Bachrach and Bachrach, *Gesta Tancredi*, pp. 56, 155; *Gesta Francorum*, p. 59.

60. Riley-Smith, *First Crusaders*, p. 109.

61. Murray, 'Money and Logistics', pp. 240–41 (pennies into pounds, divide by 240); to convert Robert's 10,000 marks, one mark sterling equals 0.66 per cent of a pound sterling; Raymond of Aguilers, *Historia Francorum*, *RHC Occ.*, vol. iii, p. 271.

62. Raymond of Aguilers, *Historia Francorum*, *RHC Occ.*, vol. iii, p. 278.

63. *RHF*, vol. xv, pp. 499, 500–502, 508–9, nos. xlv, xlviii, lii, lxviii; J. M. Baldwin, *The Government of Philip Augustus* (Berkeley and Los Angeles, 1986), pp. 44–58.

64. *RHF*, vol. xv, p. 487, no. xii; for a recent account of the French expedition, see Phillips, *Second Crusade*, pp. 184–206.

65. Tyerman, *England and the Crusades*, pp. 80–81 and in general pp. 57–85.

66. Roger of Howden, *Gesta Henrici Secundi*, vol. ii, pp. 89–90; *Pipe Roll 2 Richard I*, pp. 8–9.

67. Tyerman, *England and the Crusades*, p. 82; Villehardouin, *La Conquête*, vol. i, pp. 50–53; Richard of Devizes, *Chronicle*, p. 15, although palfries and pack-horses were sent to the continent perhaps to join

Richard's retinue and his flotilla of galleys at Marseilles; see below p. 265.

68. *Pipe Roll 2 Richard I*, p. 131, cf. pp. 1, 53, 104, 112; *Pipe Roll 3 Richard I*, pp. 11, 128; and *Pipe Roll 35 Henry II*, p. 106 for supplies of iron.

69. Richard of Devizes, *Chronicle*, p. 42; *Chronica Coloniensis*, p. 157.

70. D. Carpenter, *The Struggle for Mastery. Britain 1066–1284* (London, 2003), pp. 220, 246; R. Bartlett, *England under the Angevin and Norman Kings* (Oxford, 2000), pp. 175–7; Baldwin, *Government of Philip Augustus*, pp. 50–51; Tyerman, *England and the Crusades*, p. 79.

71. Rigord, *Oeuvres*, vol. i, p. 106; *Recueil des actes de Philippe Auguste*, vol. i, no. 252.

72. Thomas of Split, *Historia pontificum Spalatensis*, ed. L. von Heineman, MGH *Scriptores in Folio et Charto* (Hanover and Leipzig, 1826–1934), vol. xxix, pp. 578–9.

73. Baldwin, *Government of Philip Augustus*, p. 173.

74. J. H. Pryor, 'The Venetian Fleet for the Fourth Crusade', in *Experience of Crusading*, vol. i, eds. Bull and Housley, pp. 103–23.

75. Robert of Clari, *La Conquête*, pp. 8, 9, 10, trans. McNeal, *Conquest*, pp. 38, 39, 40.

76. Kedar, 'Passenger List'.

77. *Registro del Cardinale Ugolino d'Ostia*, ed. G. Levi (Rome, 1890), *Fonti per la storia d'Italia*, vol. viii, pp. 128–33, no. cv; Powell, *Anatomy of Crusade*, pp. 97–102, esp. Table 5:1.

78. Baldwin, *Government of Philip Augustus*, p. 353 and n. 94; MGH *Constitutiones et Acta Publica Imperatorum et Regum*, ed. L. Weiland (Hanover, 1896), IV-ii, pp. 129–31, no. 102.

79. *RHF*, vol. xxi, pp. 404, 513–15; A. Jal, *Pacta Naulorum, Collection de documents inédits sur l'histoire de France* (Paris, 1841–8), vol. i, pp. 605–9, vol. ii, pp. 51–67; Jordan, *Louis IX and the Challenge of Crusade*, esp. pp. 70–79, 103–4.

80. Jordan, *Louis IX and the Challenge of Crusade*, p. 71.

81. See the discussion in Lloyd, *English Society*, pp. 115–19; J. R. Strayer, 'The Crusades of Louis IX', in *A History of the Crusades*, gen. ed. K. Setton (Madison, 1969), vol. ii, pp. 510–12.

82. William of Newburgh, *Historia rerum Anglicarum*, ed. R. Howlett (London, 1884–5), vol. i, pp. 360, 383.

83. N. Vincent, *Peter des Roches* (Cambridge, 1996), esp. pp. 235–6.

84. Baldwin, *Government of Philip Augustus*, p. 173.

85. Carpenter, *Struggle for Mastery*, p. 262.

86. M. Prestwich, *Edward I* (London, 1988), pp. 200 (£120,000 on Wales) and 400 (£750,000 between 1294 and 1298 on wars in France and Scotland); cf. Lloyd, *English Society*, pp. 144–8.

87. Jordan, *Louis IX and the Challenge of Crusade*, p. 67 and n. 22.

88. E. Boutaric, 'Documents relatives à l'histoire de Philippe le Bel', *Notices et Extraits*, 20 (1865), pp. 112–18, no. v; William of Poitiers, *Gesta Guillelmi*, eds. R. H. C. Davies and M. Chibnall (Oxford, 1998), p. 102.

8. PAYING FOR A CRUSADE

1. J. Brundage, *Medieval Canon Law and the Crusader* (Madison, 1969), esp. pp. 159–90.

2. Brundage, *Medieval Canon Law*, pp. 183–4; Roger of Howden, alias 'Benedict of Peterborough', *Gesta Regis Henrici Secundi*, ed. W. Stubbs (London, 1867), vol. ii, p. 31; C. Tyerman, *England and the Crusades* (Chicago, 1988), p. 70 for English exemptions.

3. Rigord, *Oeuvres*, ed. H. F. Delaborde (Paris, 1882–5), vol. i, pp. 84–5; *Recueil des actes de Philippe Auguste*, ed. H.-F. Delaborde et al. (Paris, 1916–79), no. 1360; Tyerman, *England and the Crusades*, pp. 71, 135, 204, 219, 221.

4. Tyerman, *England and the Crusades*, p. 219 and n.146; cf. papal crusade encyclicals on Jewish usury in 1145/6, 1198, 1213, 1215, 1234, etc.

5. J. Riley-Smith, *The First Crusaders* (Cambridge, 1997), pp. 123–5.

6. *Cartulaires de l'abbaye de Moslesme 916–1250*, ed. J. Laurent (Paris, 1907–11), pp. 83–4, no. 78.

7. Tyerman, *England and the Crusades*, pp. 199, 206–7.

8. As stated pointedly by Corliss Slack, *Crusade Charters* (Tempe, 2001), pp. xxix–xxx, and indicated by *Quantum praedecessores*, which forbad any challenge to the title of property pledged by crusaders.

9. Trans. J. Riley-Smith and L. Riley-Smith, *The Crusades: Idea and Reality* (London, 1981), pp. 58–9.

10. Riley-Smith, *First Crusaders*, pp. 109–35.

11. Tyerman, *England and the Crusades*, pp. 16–17.

12. Tyerman, *England and the Crusades*, pp. 75–80.

13. Roger of Howden, *Chronica*, ed. W. Stubbs (London, 1868–71), vol. iii, p. 8.

14. Roger of Howden, *Gesta Henrici Secundi*, vol. ii, p. 90.

15. Richard of Devizes, *Chronicle*, ed. J. T. Appleby (London, 1963), p. 9.

16. C. Tyerman, *God's War* (London, 2006), pp. 442, 444 and n. 82.

17. *Register of St. Benet of Holme*, ed. J. R. West, Norfolk Record Society, 2 and 3 (1932), i, 87, no. 155; cf. G. Constable, 'The Financing of the Crusades', *Crusaders and Crusading in the Twelfth Century* (Farnham, 2008), esp. p. 126 for a similar observation.
18. Orderic Vitalis, *Ecclesiastical History*, ed. and trans. M. Chibnall (Oxford, 1969–80), vol. vi, pp. 18–19.
19. Tyerman, *England and the Crusades*, pp. 46, 47 and refs.
20. W. Jordan, *Louis IX and the Challenge of Crusade* (Princeton, 1979), p. 103; S. Lloyd, *English Society and the Crusade 1216–1307* (Oxford, 1988), p. 145 and n. 150.
21. In general, C. Maier, *Preaching the Crusades: Mendicant Friars and the Cross in the Thirteenth Century* (Cambridge, 1994).
22. Peter the Venerable, *Letters*, ed. G. Constable (Cambridge, Mass., 1967), vol. i, pp. 327–30.
23. Tyerman, *England and the Crusades*, pp. 192–3.
24. Jordan, *Louis IX and the Challenge of Crusade*, pp. 84–6, 98–9.
25. *RHF*, vol. xv, pp. 496, 501–2, 508, nos. xxxvii, lii, lxvii; Roger of Howden, *Gesta Henrici Secundi*, vol. ii, p. 31; J. Bird, E. Peters and J. M. Powell, *Crusade and Christendom* (Philadelphia, 2013), pp. 126, 139;, J. M. Powell, *Anatomy of a Crusade 1213–1221* (Philadelphia, 1986), pp. 92–3; 'Ernoul', trans. P. Edbury, *The Conquest of Jerusalem and the Third Crusade* (London, 1996), pp. 35–6; MGH *Constitutiones et Acta Publica Imperatorum et Regum*, ed. L. Weiland (Hanover, 1896), IV-ii, no. 102.
26. Tyerman, *England and the Crusades*, pp. 109, 127, 129; Lloyd, *English Society*, p. 145.
27. *Calendar of Patent Rolls 1225–32*, pp. 89–90; Richard of Devizes, *Chronicle*, p. 6.
28. *Pleas before the King or his Justices, 1198–1202*, ed. D. M. Stenton (London, 1948–9), vol. i, pp. 135–6, vol. ii, p. 49, no. 248; on gold supply, see in general P. Spufford, *Money and its Use in Medieval Europe* (Cambridge, 1988).
29. M. S. Giuseppi, 'On the Testament of Sir Hugh de Nevill', *Archaeologia*, 56 (1899), pp. 352–4.
30. A. V. Murray, 'Money and Logistics in the Forces of the First Crusade', in *Logistics of Warfare in the Age of the Crusades*, ed. J. H. Pryor (Aldershot, 2006), p. 239 n. 30 for full references; Albert of Aachen, *Historia Ierosolimitana*, ed. and trans. S. Edgington (Oxford, 2007), pp. 24–5; Constable, 'Financing the Crusades', pp. 117–18 and n. 3.

31. Roger of Howden, *Gesta Henrici Secundi*, vol. ii, p. 116; idem, *Chronica*, vol. iv, pp. 5–6.
32. Rigord, *Oeuvres*, vol. i, p. 106.
33. *Chronica Regis Coloniensis cont. a 1195*, ed. G. Waitz (Hanover, 1880), p. 157; Richard of San Germano, *Chronica, MGHS*, vol. xix, pp. 348–9; D. Abulafia, *Frederick II* (London, 1988), pp. 220–23.
34. D. Carpenter, 'The Gold Treasure of King Henry III', *The Reign of Henry III* (London, 1996), pp. 107–36; N. Vincent, *Peter des Roches* (Cambridge, 1996), pp. 238–9 and n. 53.
35. Powell, *Anatomy of a Crusade*, pp. 100–101.
36. See, e.g., the letters trans. E. Peters, *The First Crusade* (Philadelphia, 1998), pp. 283–4, 296–7; J. Riley-Smith, *The First Crusade and the Idea of Crusading* (London, 1986), pp. 23, 40–41, 72, 123–5, 162; Brundage, *Medieval Canon Law*, pp. 127–38.
37. *Chronica Monasterii de Melsa*, ed. E. A. Bond (London, 1866–8), vol. i, p. 76.
38. Urban II to his supporters in Bologna, 19 Sept. 1096, trans. Peters, *First Crusade*, p. 44; still going in 1188, Tyerman, *England and the Crusades*, p. 61; cf. *Quia Maior* (1213) and *Rachel suum videns* (1234) dispensing with suitability tests, Bird et al., *Crusade and Christendom*, pp. 110, 274–5.
39. Tyerman, *England and the Crusades*, pp. 64–5 and refs.
40. Gerald of Wales, *De principis instructione, Opera omnia*, ed. J. S. Brewer, Rolls Series (London, 1861–91), vol. viii, pp. 236–9, trans W. Lunt, *Papal Revenues in the Middle Ages* (New York, 1965), vol. ii, pp. 485–7 and, generally, for redemptions legacies and donations, vol. i, p. 125, vol. ii, pp. 485–97, 512–28; Maier, *Preaching the Crusades*, pp. 135–60.
41. Bird et al., *Crusade and Christendom*, pp. 47–52 and refs. p. 49 for docs. and a convenient summary.
42. A. Andrea, *Contemporary Sources for the Fourth Crusade* (Leiden, 2000), pp. 30–31 (Innocent III, 31 Dec. 1199); Bird et al., *Crusade and Christendom*, pp. 49–50 (Innocent III, 1200).
43. Bird et al., *Crusade and Christendom*, pp. 110, 129, and pp. 119, 135–41 for attendant confusion.
44. Bird et al., *Crusade and Christendom*, pp. 270–76; in general, M. Lower, *The Barons' Crusade* (Philadelphia, 2005).
45. Tyerman, *England and the Crusades*, pp. 193–4 and refs.; Lloyd, *English Society*, pp. 22, 149, 151, 178; Jordan, *Louis IX and the Challenge of Crusade*, pp. 67–8.

46. Lunt, *Papal Revenues*, vol. ii, pp. 488–90.

47. Matthew Paris, *Chronica Majora*, ed. H. R. Luard (London, 1872–84), vol. iv, pp. 133–4; Tyerman, *England and the Crusades*, pp. 194–5.

48. Bird et al., *Crusade and Christendom*, p. 398.

49. Tyerman, *England and the Crusades*, p. 162; Maier, *Preaching the Crusades*, pp. 139–43 and refs.

50. Bird et al., *Crusade and Christendom*, p. 455.

51. Lloyd, *English Society*, p. 149; Jordan, *Louis IX and the Challenge of Crusade*, p. 100 and n. 214.

52. Innocent IV, *Registres*, ed. E. Berger (Paris, 1884–1921), no. 3708.

53. *Calendar of Papal Registers*, ed. W. T. Bliss et al. (London, 1893–1960), vol. i, 444, 445; Tyerman, *England and the Crusades*, p. 195 and n. 38; Lloyd, *English Society*, p. 146 and n. 157.

54. Lunt, *Papal Revenues*, vol. i, pp. 111–25, vol. ii, pp. 448–85; *Historical Papers and Letters from Northern Registers*, ed. J. Raine (London, 1873), pp. 200–201 for redemptions worth only £25 14s 8d out of £500 raised in the archdiocese of York for the 1308 Hospitaller crusade; the bulk of the balance came from indulgence sales.

55. Lunt, *Papal Revenues*, vol. i, pp. 71–7, vol. ii, pp. 82–152; cf. Constable, 'Financing the Crusades', pp. 117–23.

56. Bird et al., *Crusade and Christendom*, p. 271.

57. Ibid, p. 34.

58. Ibid, p. 108.

59. Andrea, *Contemporary Sources*, p. 29.

60. *Recueil des chartes de l'abbaye de Saint-Benoît-sur-Loire*, ed. M. Prou et al. (Paris, 1900–1907), vol. i, pp. 340–43, no. 150; Constable, 'Financing the Crusades', pp. 116–17.

61. *Actes de Philippe Auguste*, vol. i, no. 252; Roger of Howden, *Gesta Henrici Secundi*, vol. ii, pp. 44–5; Ralph Niger, *Chronica*, ed. H. Krause (Frankfurt, 1985), p. 288.

62. Richard of San Germano, *Chronica*, *MGHS*, vol. xix, pp. 348–9; *Registro del Cardinale Ugolino d'Ostia*, ed. G. Levi (Rome, 1890), *Fonti per la storia d'Italia*, vol. viii, pp. 7–9, 11–13, 19–24, 101, 109–10, 113–14, 121–3, 128–33, 138–40, 152–3; Bird et al., *Crusade and Christendom*, pp. 274–5; Jordan, *Louis IX and the Challenge of Crusade*, pp. 35–64; J. R. Maddicott, 'The Crusade Taxation of 1268–70', *Thirteenth Century England*, 2 (1988), pp. 93–117; idem, *The Origins of the English Parliament 924–1327* (Oxford, 2010), pp. 266–72; C. Tyerman, 'Philip V of France, the Assemblies of 1319–20 and the Crusade', *Practices of*

Crusading: Image and Action from the Eleventh to the Sixteenth Centuries (Farnham, 2013), no. II, pp. 15–34.

63. Lloyd, *English Society*, p. 77; Tyerman, *England and the Crusades*, pp. 91–2, 121.

64. Bird et al., *Crusade and Christendom*, pp. 387–8, trans. from the Register of Archbishop Eudes of Rouen, and pp. 454–65 for some Lyons II material; on the Lyons II reports, see P. Throop, *Criticism of the Crusade* (Amsterdam, 1940); M. Aurell, *Des chrétiens contre les croisades* (Paris, 2013), pp. 310–27.

65. Tyerman, *England and the Crusades*, pp. 45–6 and nn. 37, 38 for refs, pp. 75–80.

66. *Decrees of the Ecumenical Councils*, ed. N. P. Tanner, vol. i (Washington, DC, 1990), pp. 227–71; Powell, *Anatomy of a Crusade*, p. 50 n. 46.

67. Lunt, *Papal Revenues*, vol. i, pp. 71–7; Tyerman, *God's War*, pp. 616–17, 778–9, 815–16, 829–31.

68. Tyerman, *England and the Crusades*, p. 17 and nn. 37, 45, 96; Riley-Smith and Riley-Smith, *Crusades: Idea and Reality*, p. 144 and above note 62.

69. Discussed in Constable, 'Financing the Crusades', pp. 118–20; cf. Tyerman, 'Paid Crusaders', *Practices of Crusading*, no. XIV, p. 27 and n. 116.

70. Ralph Niger, *Chronica*, p. 288.

71. Bird et al., *Crusade and Christendom*, pp. 110, 126; Powell, *Anatomy of a Crusade*, p. 94; *Registro Ugolino*, p. 7, no. iv, pp. 11–12, no. ix (viii (sic) in text).

72. Jordan, *Louis IX and the Challenge of Crusade*, pp. 94–9.

73. G. Loud, *The Crusade of Frederick Barbarossa* (Farnham, 2010), p. 121; *Actes de Philippe Auguste*, vol. i, no. 237, vol. iv, no. 1708; Tyerman, *God's War*, p. 508 and n. 20; *Histoire générale de Languedoc*, ed. C. de Vic and J. Vaisete (Toulouse, 1872–1905), vol. viii, cols. 1489–90 (cf. Jordan, *Louis IX and the Challenge of Crusade*, p. 100 for an earlier, limited hearth tax of Alphonse).

74. Tyerman, *England and the Crusades*, pp. 101, 191, although the suggestion that Peter des Roches took some of this tax money with him on crusade is unjustified, Vincent, *Peter des Roches*, p. 238, n. 51.

75. Tyerman, *England and the Crusades*, p. 45 and refs. n. 37 and p. 47, n. 48.

76. Gervase of Canterbury, *Historical Works*, ed. W. Stubbs (London, 1879–80), vol. i, pp. 422–3; Tyerman, *England and the Crusades*, esp.

pp. 75–80; for details on the Pipe Rolls *34 Henry II*, pp. 11, 106, 216; *1 Richard I*, pp. 1, 5, 12, 53, 104, 112, 131; *2 Richard I*, p. 112.

77. Roger of Howden, *Gesta Henrici Secundi*, vol. i, pp. 336–7, vol. ii, p. 32; idem, *Chronica*, vol. ii, p. 302.

78. Powell, *Anatomy of a Crusade*, pp. 100–101; *Regestro Ugolino*, pp. 128–33; Jordan, *Louis IX and the Challenge of Crusade*, pp. 82, 98; P. Guido, *Rationes decimarum Italiae nei secoli XIIIe: Tuscia: la decima degli anni 1274–90, Studi e Testi*, vol. lviii (Vatican City, 1932), pp. xli–xliii.

79. Tyerman, *God's War*, pp. 586, 600–601.

80. R. Bartlett, *The Making of Europe* (London, 1993), p. 268.

81. Jordan, *Louis IX and the Challenge of Crusade*, p. 100.

82. Tyerman, *God's War*, pp. 802–4 and refs.

83. Bird et al., *Crusade and Christendom*, pp. 274–5, 455, 462.

84. Strayer, 'Crusades of Louis IX', p. 508; William Rishanger, *Chronica*, ed. H. T. Riley (London, 1865), p. 78.

85. E. Christiansen, *The Northern Crusades* (London, 1997), esp. pp. 82–92, 123–38.

86. For these and other schemes, see A. Leopold, *How to Recover the Holy Land* (Aldershot, 2000) and S. Schein, *Fideles Crucis* (Oxford, 1991).

87. P. Dubois, *The Recovery of the Holy Land*, ed. W. I. Brandt (New York, 1956) and comments in P. Biller, *The Measure of Multitude* (Oxford, 2000), pp. 242–4; J. Bongars, *Gesta Dei per Francos* (Hanau, 1611), vol. ii, p. 23.

88. N. Housley, 'Costing the Crusade', in *The Experience of Crusading*, vol. i, *Western Approaches*, eds. M. Bull and N. Housley (Cambridge, 2003), p. 49; F. Cardini, 'I costi della crociata', *Studi in memoria di Federigo Melis* (Naples, 1978), vol. iii, p. 188.

89. *Political Songs of England*, ed. T. Wright (London, 1839), p. 128.

9. CO-ORDINATION

1. H. Hagenmeyer, *Die Kreuzzugsbriefe aus den Jahren 1088–1100* (Innsbruck, 1902), pp. 165–7 and p. 136 for departure date, trans. E. Peters, *The First Crusade* (Philadelphia, 1998), pp. 42, 291–2; for English involvement, C. Tyerman, *England and the Crusades* (Chicago, 1988), pp. 19–21; Fulcher of Chartres, *Historia Hierosolymitana*, *RHC Occ.*, vol. iii, p. 327, trans. F. R. Ryan and H. Fink, *A History of the Expedition to Jerusalem* (Knoxville, 1969), pp. 71–2 for harvest; in general, C. Tyerman, *God's War* (London, 2006), chs. 2–3; J. Riley-Smith, *The*

First Crusade and the Idea of Crusading (London, 1986), chs. 1–2; J. France, *Victory in the East* (Cambridge, 1994), ch. 4.

2. *RHC Occ.*, vol. iv, p. 149, trans. R. Levine, *The Deeds of God Through the Franks* (Woodbridge, 1997), p. 251.

3. Albert of Aachen, *Historia Ierosolimitana*, ed. and trans. S. Edgington (Oxford, 2007), pp. 60–63.

4. J. Riley-Smith, *The First Crusaders* (Cambridge, 1997), pp. 139–43.

5. Albert of Aachen, *Historia*, pp. 12–13, 18–21, 62–71.

6. For a robust view of such Byzantine–crusader relations, P. Frankopan, *The First Crusade: The Call from the East* (London, 2012), esp. chs. 6–8.

7. See now C. West, 'All in the Same Boat: East Anglia, the North Sea World and the 1147 Expedition to Lisbon', in *East Anglia and its North Sea World in the Middle Ages*, ed. D. Bates and R. Liddiard (Woodbridge, 2013), pp. 286–300.

8. *De expugnatione Lyxbonensi*, ed. C. W. David (New York, 1976), pp. 112–13.

9. For general accounts of these, see Tyerman, *God's War*, pp. 54–5, 398, 413–14, 627–8, 664–5, 685, 689–92.

10. Odo of Deuil, *De profectione Ludovici VII in Orientem*, ed. V. G. Berry (New York, 1948), pp. 32–3.

11. Odo of Deuil, *De profectione*, pp. 70–71.

12. The *De expugnatione Lyxbonensi*.

13. For general information, J. Phillips, *The Second Crusade* (New Haven, 2007), esp. chs. 4, 5, 7; for a key assessment of the lack of overarching strategy, A. Forey, 'The Second Crusade: Scope and Objectives', *Durham University Journal*, 86 (1994), pp. 165–75.

14. For these, Phillips, *Second Crusade*, p. 169; Odo of Deuil, *De profectione*, pp. 22–3, 66–9, 78–9.

15. Roger of Howden alias 'Benedict of Peterborough', *Gesta Regis Henrici Secundi*, ed. W. Stubbs (London, 1867), vol. ii, p. 56; in general, Tyerman, *God's War*, chs. 12–13.

16. G. Loud, *The Crusade of Frederick Barbarossa* (Farnham, 2010), pp. 15–18 and refs., 43–4, 47–55; Roger of Howden, *Gesta Henrici Secundi*, vol. ii, p. 56.

17. Guy of Bazoches, *Liber Epistularum*, ed. H. Adolfsson (Stockholm, 1969), no. xxxiv, p. 148.

18. Loud, *Crusade of Frederick Barbarossa*, pp. 92, 145; Ralph of Diceto, *Ymagines Historiarum, Opera Historica*, ed. W. Stubbs (London, 1876), vol. ii, pp. 51–4.

19. Guy of Bazoches, *Liber Epistolarum*, no. xxxv, pp. 152–3; Tyerman, *God's War*, pp. 440–41; *The Chronicle of Ibn al-Athir for the Crusading Period*, trans. D. S. Richards (Aldershot, 2007), vol. ii, p. 374; Baha al-Din Ibn Shaddad, *The Rare and Excellent History of Saladin*, trans. D. S. Richards (Aldershot, 2002), p. 106.

20. *Itinerarium Ricardi Regis*, ed. W. Stubbs, Rolls Series (London, 1864), pp. 64–8, trans. H. Nicholson, *The Chronicle of the Third Crusade* (Aldershot, 1997), pp. 73–7; Tyerman, *God's War*, pp. 402–17.

21. *Itinerarium Ricardi Regis*, pp. 92–4, trans. Nicholson, *Chronicle*, pp. 97–9; *The Old French Continuation of William of Tyre 1184–97*, trans. P. Edbury (Aldershot, 1998), p. 94.

22. Roger of Howden, *Gesta Henrici Secundi*, vol. ii, pp. 112–26; Tyerman, *England and the Crusades*, pp. 80–82; Tyerman, *God's War*, pp. 431–41.

23. Roger of Howden, *Gesta Henrici Secundi*, vol. ii, p. 112; Ambroise, *L'Estoire de la Guerre Sainte*, ed. G. Paris (Paris, 1877), ll. 449–90, trans. M. J. Hubert, *The Crusade of Richard the Lion-Heart* (New York, 1976), pp. 46–7; *Itinerarium Ricardi Regis*, p. 152, trans. Nicholson, *Chronicle*, p. 153.

24. Geoffrey of Villehardouin, *La Conquête de Constantinople*, ed. E. Faral (Paris, 1938–9), esp. vol. i, pp. 1–57, trans. M. R. B. Shaw, *Chronicles of the Crusades* (London, 1963), pp. 29–39; Robert of Clari, *La Conquête de Constantinople*, pp. 1–8, trans. E. H. McNeal, *The Conquest of Constantinople* (New York, 1966), pp. 31–9; J. Riley-Smith, 'Towards an Understanding of the Fourth Crusade as an Institution', in *Urba Capta*, ed. A. Laiou (Paris, 2005), pp. 71–88; in general Tyerman, *God's War*, pp. 501–60 and refs.

25. Villehardouin, *La Conquête*, vol. i, pp. 50–53, 102–5, vol. ii, pp. 28–9.

26. I. Fonnesberg-Schmidt, *The Popes and the Baltic Crusades 1147–1254* (Leiden, 2007), pp. 79–131; C. Tyerman, 'Henry of Livonia and the Ideology of Crusading', *Practices of Crusading: Image and Action from the Eleventh to the Sixteenth Centuries* (Farnham, 2013), no. VII, pp. 32–7; Tyerman, *God's War*, pp. 596–9.

27. *Ad Liberandam*, trans. J. Bird, E. Peters and J. M. Powell, *Crusade and Christendom* (Philadelphia, 2013), pp. 124–9.

28. Oliver of Paderborn, *Historia Damiatina*, trans. Bird et al., *Crusade and Christendom*, pp. 166–7.

29. J. P. Migne, *Patrologia Latina* (Paris, 1844–64), vol. ccxvi, col. 830, no. xxxv.

30. Tyerman, *God's War*, pp. 626–7; Bird et al., *Crusade and Christendom*, p. 158.

31. For some relevant trans. documents, see Bird et al., *Crusade and Christendom*, pp. 133–41.

32. M. Lower, *The Barons' Crusade* (Philadelphia, 2005), passim; Tyerman, *God's War*, pp. 755–69.

33. W. Jordan, *Louis IX and the Challenge of Crusade* (Princeton, 1979), esp. pp. 65–104, remains the best study; for Richard, see Tyerman, *England and the Crusades*, pp. 57–85 and above pp. 197–9 and below pp. 262–3.

34. Jordan, *Louis IX and the Challenge of Crusade*, pp. 3–64.

10. HEALTH AND SAFETY

1. T. F. Crane, *The Exempla of Jacques de Vitry* (London, 1890), p. 57, no. cxxiv; John of Joinville, *Histoire de Saint Louis*, ed. N. de Wailly (Paris, 1868), trans. M. R. B. Shaw, *Chronicles of the Crusades* (London, 1963), p. 191; cf. Fulcher of Chartres, *Historia Hierosolymitana*, *RHC Occ.*, vol. iii, p. 328, trans. F. R. Ryan and H. Fink, *A History of the Expedition to Jerusalem* (Knoxville, 1969), p. 74.

2. *De expugnatione Lyxbonensi*, ed. C. W. David (New York, 1976), pp. 130–31.

3. J. Brundage, *Medieval Canon Law and the Crusader* (Madison, 1969), pp. 139–90; C. Tyerman, *The Invention of the Crusades* (Basingstoke, 1998), pp. 14–28, 30–41, 55–62.

4. Cf. J. Riley-Smith, *The First Crusaders* (Cambridge, 1997), pp. 81–143; C. Tyerman, *England and the Crusades* (Chicago, 1988), pp. 195–228.

5. *Pipe Rolls 3 and 4 Richard I*, p. 285.

6. *Calendar of Close Rolls 1251–53*, p. 210; Tyerman, *England and the Crusades*, pp. 209–11.

7. J. Brundage, 'The Crusader's Wife: A Canonistic Quandary' and 'The Crusader's Wife Revisited', *Studia Gratiana*, 12 (1967), ii, pp. 425–41, iv, pp. 241–52; cf. *Quia Maior*, trans. J. Bird, E. Peters and J. M. Powell, *Crusade and Christendom* (Philadelphia, 2013), p. 110.

8. Raymond of Aguilers; cf. C. Tyerman, '"Principes et Populus": Civil Society and the First Crusade', *Practices of Crusading: Image and Action from the Eleventh to the Sixteenth Centuries* (Farnham, 2013), no. XII, pp. 1–23.

9. Urban II to the Flemish, H. Hagenmeyer, *Die Kreuzzugsbriefe aus den Jahren 1088–1100* (Innsbruck, 1902), p. 136, trans. E. Peters, *The First*

Crusade (Philadelphia, 1998), p. 42; Riley-Smith, *First Crusaders*, pp. 106–9.

10. Trans. J. Riley-Smith and L. Riley-Smith, *The Crusades: Idea and Reality* (London, 1981), pp. 57–9.

11. *De expugnatione Lyxbonensi*, pp. 56–7, 176–7 (breaking a secondary deal with the king of Portugal collectively agreed).

12. Odo of Deuil, *De profectione Ludovici VII in Orientem*, ed. V. G. Berry (New York, 1948), pp. 124–5.

13. See trans. of *Historia de expeditione Friderici Imperatoris*, in G. Loud, *The Crusade of Frederick Barbarossa* (Farnham, 2010), pp. 47, 57–8, 64–5.

14. Roger of Howden alias 'Benedict of Peterborough', *Gesta Regis Henrici Secundi*, ed. W. Stubbs (London, 1867), vol. ii, pp. 30–33; Gervase of Canterbury, *Historical Works*, ed. W. Stubbs (London, 1879–80), vol. i, pp. 409–10; *Councils and Synods with other documents relating to the English Church*, ed. F. M. Powicke et al., vol. i (Oxford, 1961), pt. 2, pp. 1025–9; Tyerman, *England and the Crusades*, pp. 61–4.

15. Richard of Devizes, *Chronicle*, ed. J. T. Appleby (London, 1963), p. 22; cf. M. Strickland, *War and Chivalry* (Cambridge, 1996), p. 37.

16. Roger of Howden, *Gesta Henrici Secundi*, vol. ii, pp. 110–11.

17. Roger of Howden, *Gesta Henrici Secundi*, vol. ii, pp. 129–32; idem, *Chronica*, ed. W. Stubbs (London, 1868–71), vol. iii, pp. 58–60.

18. Ralph of Diceto, *Ymagines Historiarum, Opera Historica*, ed. W. Stubbs (London, 1876), vol. ii, p. 88.

19. Roger of Howden, *Gesta Henrici Secundi*, vol. ii, p. 132; *Itinerarium Ricardi Regis*, ed. W. Stubbs, Rolls Series (London, 1864), trans. H. Nicholson, *The Chronicle of the Third Crusade* (Aldershot, 1997), pp. 136–7.

20. R. Röhricht, ed., *Quinti Belli Sacri Scriptores Minores* (Geneva, 1879), *Gesta crucigerorum Rhenanorum*, pp. 29, 31–4, *De intinere Frisonum*, p. 59.

21. For Alcazar, *Gesta crucegerorum Rhenanorum*, in Röhricht, ed., *Quinti Belli Sacri Scriptores Minores*, pp. 31–4; Robert of Clari, *La Conquête de Constantinople*, trans. E. H. McNeal, *The Conquest of Constantinople* (New York, 1966), pp. 100–102; Raymond of Aguilers, *Historia Francorum, RHC Occ.*, vol. iii, p. 270 for discontent at stitch-up after the siege of Ma'arrat al-Numan.

22. Odo of Deuil, *De profectione*, pp. 20–21.

23. What follows relies on the research by Piers Mitchell, *Medicine in the Crusades* (Cambridge, 2004); cf. S. Edgington, 'Medical Knowledge of

the Crusading Armies', in *The Military Orders*, ed. M. Barber, vol. i (Aldershot, 1994), pp. 320–26.

24. Joinville, *Histoire de Saint Louis*, p.109, trans. Shaw, *Chronicles*, p. 241.

25. Albert of Aachen, *Historia Ierosolimitana*, ed. and trans. S. Edgington (Oxford, 2007), pp. 142–5; Mitchell, *Medicine*, pp. 149–50.

26. Mitchell, *Medicine*, pp. 26–7.

27. *Itinerarium Ricardi Regis*, p. 43, trans. Nicholson, *Chronicle*, p. 55.

28. H. E. Mayer, *The Crusades*, 2nd edn (Oxford, 1988), p. 142; *Continuation of William of Tyre*, trans. P. Edbury, *The Conquest of Jerusalem and the Third Crusade* (Aldershot, 1998), p. 90; Mitchell, *Medicine*, pp. 90–91.

29. Ralph of Diceto, *Ymagines, Opera*, vol. ii, pp. 80–81; Roger of Howden, *Gesta Henrici Secundi*, vol. ii, pp. 89–90, 116–18; A. Forey, 'The Military Order of St. Thomas of Acre', *English Historical Review*, 92 (1977), pp. 481–503; Joinville, *Histoire de Saint Louis*, trans. Shaw, *Chronicles*, pp. 196–7; James of Vitry, *Lettres*, ed. R. B. C. Huygens (Leiden, 1960), no. II, pp. 80–83.

30. *Itinerarium Ricardi Regis*, pp. 249–50, 272, trans. Nicholson, *Chronicle*, pp. 237, 255.

31. *Continuation of William of Tyre*, trans. Edbury, *Conquest of Jerusalem*, p. 90.

32. Mitchell, *Medicine*, pp. 143–5, 176–7.

33. Discussed by Mitchell, *Medicine*, pp. 185–6.

34. Albert of Aachen, *Historia*, pp. 664–7; Guibert of Nogent, *Gesta Dei per Francos*, *RHC Occ.*, vol. iv, p. 231; discussed by Mitchell, *Medicine*, pp. 159–63; and above pp. 14–15.

35. Bibliothèque nationale de France MS Latin 11015, fols. 32–41; cf. A. Leopold, *How to Recover the Holy Land* (Aldershot, 2000), pp. 42–3.

II. SUPPLIES

1. *The Bayeux Tapestry*, ed. F. Stenton (London, 1957), esp. scenes 37–42, 46–51; Napoleon's remark that 'an army marches on its stomach' has also been attributed to Frederick the Great of Prussia.

2. *Bayeux Tapestry*, scenes 37, 49, 50 and 68 for the militant Odo.

3. C. Tyerman, *God's War* (London, 2006), plate 10.

4. *Mappae Clavicula: A Little Key to the World of Medieval Techniques*, ed. C. S. Smith and J. G. Hawthorne, *Transactions of the American Philosophical Society*, 64 (1974), pt. 4, esp. pp. 68–9.

5. See above p. 15 and, for example, Theophilus, *De Diversis Artibus*, ed. C. R. Dodwell (Oxford, 1986), pp. ix–x, xix, xxxiii–xxxix, 20, 64–5, 71, 142–58.

6. R. Rogers, *Latin Siege Warfare in the Twelfth Century* (Oxford, 1984), pp. 3, 21–2, 238–43; J. Harvey, *The Medieval Architect* (London, 1972), pp. 87–100; for an international architects' competition for the rebuilding of Canterbury Cathedral in the 1170s, Gervase of Canterbury, *Historical Works*, ed. W. Stubbs (London, 1879–80), vol. i, p. 6.

7. For a discussion, Rogers, *Siege Warfare*, pp. 237–9; for Geoffrey and the crusading engineers, above pp. 15, 23–4; for Henry, Orderic Vitalis, *Ecclesiastical History*, ed. and trans. M. Chibnall (Oxford, 1969–80), vol. vi, pp. 340–43.

8. N. Tanner, *Decrees of the Ecumenical Councils* (Washington, DC, 1990), pp. 223, 267–71; see now S. Stantchev, *Spiritual Rationality: Papal Embargo as Cultural Practice* (Oxford, 2014), esp. pp. 17–89.

9. B. Bachrach, '*Caballus et caballarius* in Medieval Warfare', *Warfare and Military Organisation in pre-Crusade Europe* (Aldershot, 2002), ch. 12, p. 183.

10. F. Gabrieli, *Arab Historians of the Crusades* (London, 1984), pp. 204–6.

11. John of Joinville, *Histoire de Saint Louis*, ed. N. de Wailly (Paris, 1868), trans. M. R. B. Shaw, *Chronicles of the Crusades* (London, 1963), p. 197; W. Jordan, *Louis IX and the Challenge of Crusade* (Princeton, 1979), pp. 76–7; S. Lloyd, *English Society and Crusade 1216–1307* (Oxford, 1988), p. 140, n. 122 and refs.

12. Albert of Aachen, *Historia Ierosolimitana*, ed. and trans. S. Edgington (Oxford, 2007), pp. 220–23; Oliver of Paderborn, *Historia Damiatina*, trans. J. Bird, E. Peters and J. M. Powell, *Crusade and Christendom* (Philadelphia, 2013), p. 200.

13. On the latter, T. Madden, 'Food and the Fourth Crusade', in *Logistics of Warfare in the Age of the Crusades*, ed. J. H. Pryor (Aldershot, 2006), pp. 209–28.

14. J. H. Pryor, 'Modelling Bohemond's March to Thessalonica', in *Logistics of Warfare in the Age of the Crusades*, ed. J. H. Pryor (Aldershot, 2006), pp. 9–15 and refs.; R. W. Unger, 'The Northern Crusaders', in *Logistics of Warfare*, ed. Pryor, p. 262.

15. Tyerman, *God's War*, p. 251 and refs.

16. Pryor, 'Modelling Bohemond's March', pp. 15–20.

17. Above p. 136; Pryor, 'Modelling Bohemond's March', pp. 10–11 and nn. 24–7.

18. Madden, 'Food', pp. 211–19.

19. *Secreta Fidelium Crucis*, ed. J. Bongars, *Gesta Dei per Francos* (Hanau, 1611), vol. ii, pp. 60–64 (bk II, pt IV, ch. 10), trans. P. Lock (Farnham, 2011), pp. 108–13 (in general, bk II, pt IV).

20. Albert of Aachen, *Historia*, pp. 26–7 (cf. pp. 24–5 for the profusion of carts with Peter's army), 62–71.

21. Odo of Deuil, *De profectione Ludovici VII in Orientem*, ed. V. G. Berry (New York, 1948), pp. 24–5.

22. G. Loud, *The Crusade of Frederick Barbarossa* (Farnham, 2010), pp. 64–5.

23. Rigord, *Oeuvres*, ed. H. F. Delaborde (Paris, 1882–5), vol. i, pp. 99, 107.

24. Richard of Devizes, *Chronicle*, ed. J. T. Appleby (London, 1963), p. 15; cf. Roger of Howden alias 'Benedict of Peterborough', *Gesta Regis Henrici Secundi*, ed. W. Stubbs (London, 1867), vol. ii, p. 117; C. Tyerman, *England and the Crusades* (Chicago, 1988), pp. 67, 80–84.

25. *Pipe Rolls 2 Richard I*, pp. 1, 8–9, 53 104, 112, 131–2, 178; *3 Richard I*, p. 11.

26. The calculations are those of Bachrach, '*Caballus et caballarius*', pp. 198–9.

27. Roger of Howden, *Gesta Henrici Secundi*, vol. ii, p. 186.

28. For examples of the system on crusade, in these cases in Languedoc, and how it could come unstuck, *Querimoniae Normannorum 1247*, *RHF*, vol. xxiv, pp. 22, 23, 29, 38, nos. 157, 168, 230, 282.

29. In general, J. H. Pryor, 'Transportation of Horses by Sea During the Era of the Crusades', *The Mariner's Mirror*, 68 (1982), pp. 9–30, 103–25, 389–90; idem, 'The Naval Architecture of Crusader Transport Ships', *The Mariner's Mirror*, 70 (1984), pp. 171–219, 275–92, 363–86; cf. C. D. Stanton, *Norman Naval Operations in the Mediterranean* (Woodbridge, 2011); Unger, 'Northern Crusaders', pp. 253–73.

30. Fulcher of Chartres, *Historia Hierosolymitana*, *RHC Occ.*, vol. iii, p. 330, trans. F. R. Ryan and H. Fink, *A History of the Expedition to Jerusalem* (Knoxville, 1969), p. 76 for horses coming to grief crossing the Adriatic in 1097.

31. *De expugnatione Lyxbonensi*, ed. C. W. David (New York, 1976), passim; cf. M. Bennett, 'Military Aspects of the Conquest of Lisbon', in *The Second Crusade*, ed. J. Phillips and M. Hoch (Manchester, 2001), pp. 71–89.

32. Fulcher of Chartres, *Historia*, *RHC Occ.*, vol. iii, p. 384, trans. Ryan and Fink, *History*, p. 150.

33. Fulcher of Chartres, *Historia, RHC Occ.*, vol. iii, p. 449, trans. Ryan and Fink, *History*, p. 239.

34. Extrapolated from Bachrach, '*Caballus et caballarius*', p. 182 and various modern estimates accessed online; cf. Pryor, 'Modelling Bohemond's March', pp. 15–23 for horse feed.

35. *Pipe Roll 2 Richard I*, pp. 53, 131; Bachrach, '*Caballus et caballarius*', pp. 198–9; Loud, *Crusade of Frederick Barbarossa*, p. 19.

36. See trans. of 1190 Genoa deal, in M. Hall and J. Phillips, *Caffaro, Genoa and the Twelfth Century Crusades* (Farnham, 2013), pp. 218–20 and n. 150; for Venice treaty and Louis's contracts, above pp. 200–202.

37. See the discussions at the Second Council of Lyons in 1274, P. Throop, *Criticism of the Crusade* (Amsterdam, 1940), pp. 231–2; for prayers from the Lambrecht rite, see Bird et al., *Crusade and Christendom*, p. 45; the blessing, Joinville, *Histoire de Saint Louis*, trans. Shaw, *Chronicles*, p. 196.

38. Trans. J. H. Pryor, 'Ships', in *The Crusades: An Encyclopedia*, ed. A. V. Murray (Santa Barbara, 2006), p. 1102 and generally, pp. 1096–103.

39. Matthew Paris, *Chronica Majora*, ed. H. R. Luard (London, 1872–84), vol. v, p. 93; Pryor, 'Ships', p. 1102; cf. for crusade sea power, J. Prestwich, *The Place of War in English History 1066–1214* (Woodbridge, 2004), esp. pp. 33–40.

40. P. Jaffé, *Regesta pontificum Romananorum ad 1198* (Leipzig, 1885–8), no. 16373.

41. Unger, 'Northern Crusaders', p. 264 and n. 39.

42. Richard of Devizes, *Chronicle*, pp. 15, 28; Roger of Howden, *Gesta Henrici Secundi*, vol. ii, p. 112.

43. *Pipe Roll 2 Richard I*, pp. 8–9; J. H. Pryor, 'The Venetian Fleet for the Fourth Crusade', in *The Experience of Crusading*, vol. i, *Western Approaches*, eds. M. Bull and N. Housley (Cambridge, 2003), pp. 115–23.

44. Pryor, 'Venetian Fleet', pp. 102, 121–3; for the variety of vessels, see, as e.g., index to Nicholson's translation of the *Itinerarium Ricardi Regis* under 'ships': H. Nicholson, *The Chronicle of the Third Crusade* (Aldershot, 1997).

45. Robert of Clari, *La Conquête de Constantinople*, p. 43, trans. E. H. McNeal, *The Conquest of Constantinople* (New York, 1966), p. 68.

46. Discussed Pryor, 'Transportation of Horses', pp. 23–4.

47. Jordan, *Louis IX and the Challenge of Crusade*, pp. 70–71, 76; Pryor, 'Transportation of Horses', pp. 103–6; idem, 'Ships', p. 1101.

48. Joinville, *Histoire de Saint Louis*, trans. Shaw, *Chronicles*, pp. 164, 203–4.

49. Richard of Devizes, *Chronicle*, p. 15; J. H. Pryor, *Business Contracts of Medieval Provence. Selected Notulae from the Cartulary of Giraud Amalric of Marseilles 1248* (Toronto, 1981), pp. 194–6, *Notula* 72; Pryor, 'Ships', p. 1102.

50. B. Kedar, 'The Passenger List of a Crusader Ship', *Studi Medievali*, 13 (1972); Joinville implies 800 in the laudatory preface but over 500 in *Histoire de Saint Louis*, pp. 5, 224, trans. Shaw, *Chronicles*, pp. 165, 321; Pryor, 'Ships', p. 1102; Richard of Devizes, *Chronicle*, p. 15; Roger of Howden, *Gesta Henrici Secundi*, vol. ii, p. 117 (says 80 for London ship's company); cf. idem, *Chronica*, ed. W. Stubbs (London, 1868–71), vol. iii, p. 43 (amended to 100, perhaps by including the crew); Ralph of Diceto, *Ymagines Historiarum, Opera Historica*, ed. W. Stubbs (London, 1876), vol. ii, pp. 65–6.

51. Albert of Aachen, *Historia*, pp. 158–61 (*'in hoc navali collegio'* was a *'magister universorum consodalium'*).

52. Geoffrey of Villehardouin, *La Conquête de Constantinople*, ed. E. Faral (Paris, 1938–9), vol. ii, pp. 44–5, trans. M. R. B. Shaw, *Chronicles of the Crusades* (London, 1963), p. 90; Pryor, 'Venetian Fleet', pp. 116–17.

53. Pryor, *Business Contracts*, pp. 77–81; idem, 'Ships', p. 1102.

54. Villehardouin, *La Conquête*, vol. ii, pp. 44–5, trans. Shaw, *Chonicles*, p. 90; Robert of Clari, *La Conquête*, p. 44, trans. McNeal, *Conquest*, pp. 70–71; Oliver of Paderborn, *Historia Damiatina*, trans. Bird et al., pp. 169–70; Phillips, *Second Crusade*, p. 157.

55. *The Chronicle of Ibn al-Athir for the Crusading Period*, trans. D. S. Richards (Aldershot, 2007), vol. ii, p. 289.

56. *Itinerarium Ricardi Regis*, ed. W. Stubbs, Rolls Series (London, 1864), p. 313, trans. H. Nicholson, *The Chronicle of the Third Crusade* (Aldershot, 1997), p. 287.

57. Raymond of Aguilers, *Historia Francorum*, *RHC Occ.*, vol. iii, p. 298.

58. Unger, 'Northern Crusaders', p. 270.

59. *Itinerarium Ricardi Regis*, pp. 218–19, trans. Nicholson, *Chronicle*, pp. 208–9; above p. 253.

60. Albert of Aachen, *Historia*, pp. 112–13.

61. Rogers, *Siege Warfare*, pp. 25, 237–8; Tyerman, *God's War*, pp. 586, 595, 608.

62. *Itinerarium Ricardi Regis*, p. 209, trans. Nicholson, *Chronicle*, p. 199.

63. *Continuation of William of Tyre*, trans. P. Edbury, *The Conquest of Jerusalem and the Third Crusade* (London, 1996), p. 94.

64. *Itinerarium Ricardi Regis*, pp. 215, 352, trans. Nicholson, *Chronicle*, pp. 205, 316.
65. *Itinerarium Ricardi Regis*, pp. 218–19, trans. Nicholson, *Chronicle*, pp. 208–9; Villehardouin, *La Conquête*, vol. i, pp. 76–7, trans. Shaw, *Chronicles*, p. 46. For a trebuchet's throwing power, R. L. Toms, *Catapult Design* (San Antonio, 2006), pp. 27–30.
66. *Itinerarium Ricardi Regis*, pp. 168, 172–3, 214, trans. Nicholson, *Chronicle*, pp. 167, 171, 204; Wace, *Roman de Rou*, ed. H. Andresen (Heilbronn, 1877–9), ll. 6509 ff.

12. STRATEGY

1. Albert of Aachen, *Historia Ierosolimitana*, ed. and trans. S. Edgington (Oxford, 2007), pp. 158–61; Orderic Vitalis, *Ecclesiastical History*, ed. and trans. M. Chibnall (Oxford, 1969–80), vol. iii, pp. 134–6, vol. v, pp. 156–9; C. Tyerman, *God's War* (London, 2006), pp. 82–3.
2. As in Albert of Aachen, *Historia*, pp. 2–45 (pp. 4–5 for '*primus auctor*').
3. See P. Frankopan's suggestion in *The First Crusade: The Call from the East* (London, 2012), pp. 115–16.
4. *Gesta Francorum*, trans. R. Hill (London, 1962), p. 2.
5. Fulcher of Chartres, *Historia Hierosolymitana*, *RHC Occ.*, vol. iii, pp. 380–81, 475–6, trans. F. R. Ryan and H. Fink, *A History of the Expedition to Jerusalem* (Knoxville, 1969), pp. 41, 44 and refs., 145–6, 284–8; for pilgrims' accounts, J. Wilkinson, *Jerusalem Pilgrimage 1099–1185* (London, 1988); D. Pringle, *Pilgrimage to Jerusalem and the Holy Land 1187–1291* (Farnham, 2012).
6. Matthew Paris, 'Itinerary from London to Jerusalem (1250–9)', Pringle, *Pilgrimage*, p. 207; in general R. Allen, ed., *Eastward Bound: Travel and Travellers 1050–1550* (Manchester, 2004), esp. B. Hamilton, 'The Impact of the Crusades on Western Geographical Knowledge', pp. 15–34, although his acceptance of an early date for the information on the Atlantic in Adam of Bremen's chronicle (p. 15) should not necessarily be followed, as the passage is likely to be a twelfth-century interpolation. For an older view, J. K. Wright, *Geographical Lore of the Time of the Crusades*, 2nd edn (New York, 1965); P. D. A. Harvey, *Medieval Maps* (London, 1991); idem, *Medieval Maps of the Holy Land* (London, 2012); J. B. Harley et al., *The History of Cartography*, vol. i (Chicago, 1987).

7. Guy of Bazoches, *Liber Epistularum*, ed. H. Adolfsson (Stockholm, 1969), pp. 145–56.
8. P. Gautier Dalché, *Carte marine et portulan au xiie siècle* (Rome, 1995), esp. pp. xi, 6–7, 15–16, 20–21, 36–82, 183–203, 304–5; but cf. D. Jacoby, 'An Unpublished Portolan of the Mediterranean in Minneapolis', *Shipping, Trade and Crusade in the Medieval Mediterranean* (Farnham, 2013), esp. pp. 65, 71–2.
9. R. Röhricht, *Regesta regni hierosolymitani* (Innsbruck, 1893–1904), no. 1083; in general A. Leopold, *How to Recover the Holy Land* (Aldershot, 2000), pp. 8–51; cf. J. Riley-Smith's hyperbole in *The First Crusaders* (Cambridge, 1997), p. 143, 'the crusaders might almost have been on the moon for all their relations could tell'.
10. Leopold, *How to Recover the Holy Land*, passim, esp. re William Adam, Hetoum and Roger Stanegrave.
11. See esp. Fulcher of Chartres, *Historia*, *RHC Occ.*, vol. iii, pp. 329–39, trans. Ryan and Fink, *History*, pp. 74–8 and 79–92.
12. Odo of Deuil, *De profectione Ludovici VII in Orientem*, ed. V. G. Berry (New York, 1948), pp. 28–33, 88–9.
13. *De expugatione Lyxbonensi*, ed. C. W. David (New York, 1976), pp. 58–69, 86–93; cf. the so-called letter of Duodechin, *MGHS*, vol. xvii, pp. 27–8.
14. G. Loud, *The Crusade of Frederick Barbarossa* (Farnham, 2010), pp. 193–6; Roger of Howden alias 'Benedict of Peterborough', *Gesta Regis Henrici Secundi*, ed. W. Stubbs (London, 1867), vol. ii, pp. 112–26, 192–206; R. Röhricht, ed., *Quinti Belli Sacri Scriptores Minores* (Geneva, 1879), *Gesta crucigerorum Rhenanorum*, pp. 29–34, *De itinere Frisonum*, pp. 59–62.
15. Caffaro, *De liberatione civitatum Orientis*, ed. L. Belgrano, *Fonti per la storia d'Italia* (Rome, 1887–1993), vol. xi, pp. 114–16, trans. M. Hall and J. Phillips, *Caffaro, Genoa and the Twelfth Century Crusades* (Farnham, 2013), pp. 118–20; Gautier Dalché, *Carte marine*, pp. 62–3.
16. Roger of Howden, *Gesta Henrici Secundi*, vol. ii, p. 198.
17. P. Gautier Dalché, *De Yorkshire à l'Inde. Une 'Géographie' urbaine et maritime de la fin di xiie siècle (Roger de Howden?)* (Geneva, 2005), esp. pp. 24–30, 172 for *conductors*; cf. J. Gillingham, 'Roger of Howden on Crusade', in *Medieval Historical Writing*, ed. D. O. Morgan (London, 1983), pp. 60–75; idem, 'The Travels of Roger of Howden', *Anglo-Norman Studies*, 20 (1997), pp. 151–69.
18. Gautier Dalché, *Carte marine*, pp. 6, 63.

19. Harvey, *Medieval Maps of the Holy Land*, pp. 60–93, plates 35, 40–44; cf. L. Donkin and H. Vorholt, *Imagining Jerusalem in the Medieval West* (Oxford, 2012).

20. Harvey, *Medieval Maps of the Holy Land*, pp. 94–154, p. 99 for quotation; for Burchard's text, *Peregrinatores medii aevi quatuor*, ed. J. C. M. Laurent (Leipzig, 1893), pp. 19–94, trans. Pringle, *Pilgrimage*, pp. 241–320.

21. In general, R. J. Pujades i Bataller, *Les cartes portolanes* (Barcelona, 2007); E. Edson, 'Reviving the Crusade: Sanudo's Scheme and Vesconte's Maps', in *Eastward Bound*, ed. Allen, pp. 131–55, esp. p. 137; Harvey, *Medieval Maps of the Holy Land*, pp. 29–30, 112–13, plates 7, 20; cf. J. Prawer's introduction to the Jerusalem 1972 reprint of Bongars' edition of Sanudo's *Secreta*, plate p. XII; on the compass, Gautier Dalché, *Carte marine*, pp. 76–8.

22. B. Z. Kedar, 'Reflections on Maps, Crusading and Logistics', in *Logistics of Warfare in the Age of the Crusades*, ed. J. H. Pryor (Aldershot, 2006), pp. 159–83.

23. Guillaume de Nangis, *Gesta Sancti Ludovici*, *RHF*, vol. xx, pp. 444–5.

24. Sanudo, *Secreta Fidelium Crucis*, ed. J. Bongars, *Gesta Dei per Francos* (Hanau, 1611), vol. ii, pp. 5, trans. P. Lock (Farnham, 2011), p. 25; Harvey, *Medieval Maps of the Holy Land*, p. 107, n. 1 and 107–27.

25. Sanudo, *Secreta*, bk III, pt. 14, ch. 3, ed. Bongars, *Gesta Dei per Francos*, vol. ii, pp. 246–9, trans. Lock, pp. 392–8; for plate, see Prawer's edn of *Secreta*, plate IX, and above, plate 29.

26. Bongars, *Gesta Dei per Francos*, vol. ii, p. 296; C. Tyerman, 'Court, Crusade and City: The Cultural Milieu of Louis I Duke of Bourbon', *Practices of Crusading: Image and Action from the Eleventh to the Sixteenth Centuries* (Farnham, 2013), no. IV, p. 59, n. 52; F. Kunstmann, 'Studien über Marin Sanudo', *Königliche Bayerische Akademie der Wissenschaften. Abhanglungen Phil- Historische Classe*, 7 (1855), p. 794.

27. E. Edson, 'Jerusalem under Siege: Marino Sanudo's Map of the Water Supply, 1320', in Donkin and Vorholt, *Imagining Jerusalem*, esp. pp. 211–17; Harvey, *Medieval Maps of the Holy Land*, pp. 107–27; for Acre and Jerusalem maps, Prawer, *Secreta*, pls. X and XI.

28. P. Throop, *Criticism of the Crusade* (Amsterdam, 1940), p. 232; on discussions after 1274, S. Schein, *Fideles Crucis* (Oxford, 1991); Leopold, *How to Recover the Holy Land*; for the 1274 crusade bull *Zelus fidei*, trans. J. Bird, E. Peters and J. M. Powell, *Crusade and Christendom* (Philadelphia, 2013), pp. 466–73.

29. For an overview, Tyerman, *God's War*, pp. 45–51, 54–7, 66–71; cf. a different view of papal strategy, P. Chevedden, 'The Islamic View and the Christian View of the Crusades', *History*, 93 (2008), pp. 181–200; idem, 'The View of the Crusades from Rome and Damascus', *Oriens* 39/2 (2011), pp. 257–329.

30. E. de Rozière, *Cartulaire de l'église du saint Sépulchre de Jérusalem* (Paris, 1849), p. 8 no. 9; I am grateful to Dr Kevin Lewis for discussion of this document.

31. *Gesta Francorum*, pp. 20–21, 73; Fulcher of Chartres, *Historia*, *RHC Occ.*, vol. iii, p. 468, trans. Ryan and Fink, *History*, p. 271; B. Z. Kedar, *Crusade and Mission* (Princeton, 1984), esp. pp. 57–74, 108.

32. Odo of Deuil, *De profectione*, pp. 70–71; J. Tolan, *Saracens: Islam in the Medieval Imagination* (New York, 2002).

33. Kedar, *Crusade and Mission*, esp. chs. 3–5.

34. J. Bédier, *Les chansons de croisade* (Paris, 1909), pp. 8–11.

35. Above p. 35.

36. J. Muldoon, *Popes, Lawyers and Infidels* (Liverpool, 1979).

37. Albert of Aachen, *Historia*, pp. 594–7, but see n. 28.

38. M. A. Köhler, *Allianzen und Verträge zwischen frankischen und islamischen Herrschern im Vorderren Orient* (Berlin, 1991), pp. 1–72; C. Hillenbrand, *The Crusades: Islamic Perspectives* (Edinburgh, 1999), pp. 44–7; J. France, *Victory in the East* (Cambridge, 1994), pp. 165–6, 211, 252–4, 302, 304, 317, 325–6, 334, 358, 368.

39. Urban II's letter to the Flemish, trans. E. Peters, *The First Crusade* (Philadelphia, 1998), p. 42; Raymond of Aguilers, *Historia Francorum*, *RHC Occ.*, vol. iii. pp. 301, 302; de Rozière, *Cartulaire de l'église du saint Sépulchre*, p. 8, no. 9; J. Shepherd, 'When Greek meets Greek: Alexius Comnenus and Bohemund in 1097–8', *Byzantine and Modern Greek Studies*, 12 (1988), pp. 185–277. Cf. a sceptical view of co-ordinated planning, J. H. Pryor, 'A View From a Masthead: The First Crusade at Sea', *Crusades*, 7 (2008), esp. pp. 125–43.

40. For considered views on Outremer strategy, M. Barber, *The Crusader States* (New Haven and London, 2012).

41. This is the argument pursued in Tyerman, *God's War*; cf. J. Harris, *Byzantium and the Crusades* (London, 2003); M. Angold, *The Fourth Crusade* (London, 2003), pp. 3–108.

42. *God's War*, pp. 488–96, 736–55, 761–3.

43. Raymond of Aguilers, *Historia Francorum*, *RHC Occ.*, vol. iii, p. 292, trans. J. H. Hill and L. L. Hill (Philadelphia, 1968), p. 115.

44. William of Tyre, *Historia*, bk 21, ch. 7, trans. E. A. Babcock and A. C. Krey, *A History of Deeds Done Beyond the Sea* (New York, 1976), p. 408; P. Edbury, *The Conquest of Jerusalem and the Third Crusade* (London, 1996), pp. 3–7.

45. Richard I to the Genoese, trans. Edbury, *Conquest of Jerusalem*, pp. 181–2; for Richard's strategy in Palestine, Tyerman, *God's War*, pp. 448–74; cf. J. Gillingham, *Richard I* (New Haven and London, 1999), pp. 172–221.

46. Guillaume de Nangis, *Gesta Sancti Ludovici, RHF*, vol. xx, pp. 446–9.

47. Pierre Dubois, *The Recovery of the Holy Land*, trans. W. I. Brandt (New York, 1956); Sanudo, *Secreta*, above note 24.

48. Matthew Paris, *Chronica Majora*, ed. H. R. Luard (London, 1872–84), vol. v, p. 107, vol. vi, p. 163; Tyerman, *God's War*, pp. 799–802, cf. pp. 638–41, 739–55, 770–71.

49. Dubois, *Recovery*, pp. 124, 138–9.

50. Sanudo, *Secreta*, bks I and II; Leopold, *How to Recover the Holy Land*, chs. 2 and 4; S. Stantchev, *Spiritual Rationality: Papal Embargo as Cultural Practice* (Oxford, 2014); S. Menache, 'Papal Attempts at a Commercial Boycott of the Muslims in the Crusader Period', *Journal of Ecclesiastical History*, 63 (2012), pp. 236–59.

51. John of Joinville, *Histoire de Saint Louis*, ed. N. de Wailly (Paris, 1868), trans. M. R. B. Shaw, *Chronicles of the Crusades* (London, 1963), pp. 197–8; P. Jackson, *The Mongols and the West* (Harlow, 2005), pp. 1–195 for the best accessible recent account; Tyerman, *God's War*, esp. pp. 784–6.

52. Jackson, *Mongols and West*, p. 104.

53. Sanudo, *Secreta*, ed. Bongars, *Gesta Dei per Francos*, vol. ii, p. 36, trans. Lock, pp. 71–2; cf. in general, Leopold, *How to Recover the Holy Land*, esp. pp. 111–19.

54. Leopold, *How to Rercover the Holy Land*, p. 118; for Hetoum's gazetteer of Asia and Mongol history, *La Flor des estoires de la terre d'Orient, RHC Documents Arméniens* (Paris, 1869–1906), vol. ii, pp. 113–219, and pp. 521–55 for William Adam's similarly well-informed *De Modo Saraceni Extirpandi*.

Bibliography

ABBREVIATIONS

MGH   Monumenta Germaniae Historica
MGHS   *Monumenta Germaniae Historica Scriptores*, ed. G. H. Pertz
           et al. (Hanover and Leipzig, 1826–)
RHC   *Recueil des historiens des croisades*
RHC Occ.   *Recueil des historiens des croisades. Historiens Occidentaux*
           (Paris, 1844–95)
RHF   *Recueil des historiens des Gaules et de la France*, ed. M. Bou-
           quet et al. (Paris, 1738–1876)

PRIMARY SOURCES

Abelard, Peter, *Sic et Non: A Critical Edition*, ed. B. B. Bryer and R. McKeon
  (Chicago, 1976–7)
Actes des comtes de Namur 946–1196, ed. F. Rousseau (Brussels, 1936)
Adam, William, *De modo Saraceni extirpandi, RHC Documents Arméniens*
  (Paris, 1869–1906), vol. ii
Alan of Lille, *Sermo de cruce domini, Textes inédits*, ed. M. T. Alverny (Paris,
  1965)
Albert of Aachen, *Historia Ierosolimitana*, ed. and trans. S. Edgington
  (Oxford, 2007)
Albert von Beham und Regesten Innocenz IV, ed. C. Hofler (Stuttgart, 1847)
Ambroise, *Estoire de la guerre sainte*, ed. G. Paris (Paris, 1877), trans. M. J.
  Hubert, *The Crusade of Richard Lionheart* (New York, 1941, 1976)
Analecta Novissima, ed. J. B. Pitra (Paris, 1885–8)
Anna Komnene, *The Alexiad*, trans. E. R. A. Sewter and P. Frankopan (Lon-
  don, 2003)
Annales Paulini, Chronicles of the Reigns of Edward I and II, ed. W. Stubbs
  (London, 1882–3)

Anselm, *Prayers and Meditations with the Proslogion*, trans. B. Ward (London, 1973)

Arab Historians of the Crusades, ed. F. Gabrieli (London, 1984)

Archives de l'Hôtel Dieu de Paris, ed. L. Briele (Paris, 1894)

Arnold of Lübeck, *Chronica Slavorum*, ed. J. M. Lappenberg (Hanover, 1868)

Baha al-Din Ibn Shaddad, *The Rare and Excellent History of Saladin*, trans. D. S. Richards (Aldershot, 2001)

Baldric of Bourgueil, *Historia Jerosolimitana*, RHC Occ., vol. iv

Baldwin of Forde, *De commendatione fidei, Opera*, ed. D. H. Bell (Turnhout, 1991)

Bayeux Tapestry, ed. F. M. Stenton (London, 1957)

Benedict of Peterborough (Roger of Howden), *Gesta Regis Henrici Secundi*, ed. W. Stubbs (London, 1867)

Benzonis Episcopi Albanesis ad Henricum IV Imperatorem Libri VII, ed. K. Pertz, *MGHS*, vol. xi

Bernard of Clairvaux, *Opera*, vol. viii, *Epistolae*, ed. J. Leclerq and H. Rochais (Rome, 1977)

— *Letters*, trans. B. S. James (London, 1953, 1998)

— *De laude novae militiae*, trans. M. Barber and K. Bate, *The Templars* (Manchester, 2002)

Bernold of St Blasien, *Chronicon, MGHS*, vol. v

Bonizo of Sutri, *Liber de Vita Christiana*, ed. E. Perels (Berlin, 1950)

Book of the Foundation of Walden Monastery, eds. D. Greenway and L. Watkiss (Oxford, 1999)

Burchard of Mount Sion, *Descriptio Terrae Sanctae*, ed. J. C. M. Laurent, *Peregrinationes medii aevi quatuor* (Leipzig, 1893), trans., *Pilgrimage to Jerusalem*, ed. Pringle

Caesarius of Heisterbach, *Dialogus Miraculorum*, ed. J. Strange (Cologne, 1851)

Caffaro, *De liberatione civitatum orientis*, RHC Occ., vol. v and ed. L. Belgrano, *Fonti per la storia d'Italia* (Rome, 1887–1993), vol. xii, trans. Hall and Phillips, *Caffaro*

Caffaro, Genoa and the Twelfth Century Crusades, ed. M. Hall and J. Phillips (Farnham, 2013)

Calendar of Close Rolls

Calendar of Papal Registers, ed. W. T. Bliss et al. (London, 1893–1960)

Calendar of Patent Rolls

Canso d'Antioca, ed. and trans. C. Sweetenham and L. M. Paterson (Aldershot, 2007)

Cartulaire générale de l'Yonne, ed. M. Quantin (Auxerre, 1854–60)

Cartulaire de l'église de Saint Sépulchre de Jérusalem, ed. E. de Rozière (Paris, 1849)

Cartulaire de Montier-le-Celle, ed. C. Lalone (Paris-Troyes, 1882)

Cartulaires de l'abbaye de Moslesme 916–1250, ed. J. Laurent (Paris, 1907–11)

Cartulary of Oseney Abbey, ed. H. E. Salter, *Oxford Historical Society*, 89 (1929)

Cartulary of St Frideswide's, Oxford, ed. S. R. Wigram, *Oxford Historical Society*, 28 and 31 (1894, 1896)

Cartulary of the Hospital of St John the Baptist, ed. H. E. Salter, *Oxford Historical Society*, 68 (1915)

Chanson d'Antioche, ed. S. Duparc-Quioc (Paris, 1977)

Chanson de la croisade albigeoise, ed. E. Martin-Chabot (Paris, 1931–61)

Chanson de Roland, ed. J. Dufornet (Paris, 1973)

Chansons de croisade, ed. J. Bédier and P. Aubry (Paris, 1909)

Chartes et documents pour server à l'histoire de l'abbaye de Saint-Maixent, ed. A. Richard, *Archives historiques de Poitou*, 16 (Poitiers, 1886)

Chronica Monasterii de Melsa, ed. E. A. Bond (London, 1866–8)

Chronica regia Coloniensis, ed. G. Waitz, *MGHS*, vol. xviii

Chronicon S. Andreae in Castro Cameracesii, ed. L. C. Bethmann (Hanover, 1846)

Chroniques des comtes d'Anjou et des seigneurs d'Amboise, ed. L. Halphen et al. (Paris, 1913)

Clement V, *Regestum* (Rome, 1885–92)

Codice diplomatic della republica de Genova, ed. C. Imperiale de Saint'Angelo (Genoa, 1936–42)

Conquest of Jerusalem and the Third Crusade, The, trans. P. Edbury (Aldershot, 1998)

Constitutio Domus Regis, ed. Johnson, *Dialogus de Scaccario*

Constitutiones Concilii quarti Lateranensis una cum Commentariis glossatorum, ed. A. Garcià y Garcià (Vatican City, 1981)

Contemporary Sources for the Fourth Crusade, trans. A. J. Andrea (Leiden, 2000)

Councils and Synods with Other Documents Relating to the English Church, ed. F. M. Powicke et al., vol. i (Oxford, 1961)

Crusade Charters, ed. C. Slack (Tempe, 2001)

Crusade and Christendom, ed. and trans. J. Bird, E. Peters and J. M. Powell (Philadelphia, 2013)

Crusade of Frederick Barbarossa, The, ed. and trans. G. Loud (Farnham, 2010)

Crusades, Idea and Reality, The, ed. and trans. J. Riley-Smith and L. Riley-Smith (London, 1981)

Curia Regis Rolls

Decrees of the Ecumenical Councils, trans. N. P. Tanner (London and Washington, DC, 1990)

De expugnatione Lyxbonensi, ed. and trans. C. W. David (New York, 1976)

De itinere Frisonum, Quinti Belli Sacri Scriptores Minores, ed. Röhricht

De profectione Danorum in Hierosolymam, ed. M. C. Gertz, *Scriptores Minores Historiae Danicae* (Copenhagen, 1970)

Dialogus de Scaccario, see under Richard FitzNeal

Directorium, RHC Documents Arméniens (Paris, 1869–1906), vol. ii

'Documents relatives à l'histoire de Philippe le Bel', ed. E. Boutaric, *Notices et Extraits,* 20 (1865)

Domesday Book, trans. A. Williams and G. H. Martin (London, 1992)

Dubois, Pierre, *The Recovery of the Holy Land,* ed. W. I. Brandt (New York, 1956)

Eadmer, *Historia novorum,* ed. M. Rule (London, 1884)

Ekkehard of Aura, *Hierosolymita, RHC Occ.,* vol. v

English Historical Documents, vol. ii, ed. D. C. Douglas (London, 1953)

English Lawsuits from William I to Richard I, ed. R. C. van Caenegem (London, 1990–91)

Episcopal Acts and Cognate Documents Relating to Welsh Dioceses 1066–1272, ed. J. Conway Davies (Cardiff, 1946)

Epistolae Cantuariensis, ed. W. Stubbs, *Chronicles and Memorials of Richard I,* vol. ii (London, 1865)

Epistolae selectae saeculi XIII, ed. C. Rodenberg (Berlin, 1883–94)

Eudes of Rouen, *Register,* ed. S. Brown and J. O'Sullivan (New York and London, 1964)

Exuviae Sacrae Constantinopolitanae, ed. P. Riant (Geneva, 1876–7)

First Crusade, The, ed. E. Peters (Philadelphia, 1998)

Fiscal Accounts of Catalonia under the Early Count-Kings (1151–1213), ed. T. N. Bisson (Berkeley, 1984)

Foedera, ed. T. Rymer, 3rd edn (London, 1745)

Fulcher of Chartres, *Historia Hierosolymitana, RHC Occ.,* vol. iii, ed. H. Hagenmeyer (Heidelberg, 1913), trans. F. R. Ryan and H. Fink, *A History of the Expedition to Jerusalem* (Knoxville, 1969)

Fulk le Réchin, *Fragmentum historiae Andegavensis, Chroniques des comtes d'Anjou*

Galbert of Bruges, *Histoire du meutre de Charles le Bon, comte de Flandre*, ed. H. Pirenne (Paris, 1891), trans. J. Ross, *The Murder of Charles the Good of Flanders* (New York, 1967)

Geffrei Gaimar, *Estoire des Engleis*, ed. and trans. I. Short (Oxford, 2009)

Geoffrey of Auxerre, *S. Bernardi Vita Prima, Patrologia Latina*, ed. Migne, vol. clxxxv

Geoffrey of Villehardouin, *La Conquête de Constantinople*, ed. E. Faral (Paris, 1938–9), trans. M. R. B. Shaw, *The Conquest of Constantinople, Chronicles of the Crusades* (London, 1963)

Gerald of Wales, *Opera Omnia*, ed. J. Brewer et al. (London, 1861–91)

— *Autobiography of Giraldus Cambrensis*, trans. H. E. Butler (London, 1937)

— *Journey Through Wales*, trans. L. Thorpe (London, 1978)

Gervase of Canterbury, *Opera historica*, ed. W. Stubbs (London, 1879–80)

Gesta crucigerorum Rhenanorum, Quinti Belli Sacri Scriptores Minores, ed. Röhricht

Gesta Francorum, ed. and trans. R. Hill (London, 1962)

Gesta Normannorum Ducum, ed. E. M. C. Van Houts (Oxford, 1992–5)

Gilbert of Mons, *Chronicle of Hainault*, trans. L. Naplan (Woodbridge, 2005)

Gratian of Bologna, *Decretum*, ed. A. Frieberg, *Corpus Iuris Canonici*, vol. i (Leipzig, 1879)

Great Rolls of the Pipe (Pipe Roll Society, London, 1884–)

Gregory VII, *Register*, trans. H. E. J. Cowdrey (Oxford, 2002)

Gregory IX, *Registres*, ed. L. Auvray et al. (Paris, 1890–1955)

Guibert of Nogent, *Gesta Dei per Francos, RHC Occ.*, vol. iv

— *Monodies and On the Relics of Saints*, trans. J. McAlhany and J. Rubinstein (London, 2011)

Guillaume de Nangis, *Gesta Sancti Ludovici, RHF*, vol. xx

Gunther of Pairis, *Historia Constantinopolitana*, ed. P. Riant, *Exuviae Sacrae Constantinopolitanae*, vol. i (Geneva, 1877), trans. A. J. Andrea (Philadelphia, 1997)

Guy of Bazoches, *Liber Epistolarum*, ed. H. Adolfsson (Stockholm, 1969)

Hayton (or Hethoum/Hetoum), *La Flor des estoires de la Terre Sainte, RHC Documents Arméniens* (Paris, 1869–1906), vol. ii

Henry of Huntingdon, *Historia Anglorum*, ed. D. Greenway (Oxford, 1996)

Henry of Livonia, *Chronicle*, trans. J. A. Brundage (New York, 2003)

Henry of Marcy, cardinal bishop of Albano, *De peregrinante, Patrologia Latina*, ed. Migne, vol. cciv

Histoire générale de Languedoc, ed. C. de Vic and J. Vaisete (Toulouse, 1872–1905)

Historia de Expeditione Friderici, Quellen, ed. Chroust

Historia peregrinorum, Quellen, ed. Chroust

Historical Papers and Letters from the Northern Registers, ed. J. Raine (London, 1873)

History of William Marshal, ed. A. J. Holden (London, 2001–6)

Humbert of Romans, *Treatise on Preaching*, trans. W. M. Conlon (London, 1955)

Ibn al-Athir, *Chronicle for the Crusading Period*, trans. D. Richards (Aldershot, 2007)

Innocent III, *Die Register*, ed. O. Hageneder et al. (Cologne, Rome and Vatican City, 1964–)

— *Epistolae, Patrologia Latina*, ed. Migne, vol. ccxvi

Innocent IV, *Registres*, ed. E. Berger et al. (Paris, 1884–1921)

Isidore of Seville, *Etymologia*, ed. W. M. Lindsay (Oxford, 1911)

Itinerarium Ricardi Regis, ed. W. Stubbs (London, 1864), trans. H. Nicholson, *The Chronicle of the Third Crusade* (Aldershot, 1997)

James of Vitry, *Lettres*, ed. R. B. C. Huygens (Leiden, 1960)

— *Historia Occidentalis*, ed. J. F. Hinnebusch (Freiburg, 1972)

— *Exempla. Sermones Vulgares*, ed. T. F. Crane (London, 1890)

— *Die Exempla*, ed. G. Frenken (Munich, 1914)

Jerusalem Pilgrimage 1099–1185, ed. J. Wilkinson (London, 1988)

Jews and the Crusaders, Hebrew Chronicles of the First and Second Crusades, The, ed. and trans. S. Eidelberg (Madison, 1977)

Jocelin of Brakelond, *Chronicle*, ed. and trans. H. E. Butler (London, 1949)

John of Joinville, *Histoire de Saint Louis*, ed. N. Wailly (Paris, 1874), trans. M. R. B. Shaw, *Chronicles of the Crusades* (London, 1963)

John of Marmoutier, *Historia Gaufredi, Chroniques des comtes d'Anjou*

John of Salisbury, *Historia Pontificalis*, ed. M. Chibnall (London, 1962)

— *Policraticus*, ed. C. C. I. Webb (Oxford, 1909)

John of Tubia (Tolve), *De Iohanne Rege Ierusalem, Quinti Belli Sacri Scriptores Minores*, ed. Röhricht

Kreuzzugsbriefe aus den Jahren 1088–1100, Die, ed. H. Hagenmeyer (Innsbruck, 1901)

Landulph of St Paul, *Liber Hystoriarum Mediolanensis Urbis*, ed. C. Castiglioni (Bologna, 1935)

Layettes du Trésor des Chartes, vol. iii, ed. J. Delaborde (Paris, 1875)

Liber Eliensis, ed. E. O. Blake (London, 1962)

Lost Letters of Medieval Life, ed. and trans. M. Carlin and D. Crouch (Philadelphia, 2013)

Mappae Clavicula: A Little Key to the World of Medieval Techniques, ed. C. S. Smith and J. G. Hawthorne, *Transactions of the American Philosophical Society*, 64 (1974)

Matthew Paris, *Chronica Majora*, ed. H. R. Luard (London, 1872–84)

— *Historia Anglorum*, ed. F. Madden (London, 1886–9)

Monitum Willelmi Grassegals militis ad historias belli sacri, RHC Occ., vol. iii

Narratio de itinere navali peregrinorum, Quellen, ed. Chroust

Odo of Deuil, *De profectione Ludovici VII in orientem*, ed. V. G. Berry (New York, 1948)

Oliver of Paderborn, *Schriften*, ed. H. Hoogeweg (Tübingen, 1894)

— *The Capture of Damietta*, trans. E. Peters, *Christian Society and the Crusades 1198–1221* (Philadelphia, 1971)

Orderic Vitalis, *Historia Ecclesiastica*, ed. and trans. M. Chibnall (Oxford, 1969–80)

Ordinatio de predicatione S. Crucis in Angliae, Quinti Belli Sacri Scriptores Minores, ed. Röhricht

Otto of Freising, *The Deeds of Frederick Barbarossa*, trans. C. C. Mierow (New York, 1966)

Otto of St Blasien, *Chronica*, ed. H. Hofmeister (Hanover, 1912)

Pacta Naulorum, ed. A. Jal, *Collection de documents inédits sur l'histoire de France*, ed. A. Champollion-Figeac (Paris, 1841–8), vol. i

Patrologia Latina, ed. J. P. Migne (Paris, 1841–65)

Peter of Blois, *Opera, Patrologia Latina*, ed. Migne, vol. ccvii

Peter of Les Vaux-de-Cernay, *Historia Albigensis*, ed. P. Guébin and E. Lyon (Paris, 1926–39), trans. *The History of the Albigensian Crusade* by W. A. Sibly and M. D. Sibly (Woodbridge, 1998)

Peter Tudebode, *Historia de Hierosolymitana Itinere, RHC Occ.*, vol. iv

Peter the Venerable, *Letters*, ed. G. Constable (Cambridge, Mass., 1967)

Pilgrimage to Jerusalem and the Holy Land 1187–1291, ed. D. Pringle (Farnham, 2012)

Pleas before the King or his Justices 1198–1202, ed. D. M. Stenton (London, 1948–9)

Political Songs of England, ed. T. Wright (London, 1839)

Querimonium Normannorum, RHF, vol. xxiv

Quellen zur Geschichte des Kruzzuges Kaiser Freidrichs I, MGH, ed. A Chroust (Berlin, 1928)

Quinti Belli Sacri Scriptores Minores, ed. R. Röhricht, *Société de l'Orient Latin*, vol. ii (Geneva, 1879)

Ralph of Caen, *Gesta Tancredi, RHC Occ.*, vol. iii, trans. B. Bachrach and D. S. Bachrach, *The Gesta Tancredi of Ralph of Caen* (Aldershot, 2005)

Ralph of Diceto, *Opera Historica*, ed. W. Stubbs (London, 1876)

Ralph Glaber, *Opera*, ed. J. France et al. (Oxford, 1989)

Ralph Niger, *De Re Militari et Triplici Via Peregrinationis*, ed. L. Schmugge (Berlin, 1977)

— *Chronica*, ed. H. Krause (Frankfurt, 1985)

Ramon Muntaner, *Crònica*, ed. F. Soldevila (Barcelona, 2011)

Raymond of Aguilers, *Historia Francorum qui ceperunt Iherusalem, RHC Occ.*, vol. iii, trans. J. H. Hill and L. L. Hill (Philadelphia, 1968)

Recueil des actes de Philippe Auguste, ed. H.-F. Delaborde et al. (Paris, 1916–79)

Recueil des chartes de l'abbaye de Saint-Benoît-sur-Loire, ed. M. Prou et al. (Paris, 1900–1907)

Regesta Chartarum Pistoriensium. Canonica di S. Zenone Secolo XI, ed. N. Rauty, *Fonti Storiche Pistoiesi*, 7 (Pistoia, 1985)

Regesta pontificum Romanorum ad 1198 (Leipzig, 1885–8)

Regesta regni hierosolymitani, ed. R. Röhricht (Innsbruck, 1893–1904)

Regesten des Kaiserreiches unter Heinrich VI, ed. G. Baaken (Cologne, Vienna, 1972)

Register of Archbishop J. Le Romeyn, ed. W. Brown (Durham, 1913–16)

Register of Bishop John de Pontissara of Winchester, Surrey Record Society (London, 1913–24)

Register of St Benet Holme, ed. J. R. West, Norfolk Record Society (Norwich, 1932)

Registri dei Cardinale Ugolino d'Ostia e Ottaviano degli Ubaldini, ed. G. Levi (Rome, 1890)

Richard of Devizes, *Chronicle*, ed. J. T. Appleby (London, 1963)

Richard FitzNeal, *Dialogus de Scaccario: The Dialogue of the Exchequer*, ed. C. Johnson (London, 1950)

Richard of San Germano, *Chronica*, ed. G. H. Pertz (Hanover, 1866)

Robert of Clari, *La Conquête de Constantinople*, ed. P. Lauer (Paris, 1924), trans. E. H. McNeal, *The Conquest of Constantinople* (New York, 1966)

Robert of Rheims, *Historia Iherosolimitana, RHC Occ.*, vol. iii, trans. C. Sweetenham, *Robert the Monk's History of the First Crusade* (Farnham, 2006)

— *Historia Iherosolimitana*, ed. D. Kempf and M. G. Bull (Woodbridge, 2013)

Roger of Howden, *Chronica*, ed. W. Stubbs (London, 1868–71)

— *Gesta Regis Henrici Secundi*, see above under 'Benedict of Peterborough'

Roger of Wendover, *Flores historiarum*, ed. H. G. Hewlett (London, 1886–9)

Royal Commission on Historical Manuscripts, *Report on Various Collections*, vol. i (1901)

— *Fifth Report*, Appendix (London, 1972)

Rutebeuf, *La desputizons dou croisié et dou descroisié: Onze poems concernant la croisade*, ed. J. Bastin and E. Faral (Paris, 1946)

Sanudo, Marino Torsello, *Liber Secretorum Fidelium Crucis*, ed. J. Bongars, *Gesta Dei per Francos* (Hanau, 1611, reprint ed. J. Prawer, Jerusalem, 1972), trans. P. Lock (Farnham, 2011)

Select Charters, ed. W. Stubbs, 9th edn ed. H. W. C. Davies (Oxford, 1921)

Seventh Crusade 1244–54, The, ed. P. Jackson (Aldershot, 2007)

Sigebert of Gembloux, *Chronica, MGHS*, vol. vi

Stephen of Bourbon, *Anecdotes historiques et apologues d'Etienne de Bourbon*, ed. A. Lecoy de la Marche (Paris, 1877)

Stephen of Rouen, *Draco Normannicus*, ed. R. Howlett, *Chronicles of the Reigns of Stephen, Henry II and Richard I*, vol. ii (London, 1885)

Suger, *Vie de Louis VI le Gros*, ed. H. Waquet (Paris, 1964)

— *Oeuvres*, ed. F. Gaspari (Paris, 1996–2001)

Table chronologiques des chartes et diplômes imprimés concernant l'histoire de la Belgique, ed. A. Wauters (Brussels, 1866–1971)

Theophilus, *De Diversis Artibus*, ed. and trans. C. R. Dodwell (Oxford, 1986)

Thomas of Chobham, *Summa de Arte Praedicandi*, ed. F. Mornezoni (Turnholt, 1988)

Thomas of Split, *Historia pontificum Spalatensis*, ed. L. von Heinemann, *MGHS*, vol. xxix

Titres de la maison ducale de Bourbon, ed. A. Huillard-Bréholles (Paris, 1867–74)

Traditionem des Klosters Tegernsee 1003–1242, ed. P. Acht (Munich, 1952)

Urban IV, *Registres*, ed. J. Guiraud (Paris, 1899–1958)

Urkunden Konrads III, ed. F. Hausmann (Vienna, 1969)

Urkunden zur alteren Handels- und Staatsgeschichte der Republik Venedig, ed. G. L. Tafel and G. M. Thomas (Vienna, 1856–7)

Vita Altmanni episcopi Pataviensis, MGHS, vol. xii

Wace, *Roman de Rou*, ed. A. J. Holden (Paris, 1970–73), trans. G. Burgess, *History of the Norman People* (Woodbridge, 2004)

Walter Map, *De Nugis Curialium*, ed. and trans. M. R. James et al. (Oxford, 1983)

Westminster Chronicle, The, ed. L. C. Hector and B. F. Harvey (Oxford, 1982)

William of Malmesbury, *De gestis regum Anglorum*, ed. W. Stubbs (London, 1887–9)

William of Newburgh, *Historia rerum Anglicarum*, ed. R. Howlett (London, 1884–5)

William of Poitiers, *Gesta Guillelmi*, eds. R. H. C. Davies and M. Chibnall (Oxford, 1998)

William of Puylaurens, *Chronicle*, trans. W. A. Sibly and M. D. Sibly (Woodbridge, 2003)

William Rishanger, *Chronica*, ed. H. T. Riley (London, 1865)

William of Tyre, *Historia*, ed. R. B. C. Huygens (Turnhout, 1986); trans. in E. Babcock and A. Krey, *A History of Deeds done beyond the Sea* (New York, repr. 1976)

SECONDARY SOURCES

Abulafia, A., *Christians and Jews in the Twelfth Century Renaissance* (London, 1995)

— *Christians and Jews in Dispute 1000–1150* (Aldershot, 1998)

Abulafia, D., *Frederick II* (London, 1988)

Aird, W. M., *Robert Curthose* (Woodbridge, 2004)

Allen, R., ed., *Eastward Bound: Travel and Travellers 1050–1550* (Manchester, 2004)

Alphandéry, P., *La chrétienté et l'idée de croisade*, ed. A. Dupront (Paris, 1954–9)

Andressohn, J. C., *The Ancestry and Life of Godfrey de Bouillon* (Bloomington, 1947)

Angold, M., *The Fourth Crusade* (Harlow, 2003)

Arnold, B., *German Knighthood 1050–1300* (Oxford, 1985)

Aurell, M., *Le chevalier lettré* (Paris, 2011)

— *Des chrétiens contre les croisades* (Paris, 2013)

Bachrach, B, 'Caballus et caballarius in Medieval Warfare', *Warfare and Military Organisation in Pre-Crusade Europe* (Aldershot, 2002)

Baldwin, J. M., *The Government of Philip Augustus* (Berkeley and Los Angeles, 1986)

Baldwin, J. W., *Masters, Princes and Merchants: The Social Views of Peter the Chanter and His Circle* (Princeton, 1970)

Baratier, E., 'Une prédication de la croisade à Marseille en 1224', *Economies et sociétés au moyen âge: Mélanges offerts à Edouard Perroy* (Paris, 1973)

Barber, M., *The New Knighthood* (Cambridge, 1994)

— *The Crusader States* (New Haven and London, 2012)

Barker, E., *The Crusades* (London, 1923)

Barlow, F., *Thomas Becket* (London, 1986)

Bartlett, R., *Gerald of Wales* (Oxford, 1982)

— *The Making of Europe* (London, 1993)

— *England under the Angevin and Norman Kings* (Oxford, 2000)

— *The Natural and Supernatural in the Middle Ages* (Cambridge, 2008)

Bataillon, J.-L., 'Approaches to the study of medieval sermons', *La prédication au xiiie siècle en France et Italie* (Aldershot, 1993)

Bennett, H. S., *Life on the English Manor* (Cambridge, 1956)

Bennett, M., 'Military aspects of the conquest of Lisbon', in *The Second Crusade*, ed. Phillips and Hoch

Berlière, U., 'A propos de Jacques de Vitry', *Revue Bénédictine*, 27 (1910)

Biller, P., *The Measure of Multitude* (Oxford, 2000)

Blake, E. O. and Morris, C., 'A Hermit Goes to War: Peter and the Origins of the First Crusade', in *Monks, Hermits and the Ascetic Tradition*, ed. W. J. Shields, Studies in Church History, vol. xxii (Oxford, 1985)

Borelli de Serres, C., 'Compte d'une mission de prédication pour secours à la Terre Sainte', *Mémoires de la Société de l'histoire de Paris et de l'Île de France*, 30 (1903)

Brown, E. A. R. and Cothren, M.W., 'The Twelfth-Century Crusading Window of the Abbey of St Denis', *Journal of the Warburg and Courtauld Institutes*, 49 (1986)

Brown, E. A. R. and Regalado, N. F., '*La grant feste*', in *City and Spectacle in Medieval Europe*, eds. B. A. Hanawalt and K. L. Reyerson (Minneapolis, 1994)

Brown, S., 'Military Service and Monetary Reward in the 11th and 12th Centuries', *History*, 74 (1989)

Brundage, J. A., 'Crucesignari: The Rite for Taking the Cross in England', *Traditio*, 22 (1966)

— 'The Crusader's Wife. A Canonistic Quandary', *Studia Gratiana*, 12 (1967)

— 'The Crusader's Wife Revisited', *Studia Gratiana*, 14 (1967)

— *Medieval Canon Law and the Crusader* (Madison, 1969)

Bull, M., 'The Capetian Monarchy and the Early Crusading Movement', *Nottingham Medieval Studies*, 40 (1996)

Bull, M. and Housley, N., *The Experience of Crusading*, vol. i, *Western Approaches* (Cambridge, 2003)

Bumke, J., *The Concept of Knighthood in the Middle Ages* (New York, 1982)

Burnett, C., ed., *Adelard of Bath* (London, 1987)

— 'Adelard of Bath', *Oxford Dictionary of National Biography*, ed. C. Mathew et al. (Oxford, 2004–)

Cardini, F., 'I costi della crociata', *Studi in Memoria di Federigo Melis* (Naples, 1978)

— 'Crusade and "Presence of Jerusalem" in Medieval Florence', in *Outremer*, ed. B. Z. Kedar et al. (Jerusalem, 1982)

Carpenter, D., 'English Peasants in Politics 1258–1267', *Past and Present*, 136 (1992)

— 'The Gold Treasure of King Henry III', *The Reign of Henry III* (London, 1996)

— *The Struggle for Mastery. Britain 1066–1284* (London, 2003)

Cate, J. L., 'The English mission of Eustace of Flay', *Etudes d'histoire dédiées à la mémoire de Henri Pirenne* (Brussels, 1937)

Cazel, F. A., 'The Tax of 1185 and the Holy Land', *Speculum*, 30 (1955)

Chazan, R., *European Jewry and the First Crusade* (London, 1987)

Chevedden, P., 'The Islamic View and the Christian View of the Crusades', *History*, 93 (2008)

— 'The View of the Crusades from Rome and Damascus', *Oriens*, 39/2 (2011)

Chibnall, M., 'Military Service in Normandy before 1066', *Anglo-Norman Studies*, 5 (1982)

Christiansen, E., *The Northern Crusades* (London, 1997)

Clanchy, M., *From Memory to Written Record* (London, 1979)

— *Peter Abelard: A Medieval Life* (Oxford, 1997)

Cole, P., *The Preaching of the Crusades to the Holy Land 1095–1291* (Cambridge, Mass., 1991)

Congar, Y., 'Henri de Marcy', *Analecta Monastica*, v (*Studia Anselmiana*, fasc. 43, Rome, 1958)

Constable, G., 'The Language of Preaching in the Twelfth Century', *Viator*, 25 (1994)

— 'The Financing of the Crusades', *Crusaders and Crusading in the Twelfth Century* (Farnham, 2008)

Copeland. R. and Sluiter, I., *Medieval Grammar and Rhetoric. Language, Arts and Literary Theory* AD *300–1475* (Oxford, 2009)

Cowdrey, H. E. J., 'Pope Gregory VII's "Crusading" Plans of 1074', in *Outremer*, ed. B. Z. Kedar et al. (Jerusalem, 1982)

— 'Pope Urban II and the Idea of the Crusade', *Studi Medievali*, 3rd ser., 36 (1995)

— 'Pope Gregory VII and the Bearing of Arms', in *Montjoie*, ed. B. Z. Kedar et al. (Aldershot, 1997)

— 'Christianity and the Morality of War', in *Experience of Crusading*, vol. i, ed. Bull and Housley

Crouch, D., *The Beaumont Twins* (Cambridge, 1986)

— *The English Aristocracy 1070–1272: A Social Transformation* (New Haven, 2011)

Crusades, The: An Encyclopedia, ed. A. V. Murray (Santa Barbara, 2006)

David, E. R., 'Apocalyptic Conversion: The Joachite Alternative to the Crusades', *Traditio*, 125 (1969)

Davis, H. W. C., 'Henry of Blois and Brian FitzCount', *English Historical Review*, 25 (1910)

D'Avray, D., *Medieval Religious Rationalities* (Cambridge, 2010)

Dickson, G., *The Children's Crusade* (Basingstoke, 2008)

Donkin, L. and Vorholt, H., *Imagining Jerusalem in the Medieval West* (Oxford, 2012)

Duby, G., *The Chivalrous Society* (London, 1977)

Edbury, P., *The Kingdom of Cyprus and the Crusades 1191–1374* (Cambridge, 1991)

— 'Preaching the Crusade in Wales', in *England and Germany in the High Middle Ages*, ed. A. Haverkamp et al. (Oxford, 1996)

Edbury, P. and Rowe, J., *William of Tyre* (Cambridge, 1988)

Edgington, S., 'Medical Knowledge of the Crusading Armies', in *The Military Orders*, ed. M. Barber, vol. i (Aldershot, 1994)

Edgington, S. and Lambert, S., *Gendering the Crusades* (New York, 2002)

Edson, E., 'Reviving the Crusade: Sanudo's Scheme and Vesconte's Maps', in *Eastward Bound*, ed. Allen

— 'Jerusalem under Siege: Marino Sanudo's Map of the Water Supply, 1320', in *Imagining Jerusalem*, ed. Donkin and Vorholt

Erdmann, C., *Die Entstehung des Kreuzzugsgedanken* (Stuttgart, 1935), trans. M. W. Baldwin and W. Goffart, *The Origins of the Idea of Crusade* (Princeton, 1977)

Flanagan, S., *Doubt in an Age of Faith: Uncertainty in the Long Twelfth Century* (Turnhout, 2008)

Flori, J., *L'Essor de Chevalerie xie–xiie siècle* (Geneva, 1986)

— *Pierre l'Ermite et la première croisade* (Paris, 1999)

— *Chroniqueurs et propagandistes* (Geneva, 2010)

Fonnesberg-Schmidt, I., *The Popes and the Baltic Crusades 1147–1254* (Leiden, 2007)

Forey, A., 'The Military Order of St Thomas of Acre', *English Historical Review*, 92 (1977)

— 'The Second Crusade: Scope and Objectives', *Durham University Journal*, 86 (1994)

France, J., *Victory in the East* (Cambridge, 1994)

— ed., *Mercenaries and Paid Men* (Leiden, 2000)

Frankopan, P., *The First Crusade: The Call from the East* (London, 2012)

Gabriele, M., *An Empire of Memory. The Legend of Charlemagne, the Franks and Jerusalem before the First Crusade* (Oxford, 2011)

Galbraith, V. H., 'The Literacy of Medieval English Kings', *Proceedings of the British Academy*, 21 (1935)

Gaposchkin, M. C., 'The Pilgrimage and Cross Blessings in the Roman Pontificals of the Twelfth and Thirteenth Centuries', *Medieval Studies*, 73 (2011)

Gautier Dalché, P., *Carte marine et portulan au xiie siècle* (Rome, 1995)

— *De Yorkshire à l'Inde. Une 'Géographie' urbaine et maritime de la fin de xiie siècle (Roger de Howden?)* (Geneva, 2005)

Geary, P. J., *Furta Scara: Theft of Relics in the Central Middle Ages* (Princeton, 1978)

Gillingham, J., 'Roger of Howden on Crusade', in *Medieval Historical Writing in the Christian and Islamic Worlds*, ed. D. O. Morgan (London, 1982)

— 'The Travels of Roger of Howden', *Anglo-Norman Studies*, 20 (1997)

— *Richard I* (New Haven and London, 1999)

Giuseppi, M. S., 'On the Testament of Sir Hugh de Nevill', *Archaeologia*, 56 (1899)

Glass, D. F., *Portals, Pilgrimages and Crusade in Western Tuscany* (Princeton, 1997)

Grant, E., *God and Reason in the Middle Ages* (Cambridge, 2001)

Guard, T., *Chivalry, Kingship and Crusade. The English Experience in the Fourteenth Century* (Woodbridge, 2013)

Guido, P., *Rationes decimarum Italiae nei secoli XIIIe: Tuscia: la Decoma degli anni 1274–90, Studi e Testi*, vol. lvii (Vatican City, 1932)

Guilhiermoz, P., *Essai sur l'origine de la noblesse en France au moyen âge* (Paris, 1902)

Hagger, M., 'A Pipe Roll for 25 Henry I', *English Historical Review*, 122 (2007)

Hamilton, B., 'The Impact of the Crusaders on Western Geographical Knowledge', in *Eastward Bound*, ed. Allen

Hannam, J., *God's Philosophers* (London, 2009)

Hanska, J., 'Reconstructing the Mental Calendar of Medieval Preaching' in *Preacher, Sermon and Audience*, ed. Muessig

Harley, J. B. et al., *The History of Cartography*, vol. i (Chicago, 1987)

Harris, J., *Byzantium and the Crusades* (London, 2003)

Harris, J. W., *Medieval Theatre in Context* (London, 1992)

Harvey, J. H., *The Master Builders: Architecture in the Middle Ages* (London, 1971)

— *The Medieval Architect* (London, 1972)

— *English Medieval Architects* (London, 1987)

Harvey, P. D. A., *Medieval Maps* (London, 1991)

— *Medieval Maps of the Holy Land* (London, 2012)

Haskins, H. A., *Norman Institutions* (New York, 1918)

Hehl, E.-D., *Kirche und Krieg im 12 Jahrhundert* (Stuttgart, 1980)

Henneman, J. B., *Royal Taxation in Fourteenth Century France: The Development of War Finance 1322–1356* (Princeton, 1971)

Hillenbrand, C., *The Crusades. Islamic Perspectives* (Edinburgh, 1999)

Hodgson, N., *Women, Crusading and the Holy Land in Historical Narrative* (Woodbridge, 2007)

Housley, N., *The Italian Crusades* (Oxford, 1982)

— *The Avignon Papacy and the Crusades 1305–78* (Oxford, 1986)

— *The Later Crusades. From Lyons to Alcazar* (Oxford, 1992)

— 'Costing the Crusade', in *Experience of Crusading*, vol. i, ed. Bull and Housley

Houts, E. Van, *The Normans in Europe* (Manchester, 2000)

Hurlock, K., *Wales and the Crusades c.1095–1291* (Cardiff, 2011)

Huygens, R., 'Guillaume de Tyre étudiant', *Latomus*, 31 (1962)

Jackson, P., *The Mongols and the West* (Harlow, 2005)

Jacoby, D., 'An Unpublished Portolan of the Mediterranean in Minneapolis', *Shipping, Trade and Crusade in the Medieval Mediterranean* (Farnham, 2013)

Jordan, W. C., *Louis IX and the Challenge of the Crusade* (Princeton, 1979)

— 'The Representation of the Crusade in the Songs Attributed to Thibaud, Count Palatine of Champagne', *Journal of Medieval History*, 25 (1999)

Kedar, B. Z., 'The Passenger List of a Crusader Ship', *Studi Medievali*, 13 (1972)

— *Crusade and Mission* (Princeton, 1984)

— 'Reflections on Maps, Crusading and Logistics', in *Logistics of Warfare*, ed. Pryor

Keen, M., *Chivalry* (New Haven, 1984)

Kempf, F., 'Das Rommersdorfer Briefbuch des 13 Jahrhunderts', *Mitteilungen des Österreichen Instituts für Geschichtsforschung. Erganzungsband*, 12 (1933)

Kienzle, B. M., 'Medieval Sermons and their Performance', in *Preacher, Sermon and Audience*, ed. Muessig

King, E., 'The Memory of Brian FitzCount', *Haskins Society Journal*, 13 (2004)

Köhler, M. A., *Allianzen und Verträge zwischen frankischen und islamischen Herrschern in Vorderren Orient* (Berlin, 1991)

Kümper, H., 'Oliver of Paderborn', in *Encyclopaedia of the Medieval Chronicle*, ed. G. Dunphy (Leiden, 2010)

Kunstmann, F., 'Studien über Marin Sanudo', *Königliche Bayerische Akademie der Wissenschaften. Abhandlungen Phil- Historische Classe*, 7 (1855)

Lecoy de la Marche, A., 'La prédication de la croisade au treizième siècle', *Revue des questions historiques*, 48 (1890)

Leopold, A., *How to Recover the Holy Land* (Aldershot, 2000)

Linder, A., *Raising Arms. Liturgy in the Struggle to Liberate Jerusalem in the Late Middle Ages* (Turnhout, 2003)

Lloyd, S., 'Political Crusades in England', in *Crusade and Settlement*, ed. P. Edbury (Cardiff, 1985)

— *English Society and the Crusade 1216–1307* (Oxford, 1988)

Lower, M., *The Barons' Crusade* (Philadelphia, 2005)

Lun, P. van, 'Les milites dans la France du XIe siècle', *Le Moyen Age*, 77 (1971)

Lunt, W., *Papal Revenues in the Middle Ages* (New York, 1965)

Madden, T., 'Food and the Fourth Crusade', in *Logistics of Warfare*, ed. Pryor

Maddicott, J., 'The Crusade Taxation of 1268– 70 and the Development of Parliament', *Thirteenth Century England*, 2 (1988)

— *The Origins of the English Parliament 924–1327* (Oxford, 2010)

Maier, C. T., *Preaching the Crusades* (Cambridge, 1994)

— *Crusade Propaganda and Ideology: Model Sermons for the Preaching of the Cross* (Cambridge, 2000)

Marvin, L. W., 'The White and Black Confraternities of Toulouse and the Albigensian Crusade 1210–11', *Viator*, 40 (2009)

Mayer, H. E., *The Crusades*, 2nd edn (Oxford, 1988)

Menache, S., *The Vox Dei: Communication in the Middle Ages* (Oxford, 1990)

— 'Papal Attempts at a Commercial Boycott of the Muslims in the Crusader Period', *Journal of Ecclesiastical History*, 63 (2012)

Michel, K., *Das Opus Tripartitum des Humbertus de Romans OP* (Graz, 1926)

Mitchell, P., *Medicine in the Crusades* (Cambridge, 2004)

Mollat, M., *The Poor in the Middle Ages* (London, 1986)

Morris, C., 'Propaganda for War. The Dissemination of the Crusading Ideal in the Twelfth Century', in *Studies in Church History*, ed. W. Shields, vol. xx (Oxford, 1983)

— 'Policy and Visions: The Case of the Holy Lance', in *War and Government in the Middle Ages*, ed. J. Gillingham and J. C. Holt (Woodbridge, 1984)

— 'Picturing the Crusades: The Uses of Visual Propaganda', in *The Crusades and their Sources*, ed. J. France et al. (Aldershot, 1998)

— *The Sepulchre of Christ and the Medieval West* (Oxford, 2005)

Mortimer, R., 'The Family of Ranulf de Glanville', *Bulletin of the Institute of Historical Research*, 54 (1981)

Muessig, C., ed., *Preacher, Sermon and Audience in the Middle Ages* (Leiden, 2002)

Muldoon, P., *Popes, Lawyers and Infidels* (Liverpool, 1979)

Murray, A., *Reason and Society in the Middle Ages* (Oxford, 1978)

Murray, A. V., 'The Army of Godfrey de Bouillon', *Revue belge de philologie et d'histoire*, 70 (1992)

— 'Money and Logistics in the First Crusade', in *Logistics of Warfare*, ed. Pryor

— 'Finance and Logistics of the Crusade of Frederick Barbarossa', in *In Laudem Hierosolymitani*, ed. I. Shagrir et al. (Aldershot, 2007)

O'Callaghan, J. F., *Reconquest and Crusade in Medieval Spain* (Philadelphia, 2003)

Oksanen, E., 'The Anglo-Flemish Treaties and Flemish Soldiers in England 1101–1163', in *Mercenaries and Paid Men*, ed. France

Opll, F., *Das Itinerar Kaiser Friedrich Barbarossas (1152–1190)*, (Cologne-Graz, 1978)

Orme, N., *Medieval Children* (New Haven, 2001)

Owst, G. R., *Preaching in Medieval England* (Cambridge, 1926)

Oxford Dictionary of National Biography, ed. C. Mathew et al. (Oxford, 2004–)

Paterson, L., *The World of the Troubadours* (Cambridge, 1993)

Paul, N. L., 'A Warlord's Wisdom: Literacy and Propaganda at the Time of the First Crusade', *Speculum*, 85 (2010)

— *To Follow in Their Footsteps* (Ithaca, 2012)

Pennington, K., 'The Rite for Taking the Cross in the Twelfth Century', *Traditio*, 30 (1974)

Perry, G., *John of Brienne* (Cambridge, 2013)

Petersen, N. H., 'The Notion of a Missionary Theatre: The *ludus magnus* of Henry of Livonia's Chronicle', in *Crusading and Chronicle Writing on the Medieval Baltic Frontier*, ed. M. Tamm et al. (Farnham, 2011)

Phillips, J., 'Odo of Deuil's *De profectione* as a source', in *Experience of Crusading*, vol. i, ed. Bull and Housley

— *The Second Crusade* (New Haven, 2007)

Phillips, J. and Hoch, M., eds., *The Second Crusade* (Manchester, 2001)

Powell, J., *Anatomy of a Crusade 1213–1221* (Philadelphia, 1986)

Power, D., 'Who Went on the Albigensian Crusade?', *English Historical Review*, 128 (2013)

Prestwich, J. O., 'The Military Household of the Norman Kings', *English Historical Review*, 96 (1981)

— 'Mistranslations and Misinterpretations in Medieval English History', *Peritia*, 10 (1996)

— *The Place of War in English History 1066–1214* (Woodbridge, 2004)

Prestwich, M., *Edward I* (London, 1988)

— *Armies and Warfare in the Middle Ages: The English Experience* (New Haven and London, 1996)

Pryor, J. H., *Business Contracts of Medieval Provence* (Toronto, 1981)

— 'Transportation of Horses by Sea During the Era of the Crusades', *The Mariner's Mirror*, 68 (1982)

— 'The Naval Architecture of Crusader Transport Ships', *The Mariner's Mirror*, 70 (1984)

— *Geography, Technology and War* (Cambridge, 1988)

— 'Modelling Bohemund's March to Thessalonica', in *Logistics of Warfare*, ed. Pryor

— 'The Venetian Fleet for the Fourth Crusade', in *Experience of Crusading*, vol. i, ed. Bull and Housley

— ed., *The Logistics of Warfare in the Age of the Crusades* (Aldershot, 2006)

— 'A View From a Masthead: The First Crusade at Sea', *Crusades*, 7 (2008)

— 'Two *excitationes* for the Third Crusade', *Mediterranean Historical Review*, 25 (2010)

Pujades i Bataller, R. J., *Les cartes portolanes* (Barcelona, 2007)

Purcell, M., *Papal Crusading Policy 1244–91* (Leiden, 1975)

Queller, D. E. and Madden, T. F., *The Fourth Crusade* (Philadelphia, 1997)

Reuter, T., 'Assembly Politics in Western Europe from the Eighth to the Twelfth Centuries', in *The Medieval World*, ed. P. Linehan and J. Nelson (London, 2001)

Reynolds, S., *Kingdoms and Communities in Western Europe 900–1300* (Oxford, 1997)

Richard, J., 'La papauté et la direction de la première croisade', *Journal des savants* (1960)

Riley-Smith, J., 'Crusading as an Act of Love', *History*, 65 (1980)

— *The First Crusade and the Idea of Crusading* (London, 1986)

— *The First Crusaders* (Cambridge, 1997)

— 'Towards an Understanding of the Fourth Crusade as an Institution', in *Urbs Capta*, ed. A. Laiou (Paris, 2005)

Rogers, R., *Latin Siege Warfare in the Twelfth Century* (Oxford, 1992)

Rosenthal, J. T., 'The Education of the Early Capetians', *Traditio*, 25 (1969)

Rubinstein, J., 'Fitting History to Use: Three Crusade Chronicles in Context', *Viator*, 35 (2004)

— *Armies of Heaven. The First Crusade and the Quest for the Apocalypse* (New York, 2011)

Russell, F. H., *The Just War in the Middle Ages* (Cambridge, 1977)

Sarris, P., *Empires of Faith* (Oxford, 2011)

Scheeben, H. C., *Albert der Grosse* (Leipzig, 1931)

Schein, S., *Fideles Crucis* (Oxford, 1991)

Schenk, J., *Templar Families* (Cambridge, 2012)

Shepard, J., 'When Greek meets Greek', *Byzantine and Modern Greek Studies*, 12 (1988)

Siberry, E., 'The Crusading Counts of Nevers', *Nottingham Medieval Studies*, 34 (1990)

Smail, R. C., 'Latin Syria and the West, 1149–87', *Transactions of the Royal Historical Society*, 5th ser., 19 (1969)

Somerville, R., *The Councils of Urban II, i, Decreta Claromontensia, Annuarium Historiae Conciliorum: Supplementum*, vol. i (Amsterdam, 1972)

— 'The Council of Clermont', in *Papacy, Councils and Canon Law* (London, 1990)

Spufford, P., *Money and its Use in Medieval Europe* (Cambridge, 1988)

Stantchev, S., *Spiritual Rationality: Papal Embargo as Cultural Practice* (Oxford, 2014)

Stanton, C. D., *Norman Naval Operations in the Mediterranean* (Woodbridge, 2011)

Stenton, D. M., 'Roger of Howden and Benedict', *English Historical Review*, 68 (1953)

— 'King John and the Courts of Justice', *Proceedings of the British Academy*, 44 (1958)

Stenton, F. M., 'Early Manumissions at Staunton', *English Historical Review*, 26 (1911)

Strayer, J. R., 'The Crusades of Louis IX', in *A History of the Crusades*, ed. K. Setton et al. (Madison, 1969–)

Strickland, M., *War and Chivalry* (Cambridge, 1996)

Sweeney, J. R., 'Hungary in the Crusades 1169–1218', *International History Review*, 3 (1981)

Thijssen, J., *Censure and Heresy at the University of Paris 1200–1400* (Philadelphia, 1998)

Thorndyke, L., *The Sphere of Sacrobosco and its Commentators* (Chicago, 1949)

Throop, P., *Criticism of the Crusade* (Amsterdam, 1940)

Throop, S., *Crusading as an Act of Vengeance 1095–1216* (Farnham, 2011)

Tolan, J., *Saracens: Islam in the Medieval Imagination* (New York, 2002)

Turner, R. V., 'The *Miles Literatus* in Twelfth and Thirteenth Century England', *American Historical Review*, 83 (1978)

Tyerman, C. J., *England and the Crusades* (Chicago, 1988)

— *The Invention of the Crusades* (London, 1998)

— *God's War. A New History of the Crusades* (London, 2006)

— *The Debate on the Crusades* (Manchester, 2011)

— *The Practices of Crusading* (Farnham, 2013)

— 'Henry of Livonia and the Ideology of Crusading', in *Practices of Crusading*, VII

— 'Who Went on Crusade to the Holy Land?', in *Practices of Crusading*, XIII

— 'Paid Crusaders', in *Practices of Crusading*, XIV

— 'Court, Crusade and City: The Cultural Milieu of Louis I, Duke of Bourbon', in *Practices of Crusading*, IV

— '"Principes et Populus": Civil Society and the First Crusade', in *Practices of Crusading*, XII

— 'Philip VI and the Recovery of the Holy Land', in *Practices of Crusading*, V

— 'Philip V of France, the Assemblies of 1319–20 and the Crusade', in *Practices of Crusading*, II

Unger, R. W., 'The Northern Crusaders', in *Logistics of Warfare*, ed. Pryor

Villey, M., *La Croisade: essai sur la formation d'une théorie juridique* (Paris, 1942)

Vincent, N., *Peter des Roches* (Cambridge, 1996)

Warren, W. L., *Henry II* (London, 1977)

West, C., 'All in the Same Boat: East Anglia, the North Sea World and the 1147 Expedition to Lisbon', in *East Anglia and its North Sea World in the Middle Ages*, ed. D. Bates and R. Liddiard (Woodbridge, 2013)

Wilms, H., *Albert the Great* (London, 1933)

Wright, J. K., *Geographical Lore of the Time of the Crusades*, 2nd edn (New York, 1965)

Index